Landmark Essays

Landmark Essays

on

Contemporary Rhetoric

Edited by Thomas B. Farrell

LEA Hermagoras Press
An Imprint of Lawrence Erlbaum Associates, Publishers

Landmark Essays Volume Fifteen

Cover design by Kathi Zamminer

Lawrence Erlbaum Associates, Inc., Publishers
10 Industrial Avenue
Mahwah, New Jersey 07430

Library of Congress Cataloging-in-Publication Data

Landmark essays on contemporary rhetoric/edited by Thomas B. Farrell.
        p. cm. — (Landmark essays : v. 15)
     Includes bibliographical references and index.
     ISBN 1-880393-10-7 (pbk. : alk. paper)
        1. Rhetoric.   I. Farrell, Thomas B., 1947-   II. Series.
   P301.L29 1998
   808—dc21   98-26841
                                                          CIP

Books published by Lawrence Erlbaum Associates are printed on
acid-free paper, and their bindings are chosen for strength and durability.

Printed in the United States of America

To My Teacher,
Lloyd F. Bitzer

About the Editor

Thomas B. Farrell (PhD. 1974, University of Wisconsin) is a professor of rhetoric and political communication at Northwestern University. Farrell is interested in the ways public symbols, images, and figures channel our participation toward partisan ends and collective projects. He has published over seventy articles and monographs dealing with rhetoric and public culture. Four of his graduate students have been awarded national honors for "dissertation of the year." His study of modernity and rhetorical tradition, *Norms of Rhetorical Culture* (Yale University Press, 1993) was awarded the 1994 Winans-Wichelns prize for "distinguished scholarship in rhetoric and public address." In 1990, Farrell received the Charles H. Woolbert Award for "scholarship of exceptional originality and influence." This is his first edited collection.

Table of Contents

By Way of Introduction

By Way of Introduction
by Thomas B. Farrell

The alert reader will have already noticed that the title of this collection is something of an oxymoron. Landmarks are usually thought to be creations that stand the test of time. That which is contemporary, again by definition, usually is something that has not. We also have, it seems (and particularly so in rhetorical studies), an engrained bias against the contemporary. The allegedly frayed and tattered condition of our modern discourse practices is itself a convention of contemporary scholarship. How, then, to select a fair and representative sampling from the medley of scholarly craft that any locally situated branch of the Humanities must offer?

Candor requires the admission that any "contemporary" collection must be, at least in part, the result of hunches and guesswork. One accepts the risk of being wrong or out of fashion in the productive arts of rhetoric for the same reasons one would support a museum of contemporary art. Contradictions notwithstanding, it is worth having and appreciating at least a provisional collection of prevailing influences on our scholarship.

I

All collections have themes and, unfashionable as the term is, admission criteria. So a few words are in order about the context and themes presented here, before overviewing the essays themselves. First, I have limited our understanding of "contemporary" rhetorical theory to roughly the last quarter century. This will seem to some an unduly narrow span of time. Most of our contemporary seminars include the pivotal figures of the twentieth century; but no collection could do justice to such a span. I have instead decided on a range marking, in part, a generational limit—the time when scholars from Cornell, Pittsburgh, and the prairie universities of America were able to define and articulate curricula for teaching the doctrines of rhetorical theory. It is also the period marking a conspicuous turn toward productive work in theory-building throughout scholarly books and journals. Whether the resulting flurry of activity qualifies as a golden age, a misguided experiment, or just a blip on the radar screen of rhetorical study's overall demise is still a lively question engaging many of the essays included here.

The themes and issues are therefore complex, continuing, and intrinsic to rhetorical study's own prospects as a discipline. Perhaps the most basic question was whether rhetoric, traditionally the wayward child of philosophy and the arts, could be theorized at all. In the late 1960's and early 1970's, a general cult of scientized theory (grand theory, systems theory, covering law theory) held sway through much of the social sciences. Even in philosophy departments, philosophical inquiry was largely construed as philosophy of science or ordinary language philosophy. In one department of communication, this editor was told by a persuasion teacher that rhetoric was just "bad social science."

Although the authors included in this collection differ widely in the directions their work takes, I think they would all agree (at least in the pages included here) that rhetoric may be theorized. This realization also helps us to identify one loosely thematic admission criterion. I have limited the essays to those making some meaningful attempt to craft or refine theory in rhetoric. Certainly there is very good work emanating from the proposition that theory in rhetoric is bad or impossible (Edwin Black's scholarship comes to mind). But we follow a different course here.

But having set forth this minimalist condition of attempting to theorize rhetoric, it becomes notoriously difficult to identify just what such theorizing actually involves. My minimalist solution to this problem has been to include essays in which authors are *doing* theory and not just talking about it. So for beginning graduate students who may want to know what rhetorical theorists do when they are doing rhetorical theory, one answer would be to open the pages of these essays and say: "They do stuff like this." It is, I grant you, a facile answer. But it is better than many others I have heard.

As our students quickly discover, however, rhetoric itself eludes precise formulation; and this has led to lamentations across the milennia. I am going to approach heresy by suggesting that perhaps this evasion of precision is not such a bad thing. What one of our authors would call rhetoric's "productive ambiguity" encourages reformulations of its principles, genres, topoi, styles of influence, and so forth. Because rhetoric is a self authored, other-directed, and culturally situated activity, we would expect lively and ongoing differences of opinion as to its best or most useful formulation.

Can we theorize something when we cannot even agree on its preferred meanings? I believe that we can if we relax somewhat our grandiose received opinions about what theory is expected to do. For instance, there may be no finalized agreement about what music precisely *is*. But this does not inhibit modern teachers from imparting knowledge of harmonics, dynamics, and forms of composition to generations of music students.

The analogy to music, and the other arts, has resonances in at least two directions. First, it suggests that theory in rhetoric is concerned with the creation and appreciation of its subject more than with the exhaustive explanation of its "components." One may know all 88 keys on the piano board, every string on the guitar, and never be able to play the simplest tune. Second, it suggests that "theory" in rhetoric is implicated directly in the formulation of a subject so that it may be grasped communicatively and emulated, in other words *taught*. Though I doubt that every author represented here would agree, the only condition which would preclude the activity of theorizing rhetoric (in my view) is the condition where there were no such thing/activity as rhetoric. This is notoriously not the case, for instance, in philosophy, as in Burke's hilariously scandalous discovery that one could replace Kant's concept of pure reason with the concept "nothing" at no loss to overall rigor and coherence of the "theory." Rhetoric, in other words, is more than thought. It is performed and taught, and *therefore* theorized.

Although there are probably more differences than similarities in these essays, I would hazard one further commonality. In the arts and humanities generally, the rule is to agree to disagree. Long before "identity and contradiction" were seen to be oppressive hegemony (the conceptual knock on the door in the middle of the night) these authors, to a person, do not find rhetoric's defiance of precision as an identity crisis, but rather as a sign of its complexity and resilience. Consistent with the practice of distinguished humanities scholarship everywhere, rhetorical theorists caption an aspect of rhetorical practice they find interesting and important and work toward a framework that enhances our appreciation of its nuances and possibilities.

For the most part, the essays included here also eschew "grand theory." This is also in keeping with my own editorial bias (my practices to the contrary notwithstanding). The exceptions are so obvious they do not even need to be named; they were included because they are, well, "landmarks." Grand theory, like its close conceptual relation, monological theory, offers wonderful insights. But it invariably turns out to be "wrong," at least in the sense of being outstripped by the aforementioned undisciplinable rhetorical practice.

Perhaps this is enough to acquaint the reader with the reason these essays are here. But our earlier allusion to music and theory has some more discordant implications for the overall issues encountered and defined by contemporary rhetorical theory. To the extent that any culture is defined by the issues over which it chooses to institutionalize disagreement, our own disciplinary culture's pulse is still lively.

For openers, theory in the "fine arts" (as well as in the Humanities pantheon) has usually managed to avoid "guilt by association" with the practical. So far as I know, people do not approach theorists of music with the charge, "If you are such a fine theorist, how do you explain *Cats*?" But as we know, a less figurative version of this charge finds itself directed at rhetorical theory all the time. A possibly related point is that both the fine arts and philosophies of the fine arts are notoriously shrewd at distancing themselves from the arts of rhetoric. Brian Vickers' *In Defense of Rhetoric*[1] documents this process of marginalization over the centuries, where philosophy has been concerned. In our own field, Robert Hariman[2] has argued that such normatively loaded differentiation may be all but endemic to theorizing in the humanities. When I suggest that this point is possibly related, I mean no dark intergenerational "conspiracy," but only the fact that theories of the arts have usually worked with touchstone prototypes of practice, whatever portrays their art in the best of light. All the better not to fall victim to "guilt by association" with the crude currency of style and fashion. The better part of valor would seem to dictate avoiding the questionable company of rhetoric.

A first issue for these pages, then, is the question whether we who theorize rhetoric may rehabilitate the art *without* disparaging or "deconstructing" those branches of humanities inquiry on our *borders*. For the most part, those defenders of rhetoric who do not "philosophize" the practice (as Aristotle purportedly did), rehabilitate rhetoric by showing that its traces and features are found throughout the activities of its border practices. Brian Vickers does this with the work of philosophy, as do Samuel Ijsseling and Ernesto Grassi.

The problem with this tack is not what happens to other branches of the humanities; literature, philosophy, the arts are more likely to be undone by comparative literature departments than by anything we rhetoricians do. Rather the problem is what happens to rhetoric. Vickers' impressive work concludes with rhetoric in the modern novel.[3] Ijsseling tells us that metaphor is to be found throughout philosophy.[4] Grassi tells us that language is the first presupposition of religion.[5] I do not mean to suggest that this reciprocal "thinning out" and ornamentalizing of rhetoric by rhetoric is inevitable, but only that it is highly likely.

For the most part, the authors presented in this collection avoid the above tactic. Their theoretical work proceeds largely on its own terms: through the groundings of tradition, the refinements of previous principles, genre, argument types, and cases, the call of a new "uncovering" of form and function. Although the problem of differentiation and marginality does not disappear in these essays, it is left, where else? On the sidelines, so as not to distract from more serious scholarly agendas.

A second, and closely related issue is that of compass or breadth. The novel, religion, and metaphors in science and philosophy all surely partake of rhetorical elements. But do we wish to conceptualize the boundaries of inclusion and convention so that these become the "prototypes" of rhetoric? Bluntly put, how narrowly or broadly do we define the area of rhetorical activity itself? Some time ago, with glib disregard for its political repercussions, I coined "Farrell's rule" for the rhetoric as epistemic movement. My rule was that all knowledge is rhetorical in direct proportion to how trivial one's conception of rhetoric happened to be.[6] The point I was trying to make had to do with corollaries of attribution. A "thin" conception of a subject will see its traces everywhere, sometimes with startling rediscovery. Is the bird "singing"? Well, from one minimalist conception of music (with poetic overtones) it certainly is. But there may be more to music than the "thin" reading, however charming, allows. The point is not to turn away foreigners at the gate (much less to silence birds) so much as it is to refine the concepts within theory sufficiently to know what we are talking about.

The scholarship presented here does not take a unified position on the matter of breadth and boundaries. Instead, it is sufficiently rich and complex as to refute my glib codicil. It is safe to say, for instance, that Richard McKeon did not have a trivial conception of rhetoric. And yet he fashioned an impossibly broad and analytically inclusive range of interpretative practices for the art itself. And although Bitzer's work is overtly much narrower in scope, it holds out a richly textured promise for civic life that will strike modern readers as close to utopian. Campbell begins with a quite specific and grounded ontological vision of rhetoric, but translates the modern "symbolist" version of this vision into a redefinition of the rhetorical that blurs its boundaries. In their respectively different ways, Dilip Gaonkar and Carole Blair take dead aim at the very way I and others have raised and defined these issues, suggesting that it is our unreflective historicized "theme" that needs to be challenged. But the fact that no one evades the issue of boundaries suggests that the problem of breadth and "largesse" will continue to haunt the development and refinement of rhetorical theory.

A third important issue confronting any theory of rhetoric, and surely the essays included here, involves the normative or value component. Whereas "values" once upon a time were thought to be a corruption of theory (objectively construed), some sense of normative trajectory now seems intrinsic to any coherent theory of rhetoric. There are many reasons for this. Rhetorical practice, however else it is construed, is sermonic and value laden. As Bitzer long ago observed, in a perfect world there would be no rhetoric; for rhetoric comes into existence for the sake of something beyond itself.[7] This means it not only can make things better than they were, but, as our millenium never ceased to witness, far, far worse. Any informed general observation about rhetoric that did not take into account the matter of critical reckoning would be empty. Then there is the matter of manner, craft, and accomplishment. As any other productive art, rhetoric can be performed well or badly. It does not succeed or fail in private but in full sight of not always charitable "others." Theorists, as would-be ideal addressees, need to account for this brute fact. Finally, as I have noted before, rhetorical practice, by virtue of being a practice, cultivates qualities of character that are not value-neutral, but rather charged with normative content. To present the value component of rhetoric as an issue for theory, then, would be to ask how a theory mediates the value aspects of rhetoric as practiced well with the more culturally specific adaptative conditions counting as success and failure.

There is no single preferred or even common way these writings engage the value question. I would say that every theorist is aware of rhetoric's pragmatic dimension. This awareness is most fully apparent in the work of Miller, Cox, McGee, and Bitzer. It is perhaps least apparent in essays by McKeon, Hyde and Smith, and Frentz because their very different construals of rhetoric tend to eschew the immediacy of pragmatics. Campbell locates the virtues of rhetoric in an enhanced humanist understanding of human nature. For Frentz, and to some degree, Hyde and Smith, there is the sense of rhetoric as a higher calling where "habits of the heart" may be refined and cultivated. McGee is, I think, the most difficult to pin down on the values "of theory." He has, at various times, claimed to be a materialist, a social constructivist, and an off-center avatar of post-modernism. But as to the values surrounding the critic's project, just as the value component to theory, there can be no doubt.

How do we go about evaluating theory? I suggest to beginning students that the best sort of rhetorical theory is one that is philosophically consistent, conceptually coherent, definitionally clear, open to new cases and recognizable to old ones, and heuristically interesting. The job of theory in humanities arts such as rhetoric is not to predict so much as it is to provide an appreciative, and anticipatory explanation of things rhetorical. Ultimately we read and attempt to craft rhetorical theory to help each other grasp and perform the rich mechanics, dynamics, and harmonics that is rhetorical practice itself. On this lofty instrumental criterion, each of the essays here makes important and (in my anticipatory view) enduring contributions to a contemporary understanding of rhetorical theory. And despite the very different, and even incompatible ways they address many of the issues I have mentioned, these essays are exemplars of rich and rigorous inquiry in our still-developing humanities project. To the essays themselves.

II

Lloyd Bitzer's "Political Rhetoric" opens our collection not only because it is an eloquent reinterpretation of 'beginnings' where rhetorical theory is concerned. It also deserves a much wider audience than it has received. May an essay be a landmark without a large initial audience? See the work of Charles Sanders Peirce. In any case, I am grateful to Lloyd Bitzer for personally endorsing my idea for the essay's appearance in this volume. And I am delighted to be able to give it the marquee position on our little screen.

Bitzer's "Political Rhetoric" is a masterpiece of clear and judicious theoretical reasoning designed to expand and extend traditional prototypes. In this case, the prototype is Aristotelian deliberative rhetoric; it was Aristotle's prototype too. This essay finds a most traditional scholar "stretching" the tradition to accommodate such diverse and challenging modern phenomena as "political imagery" and what used to be known (in the pre-broadcast journalist era) as expository discourse. And while narrowly traditional in its foundations, the trajectory of this study is grand and ambitious. I take this ambition to be nothing less than an expansion and reform of what counts as the public's rhetorical business. Finally, Bitzer's essay serves to remind us that, first and foremost, rhetoric is a practical activity situated in institutional contexts, and driven by conflicted notions of the good as "expedient." Same as it ever was.

Before Karlyn Kohrs Campbell's foundational essay on "The Ontological Foundations of Rhetorical Theory," aspiring scholars were taught that rhetoricians worked from certain epistemological and metaphysical assumptions; i.e., what we can be said to know, how we come to know, what is real. But for several generations, nary a word was written about whether these assumptions might have changed, and whether theory might therefore need to be changed as well.

With characteristic directness, Campbell tackles head on the prevailing (albeit unexamined) philosophical assumptions, as these constrain rhetorical theory. What she calls traditional theory receives just condemnation for its antiquarian rationalization of human nature. Behavioral theory, our once and future social science antagonist, takes equally harsh critique for its exclusion of all creative choice and subjectivity from human nature. Campbell's rhetorical agenda calls for a bold transcendence of these two incompatible world views. What emerges in an almost Deweyesque middle is a symbolist vision of human nature, owing in equal parts to Burke and Langer by way of Ernst Cassirer. Campbell unflinchingly follows her ontology to its logical consequence: a broad and somewhat blurry expansion of rhetoric's domain. This is, one senses, the dizzying conceptual alternative to Bitzer's focused traditional vision. With the passing of years, it can also be seen that Bitzer's path proved to be the road not taken. But in her pivotal essay, Campbell does more than lead the charge through this uncertain terrain. Contemporary readers will discover that Campbell has anticipated the immediate future of her discipline in a voice that is nearly prophetic.

Richard McKeon, to my knowledge, never expressed his precise philosophical assumptions about human nature. I expect that he would have responded to any such query the way he responded to most drives toward grounded precision: "It depends." For all that, the world view of Campbell's symbolism runs through all of McKeon's writings, including his graceful *tour de force* essay presented here. "Creativity and the Commonplace," functions as something of an overview of McKeon's thought, featuring the centrality of ambiguity to invention and creativity.

A word to those encountering McKeon's prose for the first time. Even in the stripped down stylistic presented here, McKeon's writing presents the reader with an hermeneutic challenge. Whereas other students of the humanities employ clauses and phrases to reference an idea or theory, McKeon's notoriously complex prose style often deploys quite similar sentence patterns to reference entire (and often obscure) traditions of thought. I have come to think of these sentences as analogous to file headings in a vast cognitive computer. There are entire lifeworld horizons in McKeon's encompassing analytic screen. And if I may paraphrase an old patriarchal joke, the more one's maturation and competence in the history of ideas deepens, the more thoughtful and luminous McKeon's prose style becomes.

So it is with this deceptively ordinary subject of "the commonplace." Far from juxtaposing the commonplace to "the new," as is commonly done in ordinary language, McKeon brilliantly develops their historical interdependence. Of course, history (McKeon would pluralize this) implies trajectories of corruption as well as generation. And McKeon has ample evidence to show just how commonplaces may become all too wedded to obstinate conventions. Not too thinly veiled is the suggestion that our own time presents one such era. But the agenda behind this highly engaging (even amusing) essay is that of a flourishing inventional art of rhetoric that challenges received opinion, welcomes the plural, and invents the new. Anyone who believes that analysis is a conceptual arm of intellectual hegemony should read this essay. Everyone else should too.

Taken together, the Bitzer, Campbell, and McKeon essays suggest three quite different paths toward the development of rhetorical theory. McKeon's essay is also part of a larger story that informs the next several essays included here. The vision of a grand archetectonic art that might enrich existing disciplines, while inventing new ones, dazzled many scholars in the field. My own view is that McKeon's sense of the primacy of rhetorical invention rather mysteriously mutated into something called, "rhetoric as epistemic." There have been a great many different positions, variations, and sometimes heated confrontations in this episode of disciplinary history, too many to be depicted fairly here. Instead, I am including Michael Leff's outstanding review of the "rhetoric as epistemic" literature circa the late 1970's, "In Search of Ariadne's Thread: A Review of the Recent Literature on Rhetorical Theory." Billing itself as a literature review, Leff's essay is considerably more than this. It is a highly rigorous and tough-minded inquiry into just what the speculations over epistemology and rhetoric have contributed to the discipline. Acknowledging the need for both historically grounded studies as well as theoretical work, Leff nonetheless finds little outward coherence in the epistemic literature. Working through minimal theoretical aspirations (to cohere, to build upon itself), Leff emerges with four variations on the "rhetoric as epistemic," position. The most radical of these, he discovers, actually finds the paired terms exchanging places, with epistemology (e.g. all knowing) becoming rhetorical.

And therein lies the problem. How is rhetoric able to maintain any normative integrity as a practice if it can slip so easily into the blurred sidelines of all thought, all language, all perception? Using the traditional resources of rhetoric as his guide, Leff concludes by calling for a more careful development of grounded, case-related, middle-range theory. It is a call to which several essays in this volume pay heed.

An important collaborative essay that explores the relationship between interpretation and rhetoric is "Hermeneutics and Rhetoric: a Seen but Unobserved Relationship," by Michael J. Hyde and Craig R. Smith. This essay realizes ironically Campbell's pronouncement of rhetoric's expansionism, even as it offers a groundbreaking synthesis of philosophical foundationalism and historical touchstones.

Hyde and Smith wed their rhetorical hermeneutic to ongoing work calling for renewed attention to ontological foundations, Campbell's included. But more than a general category, they have something doctrinally specific in mind with both "hermeneutics" and "ontology." Following Gadamer and Heidegger, hermeneutics is the way human "Being" is disclosed through primordial interpretative understanding. Rhetoric makes this understanding known to self and other. Hyde and Smith take this insight in an unexpected direction by reexamining several more and less known rhetorical texts. The beginning problematic of how rhetoric relates to the human condition eventuates into the vexing question of why certain "successful" instances of rhetoric lack durability, while immediate failures live on. Hyde and Smith's speculations on these and other issues remain as fascinating and provocative today as when they were first written.

The aforementioned essay is paired with one coming from a very different, though equally foundational, set of assumptions. Michael McGee's, "The 'Ideograph': A Link Between Rhetoric and Ideology," presents itself in open and direct opposition to "the symbolist view" espoused by Burke, Campbell and (according to McGee) many others. McGee's argument is designed to bring into open discussion what he regards as the repressed domain of power and "mass consciousness" in rhetorical persuasion. Crucial to McGee's understanding of this domain of power is that it bypass normal processes of critical reflection; indeed "critical reflection" itself would appear to be a rhetorical apology for the myth of participation in McGee's deadened political landscape.

And so McGee the theorist (traversing the heady terrain of superstructure) invents, presents, and illustrates the seductive concept of "ideograph" as a discursive link to this power and warped consciousness. Ideographs are condensed arguments, terms loaded with inferential components that have already been smuggled aboard so as to avoid inference itself. They goad, without giving away their motive origins. And they are unavoidably embedded in an already asymmetrical system of power relations. McGee's theory is of the rhetorical text as weapon. And in an unlikely anticipation of the deconstructionist movement throughout all the arts, McGee's cadre of ideographic critics becomes a kind of rhetorical "bomb squad."

In differing ways, what Hyde and Smith's essay and McGee's work represent are attempts to essentialize rhetoric and its materials. May true rhetoric be the disclosure of primordial Being and be the agency of false consciousness all at the same time? In witholding our assent, we do not so much deny the strength of these fine essays as qualify the extremity of their pronouncements.

As scholars in the field were quick to learn, the lofty aspiration toward timeless truths does not yield the floor quietly. Thomas S. Frentz's thoughtful essay, "Rhetorical Conversation, Time, and Moral Action," presents a bold reworking of contemporary rhetorical philosophy as well as a fascinating case study. Frentz's analysis grants much of the dire diagnostic of Alasdair MacIntyre (author of one of the most influential works in the humanities generally),[8] as well as Fisher's vision of the centrality of narrative. His question might beposed as: Where does rhetoric figure in all of this?

The surprising answer builds upon our mutual work in conversational theory and analysis known as "language-action." Frentz suggests that, in the arid and emptied sphere of post-modern politics, we are more likely to find rhetoric as "moral action" in those privileged moments of mutual recognition occasionally yielded by conversation. His extended example is a beautifully realized allegorical criticism of the film, *My Dinner With Andre*, by Louis Malle. This most unconventional film culminates in an even less conventional "still-moment" (*ecstasis*) where the conversants each recognize a mutual need for a richer human life. Those charmed by the film will find, as I have, much to ponder and appreciate in Frentz's inventive hybrid form of "rhetorical conversation." The larger question of whether such moral action as this is the only available prelude to a revitalized public life does give pause. If Wally and Andre are seen as an extended illustration, the implications are more benign than if they are viewed as a prototype.

Carolyn R. Miller takes us in a more worldly direction with her fine contribution, "Genre as Social Action." Miller's invaluable essay is driven by two unfashionable insights: first, that some form of classification is inevitable in the theory of rhetoric, indeed in all disciplined thought; and second, that what uniquely characterizes rhetorical *genre* is that these types of discourse are possessed of an actional component. Miller also builds upon touchstone research in speech communication as well as compositional studies and philosophy of language. This essay works from one of the most wide-ranging bases of literature available to the field. Yet the result is a meticulously developed argument that gives new force to "genre" as a governing term in rhetorical theory.

Miller's overall aim is to offer greater precision to the meaning of "genre" while offering an interpretative framework that integrates previous speculations on the subject. because the term, "genre" is necessarily a generalization, Miller needs to confront the most serious deficiency of genre studies to this point i.e., a failure to adhere consistently to the level of abstraction at which definitions occur. So, there are definitions driven by motive, by situation, by utterance type, and a myriad of other factors. To help clarify and integrate these diverse senses, Miller introduces a helpful modification of Frentz and Farrell's "language-Action" paradigm. Her model is unavoidably hierarchical, but heuristically so; it shows how more basic language and utterance elements are able to be combined so as to enact recognizably public meanings. To acquire competency in a rhetorical genre, for Miller, is to learn rules for practicing reflective social action.

Every now and then, a theorist finds an old notion realized in startling new ways. The result is theory on the cusp of rediscovery, and an exhilarating sense of variation as invention. This is what happens, I think, in J. Robert Cox's essay, "The Die is Cast: Topical and Ontological Dimensions of the *Locus* of the Irreparable." Beyond his daunting title, Cox is interested in gathering together previous theory on the peculiar power of the irreparable, "that which cannot be undone" in our personal and public lives. Beginning with the work of Aristotle, Perelman, and Olbrechts-Tyteca, Cox finds that most treatments of the irreparable tend to treat it under the domain of the preferable or expedient. Clearly, an expanded treatment is warranted.

The body of Cox's essay uses poignant contemporary illustrations to show how *uniqueness*, *precariousness*, and *timeliness* or urgency of what is chosen may contribute to the power of the irreparable as an appeal. But Cox moves beyond these features to reintroduce an ontological orientation to time and lived existence; unlike sacred time, which is repeatable, confrontation with the irreparable assumes our own positioned understanding of the precariousness of existence itself.

It might seem, with Cox's essay, that we have come full circle back to Campbell's and Hyde's foundationalism. But not exactly. Whereas Campbell and Hyde actually call for "filled in" ontologies of human nature or "Being," Cox is more interested in invoking a particular ontology to help explain a powerful contemporary appeal. Among the many qualities that stand out in this essay are its groundbreaking meditations on the mystery of "weight," value, and its appreciation. Also, the irreparable as a contemporary appeal may be at least a partial rebuke to some earlier dismissals of public moral argument. My hope is that the essay's reappearance here will stir many such discussions.

The collection closes with two "counter-statements," by Dilip Gaonkar and Carole Blair. Each might be considered a sort of metarhetoric, a commentary on and challenge to the way rhetorical theory is formed and rationalized. Gaonkar's brilliant and provocative essay offers a sort of non-therapeutic diagnostic for an afflicted field. Constantly running from its "mereness," as he puts it, rhetoric (personified in its theories) is always searching for this doubled "other" that will lend it coherence and "substance." The two ways in which this yearning manifests itself are: *first*, a seductive rewriting of the history of rhetoric; *second*, a much-publicized rhetorical turn toward discovering rhetoric in other unlikely disciplinary places. Gaonkar finds each path to be a hollow refuge at best. In the end, he is content to accept the scandal of rhetoric's emptiness, and its marginal status as the medium of crisis. This is what I mean by "non-therapeutic." Gaonkar seems to be saying, "You're not well and you're never going to be."

Blair's challenging study places the entire array of historical discourse practices for the study of rhetoric in radical question. She correctly (in my vew) identifies two overarching, and largely unquestioned sets of assumptions in the historical study of rhetoric: first, a sort of veneration of ancient theory where anything contemporary is at best a footnote to already accomplished "lore;" and second, a sort of unquestioned progressivism where old and simplistic rhetorical theory is supplanted by modern improvements. Her example of the latter tendency turns on a bold, Foucauldian rereading of Douglas Ehninger's "systems of rhetoric."

Blair's point, I think, is that each of these approaches (we could dub them negative and positive teleologies) has the side-effect of effacing contemporary attempts to actually *do* original rhetorical theory. In calling for a critical historiography of rhetorical theory, Blair introduces a series of "metatopoi" to help textualize, pluralize, change, and critique what she would regard as the sedimented state of rhetorical inquiry.

Taken together, the essays included here help to chart a partial narrative about the study of rhetoric in the late Twentieth century. We began in mid-stream, as in all disciplinary stories: a fledgling discipline abiding both ancient roots and utopian aspirations. While the theorizing of rhetoric matured, its vision broadened and the turbulent currents in philosophy, cultural theory, and hermeneutics emboldened some to more expansive claims for the subject matter and methods of rhetoric itself. As Campbell prophesied, borders and focus were early casualties in this enthusiastic quest for new humanities frontiers. Ironically, the most enduring contributions of this exciting period were actually enhanced appreciations of rhetorical practice: in texts, in conversation, in neglected inventional **topoi**. And as might have been expected, with the reliable benefit of hindsight, the progressive totalities inherent in grand theory-building would sooner or later turn back against themselves: in rhetorical history's "dark side," its double, its patriarchical secret. From Bitzer to Blair is thus a kind of parabola, with a politics no clearer at the end than in the beginning.

May an introduction have a conclusion? This one does. The essays as assembled here are a story of both a discipline and an editor in transition. Of the discipline, wayward marginalized creature that it is, lively issues in method, foundations, scope, and judgment of theory abound and persist. The paths sketched and modeled by Bitzer, McKeon, and Campbell have been pursued with results that are still being evaluated and revised. To some extent, the charges of Gaonkar and Blair are both confirmed and refuted in these pages. We continue to do good work. We long perhaps for an abiding stability that is just not there. This might explain the philosophical adventurism, as well as the latent progressive agenda detected by Blair and others.

III

As for the charge of exclusion, any collection must be the most glaring prototype of the practice. A personal note. When I took on this assignment, it was implied that there would be not much to it. Just assemble the essays I had been foisting on my colleagues anyway, copy them, get permissions. Voila! Instead, I discovered this task to be one of the more difficult things I have ever taken on. I decided to exclude entire movements at least related to rhetorical theory on the grounds that one essay would not adequately represent them, and in the hope that perhaps they would be collected elsewhere. I decided to exclude all my own work. There are other painful exclusions. And for all this, the entire process of *dispositio* still became obtrusively personal. More than once, I found myself absent-mindedly underlining a favorite passage on a freshly copied manuscript—only to have to return to the copier one more time.

And so, better late than never. My appreciation to Senior Editor Murphy for his infinite patience. To Northwestern University, and my Department, for a (seemingly) infinite copying budget. To all the journals and collections that graciously consented to having this valued material reprinted. And to all my colleagues included here (or not), may you find here no party line, no relics, no finalized sacred truth. Instead, as always in rhetorical inquiry, may propriety and provocation go hand in hand.

Notes

1. Brian Vickers, *In Defense of Rhetoric*. Oxford: Clarendon Press, 1988.
2. Robert Hariman, "Status, Marginality, and Rhetorical Theory," *Quarterly Journal of Speech* 72 (1986), 37–50.
3. Vickers, *Op Cit.*, 375–434.
4. Samuel Ijsseling, *Rhetoric and Philosophy in Conflict: an Historical Survey*. The Hague: Martinus Nijhoff (1976), 115–126.
5. Ernesto Grassi, *Rhetoric as Philosophy: the Humanist Tradition*. University Park: the Pennsylvania State University Press (1980), 102–114.
6. Thomas B. Farrell, "From the Parthenon to the Bassinet: Death and Rebirth Along the Epistemic Trail, *Quarterly Journal of Speech* 76 (1990): 78–84.
7. Lloyd F. Bitzer, "The Rhetorical Situation," *Philosophy and Rhetoric*, I (1968), 1–14.
8. Alasdair MacIntyre, *After Virtue* (Notre Dame, Indiana: University of Notre Dame Press, 1981).

Political Rhetoric
by Lloyd F. Bitzer

If study of past and present political rhetoric merely commits us to consider bombastic language, sophistic word tricks, and deceptive speech, we should abandon this subject to those who analyze errant forms of communication. If review of classical theories of political rhetoric leads us only to resurrect arcane notions that have little bearing on contemporary political communication, then we should leave to historians the study of ancient texts and turn to other matters. However, the practice of political rhetoric is far more than uses or misuses of language; it is the engagement of motives, principles, thoughts, arguments, and sentiments in communications—an engagement which functions pragmatically to form attitudes and assist judgments regarding the broad range of civic affairs. Political rhetoric serves the art of politics at every turn, both as a mode of thought and as an instrument of expression and action. The classical theories of political rhetoric provide for us rich principles and distinctions won through dialectical struggle with hard problems of government and civic affairs: Where is the location and what is the use of power and authority? Where and what are the sources of premises? To what extent must political discourse exhibit truth and moral quality? Therefore, any inquiry into political thought and communication should undertake the subject of political rhetoric with appreciation of its proper definition and attention to the contributions of its foremost theorists.

This chapter begins with a sketch of the kind of rhetoric which links easily and naturally with political thought and action. Thereafter topics and problems relevant to the study of political rhetoric are taken up, and along the way concepts useful to critics, theorists, and students are surveyed.

Reprinted from Nimmo and Keith (eds.) *Handbook of Political Communication* (Beverly Hills: Sage Publications, 1981). Reprinted by permission of Sage Publications.

The Concept of Rhetoric

Rhetoric has received virtually uninterrupted study for nearly 2500 years—from the time of Plato and Aristotle to the present. Until print became a practical medium of communication, rhetoric and public speaking throughout most of these centuries were nearly synonymous. Numerous definitions strongly imply this historic connection: Quintilian, for example, defined rhetoric as "the art of speaking well" (1958). In discussions of rhetoric, theorists spoke typically of public speaking or oratory; they explained the talents and duties of the speaker, the types of speeches, and the methods of invention, arrangement, style, memory, and delivery by which a speech could be created and presented to an audience. After the advent of print, almost every book on rhetoric was composed with reference to speaking or writing. Modern and contemporary theorists regard rhetoric broadly as a method of inquiry and communication applicable to spoken and written discourse, as well as to broadcasting, film, and other media.

Common to all rhetorics is consideration of methods and techniques whereby expression and communication can be rendered effective. Beyond this element, however, different theories focus on other skills and ends. The sophistic rhetoric of ancient Greece portrayed by Plato's dialogues and other classical sources emphasized the persuasive power of the speaker and his discourse for the producing of intended effects. Plato, after refuting that view, called for a rhetoric devoted to the health of the soul—both the soul of the individual and the collective soul of the polis. His noble rhetor would be physician to the audience, the medicine being those truths, values, and persuasive messages sufficient to keep the audience in health or return it to health. While the sophists focused on the speaker's influence and Plato on the audience's well-being, Aristotle conceived rhetoric as a kind of method and communication leading to reliable judgments about practical and civic matters. Cicero and Quintilian, taking a broader view, regarded rhetoric as the theory of communication; still, politics was its principal stage. In Quintilian's view, the finished orator and the ideal statesman were identical. Thus, his *Institutes of Oratory* served both as the manual of instruction for the orator—"the good man speaking well"—and as the educational program for the Roman citizen. Numerous writers, focusing particularly on the resources of language and style, have identified the strategies and figures of language which contribute to clarity, appropriateness, energy, beauty, and other qualities (Howell, 1956).

Chaim Perelman and Kenneth Burke, the two twentieth-century theorists whose views command the widest study, assign wide scope and basic functions to rhetoric. Perelman (1969) holds rhetoric to be the theory and practice of all argumentation which aims to secure the persuasion and conviction of audiences in political and other humane fields and also in the sciences. Rhetoric is at work whenever a writer or speaker seeks through argument to secure the assent of others to theses he advances. Burke's theory commences not with attention to argumentation, but to the nature of man as the symbol-using animal. Says Burke (1962): "Rhetoric as such is not rooted in any past condition of human society. It is rooted in an essential function of language itself . . . ; the use of language as a symbolic means of inducing cooperation in beings that by nature respond to symbols." In this view, rhetoric seeks to promote cooperation by use of symbolic, linguistic, and other strategies of identification. This is enough to suggest that in Western thought rhetoric has been assigned various ends; it has been brought to the service of politics, religion, science, literary achievement, social intercourse, personal relations, and salesmanship.

The most influential rhetorics, the classical theories of ancient Greece and Rome, show three characteristics especially important to our purpose. First, they were strikingly political in conception and practice. All the major writers—Isocrates, Plato, Aristotle, Cicero, Quintilian—thought that politics was the principal locus for rhetorical thought and communication, and therefore they designed their theories for use by political agents. In the second place, their rhetorics were significantly normative. Each theorist was a reformer seeking to correct defects in political oratory and recommending methods and principles to improve practice. Plato penned history's most famous attack on rhetoric when, speaking through Socrates in *Gorgias,* he denounced sophistic rhetoric as a mere sham art, a kind of "cookery," a means of making the worse appear the better, and a "knack" which substitutes appearance for reality and probability for truth. Aristotle complained that his sophistic predecessors failed to invest rhetoric with sufficient rational character. Quintilian (1958) took pains to explain that his rhetoric aimed not at victory but at "speaking well," by which he meant saying what ought to be said—and speaking in such a way that posterity will judge the speech right, fit, becoming. These and other rhetorics incorporated regulative principles for the purpose of encouraging, though never guaranteeing, that messages and decisions would be informed by fact and wisdom and would serve the public interest. Finally, these theories treated rhetoric as an art, or systematic method, the object of which was to guide practice toward the best activity permitted by circumstances, and they assigned it tasks of the first order. Thus Aristotle defined rhetoric as the art or faculty of discovering the available means of persuasion in any given case; and he placed it alongside dialectic, the two being the arts, or organons, by which we come to judgments about subjects and problems in the field of the contingent. Of all the classical theorists, Aristotle was the most philosophical, rigorous, and at the same time the most concerned with the political realm. This chapter draws heavily from his work.

In agreement with the tradition just reviewed, we regard rhetoric as a method of inquiry and communication which functions to establish judgments, primarily in areas of practical and humane affairs, for ourselves and for the audience addressed. All persons use rhetoric to some extent, since they try to ground judgments on investigation and seek the agreement of other minds through communication. However, many do not take the trouble to acquire competence in handling subjects and problems, and consequently they often embrace viewpoints and seek to persuade others to adopt viewpoints that are weak in conception and shallow in value. It is obvious that we need to judge and persuade not on the basis of whimsy, falsehood, or inadequate information and methods, but rather on the basis of purposeful deliberation which employs as much truth as the subject admits and proceeds systematically through methods of investigation, evaluation, and communication suited to the subject, the audience, and the purpose. This rhetoric differs from both propaganda and the craft of persuasion. The former implies inculcation of beliefs in the absence of critical deliberation, while rhetoric insists on rational justification. The craft of persuasion reduces truth and value to the role of tactic for the sake of making people believe or do what the communicator desires, while rhetoric is committed to truth and value as regulative principles.

Skillful Inquiry and Communication

The notion of political rhetoric often reminds us of messages which stand out because of factors such as intrinsic importance or uniqueness, situational urgency, and short- or long-term influence, or because of the communicator's extraordinary skill, eloquence, or courage in the face of danger. Thus our anthologies contain such touchstones as the Declaration of Independence, the Federalist Papers, Milton's *Areopagitica,* Henry's Liberty or Death speech, Lincoln's Second Inaugural, Churchill's wartime addresses, and Martin Luther King's "I Have A Dream" speech. Such memorable works are only dots on a vast landscape, however. For each impressive speech by an Edmund Burke, ten thousand routine speeches also played their parts well or ill. And for each political speaker or writer who crafted a message, there were countless audience members engaged by those messages who exercised their own rhetorical skills in tasks of interpretation, argumentation, and judgment.

Every citizen who deliberates and creates messages about civic affairs—estimating ends and means, selecting arguments and evidence, weighing factors of advantage, justice, and virtue—engages in political rhetoric. And this activity of deliberation and message-making constitutes genuine political rhetoric even when self-addressed. Indeed, we should acknowledge that one of the most important competencies of the citizen is the ability to deliberate skillfully for himself, as well as for others. Walter Lippmann (1966) once reminded educators that every citizen's education ought to include an art of judging rightly. "Now that we live in a time when, as Huey Long truly said, every man is a king, it is still the prime function of education to instruct and to train the future rulers of the state." A critical task of scholarship, he concluded, is discovering "what should be taught to the future rulers of a modern state" and how citizens can "acquire that capacity of judging rightly which is the essence of wisdom." The competence to "judge rightly" should apply not only to eloquent political communications but also to the mundane; to normal communication settings as well as to private deliberation of civic matters by an individual; to the tasks of the message maker's audience as well as to the message maker.

Skill in political rhetoric must involve union of inquiry and communication. The separation of the two is both dangerous and unphilosophical. If political rhetoric were regarded simply as skillful communicative behavior, then the focus of theory, research, and instruction would go almost inevitably to such matters as causal linkages between communicative behaviors and their effects, while such matters as thought, the soundness of arguments, and the foundation of positions would be short-circuited. Politics is too important and its stakes too large for us to allow its fortunes to be committed to a theory of communication divorced from inquiry—in short, to a know-nothing rhetoric. This is one of the reasons Plato rejected the sophistic rhetoric of his time: It purported to teach tactics of persuasion to political agents who had neither motive nor means to discover the truth or probable truth of matters on which they spoke: thus it amounted to a rhetoric of ignorance, dangerous to its users and to the public. The separation of inquiry and communication is also unphilosophical. Political discourse makes claims and urges judgments about policies and actions which deserve to stand or fall on the strength of the evidence and proofs that support them. This is the very essence of rational thought. For this reason Aristotle held that the essential element of rhetorical discourse is proof, while all else is accessory. Moreover, if we view political rhetoric as a system comprised of many competing messages, we should hold that its proper function is "deliberation," using the word in its general sense of inquiry on a large scale. For example, deliberation is the proper function of all the messages in congressional committee hearings, public speeches, newspaper and magazine articles, and formal debates on the question of ratifying Panama Canal treaties.

Classical rhetoricians, particularly the Romans, tried to assure complete education regarding the whole art of political deliberation by dividing rhetoric into five essential parts—invention, arrangement, style, memory, and delivery. According to the *Rhetorica ad Herennium,*

> invention is the devising of matter, true or plausible, that would make the case convincing. Arrangement is the ordering and distribution of the matter, making clear the place to which each thing is to be assigned. Style is the adaptation of suitable words and sentences to the matter devised. Memory is the firm retention in the mind of the matter, words, and arrangement. Delivery is the graceful regulation of voice, countenance, and gesture.

These five covered practically all the concepts, rules, and methods concerning both inquiry and communication.

Theorists did not slight the first part, invention; indeed, they copiously detailed its task of discovering, creating, and judging the subject matter of discourse. Most of Aristotle's *Rhetoric* was concerned with invention, leading Quintilian to complain that Aristotle neglected the other four parts. Presupposing the speaker's wide learning and information about the subject at hand, theorists of invention provided systems of topics to aid the speaker. For example, an advocate and a prosecutor preparing to defend and accuse a party at trial—either in a formal judicial setting or in the court of public opinion—were advised to examine the basic causes of human action, which Aristotle identified and characterized as chance, nature, compulsion, habit, reason, passion, and desire. Topics were provided to guide inquiry in relation to types of discourse—deliberative, forensic, and epideictic; modes of proof—logos, ethos, and pathos; kinds of disputes—conjectural, definitional, qualitative, and procedural; arguments, according to kinds, forms, premises; audiences, according to various factors including age and social standing. The topics, singly and in combination, were heuristic methods by which to probe in the right places.

Subject Matter

The territory of political rhetoric implies some idea of the "public's business," or public affairs, and this phrase in turn implies some identity of the "public." (Bitzer, 1978). What, then, is the public, and what is the public's business? We borrow answers from John Dewey's *The Public and Its Problems*. Seeking to account for the origin of the state, Dewey distinguished between public and private actions and identified public business according to the seriousness and duration of the consequences of public action.

> We take then our point of departure from the objective fact that human acts have consequences upon others, that some of these consequences are perceived, and that their perception leads to subsequent effort to control action so as to secure some consequences and avoid others. Following this clue, we are led to remark that the consequences are of two kinds, those which affect the persons directly engaged in a transaction, and those which affect others beyond those immediately concerned. In this distinction we find the germ of the distinction between the private and the public. When indirect consequences of an action are confined, or are thought to be confined, mainly to the persons directly engaged in it, the transaction is a private one [Dewey, 1927, p. 12].

In Dewey's view, then, the consequences of some transactions are short-lived, nonrecurring, and of only minor significance; they do not require attention and control. But other transactions produce consequences that are widespread and enduring; and to the extent that they affect persons other than oneself for good or evil, the transactions and their consequences amount to the public's business. Moreover, Dewey identified as the public that class of persons significantly affected by public transactions and their consequences. The state and its machinery—laws, courts, offices, and so on—come into existence for the purpose of caring for and conducting the public's business.

We may say that political rhetoric deals with matters thought to constitute the public's business—that is, all transactions and their consequences which significantly affect the public or its parts. This includes the notion of possessions, since the public acquires things of value which need protection and nurture. Possessions in the physical sense are obvious public lands and buildings, for example, as well as such things as clean air and water. But the public also possesses much in the realm of language and thought—laws, principles, authoritative documents, values, symbols, and other elements of its mythos—which may require protection or shoring up because these, in whole or in part, are essential to the public's character and stable identity.

Ambiguous areas rather than sharp lines separate political from other kinds of rhetoric. In the first place, persons disagree over whether some transactions are actually public; whether a public transaction has or will have significant consequences; whether an alleged possession is a legitimate possession of the public; and whether a possession deserves protection or nurture. The fact that disagreements on such points attain stature as serious public issues indicates the centrality of political rhetoric even on questions of what constitutes the business of the public. In the second place, human motives and activities are often mixed in such a way that it is difficult to find the line between essentially political rhetoric and religious, aesthetic, or social rhetoric. Finally, even discourse that in its function appears to be essentially religious or philosophical or purely entertaining will often produce effects—sometimes distant—on beliefs and attitudes relevant to the public's business. This is one reason why some critics argue that the state should control activities and discourses that appear not to be political in nature.

To observe that political rhetoric is about subject matter which affects the public and is the public's business is not to say that rhetoric itself is a discipline or science with content in the sense that political science, physics, and psychology have content. Aristotle held explicitly that rhetoric must be understood as a general art (akin to dialectic, or logic) consisting not of knowledge about specialized fields but of classifications, topics, methods, lines of argument, probabilities, prudential rules, and so on. This general art is widely applicable to matters which come before citizens for judgment when there is no special discipline or science to guide choice. This point is important for two reasons: First, as a matter of theoretical cleanliness, rhetoric should be distinguished from other arts and sciences. (Readers of Plato's *Gorgias* will recall that Gorgias, muddled in his thought, momentarily confused rhetoric with mathematics.) Second, and more important practically, we should not try to prove a proposition that belongs to physiology by using rhetoric, or vice versa; in either case, a gross methodological error would be involved. It is erroneous to set out to establish by means of rhetoric that a fetus has or has not certain physiological characteristics, and equally wrong to seek to prove, by using methods and knowledge of physiology, that moral laws were or were not violated by destruction of a fetus.

Thomas DeQuincy held that rhetoric deals mainly with matters which lie in that vast field "where there is a *pro* and a *con,* with the chance of right and wrong, true and false, distributed in varying proportions between them" (1967, p. 91). Aristotle meant approximately the same thing when he said rhetoric deals with matters that are contingent rather than necessary, questions which might be answered one way or another, with problems which permit probable rather than certain conclusions. We do not deliberate rhetorically, he said, about absolute certainties or about matters that are fixed by nature. In other words, rhetoric applies to contingent and probable matters which are subjects of actual or possible disagreement by serious people, and which permit alternative beliefs, values, and positions.

Rhetorical subjects, then, are mainly probable, contingent, interest-laden, and frequently in contention. These characteristics mark the central realm of activity for rhetoric, which is the practical world of human affairs. Here rhetoric labors between the challenge and the fitting response, the imperfection and the remedy, the crisis and the calm. This, Kenneth Burke colorfully remarked, is the area of the human barnyard—the big scramble. Some arts and disciplines shun strife, discord, practical interests, and effects: They work quietly, removed from the practical business of life and free from the burdens of decision and action. Rhetoric, however, is geared for human affairs, and much of its work lies in the bustle and jostling of political and social deliberations, in courtrooms, assemblies, and in controversies of many kinds. Unlike the sciences, which may be said to deal with the realm of truth, rhetoric deals with the realm of action where truth and feeling, actuality and motive, problems, uncertainties, hopes, and visions all play a role in the formation of judgment and action.

Characteristically, political subject matter engages interests, values, emotions, and aspirations. As a natural consequence, messages designed for persuasion in courts, assemblies, political campaigns, and public ceremonies make their way on arguments linked to valued premises, facts linked to interests, descriptions and visions linked to emotions, and on language which rouses and satisfies appetites by means of its form as well as its substance. Political rhetoric which presents itself as dispassionate, purely objective, or empirical only disguises the operating forces of valuation. Even those empirical public opinion polls issued during presidential campaigns engage partisan motives and function persuasively, notwithstanding their authors' protestations of scientific and journalistic purity.

The fact that human valuation interacts with contingent subject matter helps explain why political rhetoric must ever remain unscientific; that is, why it will refuse to be held to statements of the true-false variety. Values and interests will exert such force that persons contending in the same context and about the same subject will disagree in what they perceive and say, a political speaker will be inconsistent from one situation to another, and the perceived truth of political discourse will vary markedly across contexts. This variable quality would be of little note, perhaps, if political rhetoric were inconsequential. But in fact the consequences are as large as the health of the state and the well-being of each and every citizen.

Political rhetoric has served good ends and bad, used intelligence and defied it, and harnessed the noblest of motives and the worst. It has aided the triumph of magnificent causes; but it has also furthered the reign of despots and promoted massive lies and injuries. In short, political rhetoric is dangerous. This is why practically every theorist of rhetoric has labored to identify and define principles, methods, and standards which, if observed, would bring political rhetoric under the influence of a rationality suitable to practical action, thus making it as good as it can be.

Action and Rhetorical Proof

A fundamental question is whether political persuasion is essential to the human enterprise or some part of it. This is not to ask whether it is sometimes useful in a purely utilitarian sense: Political persuasion may be useful and yet lack centrality if it is only an incidental aspect of life capable of being eliminated with no significant loss and no alteration in the nature of the human being or the human community. Let us say that political persuasion must be counted as essential if it is necessary to civic cooperation and decision-making. Should it fail this test, we would doubt its centrality.

Now, we might define man as the communicating animal, thus calling attention to the fact that communicability is essential to being human. This conception, however, does not bear closely enough on the question of whether political persuasion is essential: It is possible that human beings must communicate, but need not engage in political persuasion. Or we might hold the view that political and other kinds of persuasion are essential because those things we count as believable—from facts to laws of nature, from preferences to maxims of moral conduct—in the final analysis are objects of agreement which received that status through processes of persuasion (Ziman, 1968). But this view encounters theoretical and commonsense objections: For example, few of us are prepared to reduce facts and truths of the physical universe to the status of objects of agreement. We are inclined to think that distinctions should be made between is and ought, actuality and possibility, necessity and contingency, motion and action, and between scientific method by which we come to know and judge things capable of precision and certainty on one hand and other modes of proof and persuasion by which we properly judge and act with some degree of confidence regarding uncertain matters on the other.

One way to place political rhetoric within the whole scheme of human endeavor begins with the great fact of division. As Kenneth Burke remarks, "if men were not apart from one another, there would be no need for the rhetorician to proclaim their unity. If men were wholly and truly of one substance, absolute communication would be of man's very essence." But individuals are at odds with one another; and so also are groups, cultures, and generations. The human condition is shot through with divisiveness, separation, competition. This condition explains why the key notion in Burke's theory of rhetoric is identification, which "is affirmed with earnestness precisely because there is division. Identification is compensatory to division." Rhetoric functions through language, a kind of symbolic action, to "induce cooperation in beings that by nature respond to symbols." Human agents with competing motives, interests, meanings, and truths find themselves at odds, sometimes radically so; but at the same time they share those same elements in some degree as a condition of their common understanding and humanity. There is, then, a constant condition of both division and community; our efforts to bridge gaps, even when successful, sometimes create others; and some of our most exhausting labor toward cooperation only anticipates division, as when we take great pains to rally ourselves for war. Rhetoric's function is essentially pragmatic—to find common meaning, unifying symbols, and ways of acting together, thus promoting cooperation.

It is but a small step from the general notion of cooperation to the specific notion of political cooperation, which involves strategies of identification and ways of inducing joint action that relate to political life and, indeed, make political life possible. Says Burke (1962): "Identification ranges from the politician who, addressing an audience of farmers, says, 'I was a farm boy myself,' through the mysteries of social status, to the mystic's devout identification with the source of all being" (pp. 522, 546–547, 567). Strategies of identification, at once strategies of persuasion, are at work when divergent purposes or interests are linked, when the material and formal features of arguments bring minds to agreement on premises and conclusions, when meanings, images, and other resources of language bring us to the same thoughts and feelings, and when the regimens to which we submit succeed in harmonizing our actions. All of this takes place in the realm of action and symbolism, not in the realm of motion and physicality. In the absence of political persuasion, only motion or force might impose some discipline on the physical aspects of persons; but it could never produce a community of minds.

Aristotle's placement of rhetoric among the arts and sciences and his conception of the mission of political persuasion result from a line of reasoning different from Burke's. The main reason for the difference is that Aristotle holds judgment to be rhetoric's chief concern: Properly speaking, the audience is a judge, and the object of rhetorical transactions involving speakers and listeners is to produce reliable judgments. His concern is announced at the very beginning of the *Rhetoric* with the complaint that his sophistic predecessors placed an inappropriate emphasis on appeals to the emotions, and that this emphasis put the audience into the wrong emotional condition, thus warping their judgment: "It is not right to pervert the judge by moving him to anger or envy or pity—one might as well warp a carpenter's rule before using it." Aristotle knew that a speaker's powerful delivery and clever style can exert persuasive force; but, he said, these should not be persuasive—they should neither pain nor please, because the case should be won on the strength of the proofs. In rhetoric, only the proofs—logos, ethos, and pathos—are essential; everything else is accessory.

Logos (logical proof) refers to the probity of thought and the convincing quality of evidence and arguments, ethos (ethical proof) to the credibility and integrity of the speaker, and pathos (emotional proof) to the emotional condition of the audience. When an audience is persuaded to accept a speaker's position, all three types of proof are usually operative: The audience accepts as reliable the information and arguments set forth by the speaker (logos); the audience considers the speaker to be trustworthy, expert, authoritative (ethos); and the audience experiences interests or emotions that influence the judgment it makes (pathos). Thus, "the orator must not only try to make the argument of his speech demonstrative and worthy of belief; he must also make his own character look right and put his hearers, who are to decide, into the right frame of mind" (Aristotle, 1946, p. 1377a). Proofs of these types are called "artistic" when they are generated by the speech itself, and "inartistic" when they already exist and are operative.

Much of the first and second books of Aristotle's *Rhetoric* treat these kinds of proof. In amplifying logos, Aristotle treats the two broad forms of rhetorical argument—enthymeme, or the rhetorical syllogism, and example, the rhetorical induction. In addition, he discusses the materials of which enthymemes are made (probabilities, infallible signs, fallible signs, and examples), the premises appropriate to deliberative, forensic, and epideictic speeches, constructive and refutative arguments, sound and sophistical arguments, and 28 lines or patterns which commonly occur, such as arguments from precedent, from cause, from good and evil consequences, from opposites, and so on. He makes it clear that logical proof in rhetoric differs from proof in science: The former is less logically rigorous; it ordinarily achieves probability rather than certainty; it must engage premises credible to the audience as a condition of persuasion; and, of course, it deals with matters that are contingent rather than necessary. Ethos has reference to the speaker's trustworthiness or character as a ground of proof. The three constituents of ethos are said to be universal: In the first place, the speaker must display intelligence or knowledge; second, he must be perceived as a person of high moral character; and finally, it must be apparent that he has the best interests of his audience at heart. Aristotle indicates that there is a close tie between ethos and the virtues: The person of highest ethos will be one believed to possess the virtues in the highest degree, among which are knowledge and prudence as well as good will. Pathos is taken up in Book 2, where Aristotle discusses each emotion in detail. "The emotions," he writes, "are all those feelings that so change men as to affect their judgments, and that are also attended by pain or pleasure." Here, then, is one clear reason for the extensive discussion of pathos: The judgment of an audience will be influenced by emotion. His discussion includes the emotions of anger, calmness, friendship, enmity, fear, confidence, shame, shamelessness, kindness, unkindness, pity, indignation, envy, and emulation. At the outset he indicates the pattern of discussion for each emotion. With respect to anger,

> here we must discover (1) what the state of mind of angry people is, (2) who the people are with whom they usually get angry, and (3) on what grounds they get angry with them. It is not enough to know one or even two of these points; unless we know all three, we shall be unable to arouse anger in any one. The same is true of the other emotions. So just as earlier in this work we drew up a list of useful propositions for the orator, let us now proceed in the same way to analyze the subject before us.

At the conclusion of his discussion, Aristotle says: "This completes our discussion of the means by which the several emotions may be produced or dissipated, and upon which depend the persuasive arguments connected with the emotions" (1946, pp. 1378a, 1388b).

This brief account of Aristotle's notion of rhetorical proof leaves unanswered the question, Why are these kinds of proof—these ways of persuasion—essential to political life? Furthermore, while Aristotle recommends that the speaker know the emotions and use emotional proof—for example, to make an audience angry—he nevertheless complains that his predecessors erred by recommending and using pathos. On the surface, this amounts to an incompatibility. The search for Aristotle's view of the essential role of rhetorical proof, including the proper influence of feelings and emotions, takes us to his *Nicomachean Ethics* and *Politics,* both of which, he remarks, are closely linked to rhetoric.

First, rhetoric is put squarely to the service of politics, as a part of it and as an instrument. At the beginning of the *Ethics,* after explaining that ethical studies aim to determine what the good is, Aristotle links ethics to politics: The latter, as the "master science," considers the conditions under which human beings can achieve the good life. Oratory is said to be contained in politics, and to serve as one of its "most honored capacities" along with strategy and household management.

Second, the three problems Aristotle says are paramount in politics—problems about the good, the just, and the noble—coincide with the concerns of his three types of rhetoric: deliberative concerned with the good or expedient, forensic with the just, and epideictic with the noble or praiseworthy.

Third, in the *Politics* (Books 2 and 3) Aristotle explains that deliberation by the many is in the interest of the state. Individuals by themselves tend to form imperfect judgments, influenced in part by defects of prudence, virtue, and emotion; however, "the many, of which each individual is but an ordinary person, when they meet together may very likely be better than the few good, if regarded not individually but collectively, just as a feast to which many contribute is better than a dinner provided out of a single purse." Again: "Now any member of the assembly, taken separately, is certainly inferior to the wise man. But the state is made up of many individuals . . . [and] a multitude is a better judge of many things than any individual." These and similar comments indicate that judgment appropriate to political affairs ordinarily is better when it results from deliberation involving many minds rather than one or a few.

Fourth and most important, the *Ethics* (chiefly Books 2 and 6) explains the rationale underlying the three forms of rhetorical proof—a rationale that draws heavily on Aristotle's notions of practical wisdom, the nature of action, and the golden mean.

(a) Practical wisdom, one of five intellectual excellences or virtues, is concerned with the field of action, aims at good action, deals with matters about which human beings deliberate and particularly with "what is just, noble, and good for man," and is critical to judging rightly: "No choice will be right without practical wisdom and virtue. For virtue determines the end, and practical wisdom makes us do what is conducive to the end." The "man of practical wisdom is *ipso facto* a man of good character."

(b) Good choice in the field of action involves reasoning and desire, and both must be right. Such choice differs from decisions in science and theoretical disciplines: "In the kind of thought involved in theoretical knowledge and not in action or production, the good and the bad state are, respectively, truth and falsehood." On the other hand, "in intellectual activity concerned with action, the good state is truth in harmony with correct desire."

(c) How can desire, emotion, and the choice of ends be said to be correct? Aristotle answers that a choice, desire, or emotion is correct when it hits the right point between extremes of excess and deficiency, a point "relative to us" and dependent on circumstances. "We may thus conclude that virtue or excellence is a characteristic involving choice, and that it consists in observing the mean relative to us, a mean which is defined by a rational principle, such as a man of practical wisdom would use to determine it. It is the mean by reference to two vices: the one of excess and the other of deficiency." It is important to note that there is a mean regarding emotional experience, although selecting the mean is difficult—"it is a hard task to be good." With respect to anger, for example, "anyone can get angry," but the problem is directing anger "to the right person, to the right extent, at the right time, for the right reason, and in the right way." Thus, the moral virtues involve desire and emotion, as well as a rational principle; and these factors are essential in practical wisdom and deliberation.

Why, then, must the three modes of rhetorical proof be used? Because deliberations about the contingent and actionable require engagement of practical wisdom, virtue, and the right emotional experience, else judgment cannot be reliable. Logos, the rational element, is always required; so is ethos, the virtuous character, which is no other than the combination of excellences by which speaker and audience select the mean and aim at the right end; and pathos is required because the right emotional condition is critical to judging correctly.

Finally, why is political persuasion essential? Because when persuasion is right—involving the three modes of proof in a process of deliberation—we come to reliable judgments about matters which must be decided and which can be decided rationally in no other way. Ideally, everyone involved in political deliberations would possess practical wisdom.

Messages and Situations

The territory of contemporary political rhetoric is diverse. It ranges from campaign rallies, with their hoopla and extravagance, to the most somber deliberations in capital offices, from robust persuasive speeches in quest of victory to quiet, informative discourses meant to assist decision-making; and from passionate speeches of competing advocates to reflective statements by judges and critics on what is legally and morally just. The territory varies from press reporting and commentary to symbol-rich ceremonies of public life; from the fervent speeches of the civil rights movement to the threat-backed advocacy of special interest groups; from the televised state-of-the-union address aimed at millions to the self-deliberations of a single constituent; and from the highest congress to the local school board.

All of these messages are political in the sense that they either conduct the public's business or they bear on it. Into the former class fall the most obvious types, such as debates and deliberations in assemblies by citizens and their representatives, as well as public persuasion to rally citizen support outside such assemblies. A wide range of messages bear on the public's business—for example, some press reporting and commentary and other informative messages, social and political criticism, ceremonial discourses, and, in some cases, literary and philosophical works. The messages comprising contemporary political campaigns certainly bear on the public's business, and sometimes they conduct it. A chief characteristic of campaign rhetoric is that it aims to decide who will conduct public affairs; this explains why it plays so much on the themes of the candidates' personal character and competence.

Novels and other poetic works typically create a fictive context that is sufficient to render meaningful the utterances and actions of characters; thus our understanding of a novel or drama seldom requires study of its author's actual historical situation. Philosophical and other theoretical works typically make explicit the arguments and data needed to establish conclusions and perspectives. But political messages, unlike literary and theoretical discourses, link so closely to historical situations that we must understand details of the situation as a condition of understanding the meaning of the message. For example, on January 28, 1980, prior to important presidential primary elections in the East in which he was a candidate, Senator Edward Kennedy presented a televised speech to the people of New England. He prefaced his speech with a short message on the subject of Chappaquiddick. That brief but critically important message will be nearly unintelligible to persons unfamiliar with the Chappaquiddick incident and with Kennedy's misfortunes in the 1980 campaign. The message presumed the audience's knowledge of events, including numerous attacks on his character during the weeks preceding the speech, and its persuasive strategy made appeals to unstated presumptions and values in the audience. Anyone who examines political messages outside familiar contexts will be struck by the fact that context and message are so interactive that they can scarcely be separated: The real message, one might say, is a construction consisting of meanings supplied jointly by speaker and audience; it will seldom be explicit or even fully implied by the speaker's utterances.

Most political messages occur in specific historical situations and are essentially responsive to them. Political speakers find themselves in situations that present problems, crises, obstacles, or other kinds of exigencies which they seek to modify by addressing messages to mediating audiences—that is, to audiences which have sufficient power to modify the exigencies. In a normal situation, the speaker or writer perceives an *exigence* whose positive modification needs or requires the assistance of a message (or a campaign of messages) to engage *constraints*—facts, laws, principles, arguments, feelings, values, emotions, attitudes, motives—that are sufficient to persuade one or more *mediating audiences* to positively modify the exigence. In the absence of an exigence, there would be no motive to speak; in the absence of constraints, messages could not be effective; in the absence of a mediating audience, messages would be futile. Exigence, constraints, and mediating audience thus are the essential constituents of political situations in which discourse is invited.

When political situations are experienced as forceful or urgent, agents are inclined to respond rhetorically, although sometimes the agent does not respond and the situation, lacking response, atrophies to a point where any message would be too late. In the prior example of Senator Kennedy, the exigence—the obstacle to his success in New England primaries—was the public's perceptions about weaknesses in his character, perceptions recently aroused or generated in large part by journalists. He obviously sensed a need to respond by addressing the New England audience capable of modifying the exigence by providing a strong vote in his favor. His analysis was probably correct, but his failure to overcome the Chappaquiddick problem in that instance can be traced to his inability to find and use adequate proofs and other constraints. Kennedy's character exigence, and the situation given focus by it, persisted throughout his presidential campaign. At a broader level, we may observe that a presidential candidate's campaign develops around a set of exigencies, ranging from public issues to personal traits, and that the candidate's speeches on the stump and on special occasions consist largely of commonplaces, or set units of discourse, meant to modify the exigencies. However, in the progress of a campaign new, unanticipated exigencies and situations arise, such as one's own blunders or crisis events over which one has no control.

The exigencies to which political speakers respond are sometimes anchored in external reality, such as rampant inflation or unemployment, but at other times their location is in thought, such as the presence in some people of a dangerous intention or belief. In any case, genuine exigencies involve a real condition, whether physical or mental, coupled with one or more human interests. It is obvious that speakers and writers sometimes seek to modify unreal or fictional exigencies. This may result from misperception, ignorance, playfulness, or strategy. A common practice in political campaigns is to fabricate or purposely exaggerate an exigence (the "missile gap" in the 1960 presidential campaign) for the strategic purpose of creating an issue favorable to victory. The enthusiasm of a political agent often leads to exaggeration, but a fault in moral character leads to creation of a strategic fiction. We should notice also that persons with competing interests may disagree on the actuality of an exigence even when they perceive almost the same facts; this is because interest is a component of every exigence (Bitzer, 1968, 1980).

The dominant types of political rhetoric are those which conduct the public's business. We acknowledge Aristotle's identification of three broad types, while noting that these admit of many combinations and permutations arising from the particularities of situations. Aristotle defined the three types—deliberative, forensic, and epideictic—in terms of the kind of judgment characteristic of each: a judgment about what is expedient or good—deliberative rhetoric; a judgment about what is just or right—forensic; and a judgment regarding what is noble or worthy—epideictic. In ancient Athens the scenes of the three were the assemblies, courts, and ceremonial occasions; but, obviously, messages in all categories go beyond these scenes today.

Political discourse is deliberative when it calls for a judgment concerning the well-being of the public or some part of it. The end-term or ruling value is well-being, or some synonymous term such as the "good" or the "expedient," and the purpose in speaking is either to secure advantageous things by persuading the audience that a policy or proposal or remedy will be advantageous or by dissuading the audience from a course of action likely to lead to injurious consequences. Most political discourse of the normal sort is deliberative: legislators, school board members, political leaders of all kinds usually address audiences on matters of future policy—what should or should not be done. The arguments draw premises from the audience's stock of maxims and beliefs about what constitutes its own or the public's interest. And the speaker who anticipates disputes regarding his proposal is advised by Aristotle to consider four stock issues of deliberation—that is, four places where disputes can occur: What he proposes either can or cannot be done; what he proposes would or would not be just; what he proposes would or would not be advantageous; and what he claims regarding the degree or quality of advantages may be disputed.

Discourse is forensic, or judicial, when it calls for a judgment relative to justice. This ordinarily occurs in response to some denial or violation of law, moral principle, cultural value, and the like. The end-term or ruling value is justice, and the purpose in speaking is to secure a judgment that some act, purpose, or policy is or was just or unjust. The speaker draws premises from conceptions, values, and rules subordinate to justice (laws, constitutions, maxims of conduct) in order to prove the case. The obvious forensic scene is the courts, but numerous other contexts invite this kind of discourse—committee hearings, for example. Often, too, messages conveyed through essays and books judge past events—for instance, those written about President Nixon's conduct in the Watergate incident. There are four stock areas or topics of dispute in forensic discourse, according to Aristotle: an act was or was not done; it was or was not harmful; it did or did not cause the degree of harm attributed to it; and it was or was not justified. The clear cases for forensic deliberation lie in the past; and one cannot judge as right or wrong, lawful or unlawful, what has not yet occurred, except hypothetically. Yet some deliberative proposals involve elements of justice, and for that reason Aristotle's topics of deliberative dispute include the matter of justice. An example would be a congressional debate on whether to reinstate the selective service draft: the issue would be decided in part on a criterion of expediency, but also on whether a draft is ethnically, racially, or socially discriminatory—a question of justice.

Discourse is epideictic when it serves to show that an act, belief, person, institution, or thing deserves approval and praise because it is worthy, or disapproval and blame because it is unworthy. Aristotle said that the end-terms of epideictic are the honorable and the dishonorable (or the noble and the base); that the means are praise and blame; and that the principal topics are virtues and vices. These terms, interpreted broadly, cover all instances of epideictic discourse. There are many kinds of occasions, prompted by events and traditions, when speakers are called upon to praise someone or something—to pay tribute, celebrate, dedicate, approve, commend, compliment, endorse—or when they are called upon to do the opposite, to blame someone or something—to disapprove, belittle, defame, depreciate, reprove. The discourse of praise includes eulogies, commemorative addresses, speeches of celebration, and declarations of ideals. The aspirations, sentiments, and values treated by such messages permit eloquent style, bordering on poetry. Epideictic rhetoric is seldom argumentative; rather, it displays and amplifies the subject's virtuous traits, or vicious ones. The ideals and feelings expressed by the speaker are usually latent in the audience; the speaker gives voice to ideas and sentiments, hopes and aspirations, ideals and judgments which the audience would express if it could. The audience in epideictic situations neither decides and acts with regard to future well-being nor determines the justice of acts; rather, if conditions are right, it responds to the epideictic message with a sympathetic "yes"—it shares in praising or in blaming the subject.

Epideictic units of discourse may be employed in either deliberative or forensic messages: In deliberative, a speaker may wish to prove that a proposed action is desirable because it is honorable as well as expedient; and in forensic, the speaker may wish to strengthen his client's defense by proving that the client is virtuous as well as innocent of the alleged injustice.

Aristotle's view of the function of epideictic discourse in the state is indicated at the close of the *Ethics,* where he laments that the task of developing moral and intellectual virtues, or excellences, among citizens is very difficult. Yet, he remarks, citizens must have a capacity to apprehend what is right, and to judge rightly. It will be difficult, and perhaps impossible, to develop citizen virtues by means of teaching and argument, because most people are under the sway of emotion: "A man whose life is guided by emotion will not listen to an argument that dissuades him, nor will he understand it." What is required is this: "There must first be a character that somehow has an affinity for excellence or virtue, a character that loves what is noble and feels disgust at what is base." We assume from this and other statements of similar kind that the broad function of epideictic discourse is to cultivate and preserve those aspirations, values, beliefs, and habits which form the public's virtues and which are requisite to competent deliberation by the public in civic affairs as well as to the happiness of citizens as individuals.

Campaign rhetoric, broadly conceived, is deliberative; it asks for a judgment by citizens regarding whether one or another candidate would best administer public affairs. When substantive issues are particularly salient, campaign discourse may also decide matters of policy; but the stuff of ordinary campaigns consists of arguments, position statements, testimonials, commercials, and other materials relating to the prudence, good character, and right intentions of the candidate—to the image. This means that much campaign rhetoric, although mainly deliberative in function, works its way by taking up the topics of epideictic: by celebrating the virtues of a candidate, citing his past good deeds, and showing that on selected issues he displays prudence. And, in opposing a candidate, speakers try to show that prudence, character, and intentions are suspect. Thus, discussion of issues (deliberative) tends to be subsumed under discussion of images (epideictic). Occasionally, forensic themes of guilt or innocence enter, as they did in 1980 regarding the candidacy of Edward Kennedy.

It is important to notice that a significant part of campaign rhetoric centers on mistakes: The candidate makes an erroneous statement, or he says something contradictory, or he expresses a judgment showing lack of prudence—lack of practical wisdom. The opposition quickly dramatizes the mistake—a sign the guilty politician is unfit for office; and the press often gives a mistake front-page headlines. One example was President Gerald Ford's mistake in the second debate with Jimmy Carter in 1976: Responding to a panelist's question, Ford declared that the countries of Eastern Europe are not under the domination of the Soviet Union. That mistake dominated campaign rhetoric for about five days, until Ford admitted he had not said what he meant. During the same campaign year, Jimmy Carter suffered for weeks because of a lack of prudence in agreeing to a *Playboy* magazine interview and in the interview using language offensive to millions. What explains the attention given to such mistakes? For the competing candidates, serious mistakes obviously provide points of easy attack. For the press, mistakes are sometimes the most newsworthy matters to report. And it surely is true that a voter often enjoys learning that a candidate has made a major error: For voters, mistakes count as evidence that their assessment of a candidate is correct. But the importance of mistakes in campaign rhetoric rests on a more basic point: The public forms fairly reliable judgments about candidates by observing their mistakes—especially their flaws in reasoning, character, and prudence. Most voters are not well educated about details of issues and legislation, although they should be; consequently, most are not good judges of a candidate's pronouncements on complicated issues. But most voters do have sound views on the constituents of logical reasoning, good character, and prudence. Thus, when a candidate makes a mistake of reasoning, or of practical wisdom, or a mistake resulting from a flaw in character, the public is quick to recognize and, by and large, competent to judge it. Mistakes provide the public with tests of candidates' intelligence, character, and prudence, which accounts for why they play a most important role in campaigns.

Although Aristotle's *Rhetoric* did not provide for a class of *informative* discourse, we should do so, because the occasions for messages that inform the public are abundant. Furthermore, there exist professionals, established message forms, and industries for the purpose of presenting information to the public. The end-term or ruling value of informative discourse must be truth, or knowledge; the purpose of messages is to state and defend what is true, or deny and refute what is false. When argument is unneeded, the means are affirmation and denial, and when argument is required, the means are proof and refutation. Units of informative discourse occur subordinately in deliberative, forensic, and epideictic messages. However, in pure instances of informative discourse, information is generated and conveyed not because it serves the ends of goodness, justice, or nobility, but simply because it is truth the audience should know or would want to know—it relates to their interests. News reporters and analysts in their reports and explanations do not seek primarily to improve the well-being of their audience or to uphold the just or noble, although sometimes their discourse has these effects; they seek to provide news, interpretations, and conclusions which are true and of interest to the public. It seems self-evident that a competent public must receive a steady supply of information that is reliable and relevant to its real or perceived interests, and that "news" in the broad sense should answer that need.

Journalists have been at work for generations as reporters, interpreters, seers, agitators, critics of government, and advisors. But today's journalists, swelled by broadcasters, assisted by new technologies, and involved in the competitive merchandising of news, constitute a new class of orators. Although they would prefer not to be called orators, or rhetoricians, in fact the term fits: They form a profession of communicators including the prestige commentators and news analysts, anchorpersons, reporters, editors, and all who convey news to the public through television, radio, newspaper, and magazine. Their message-making is voluminous; they have easy access to the most available and effective channels of public communication—channels already linked to audiences prepared to read and hear them; they win our trust more easily and securely than do politicians; and perhaps the journalists, rather than the preachers and politicians, have become the dominant speakers in our political life. Whether the orators of news have an art of inquiry and communication adequate to their mission is a question of large importance.

Toward Political Competence

A sound theory of political rhetoric regards the audience as neither a terminal receiver of messages nor a passive object to be manipulated, but as an active, participating agent in deliberations. Reliable deliberations require a competent audience no less than a competent speaker, because each is a center of information, interest, and intelligence with the capacity to influence the other; and neither is assumed to be generally wiser than the other. The best audience will be the one possessing the most practical wisdom, skill, and knowledge relevant to the case at hand. Recognition of these principles is implicit in our efforts to elect wise and skillful men and women to legislative bodies, and in our expectations that biased or impractical speakers and audiences will produce biased or impractical decisions.

It follows that, ideally, a speaker would always address the audience most competent to judge the matter about which he speaks, and as a rule would not ask an incompetent audience to decide or act. However, sometimes the most competent audience is unavailable or powerless, and the situation virtually requires persuading an audience that is biased, misinformed, or otherwise incompetent. A speaker who persuades such an audience may have to use premises drawn from its field of beliefs and commitments even though these grounds of assent would be rejected by a more competent audience. For responsible speakers, such occasions pose an obvious dilemma, sometimes escaped by designing a message that would be acceptable to the most competent audience and at the same time is persuasive to the audience addressed. Occasionally the dilemma cannot be escaped, and with reference to it Quintilian remarked that the advocate might need to deceive a bad judge in order to make justice prevail.

What is the ideal condition of deliberation? Chaim Perelman provides an ideal involving address to the "universal audience," a pivotal concept in his theory of rhetoric and argumentation. The universal audience refers to a class of ideal hearers or readers to whom an arguer appeals as the perfectly reasonable and impartial audience. This audience would not be influenced by such things as flattery, prejudices, local conventions, private preferences, falsehoods, and invalid reasoning. It would be influenced instead by fact and truth, by reality, and by faultless

reasoning. Statements and arguments which win the assent of the universal audience secure authoritative confirmation as true and sound. In other words, the
universal audience is a model or standard of perfection: it provides "a norm for
objective argumentation." Any actual audience may be evaluated in terms of how
nearly it approximates this ideal. Furthermore, any message may be evaluated in
terms of how much of it would be accepted by the universal audience: "In general,
a speaker or writer who desires to win the adherence of the universal audience will
give up arguments that this audience as he conceives it—would find inadmissible,
even when he is addressing a particular audience. He will deem it almost immoral
to resort to an argument which is not, in his own eyes, a rational one." The universal
audience is never fully realized in an actual, or particular, audience, but exists as
an ideal formulated by the speaker or by a group, profession, or culture. All normal
persons are capable of membership in the universal audience at some times and on
some matters provided they accept only what is true and reasonable. But when
preferences, values, and aspirations exert influence, this audience ceases to be
"universal" (Perelman & Olbrechts-Tyteca, 1969, pp. 13–14).

Aristotle's portrait of persons ideally suited to political deliberation has features
we have already noticed. First, they have the commitment to rationality, fact, and
truth mentioned by Perelman. However, their excellence is displayed chiefly in
deliberations about matters contingent, indeterminate, and actionable, when choice
necessarily involves pleasure and pain, emotion, and preference. In the second
place, therefore, Aristotle's ideal agents exercise their perfected moral and intellectual virtues, chiefly practical wisdom, for the purpose of deliberating well and
making reliable choices. Third, this class of persons, limited to those having
practical wisdom, is small in number relative to the whole population because only
a few people possess the essential qualities.

Shifting from the ideal to the real, let us ask, What sort of group actually
deliberates about and decides most of the public's business? For the most part, the
public's business is conducted by what we may call assigned-function organizations—that is, organizations of persons elected or appointed to perform functions
mandated by law, custom, or decree of a parent organization. Such organizations
include legislative assemblies, commissions, school boards, special committees,
juries, judicial panels, and the like. Members deliberate among themselves; also
they are addressed by speakers from outside their ranks. Among the characteristics
of the assigned-function organization are these: (1) It has an assigned jurisdiction
or area of concern; that is, it is established to handle a class of problems or
exigencies. (2) It is duty-bound to fulfill its functions expeditiously, faithfully, and
with a view to the public interest. Frequently the organization's adherence to these
goals is enforced by rules. (3) It usually has considerable duration. A jury may serve
for weeks or months, and some governmental bodies have continued existence even
while membership changes. (4) As a consequence of these characteristics, the
organization tends to be well informed about matters within its scope, motivated
by the right interests, and guided by familiar principles and methods. (5) Its
members ordinarily are selected because of known qualifications; or, if elected,
there is at least the possibility that electors will select members on recognition of

their knowledge and skill. At any rate, as a result of working together for a period of time, they come to possess common knowledge and interests, and so they come to have even greater homogeneity. (6) As its experience increases, this organization becomes increasingly stable and self-confident and settles into more and more uniform procedures. (7) It has power which it appreciates and protects, and so it resists efforts to change its power, methods, and standards; also, often laws and conventions establish protections to allow the organization to do its work without undue pressures from outside. Owing to these characteristics, the assigned-function organization is far more competent than citizens selected at random. Political entities entrust to such organizations the conduct of important categories of public business. Legal decisions, legislation, policies, and similar matters result from their deliberations.

If we look for organizations and groups that conduct the public's business through somewhat formal deliberation, we can find none except assigned-function organizations. Other groups, it is true, are addressed by political speakers and sometimes make decisions—such groups as special-interest organizations, institutional and elite audiences, and the public at large; but it is very doubtful that these engage in the kind of political deliberation that would make their decisions right. The reason genuine deliberation sometimes occurs outside assigned-function organizations is either that some sponsors and speakers take special pains to promote it or that the individual citizen initiates deliberation alone or with associates.

Two facts seem ominously important. The first is that the public at large is not a deliberative organization, and the second is that great numbers of citizens live out their lives having never participated in rigorous political deliberation. Perhaps the whole public cannot become a deliberative body, and perhaps most individuals cannot become competent citizens; if so, then maybe it is a good thing that assigned-function organizations conduct the public's business. On the other hand, assigning the duties of citizenship to a few persons may actually cultivate an even larger class of incompetent citizens.

A third important fact is that political messages addressed to the general public are ordinarily shallow—a description applicable to campaign discourse, presidential messages, and some press reporting and commentary, to name a few examples. Analysis of those messages will show that they seldom invite deliberation, and we may suspect the reason traces to the fact that they are meant to engage a public that is not prepared to deliberate.

There are, then, large problems for all who hold that the public should be competent and that political communication should engage it responsibly in processes of decision-making. The problems we have noted relate to political rhetoric on local and national scales, which at once reminds us that the problems of political competence are larger. In fact, we should conceive the whole of mankind as a single massive public whose vital interests are at stake, who require proper representation in assemblies empowered to conduct their business, and who need to acquire an art of judging rightly as citizens of the world. A daring political strategy assisted by the most artful communication will be needed to create a competent world community out of the divisions that now exist.

Works Cited

Aristotle. *Rhetoric* (W. R. Roberts, trans.). Oxford: Clarendon Press, 1946.

Aristotle. *Politics* (B. Jowett, trans.). Cleveland: Fine Editions Press, 1952

Aristotle. *Nicomachacan ethics* (M. Ostwald, trans.). Indianapolis: Bobbs-Merrill, 1962

Bitzer, L. F. The rhetorical situation. *Philosophy and Rhetoric,* 1, 1968.

Bitzer, L. F. Rhetoric and public knowledge. In D. M. Burks (Ed.), *Rhetoric, philosophy and literature: An exploration.* West Lafayette: Purdue University Press, 1978.

Bitzer, L. F. Functional communication: A situational perspective. In E. E. White (Ed.), *Rhetoric in transition: Studies in the nature and uses of rhetoric.* University Park: Pennsylvania State University Press, 1980.

Burke, K. *A grammar of motives and a rhetoric of motives.* Cleveland: World Publishing, 1962.

DeQuincey, T. In F. Burwick (Ed.), *Selected essays on rhetoric.* Carbondale: Southern Illinois University Press, 1967.

Dewey, J. *The public and its problems.* Chicago: Swallow Press, 1927.

Howell, W. S. *Logic and rhetoric in England, 1500–1700.* Princeton: Princeton University Press, 1956.

Kennedy, G. A. *Classical rhetoric and its Christian and secular tradition from ancient to modern times.* Chapel Hill: University of North Carolina Press, 1980.

Lippmann, W. L. Speech presented at a convocation sponsored by the Center for the Study of Democratic Institutions, Beverly Hills, California, in *The Capital Times,* Madison, Wisconsin, May 9, 1966.

Perelman, C., & Olbrechts-Tyteca, L. *The new rhetoric: A treatise on argumentation.* Notre Dame: Notre Dame University Press, 1969.

Plato. *The Dialogues* (B. Jowett, trans.). New York: Random House, 1937.

Quintilian. *Institutes of oratory* (H. E. Butler, trans.). Cambridge: Harvard University Press, 1958.

Rhetorica ad herennium (H. Caplan, trans.). Cambridge: Harvard University Press, 1954.

Ziman, J. *Public knowledge: The social dimensions of science.* Cambridge: Cambridge University Press, 1968.

The Ontological Foundations
of Rhetorical Theory
by Karlyn Kohrs Campbell

In an article delineating the ways in which rhetoric and philosophy are mutually relevant, Henry W. Johnstone, Jr. asserted that conclusions regarding the nature of language and of rational decision-making which follow logically from philosophies assuming that man is, by nature, a rhetorical being differ significantly from those which follow logically from philosophies which do not make that assumption.1 This distinction is one which arises in human ontology, the branch of philosophy which is concerned with the study of the nature and the essential characteristics of man. Although philosophies which deny that rhetoric is an indispensable part of human experience have stimulated rhetorical scholars, all rhetorical theories make the ontological assumption that man is, by nature, subject to and capable of persuasion. In spite of this common philosophical ground, explanations of how and why persuasion occurs have produced rhetorical theories which differ from each other in important ways.

Three interpretations of this common ontological presumption have become dominant. Traditional theory explains that man is rhetorical because he is rational; behavioristic theory explains that he is rhetorical because he has certain basic, unlearned drives; theories of symbolic behavior explain that he is rhetorical because he is the symbol-using or signifying animal. In this paper I shall argue that the last interpretation is the most productive and viable basis for a complete and coherent theory of rhetoric.

Traditional Theory

The fundamental assumption underlying traditional theory is that man is capable of and subject to persuasion because he is, by nature, a rational being, and that, as

Reprinted from *Philosophy and Rhetoric* 3 (1970). Copyright 1970 by the Pennsylvania State University. Reproduced by permission of the publisher.

a consequence, rhetoric is the art of reasoned discourse or argumentation. This explanation of human persuadability is developed from the Aristotelian view that man's unique attribute is the capacity to exercise his rational faculty. Because Aristotelian ontology defines man in terms of his purpose or *telos*, it necessarily leads to the ethical principle that man is most human, most fulfilled, when he is acting in obedience to reason. Consequently, "true" or "genuine" rhetoric becomes the art by which men are induced to act in obedience to reason in contrast to "false" or "sophistic" rhetoric which uses any and all means to produce acquiescence. Traditional theory follows the Aristotelian dictum that "no rhetoric is genuine which is not based upon dialectics or the art of logical demonstration."[2]

Traditional theorists do not deny that nonrational (i.e., emotional, psychological, and physiological) factors affect persuasion, but insist that such appeals are subsidiary to or contingent upon judgments resulting from rational means of persuasion.[3] In effect, they argue that if man had no rational capacities, he would still act to satisfy his needs and be subject to certain forms of influence, but he would not be capable of persuasion. True persuasion or genuine rhetoric depends on the capacity to conceptualize alternatives and to make judgments regarding which is most consistent and valid. As judgments must be made and as men must *choose* whether or not to act in obedience to reason, rhetoric is necessary because it induces judgments and actions consistent with rational deliberation; and it is desirable because, when men act in obedience to reason, their acts are morally preferable.

A primary objection to the rationalistic interpretation of human persuadability is that, by its very nature, it cannot provide a basis from which to scrutinize all persuasive uses of language; it cannot generate a complete theory of the rhetorical dimensions of language usage. "False" persuasion and "sham" or "sophistic" rhetoric, however evil and undesirable, are still instances of the persuasive use of language which may provide insight into the rhetorical process, yet the critic is enjoined from examining them or constrained to dismiss them with a general, and perhaps superficial, condemnation. Critics and theorists who adopt the rationalistic perspective are led invariably to denigrate or ignore those genres of discourse seeking acquiescence primarily through means other than appeals to reason. Moreover, these critics and theorists are tempted to fit all possible discourses into a sometimes Procrustean logical form ill-suited to the associational or convoluted structure of many discourses and to focus undue attention upon distinguishing between rational and nonrational appeals, a distinction which is dubious to say the least. Finally, because traditional theory contrasts persuasion, or all uses of language which influence, and rhetoric, the true art by which men are induced to act in obedience to reason, even the most conscientious theorist or critic is placed in a dilemma between effects and ethics. He cannot deny that nonrational appeals are often effective. At the same time he must condemn these effective uses of language as unethical and propound instead a form of rhetorical appeal which is widely believed to be less efficacious. Such a dilemma leads to self-contradiction and ridicule. A viable and productive ontological interpretation of human persuadability must allow for theorizing about all persuasive uses of language and must generate an intrinsic ethic by which they may be evaluated.

A second objection to traditional rationalistic theory is that it places a disproportionate emphasis upon the effects of the discourse on the immediate audience. Such an emphasis is, however, a logical outcome of its presuppositions. If a discourse is an instance of genuine rhetoric it will be, of necessity, directed toward inducing a rational judgment, a major step toward fulfilling traditional truth criteria. It will be ethical or socially worthy because it seeks to induce men to act in obedience to reason, a process productive of individual and social virtue. It will be of some artistic merit because, if it proceeds logically, it is likely to meet minimal criteria for arrangement and for stylistic clarity, correctness and appropriateness. Consequently, the preeminent concern of the rhetorical critic will be whether or not the discourse actually induced men to judge and act rationally, and the traditional criticism of oratory in the last three decades has been focused primarily on the effects of discourses on immediate audiences.[4] Such a narrowing of the critical vista inhibits rather than enhances much-needed creative criticism. It also should be noted that an emphasis upon effects tends to diminish the reliability and validity of critical judgments. It is difficult to measure the effects of a speech. It is difficult to distinguish the effects of a speech from the effects of other symbolic stimuli. A decision must be made regarding the relative emphasis to be given to immediate and long-range effects. Such problems tend to discredit evaluations made primarily on the basis of the effects criterion.

Finally, it may be objected that the rationalistic interpretation of human persuadability is a threat to the integrity of the very discipline for which it attempts to provide a philosophical basis. Although Aristotle described rhetoric as a combination of reasoning or the science of analysis and the ethical branch of politics[5] and as a special use of practical reason which urges one of the alternatives delineated in a dialectic,[6] traditional theory seems to imply that the means by which the alternative to be urged is selected and advocated are, fundamentally and predominantly, means which properly fall within the province of theoretic reason or philosophy. In other words, the rationalistic interpretation of the ontological presumption that man is rhetorical implies that the means and ends of rhetorical discourse ought to be determined by procedures which properly belong to the office of the philosopher. The problem is vividly illustrated in the following statement of the relationship of philosophy to rhetoric made by a contemporary rationalistic theorist:

> Philosophy provides a method by which rhetoric (communication oral and written) selects subject and subject-matter of importance; defines terms; develops ideas and their supports with full regard for their logical and psychological validity and significance to an audience; generalizes with due account of the details and then moves from the concrete to the abstract, always with due regard for logical consistency in the successive steps; views the subject in relation to related areas of knowledge; sets up goals that follow through the approaches from the simple to the complex, and that indicate a direction consistent with value judgments.[7]

If these are the services that philosophy is to render rhetoric, then the province of rhetoric appears to be indistinct and severely limited.

Behavioristic Theory

A second major group of rhetorical theorists and critics explain that man is subject to and capable of persuasion because he is a psycho-physiological being. This interpretation of human persuadability reverses the priorities of the rationalists and gives motivational primacy to man's needs, drives, and desires. It turns to the field of psychology for an explanation of the persuasive dimension of human ontology and concludes that there are "basic, unlearned drives universally present in all human beings,"[8] and that these are the "headspring" of a persuasion which occurs "not on an intellectual, but rather on a motor level."[9] In other words, man is rhetorical because he is an organism with certain innate needs, and persuasion is a process by which these are activated and directed. Rhetoric is defined as all discourse designed to induce belief and action by any means whatever, and persuasion is viewed as the manipulation of innate drives and desires.

An important element in behavioristic theory is the scientific approach that it takes to the study of human behavior, an approach which rejects the concept of choice as an unpredictable force capable of interfering with stimulus-response relationships and substitutes for it the concept of behavioral variability: in a given situation various behaviors are possible although determined by and predictable from causal factors. The individual's belief that he can make free choices is considered an illusion, but one which contributes to psychological health. Consequently, persuasion is necessary and desirable because, in the words of one theorist, "the perception of choice, illusionary or real, becomes an important internal determiner of behavior. It generates harmony between one's feelings, beliefs, and actions."[10] In other words, behavioristic theory views rhetoric as a process which uses predominantly verbal stimuli to activate, direct, and manipulate men's needs, drives, and desires so that they will be satisfied in one way rather than another. Persuasion is possible because men have fundamental drives and because they believe, whether accurately or erroneously, that they can make "free" choices. Persuasion is desirable because it contributes to psychological health by reinforcing the individual's illusion of choice, an illusion which integrates his feelings, beliefs and actions.

The behavioristic explanation of human persuadability overcomes some of the limitations implicit in traditional rationalistic theory. It is concerned with and theorizes about all persuasive uses of language. By so doing, it encourages the critic to exercise all his critical options and creative abilities in analyzing, interpreting, and evaluating the epistemological, aesthetic, and ethical dimensions of discursive acts. However, because of its behavioristic focus, it is likely to ignore discourses which do not produce measurable or observable effects, a criterion for recognition which is problematic, as already indicated. Traditional critics do scrutinize discourses which were "ineffective," and abortive attempts at persuasion may provide valuable research data. In addition, unlike traditional theory, there are no ethical principles inherent in this interpretation of human persuadability. If discourses are to be evaluated as undesirable because unethical, criteria will have to be drawn from areas distinct from the ontological interpretation on which this form of rhetorical theory rests. Because this is the case, the dilemma between effects and ethics remains, as behavioristic theory cannot aid us in distinguishing between effects which are socially desirable and those which are not.

A primary objection to behavioristic rhetorical theory is that it generates a manipulative view of the persuasive act which views the speaker and auditor as separated, alienated, even in conflict. The persuader is "hidden," suggesting, often indirectly, that he can skillfully move his listener into acquiescence, or that he is the active principal injecting a stimulus into a passive receiver, a clever switchboard operator who can plug in an appropriate message to produce the relatively predictable response he desires. Both speaker and auditor are dehumanized, and the notion of persuasion as an inter*personal*, humane, cooperative process is lost. As a consequence, such theory tends to ignore an element implicit in the very idea of rhetoric—that men tend to speak to other men, to urge their action in the face of problems which they cannot solve alone and which require concerted, group action for their solution. Although skilled manipulators may induce mass action, such theorizing leaves no place for cooperative action in which individuals deliberate, understand the implications of their action, and subordinate immediate individual needs to long-term goals for groups, sometimes groups which do not include themselves.[11] Quite simply, behavioristic theory confronts rhetorical theorists with the question whether or not persuasion, among the various means of influencing others, is to be distinguished as that means characterized by the exercise of choice or by the deliberate cooperation of the persuadee.

Finally, it may be objected that behavioristic theory also jeopardizes the integrity of the discipline for which it forms a basis. If man is as these theorists describe him, rhetoric becomes that form of applied psychology which employs predominantly verbal messages, and it would seem that the criteria for the selection, formulation, and evaluation of these messages should be drawn primarily, if not exclusively, from the field of psychology. Once again, rhetoric, as a distinct area of inquiry with peculiar capacities and functions, seems to disappear.

Theories of Symbolic Behavior

A third interpretation of human persuadability explains that man is a rhetorical being because he is a symbol-using or signifying creature capable of influencing and being influenced because of his capacity for linguistic and semantic responses. Wallace Fotheringham has termed this explanation of human behavior the "meaning arousal theory" and explains that "this mode rests on the principle that humans, particularly, assign meaning to impinging stimuli and that the meaning given is a major determinant of the subsequent behavior."[12] In such a view the receiver is an active contributor to the persuasive process who detects, identifies, and interprets the symbolic stimuli which are the message, participating in and creating its meanings which, in turn, become the most significant element in his future behavior. Persuasion becomes a consequence of the interaction between men and their language. When used symbolically, a stimulus represents the user's conception of an object, event, condition, relationship, etc., and indicates an attitude or meaning which can be detected, identified, and interpreted by the receiver which, in turn, can influence his attitude toward the object, event, condition, relationship, etc. From the point of view of these theorists, the discipline of rhetoric is generally the study of the ways in which symbols influence human behavior and specifically the study of the ways in which one man's symbolic behavior influences that of another man. In the words of Kenneth Burke, "wherever there is persuasion, there is rhetoric. And wherever there is 'meaning,' there is persuasion."[13]

Quite obviously, meaning-arousal theory presumes the uniqueness of the human individual because it views him as an acting, contributing element in the persuasive process. Because unique men are necessarily separate, distinct and divided from one another, conflict, misunderstanding and misinterpretation arise which require rhetorical statements proclaiming common interests and calling for common action. For meaning-arousal theorists, the rationale for persuasion is the need to create unity, to overcome the division to which man is, by nature, heir. Rhetoric "is rooted in an essential function of language itself, . . . the use of language as a symbolic means of inducing cooperation in beings that by nature respond to symbols."[14] From this rationale a set of intrinsic ethical principles may be developed by which to distinguish socially desirable and undesirable persuasive uses of language and persuasive effects.[15]

Finally, these theorists and critics take an original view of human motivation. They contend that human motivation is distinct from that of other beings because the nature and structure of language are themselves motivating forces and because the interaction between man and his language profoundly transforms his physical, biological, and animal needs, drives and desires. The motive forces within language arise from its nature as an instrument of transcendence; as in naming, man not only draws arbitrary boundaries about an event or object, but goes beyond it to speak of the event or object in terms of what it is not, a word, by which he codifies his experience into meanings which reflect his and his group's perspectives and attitudes. Any such term goes beyond particular objects to abstract a category, and the structure of language is such that each category can, in turn, become a part of an ever more abstract category. Man surpasses the particular, experienced and concrete, when he uses language. He makes an inductive leap from sensation to inference. Language urges man toward ever higher moments of symbolic transcendence, a motive mythically represented in the story of the tower of Babel. In addition, the interaction between man and language is viewed as a process which destroys all purely "animal" or "biological" motives. While it is true that man is an animal with basic biological needs who must "live his body," the process of becoming human, of becoming socialized and acculturated, is essentially a symbolic one in which basic, unlearned needs are linguistically transformed into socially and culturally acceptable motives which can never be divorced from their symbolic origins. The human individual, as he engages in the rhetorical process, is an inseparable compound of animality and symbolicity.

From the point of view of theories of symbolic behavior, persuasion is a process in which the individual creates his meaning through detecting, identifying, and interpreting the stimuli he receives and which is integrated into and hence influences his perceptual framework. Persuasion is necessary because men are alienated, requiring persuasive uses of language to induce identification and cooperation in order to overcome the conflicts natural to the human condition—a purpose which generates an intrinsic ethic. Persuasion is possible because men create meaning, because language itself is a motivating force, and because language may be used both to modify man's basic needs and to influence his symbolically created social and cultural motives. Man is also persuadable because the very notion of language presumes a community of users in which, of necessity, the usage of each influences the usage and hence the meanings, attitudes, and behavior, of others.

A major advantage of the symbolic interpretation of human persuadability is that it provides a basis from which to scrutinize all persuasive uses of language. In fact, it encourages theorists and critics to extend their interest from rhetorical discourses as a theoretically distinct genre to include the rhetorical dimension present in all language usage. Such a perspective avoids the constraints of a too precise discrimination between rhetorical discourse and other literary forms and provides a basis for developing techniques for critical analysis which will heighten our appreciation of discourses as works of art and will increase our insight into the symbolic strategies and linguistic transactions out of which they are formed. In other words, meaning arousal theory provides a framework more amenable to the re-creative or aesthetic dimensions of criticism, and it allows theorists and critics to avoid the problems which result from a preeminent concern with effects and a too narrow interpretation of the process of criticism as a method for judging rather than for understanding the internal workings of the discourse.[16]

A second advantage of the symbolic interpretation of the onto-logical presumption of human persuadability is that it can encompass the most significant insights of rationalistic and behavioristic theory without incurring their limitations. For instance, meaning-arousal theorists consider man's ability to reason as one facet of his symbol-using capacity and view reasoning as one type of symbolic strategy. Yet they can scrutinize all persuasive uses of language; they are not tempted to force discourses into a logical mode, nor to make questionable distinctions between logical and emotional appeals. At the same time, this theory sustains the notion that choice is an integral part of persuasion and generates an intrinsic ethic by which to judge persuasive uses of language. Similarly, meaning-arousal theory can account for the role of human needs, drives and desires without generating a dehumanizing, manipulative theory of persuasion. It can avoid much of the deterministic dilemma by positing a concept of choice as functioning in the process of detecting, identifying, and interpreting stimuli. It can also avoid the ethics-effects dilemma which develops when ethical principles must be derived from extrinsic sources. For these reasons the meaning-arousal interpretation of the ontological presumption of human persuadability seems the most productive and viable basis for developing complete and coherent theories of rhetoric.

What objections, if any, can be raised to the symbolic approach to the rhetorical facet of human ontology? First, although it avoids the problems which arise when distinctions between rhetoric and psychology or philosophy are blurred, it can be objected that the discipline of rhetoric which it posits has no distinguishable limits, that it is in effect the study of all language. The objection is, to me, an irrefutable one, as I believe that indistinct boundaries and wider horizons are precisely the price we shall have to pay in order to have the latitude needed to theorize about and examine the many language acts which do not fall easily into neat classifications of purpose or genre. In fact, it seems to me a small price for restoring rhetoric to its ancient and rightful place as one of the essential facets of language study and for expanding its role contemporaneously to the study of all persuasive uses of language.

A second related objection is that it is more difficult to develop coherent theories and systems of criticism from the symbolic approach to human behavior. If neatness and order are the criteria, analytical and empirical perspectives are clearly preferable, but they are, as I hope I have demonstrated, constraining and incomplete when adopted as exclusive bases for theorizing. This objection is not, however, irrefutable. It is quite true that symbolic approaches to human behavior do not lead to the precise analytic structures of rationalistic or behavioristic theory, but the fact that these are incomplete or dubious bases for rhetorical theory and criticism makes illegitimate the demand that they be duplicated, particularly when approaches of this sort have made the criticism of so many persuasive uses of language so difficult. In this respect, I would agree with Edwin Black that what we need is imaginative criticism rather than attempts to generate new critical systems.[17] In addition, there have been numerous attempts to suggest the outlines of theoretical and critical frameworks consistent with the presumptions underlying symbolic approaches to human behavior which might profitably be re-examined and expanded.[18] Rhetorical theorizing from a symbolic perspective may be more difficult, but difficulty surely is not a valid basis for rejecting a critical approach, particularly when that approach would seem to provide the most productive and viable ontological basis from which to develop a complete and coherent theory of rhetoric.

Notes

1. "The Relevance of Rhetoric to Philosophy and of Philosophy to Rhetoric," *The Quarterly Journal of Speech*, LII, 1 (February 1966), 43.
2. Aristotle, *Rhetoric*, trans. W. Rhys Roberts (New York: The Modern Library, 1954), i.1.1355a.11.
3. *Ibid.*, i.1.1354a.12. See also Edwin Black, *Rhetorical Criticism: A Study in Method* (New York: The Macmillan Company, 1965), 117, and Lester Thonssen and A. Craig Baird, Speech Criticism: The Development of Standards for Rhetorical Appraisal (New York: Ronald Press, 1948), 359.
4. Black, 33.
5. Aristotle, i.4.1359b.10.
6. *Ibid.*, i.1.1354a.1.
7. A. Craig Baird, *Rhetoric: A Philosophical Inquiry* (New York: Ronald Press, 1965), 22–23.
8. Jon Eisenson, J. Jeffrey Auer, and John V. Irwin, *The Psychology of Communication* (New York: Appleton-Century-Crofts, 1963), 245.

9. William N. Brigance, "Can We Re-Define the James-Winans Theory of Persuasion?" *The Quarterly Journal of Speech*, XXI, 1 (February 1935), 21. This is reiterated in Eisenson, Auer, and Irwin, 245.

10. Wallace C. Fotheringham, *Perspectives on Persuasion* (Boston: Allyn and Bacon, Inc., 1966), 12.

11. Kenneth Kenniston, summarizing available evidence on contemporary student dissent says that "in rare cases are demonstrations directed at improving the lot of the protesters themselves; identification with the oppressed is a more important motivating factor than an actual sense of immediate personal oppression," in "The Sources of Student Dissent," *Black Power and Student Rebellion: Conflict on the American Campus*, ed. James McEvoy and Abraham Miller (Belmont, California: Wadsworth Publishing Company, 1969), 312.

12. Fotheringham, 158.

13. Kenneth Burke, *A Grammar of Motives and A Rhetoric of Motives* (New York: Meridian Books, 1962), 696.

14. *Ibid.*, 567.

15. See Henry Nelson Wieman and Otis M. Walter, "Toward an Analysis of Ethics for Rhetoric," *The Quarterly Journal of Speech*, XLIII, 3 (October 1957), 266–270 and Karlyn Kohrs Campbell, "The Rhetorical Implications of the Philosophy of Jean-Paul Sartre," (unpublished Ph.D. dissertation, University of Minnesota, 1968), 287–292.

16. John Rathbun, "The Problem of Judgment and Effect in Historical Criticism: A Proposed Solution," *Western Speech*, XXXIII, 3 (Summer 1969), 146–159.

17. Black, 177.

18. Rathbun outlines and illustrates an alternative system using the three properties of formal technique: point of view, diction and imagery, 153–159. The framework for a critical system developed from the works of Kenneth Burke has been outlined by Marie Hochmuth, "Burkeian Criticism," *Western Speech*, XXI, 2 (Spring 1957), 89–95, and "Kenneth Burke and the 'New Rhetoric,'" *The Quarterly Journal of Speech*, XXXVIII, 2 (April 1952), 133–144; Virginia Holland, "Kenneth Burke's Dramatistic Approach in Speech Criticism," *The Quarterly Journal of Speech*, XLI, 4 (December 1955), 352–358, and "Rhetorical Criticism: A Burkeian Method," *The Quarterly Journal of Speech*, XXXIX, (December 1953), 444–450; and John W. Kirk, "Kenneth Burke's Dramatistic Criticism Applied to the Theatre," *The Southern Speech Journal*, XXXIII, 3 (Spring 1968), 161–177 among others. See also Richard Gregg, "A Phenomenologically Oriented Approach to Rhetorical Criticism," *Central States Speech Journal*, XVII, 2 (May 1966), 83–90; Richard Lanigan, "Rhetorical Criticism: An Interpretation of Maurice Merleau-Ponty," *Philosophy and Rhetoric*, II, 2 (Spring 1969), 61–71, and many others.

Creativity and the Commonplace
by Richard McKeon

That creativity takes its beginning in the commonplace may be taken as a familiar and accepted commonplace. Invention, discovery, and insight are creative modes of departure from accustomed circumstances of the commonplace to transform the customary or the unnoticed into novelties. Widely known and authoritatively established novelties in turn become commonplaces and provide circumstances and subjects for new innovations. Such "commonplaces" of common opinion and ordinary language, however, are examples of the changes and alterations which the "commonplace" undergoes. Both "creativity" and "commonplace" are ambiguous words. Places, topics, loci, commonplaces and proper places have had long paradoxical histories since they entered into the languages of the West. They were as ambiguous in ordinary Greek as they are in ordinary English, and the nature of "place" and "space" was a subject of dispute in the beginnings of Greek physical science. They became terms of art in Greek rhetoric, acquired fixed meanings in Roman rhetoric, and spread, with the widespread use of rhetoric in the development of the arts of practical philosophy, jurisprudence, history, and literature, to commonplace meanings which are frequently at variance with their uses as terms of art. Creativity, invention, discovery, recovery, and innovation were ambiguous in their ordinary uses and in their philosophic uses, to such an extent that Plato sought to rectify the errors of poetic invention by truths discovered in the recollection of ideas. In the subsequent history of philosophical speculation on creativity, memory is the basis of invention, invention provides the materials for memory, and commonplaces are the devices of both invention and memory.

Cicero defined places as seats (*sedes*) or sources of arguments. Since rhetoric is composed of five parts—invention, disposition, elocution, memory, and pronunciation—he used places as fundamental devices in two parts, in invention and in

Reprinted from *Philosophy and Rhetoric* 6 (1973). Copyright 1973 by the Pennsylvania State University. Reproduced by permission of the publisher.

memory. For the places of memory he went back to the poet Simonides; for the places of invention he built on the topics of Aristotle. Cicero attributes the invention of the art of memory to Simonides of Ceos. Simonides had been commissioned to present a poem in honor of his host at a banquet. In the course of his poem he also praised Castor and Pollux, and his patron, when the poem had been read, argued that the praise had been divided and proposed to pay only half of the fee that had been set for the panegyric. At that point Simonides was notified that two young men wished to see him outside. In his absence the roof of the banqueting hall collapsed, crushing the diners so badly that it was difficult to identify the corpses. Simonides used his memory of the places at which the guests had been seated to identify the persons, and he argued that the faculty of memory may be trained by selecting places, forming mental images of the things to be remembered, and placing them in the places distinguished, so that the order of the places would preserve the order of the things, likening the places to a wax tablet and the images to the letters written on it (Cicero, *De Oratore* ii. lxxxvi. 351–4). The wax tablet and the letters or images were to continue in the figurative philosophic language used in the history of the discussion of memory and thought—of impressions, likenesses, and images—together with the signet ring and its impression on the wax of a seal, and the footprint (*vestigium*) and its mark in soft earth.

At the beginning of his *Topica* Cicero recalls to his friend Trebatius that when he had picked up a copy of Aristotle's *Topics* in Cicero's library and had asked what it was about, Cicero had explained that it "contained a discipline invented by Aristotle for inventing arguments so that we might come upon them by a structure and a path (*ratione et via*) without any error" (*Topica* i. 2). He had promised to explain this discipline more fully, and the *Topica* was his fulfillment of that promise written from memory on a voyage to Greece, when he had no books with him (*ibid.* 4–5). The absence of books has provided scholars with a rich field of investigation to relate the discipline expounded by Cicero to the topics and their uses set forth in either Aristotle's *Topics* or his *Rhetoric.* Every ordered structure of discourse (*omnis ratio diligens disserendi*), Cicero argued, has two parts concerned respectively with inventing and with judging. Aristotle established both, whereas the Stoics limited themselves to the ways of judgment, which they called dialectic, and neglected the art of invention which is called topics, in spite of the fact that it is more useful and certainly prior in nature (*ibid.* ii. 6–7). Cicero divides the topics into technical and atechnical, that is, places from which arguments are derived by art and places from which arguments are derived without art. Aristotle makes a like distinction in the *Rhetoric,* but Cicero's treatment of the two kinds of topics differs from his. For Cicero the atechnical places have to do with testimony. He enumerates four technical places—"definition," "enumeration," "etymology," and "circumstances"—and divides "circumstances" into thirteen kinds—"conjugates," "genera," "species," "similarities," "differences," "contraries," "adjuncts," "antecedents," "consequents," "contradictions," "causes," "effects," and "comparisons" with things "greater," "equal," or "less." They are not Aristotle's topics, and they combine topics, with the predicables which Aristotle uses with the commonplaces in his *Topics,* with the kinds of opposites which he distinguishes in his the arrangement of what has been discovered, involves judgment; and the connections of discourse are found in the places of judgment and argument, in the figures of syllogisms and of proofs, and in the figures of speech and of thought: "tropes" have been connected closely with "topes" in the history of devices of placing and of turning. "Elocution" is language adapted to the arguments, narratives, and myths of presentation and proof; and the places of statement and judgment are the sources and determinants of lines of inferences and flows of styles. "Pronunciation" or delivery includes the motions of the body as well as those of the voice; it is action, and the places of doing govern all arts of action, not only the dramatic and oratorical actions of the stage and the podium, but also the practical arts, the liberal arts, and the fine arts, that is, the arts of prudence, the arts of wisdom, and the arts of imagination. The places of the warranted, of the asserted, and of the done have developed out of the places of the known and of the unknown; and the newly invented places are places both of memory and of invention.

The mnemotechnics and the heuristics of the Renaissance have fallen out of fashion, or have been altered beyond recognition; and we have wearied of, or forgotten, the voluminous investigations and schematizations of methodologies of the nineteenth century, which developed methods for natural sciences, cultural sciences, social sciences, human sciences or humanities, for history, bibliography, and criticism. We are more apt to remember the paradoxes, which came to life again in the controversies among proponents of those methods, concerning whether an art or method of invention and discovery can be constructed, or whether they must be regarded as products of genius and quick wit, which cannot be learned or acquired. John Stuart Mill and William Whewell agreed that there can be no "method" of discovery, while disputing for years, through several editions of Mill's *System of Logic* and through several books of Whewell on inductive logic and the philosophy of discovery, concerning the nature of discovery and its place in philosophy and logic. Yet in the twentieth century we have had books and articles on the logic of discovery as well as on the logic of chance and of the artificial. The new interest in creativity has made "creativity" a commonplace with many meanings and with many places in art and science, in practice and theory, in logic and method. "Creativity" is frequently used as a commonplace, meaning to do something differently than is customary. Used in that meaning it seldom gives rise to problems that require appeal to an art, or a method, or a logic of discovery: spontaneity, chance, obstinacy, or animosity is sufficient to account for change; and if questions of value are raised, they are reduced to commonplace disputes concerning the relative worth of the new and the conventional, or the relative attractiveness of revolution and tradition, or the relative effectiveness of innovation and revival. Considering such formulations of the questions, and using such arguments for resolving the debates, the decision may as easily go against as for novelty, and any step of progress or innovation may as easily be shown to be due to rebirth as to revolution. The battle of the books, of the ancients and the moderns, was such a commonplace battle for creativity. Commonplaces begin to emerge in the course of such set disputes of value, however, and they begin to function once more as arts of invention and as arts of memory—beginning with the commonplace

Categories, and with the "circumstances" of action which he examines in the *Nicomachean Ethics.* But some of them also call to mind topics that have recurred in later inquiries into inductive logic and logic of discovery, and others give color to objections brought, again and again, against "traditional logic" and "verbal rhetoric" and against formalisms and subjectivisms of art and authority unrelated to the concrete things of existence and experience.

Commonplaces underwent degradations and criticism. Topics of memory threatened to become as numerous as things to be remembered, and therefore to provide no aid in retaining or ordering them: the word "topic" changed periodically from meaning an empty place by which to order things to be remembered to meaning a subject matter or a placed subject, as "the topic" on which to speak, to think, or to act. The commonplaces of invention changed periodically from meaning devices for discovering something previously unknown to meaning familiar quotations in which something well known and widely esteemed is stated. Quintilian complained that many orators made collections of sayings and arguments concerning subjects likely to recur in the practice of their art instead of fortifying themselves with places by which to discover new arguments that had never occurred to them before. Commonplaces were memorized rather than used for invention, and they were recited when the occasion arose rather than used when the circumstances required. Commonplaces ceased from time to time to be ways to the new and unknown, and commonplace-books became collections of aphorisms and verses rather than arts of invention. From time to time commonplaces reappeared and were schematized as devices and in the Renaissance they were organized in numerous arts of invention or arts of discovery and arts of memory, or mnemonic arts or arts of artificial, or technical, or topical memory, and the listed commonplaces or topics underwent changes in successive versions of the arts. Seneca the Elder reports prodigies of memory and subtleties of invention in the Roman schools of rhetoric. The Second Sophistic carried the practices of adepts and the informed appreciation of audiences to new extensions and embellishments. Aristotle did not enslave men's minds during the Middle Ages in logic, science, philosophy, or even topics. Boethius did not translate Aristotle's *Topics,* but he wrote a vast work in four books, *De Differentiis Topicis,* in which he combined the topics of Cicero with those of Themistius and gave the version of Aristotle's logic which was to be studied in the Middle Ages, a Platonized form, by basing knowledge on the opinions used in dialectical syllogisms of the *Topics* rather than on the scientific principles used in demonstrative syllogisms of the *Posterior Analytics.* Commonplaces gave shape to the method of canon law and to the scholastic method which was developed from it in the twelfth century.

The commonplaces contributed, in their alternations from invention to repetition, to the aridity and obtuseness of the medieval liberal arts against which the Renaissance revolted. The Humanist revolt inspired a return to Cicero, who had also been the source and inspiration of the medieval liberal arts, and invention and the commonplaces were again prominent in the revolt. Aristotle had distinguished between commonplaces and proper places. Cicero had distinguished between particular questions about concrete events and persons and general questions about philosophical problems; and he used the "paths" or "ways" of places in both kinds of questions as part of his program to rejoin wisdom and eloquence, rhetoric and philosophy. During the Renaissance, letters were revived by proper places used in a new form of the discipline of philology, and commonplaces came into their own in new versions of logic, dialectic, and rhetoric developed in numerous treatises on method. "Method" (*methodos*) was used by Aristotle to signify a "path to" the investigation of a scientific subject matter or the solution of a scientific problem and he distinguished "methods" from "paths" or "ways" (*hodos*) constructed in universal arts for the statement of arguments or descriptions or accounts applicable to any problem or subject matter. The Ciceronian and medieval treatises were "paths" or "ways" (*via*), and "methodus" did not become a Latin word until the translation of Aristotle's *Topics* in the twelfth century. Lully devised a Combinatory Art which had an inventive part. Rudolph Agricola wrote a *De Inventione Dialectica* which influenced Ramus in his revision of the liberal arts—and for all his criticisms of Aristotle, Ramus was at pains to point out the superiority of Cicero's treatment of the topics to Quintilian's, and the superiority of Aristotle's approach to both. Nizolius wrote a treatise *On the True Principles and True Reason of Philosophizing against the Pseudophilosophers* basing metaphysics on principles derived from literature and rhetoric. The art of memory was also developed in a large number of diversified systems of mnemonic art.

The beginnings of modern philosophy were in these innovations in philology, philosophy, history, and science, and many of the heralds of the new advancement, philosophers like Francis Bacon, Leibniz, and Vico, were aware of the work of their predecessors with commonplaces and proper places. Bacon was critical of the methods of Lully and Ramus. He sought proper places for the discovery of things and of arts rather than commonplaces for the invention of words and arguments. Leibniz continued the tradition of the combinatory art and the universal characteristic, and he edited and commented on Nizolius' rhetorical metaphysics. He found place for topics in both the demonstrations of combinatory logic and the probabilities of moral science, jurisprudence, and history. The subtitle of his *Dissertation on the Combinatory Art* promises that it will sow "new seeds of the art of meditating or logic of invention." He divided logic into two parts, an inventive logic or topics and a logic of judgment or analytics. The practical sciences are based on probability logic, that is, on Topics or Dialectic, used, in the absence of analytic, as an art of estimating degrees of probation. The art of invention, however, was poorly developed, and only a few samples of it could be found. Vico attacked Descartes' method as a method craftily feigned to exalt mathematics and Descartes' own philosophy and to degrade all other studies and philosophies. Vico proposed instead a program which would exercise memory, imagination, and perception (*ingegno* from *ingenium,* a faculty of the mind comparable to what Aristotle called "quick wit," the immediate perception of middle terms, the faculty of genius or immediate perception on all levels, sensitive and intellectual, of end terms to be related). One of the pernicious practices which afflicts the study of philosophy today, he said, is to introduce philosophy by the study of the Port-Royal Logic, "full of rigorous judgments concerning recondite matters of the higher sciences, remote

from vulgar common sense." In the program he proposed, youthful men would be regulated and developed each by a separate art—memory by the s languages, imagination by the reading of poets, historians, and orators, and p tion (*ingegno*) by plane geometry, which is in a sense a graphic art which invi memory by the great number of its elements, refines imagination with its d figures as with so many drawings described in the finest lines, and qui perception (*ingegno*) by surveying all these figures and collecting among the those which are needed to demonstrate the magnitude which is required. S regime will bear fruit, at the time of mature judgment, in an eloquent, lively acute wisdom. If, on the contrary, students are led by logics prematurely criticism

(that is to say, are led to judge before properly apprehending, against the natural cours of ideas—for they should first apprehend, then judge, and finally reason), they becom arid and dry in expression, and without ever doing anything set themselves up ir judgment over all things. On the other hand if in the age of perception [*ingegno*], which is youth, they would devote themselves to Topics, the art of discovery that is the special privilege of the perceptive (as Vico [in the *Autobiography* Vico refers to himself in the third person], taking his cue from Cicero, did in his youth), they would then be furnished with matter in order later to form a sound opinion on it. For one cannot form a sound judgment of a thing without having complete knowledge of it; and topics is the art of finding in anything all that is in it. Thus nature itself would aid the young to become philosophers and good speakers. [*The Autobiography of Giambattista Vico,* trans. M. H. Fisch and T. G. Bergin (Cornell University Press, 1944), pp. 123–24.]

Vico had returned to Cicero's ideal of joining wisdom and eloquence, and he used commonplaces to form programs of study and to open up insights in research which were to guide and inspire later inquiries into literature, history, and jurisprudence.

Bacon, Leibniz, and Vico extracted, and developed from Renaissance speculations on methods of discovery and on topics, the diversity of topical uses that were implicit in Cicero's use of them to rectify the predicament of philosophy and rhetoric both of which had become "technical" disciplines in his day, producing on the one hand experts who had knowledge but were unable to express themselves, and on the other hand experts who had mastered the arts of language and communication but had nothing to say. Cicero had used them as devices by which to achieve his ideal of uniting eloquence and wisdom. But he had used them on only two of the five parts of rhetoric, while Bacon, Leibniz, and Vico had extended them to all five parts and had made them ways of advancing science, reforming philosophy, conceiving and studying culture, and framing universal history. They saw that Cicero's places of "invention" were more than sources of argument for orators and philosophers pressed or cornered in debate and controversy, and transformed them into places for the perception, discovery, and explanation of the unknown. The places of "memory" were transformed from the storage places of known facts assorted for easy reference into an organization of what has been discovered and what is known into interacting schematisms of arts and sciences. "Disposition," or of the relation of fact to value, followed by a cluster of related commonplaces of the relation of imagination to memory, of invention to judgment, of myth to logos, of history to theory, and of sequence to structure.

The places of invention and of memory are places of things, thoughts, actions, and words. They are explored as sources of invented novelty and of established fact by faculties of symbolic imagination, factual memory, discursive reason, and intuitive understanding. In communications, in sciences, and in arts, there are no things or thoughts, only known things and significant thoughts, expressed things and thoughts, ordered by actions of art which produce and make them as objects, understandings, consequences, and expressions. The inventions and discoveries, the recollections and recoveries of things and occurrences, of thoughts and imaginations, of arts and actions, and of statements and accounts, are expressed in inventions of language and in genres of discourse—fictive narration, concrete description, sequential argument, and intelligible exposition; and they are constructed by arts or actions of innovation and fixation—invention, recovery, discovery, creation. By the use of such discourses and arts, we are able to make confidently our commonplace, concrete distinctions of things, thoughts, actions, and statements. If there is a philosophy of discovery and creativity, it cannot be a philosophy established by consensus concerning the nature of things, the powers or faculties of thought, the devices of arts, or the meanings or warrants of statements. It must be a pluralistic philosophy which establishes a creative interplay of philosophies inventing their facts, their data, their methods, their universes. It must be a rediscovery of the commonplaces of invention and memory for innovation rather than the establishment of a doctrine for proselytizing and conversions among marked-off heresies and dogmas.

It is appropriate that commonplaces be transformed from collections of fixed and established, communicable clichés to neutral sources of new perceptions operative in new directions in the thought and culture and philosophy of the twentieth century. Rhetoric again has assumed a dominant place in our thought and action. Whereas the rhetoric of the Romans took its commonplaces from the practical arts and jurisprudence and the rhetoric of the Humanists took its commonplaces from the fine arts and literature, our rhetoric finds its commonplaces in the technology of commercial advertising and of calculating machines. As in past rhetorics, the art of memory has developed more elaborately and more rapidly than the art of invention, and retrieval often passes for innovation and motivation for ratiocination. The great problem of creativity is "creativity" itself. It is a commonplace, a meaningless word which assumes clear and fixed meanings in well-known commonplaces that express what everybody knows about it, or which preserves a productive systematic ambiguity from which new insights may be derived and new consequences constructed. But the products of creativity—acquired insights, made things, planned actions, composed statements—become the commonplaces of our familiar world, while the commonplaces which innovate and transform, invent and discover, may be detected in their effective use but can never be stated univocally, clearly, or distinctly. The present exposition of "creativity and the commonplace" is not designed to uncover and state truths about creativity but to explore the commonplaces which determine the varieties of meanings it assumes in statements about it and the variety of ways in which it functions in exploring the old and constructing the new. If it had been designed to be a history of commonplaces or a theory of the commonplace, it would have had the radical defect that it never defines a commonplace or enumerates commonplaces: Cicero's commonplaces are not Aristotle's, Boethius departs beyond both, Lully and Ramus innovate. and Bacon, Leibniz, and Vico refashion their innovations. The only list that is given, with unconcealed reluctance, is Cicero's list, and it was chosen obviously because it is short and its terminology is traditional and has been fashioned into the language of new and later traditions—that is, the listed commonplaces have ceased to be commonplaces of invention and have become commonplaces of repetition. If the adepts of commonplaces have used different commonplaces, what is the commonplace of commonplaces, and how are commonplaces used to depart from the commonplace?

The commonplace of commonplaces is the place in which the certainties of the familiar are brought into contact with the transformations of innovation. A commonplace term, like "creativity," is meaningless in isolation. When it is combined with another term in a statement, the statement may be true or false. and the term is ambiguous. When reasons are brought to warrant a meaning, the meaning of the term becomes a variable adjusted to the variations of other terms in the formulation of the argument. When principles are sought to ground the argument, the meaning of the term becomes a function of the system, and the doctrine of creativity becomes a comfortable commonplace in an established universe. This is the genesis of doctrines of creativity from the commonplace word "creativity"; like accounts of that genesis might be given from the commonplace thing, thought, or action "creativity." The commonplaces of creativity differ from the doctrines of creativity in all four stages of this progress: a term may be meaningless in the sense of being undefined or in the sense of being stripped methodically of vestiges of meaning; ambiguity has productive uses as well as equivocal dangers; variability appears in accounts which are variations of an argument or theme as well as in stages of arguments or occurrences; functionality is a relation among things and statements, thoughts, and arts as well as a relation among the constituent parts of what is the case. The present exposition is an account of the commonplaces of creativity: "creativity" was used as a commonplace; it was expanded to the commonplace "known-unknown" and used to distinguish and merge the arts of invention and memory, which were explored in the commonplace "term-statement-argument-system," and systematized in the creation of the commonplace "things-thoughts-actions-words." Many doctrines of creation have been moved along the first path; they have all used the structures of the commonplaces sketched along the second path. The commonplace "known and unknown" has some advantages over the customary commonplaces of philosophic discussion, like "subjective and objective," "mind and matter," "real and ideal," because it retains an easy reversibility by which the known becomes unknown as well as the unknown known, and by which its inventive openness as a commonplace is preserved and the commonplaces derived from it provide structures for all philosophies in a pluralism of philosophies of invention and of varieties of creativity.

The commonplaces of creativity operate in the interpretation of texts as well as in the writing of texts, in the interpretation of experience as well as of statements, in the interpretation and formation of character, thought, actions, and things. In the interpretation of the text of a philosopher, past or present, commonplaces of invention may open up the perception of new meanings and applications even in a familiar text, which in turn uncovers previously unperceived lines of arguments to unnoticed conclusions which were not there until they were made facts by discovery. The newly perceived facts of interpreting a text may in turn lead to the discovery of new powers of perception and their use in the discovery of new existential data and new experiential facts, set in relation by new arts and methods, to discover new universes of discourse, thought, consequential occurrence, and systematic organization. The use of the commonplaces of creativity erects and fills the commonplace as a storehouse of the familiar to provide materials for commonplaces as instruments for the perception, creation, arrangement, and establishment of the new in existence, experience, discursive exploration, and inclusive organization.

In Search of Ariadne's Thread:
A Review of the Recent Literature
on Rhetorical Theory
by Michael C. Leff

MY assignment was to review the articles on rhetorical theory that appeared in the Speech Communication journals during the years 1976 and 1977. Although the editor provided a list of the relevant journals, I was left to my own devices in selecting the articles that fell under the heading of rhetorical theory. I approached this task with profound reservations, since, as we all know through bitter experience, rhetorical theory is virtually impossible to define. Thus, I was afraid that I would either have to report on everything in the journals or appear to be arbitrary.

After reading a few essays, however, my fear dissipated. I soon learned that rhetoric was, among other things, a method for reaching decisions. Furthermore, the method worked best in situations where abstract principles were in doubt, where the rigorous standards of logic were impractical, and where the decision led directly to some sort of action. This suited my purposes entirely. What could be more appropriate than to define the literature of rhetorical theory according to a rhetorical method? If I could not devise a logically coherent definition of my subject, I could at least select those materials likely to engage the interest of rhetorical theorists.

Unfortunately, the solution of this first problem led directly to a second and far more serious one. I had gathered together a group of essays and referred to them as a body of literature. This act of classification brought with it certain assumptions, since a body of scholarly literature should reveal common agreements about the subjects and issues that delimit an area of inquiry. But the more I read, the more I

Reprinted from *Central States Speech Journal* 29 (1978), with permission of the National Communication Association.

wondered whether these essays on rhetorical theory exhibited any coherence. The literature simply did not appear to build on itself. Consequently, my original purpose had to be revised. I had intended to abstract and comment on the issues that already existed in the literature. The circumstances, however, mandated a more indirect approach, and the resulting essay is an exercise in inference. Its aim is to make a plausible conjecture about the direction of recent rhetorical theory and to suggest some potential issues that might confront us as we move in that direction.

Before turning to this task, I need to make one more point about my methodology. Two types of articles seem to dominate the recent literature. The first type may be called meta-rhetorical. Essays in this category are very abstract in character, since they deal with the scope, nature, and ethical burden of rhetoric as a concept. The second category consists of historical/textual studies, and these take several different forms. Most often, such essays deal with a single well-known figure in the rhetorical tradition (e.g. Plato, Augustine, Perelman), but some of them are comparative (e.g. Burke and Richards), and a few attempt to survey a period (e.g. the twelfth century).[1] In general, these two types are distinct, works in one category having very little to do with works in the other. Historical/textual essays sometimes make introductory or concluding remarks that apply to meta-rhetorical concerns, but the burden of these essays is explication, and they achieve general theoretical interest only as they are accumulated and interrelated. Meta-rhetorical essays use the historical tradition as a source for examples, but they rarely show a sustained interest in the traditional authorities, and there are few references to the historical/textual studies.

Obviously, both types of studies are important, since a discipline cannot proceed effectively without examining its philosophical bases and its historical tradition. Yet, the separation between the two approaches to theory creates serious problems for both. On one side, the meta-rhetorical studies are alive with items of theoretical interest, but, lacking concrete points of reference, they are often so difficult to understand that they appear vacuous. On the other side, the historical/textual essays are so wedded to the particular that it is difficult to understand their theoretical significance.

The very formulation of this problem suggests its solution, since the deficiencies of the two approaches are symmetrical. That is, the meta-rhetorical studies can provide a needed theoretical framework for the historical/textual studies, and the historical/textual studies can provide a concrete grounding for meta-rhetorical speculation. At any rate, the union of these two approaches offers a convenient strategy for reviewing the literature as a coherent whole. And in the following pages, I have attempted to isolate some of the leading tendencies in the meta-rhetorical literature and explicate them by reference to historical/textual studies that have appeared recently in the journals. The fit between the two categories is not always perfect; at times, I have not been able to find historical essays that respond to the issues raised in the more purely theoretical literature, and in some cases, I have had to interpret the historical essays in a rather loose fashion. Consequently,

Categories, and with the "circumstances" of action which he examines in the *Nicomachean Ethics.* But some of them also call to mind topics that have recurred in later inquiries into inductive logic and logic of discovery, and others give color to objections brought, again and again, against "traditional logic" and "verbal rhetoric" and against formalisms and subjectivisms of art and authority unrelated to the concrete things of existence and experience.

Commonplaces underwent degradations and criticism. Topics of memory threatened to become as numerous as things to be remembered, and therefore to provide no aid in retaining or ordering them: the word "topic" changed periodically from meaning an empty place by which to order things to be remembered to meaning a subject matter or a placed subject, as "the topic" on which to speak, to think, or to act. The commonplaces of invention changed periodically from meaning devices for discovering something previously unknown to meaning familiar quotations in which something well known and widely esteemed is stated. Quintilian complained that many orators made collections of sayings and arguments concerning subjects likely to recur in the practice of their art instead of fortifying themselves with places by which to discover new arguments that had never occurred to them before. Commonplaces were memorized rather than used for invention, and they were recited when the occasion arose rather than used when the circumstances required. Commonplaces ceased from time to time to be ways to the new and unknown, and commonplace-books became collections of aphorisms and verses rather than arts of invention. From time to time commonplaces reappeared and were schematized as devices and in the Renaissance they were organized in numerous arts of invention or arts of discovery and arts of memory, or mnemonic arts or arts of artificial, or technical, or topical memory, and the listed commonplaces or topics underwent changes in successive versions of the arts. Seneca the Elder reports prodigies of memory and subtleties of invention in the Roman schools of rhetoric. The Second Sophistic carried the practices of adepts and the informed appreciation of audiences to new extensions and embellishments. Aristotle did not enslave men's minds during the Middle Ages in logic, science, philosophy, or even topics. Boethius did not translate Aristotle's *Topics,* but he wrote a vast work in four books, *De Differentiis Topicis,* in which he combined the topics of Cicero with those of Themistius and gave the version of Aristotle's logic which was to be studied in the Middle Ages, a Platonized form, by basing knowledge on the opinions used in dialectical syllogisms of the *Topics* rather than on the scientific principles used in demonstrative syllogisms of the *Posterior Analytics.* Commonplaces gave shape to the method of canon law and to the scholastic method which was developed from it in the twelfth century.

The commonplaces contributed, in their alternations from invention to repetition, to the aridity and obtuseness of the medieval liberal arts against which the Renaissance revolted. The Humanist revolt inspired a return to Cicero, who had also been the source and inspiration of the medieval liberal arts, and invention and the commonplaces were again prominent in the revolt. Aristotle had distinguished between commonplaces and proper places. Cicero had distinguished between particular questions about concrete events and persons and general questions about philosophical problems; and he used the "paths" or "ways" of places in both kinds of questions as part of his program to rejoin wisdom and eloquence, rhetoric and philosophy. During the Renaissance, letters were revived by proper places used in a new form of the discipline of philology, and commonplaces came into their own in new versions of logic, dialectic, and rhetoric developed in numerous treatises on method. "Method" (*methodos*) was used by Aristotle to signify a "path to" the investigation of a scientific subject matter or the solution of a scientific problem and he distinguished "methods" from "paths" or "ways" (*hodos*) constructed in universal arts for the statement of arguments or descriptions or accounts applicable to any problem or subject matter. The Ciceronian and medieval treatises were "paths" or "ways" (*via*), and "methodus" did not become a Latin word until the translation of Aristotle's *Topics* in the twelfth century. Lully devised a Combinatory Art which had an inventive part. Rudolph Agricola wrote a *De Inventione Dialectica* which influenced Ramus in his revision of the liberal arts—and for all his criticisms of Aristotle, Ramus was at pains to point out the superiority of Cicero's treatment of the topics to Quintilian's, and the superiority of Aristotle's approach to both. Nizolius wrote a treatise *On the True Principles and True Reason of Philosophizing against the Pseudophilosophers* basing metaphysics on principles derived from literature and rhetoric. The art of memory was also developed in a large number of diversified systems of mnemonic art.

The beginnings of modern philosophy were in these innovations in philology, philosophy, history, and science, and many of the heralds of the new advancement, philosophers like Francis Bacon, Leibniz, and Vico, were aware of the work of their predecessors with commonplaces and proper places. Bacon was critical of the methods of Lully and Ramus. He sought proper places for the discovery of things and of arts rather than commonplaces for the invention of words and arguments. Leibniz continued the tradition of the combinatory art and the universal characteristic, and he edited and commented on Nizolius' rhetorical metaphysics. He found place for topics in both the demonstrations of combinatory logic and the probabilities of moral science, jurisprudence, and history. The subtitle of his *Dissertation on the Combinatory Art* promises that it will sow "new seeds of the art of meditating or logic of invention." He divided logic into two parts, an inventive logic or topics and a logic of judgment or analytics. The practical sciences are based on probability logic, that is, on Topics or Dialectic, used, in the absence of analytic, as an art of estimating degrees of probation. The art of invention, however, was poorly developed, and only a few samples of it could be found. Vico attacked Descartes' method as a method craftily feigned to exalt mathematics and Descartes' own philosophy and to degrade all other studies and philosophies. Vico proposed instead a program which would exercise memory, imagination, and perception (*ingegno* from *ingenium,* a faculty of the mind comparable to what Aristotle called "quick wit," the immediate perception of middle terms, the faculty of genius or immediate perception on all levels, sensitive and intellectual, of end terms to be related). One of the pernicious practices which afflicts the study of philosophy today, he said, is to introduce philosophy by the study of the Port-Royal Logic, "full of rigorous judgments concerning recondite matters of the higher sciences, remote from vulgar common sense." In the program he proposed, youthful mental gifts would be regulated and developed each by a separate art—memory by the study of languages, imagination by the reading of poets, historians, and orators, and perception (*ingegno*) by plane geometry, which is in a sense a graphic art which invigorates memory by the great number of its elements, refines imagination with its delicate figures as with so many drawings described in the finest lines, and quickens perception (*ingegno*) by surveying all these figures and collecting among them all those which are needed to demonstrate the magnitude which is required. Such a regime will bear fruit, at the time of mature judgment, in an eloquent, lively, and acute wisdom. If, on the contrary, students are led by logics prematurely into criticism

> (that is to say, are led to judge before properly apprehending, against the natural course of ideas—for they should first apprehend, then judge, and finally reason), they become arid and dry in expression, and without ever doing anything set themselves up in judgment over all things. On the other hand if in the age of perception [*ingegno*], which is youth, they would devote themselves to Topics, the art of discovery that is the special privilege of the perceptive (as Vico [in the *Autobiography* Vico refers to himself in the third person], taking his cue from Cicero, did in his youth), they would then be furnished with matter in order later to form a sound opinion on it. For one cannot form a sound judgment of a thing without having complete knowledge of it; and topics is the art of finding in anything all that is in it. Thus nature itself would aid the young to become philosophers and good speakers. [*The Autobiography of Giambattista Vico,* trans. M. H. Fisch and T. G. Bergin (Cornell University Press, 1944), pp. 123–24.]

Vico had returned to Cicero's ideal of joining wisdom and eloquence, and he used commonplaces to form programs of study and to open up insights in research which were to guide and inspire later inquiries into literature, history, and jurisprudence.

Bacon, Leibniz, and Vico extracted, and developed from Renaissance speculations on methods of discovery and on topics, the diversity of topical uses that were implicit in Cicero's use of them to rectify the predicament of philosophy and rhetoric both of which had become "technical" disciplines in his day, producing on the one hand experts who had knowledge but were unable to express themselves, and on the other hand experts who had mastered the arts of language and communication but had nothing to say. Cicero had used them as devices by which to achieve his ideal of uniting eloquence and wisdom. But he had used them on only two of the five parts of rhetoric, while Bacon, Leibniz, and Vico had extended them to all five parts and had made them ways of advancing science, reforming philosophy, conceiving and studying culture, and framing universal history. They saw that Cicero's places of "invention" were more than sources of argument for orators and philosophers pressed or cornered in debate and controversy, and transformed them into places for the perception, discovery, and explanation of the unknown. The places of "memory" were transformed from the storage places of known facts assorted for easy reference into an organization of what has been discovered and what is known into interacting schematisms of arts and sciences. "Disposition," or the arrangement of what has been discovered, involves judgment; and the connections of discourse are found in the places of judgment and argument, in the figures of syllogisms and of proofs, and in the figures of speech and of thought: "tropes" have been connected closely with "topes" in the history of devices of placing and of turning. "Elocution" is language adapted to the arguments, narratives, and myths of presentation and proof; and the places of statement and judgment are the sources and determinants of lines of inferences and flows of styles. "Pronunciation" or delivery includes the motions of the body as well as those of the voice; it is action, and the places of doing govern all arts of action, not only the dramatic and oratorical actions of the stage and the podium, but also the practical arts, the liberal arts, and the fine arts, that is, the arts of prudence, the arts of wisdom, and the arts of imagination. The places of the warranted, of the asserted, and of the done have developed out of the places of the known and of the unknown; and the newly invented places are places both of memory and of invention.

The mnemotechnics and the heuristics of the Renaissance have fallen out of fashion, or have been altered beyond recognition; and we have wearied of, or forgotten, the voluminous investigations and schematizations of methodologies of the nineteenth century, which developed methods for natural sciences, cultural sciences, social sciences, human sciences or humanities, for history, bibliography, and criticism. We are more apt to remember the paradoxes, which came to life again in the controversies among proponents of those methods, concerning whether an art or method of invention and discovery can be constructed, or whether they must be regarded as products of genius and quick wit, which cannot be learned or acquired. John Stuart Mill and William Whewell agreed that there can be no "method" of discovery, while disputing for years, through several editions of Mill's *System of Logic* and through several books of Whewell on inductive logic and the philosophy of discovery, concerning the nature of discovery and its place in philosophy and logic. Yet in the twentieth century we have had books and articles on the logic of discovery as well as on the logic of chance and of the artificial. The new interest in creativity has made "creativity" a commonplace with many meanings and with many places in art and science, in practice and theory, in logic and method. "Creativity" is frequently used as a commonplace, meaning to do something differently than is customary. Used in that meaning it seldom gives rise to problems that require appeal to an art, or a method, or a logic of discovery: spontaneity, chance, obstinacy, or animosity is sufficient to account for change; and if questions of value are raised, they are reduced to commonplace disputes concerning the relative worth of the new and the conventional, or the relative attractiveness of revolution and tradition, or the relative effectiveness of innovation and revival. Considering such formulations of the questions, and using such arguments for resolving the debates, the decision may as easily go against as for novelty, and any step of progress or innovation may as easily be shown to be due to rebirth as to revolution. The battle of the books, of the ancients and the moderns, was such a commonplace battle for creativity. Commonplaces begin to emerge in the course of such set disputes of value, however, and they begin to function once more as arts of invention and as arts of memory—beginning with the commonplace of the relation of fact to value, followed by a cluster of related commonplaces of the relation of imagination to memory, of invention to judgment, of myth to logos, of history to theory, and of sequence to structure.

The places of invention and of memory are places of things, thoughts, actions, and words. They are explored as sources of invented novelty and of established fact by faculties of symbolic imagination, factual memory, discursive reason, and intuitive understanding. In communications, in sciences, and in arts, there are no things or thoughts, only known things and significant thoughts, expressed things and thoughts, ordered by actions of art which produce and make them as objects, understandings, consequences, and expressions. The inventions and discoveries, the recollections and recoveries of things and occurrences, of thoughts and imaginations, of arts and actions, and of statements and accounts, are expressed in inventions of language and in genres of discourse—fictive narration, concrete description, sequential argument, and intelligible exposition; and they are constructed by arts or actions of innovation and fixation—invention, recovery, discovery, creation. By the use of such discourses and arts, we are able to make confidently our commonplace, concrete distinctions of things, thoughts, actions, and statements. If there is a philosophy of discovery and creativity, it cannot be a philosophy established by consensus concerning the nature of things, the powers or faculties of thought, the devices of arts, or the meanings or warrants of statements. It must be a pluralistic philosophy which establishes a creative interplay of philosophies inventing their facts, their data, their methods, their universes. It must be a rediscovery of the commonplaces of invention and memory for innovation rather than the establishment of a doctrine for proselytizing and conversions among marked-off heresies and dogmas.

It is appropriate that commonplaces be transformed from collections of fixed and established, communicable clichés to neutral sources of new perceptions operative in new directions in the thought and culture and philosophy of the twentieth century. Rhetoric again has assumed a dominant place in our thought and action. Whereas the rhetoric of the Romans took its commonplaces from the practical arts and jurisprudence and the rhetoric of the Humanists took its commonplaces from the fine arts and literature, our rhetoric finds its commonplaces in the technology of commercial advertising and of calculating machines. As in past rhetorics, the art of memory has developed more elaborately and more rapidly than the art of invention, and retrieval often passes for innovation and motivation for ratiocination. The great problem of creativity is "creativity" itself. It is a commonplace, a meaningless word which assumes clear and fixed meanings in well-known commonplaces that express what everybody knows about it, or which preserves a productive systematic ambiguity from which new insights may be derived and new consequences constructed. But the products of creativity—acquired insights, made things, planned actions, composed statements—become the commonplaces of our familiar world, while the commonplaces which innovate and transform, invent and discover, may be detected in their effective use but can never be stated univocally, clearly, or distinctly. The present exposition of "creativity and the commonplace" is not designed to uncover and state truths about creativity but to explore the commonplaces which determine the varieties of meanings it assumes in statements about it and the variety of ways in which it functions in exploring the old and constructing the new. If it had been designed to be a history of commonplaces or a theory of the commonplace, it would have had the radical defect that it never defines a commonplace or enumerates commonplaces: Cicero's commonplaces are not Aristotle's, Boethius departs beyond both, Lully and Ramus innovate. and Bacon, Leibniz, and Vico refashion their innovations. The only list that is given, with unconcealed reluctance, is Cicero's list, and it was chosen obviously because it is short and its terminology is traditional and has been fashioned into the language of new and later traditions—that is, the listed commonplaces have ceased to be commonplaces of invention and have become commonplaces of repetition. If the adepts of commonplaces have used different commonplaces, what is the commonplace of commonplaces, and how are commonplaces used to depart from the commonplace?

The commonplace of commonplaces is the place in which the certainties of the familiar are brought into contact with the transformations of innovation. A commonplace term, like "creativity," is meaningless in isolation. When it is combined with another term in a statement, the statement may be true or false. and the term is ambiguous. When reasons are brought to warrant a meaning, the meaning of the term becomes a variable adjusted to the variations of other terms in the formulation of the argument. When principles are sought to ground the argument, the meaning of the term becomes a function of the system, and the doctrine of creativity becomes a comfortable commonplace in an established universe. This is the genesis of doctrines of creativity from the commonplace word "creativity"; like accounts of that genesis might be given from the commonplace thing, thought, or action "creativity." The commonplaces of creativity differ from the doctrines of creativity in all four stages of this progress: a term may be meaningless in the sense of being undefined or in the sense of being stripped methodically of vestiges of meaning; ambiguity has productive uses as well as equivocal dangers; variability appears in accounts which are variations of an argument or theme as well as in stages of arguments or occurrences; functionality is a relation among things and statements, thoughts, and arts as well as a relation among the constituent parts of what is the case. The present exposition is an account of the commonplaces of creativity: "creativity" was used as a commonplace; it was expanded to the commonplace "known-unknown" and used to distinguish and merge the arts of invention and memory, which were explored in the commonplace "term-statement-argument-system," and systematized in the creation of the commonplace "things-thoughts-actions-words." Many doctrines of creation have been moved along the first path; they have all used the structures of the commonplaces sketched along the second path. The commonplace "known and unknown" has some advantages over the customary commonplaces of philosophic discussion, like "subjective and objective," "mind and matter," "real and ideal," because it retains an easy reversibility by which the known becomes unknown as well as the unknown known, and by which its inventive openness as a commonplace is preserved and the commonplaces derived from it provide structures for all philosophies in a pluralism of philosophies of invention and of varieties of creativity.

The commonplaces of creativity operate in the interpretation of texts as well as in the writing of texts, in the interpretation of experience as well as of statements, in the interpretation and formation of character, thought, actions, and things. In the interpretation of the text of a philosopher, past or present, commonplaces of invention may open up the perception of new meanings and applications even in a familiar text, which in turn uncovers previously unperceived lines of arguments to unnoticed conclusions which were not there until they were made facts by discovery. The newly perceived facts of interpreting a text may in turn lead to the discovery of new powers of perception and their use in the discovery of new existential data and new experiential facts, set in relation by new arts and methods, to discover new universes of discourse, thought, consequential occurrence, and systematic organization. The use of the commonplaces of creativity erects and fills the commonplace as a storehouse of the familiar to provide materials for commonplaces as instruments for the perception, creation, arrangement, and establishment of the new in existence, experience, discursive exploration, and inclusive organization.

In Search of Ariadne's Thread:
A Review of the Recent Literature
on Rhetorical Theory
by Michael C. Leff

MY assignment was to review the articles on rhetorical theory that appeared in the Speech Communication journals during the years 1976 and 1977. Although the editor provided a list of the relevant journals, I was left to my own devices in selecting the articles that fell under the heading of rhetorical theory. I approached this task with profound reservations, since, as we all know through bitter experience, rhetorical theory is virtually impossible to define. Thus, I was afraid that I would either have to report on everything in the journals or appear to be arbitrary.

After reading a few essays, however, my fear dissipated. I soon learned that rhetoric was, among other things, a method for reaching decisions. Furthermore, the method worked best in situations where abstract principles were in doubt, where the rigorous standards of logic were impractical, and where the decision led directly to some sort of action. This suited my purposes entirely. What could be more appropriate than to define the literature of rhetorical theory according to a rhetorical method? If I could not devise a logically coherent definition of my subject, I could at least select those materials likely to engage the interest of rhetorical theorists.

Unfortunately, the solution of this first problem led directly to a second and far more serious one. I had gathered together a group of essays and referred to them as a body of literature. This act of classification brought with it certain assumptions, since a body of scholarly literature should reveal common agreements about the subjects and issues that delimit an area of inquiry. But the more I read, the more I

Reprinted from *Central States Speech Journal* 29 (1978), with permission of the National Communication Association.

wondered whether these essays on rhetorical theory exhibited any coherence. The literature simply did not appear to build on itself. Consequently, my original purpose had to be revised. I had intended to abstract and comment on the issues that already existed in the literature. The circumstances, however, mandated a more indirect approach, and the resulting essay is an exercise in inference. Its aim is to make a plausible conjecture about the direction of recent rhetorical theory and to suggest some potential issues that might confront us as we move in that direction.

Before turning to this task, I need to make one more point about my methodology. Two types of articles seem to dominate the recent literature. The first type may be called meta-rhetorical. Essays in this category are very abstract in character, since they deal with the scope, nature, and ethical burden of rhetoric as a concept. The second category consists of historical/textual studies, and these take several different forms. Most often, such essays deal with a single well-known figure in the rhetorical tradition (e.g. Plato, Augustine, Perelman), but some of them are comparative (e.g. Burke and Richards), and a few attempt to survey a period (e.g. the twelfth century).[1] In general, these two types are distinct, works in one category having very little to do with works in the other. Historical/textual essays sometimes make introductory or concluding remarks that apply to meta-rhetorical concerns, but the burden of these essays is explication, and they achieve general theoretical interest only as they are accumulated and interrelated. Meta-rhetorical essays use the historical tradition as a source for examples, but they rarely show a sustained interest in the traditional authorities, and there are few references to the historical/textual studies.

Obviously, both types of studies are important, since a discipline cannot proceed effectively without examining its philosophical bases and its historical tradition. Yet, the separation between the two approaches to theory creates serious problems for both. On one side, the meta-rhetorical studies are alive with items of theoretical interest, but, lacking concrete points of reference, they are often so difficult to understand that they appear vacuous. On the other side, the historical/textual essays are so wedded to the particular that it is difficult to understand their theoretical significance.

The very formulation of this problem suggests its solution, since the deficiencies of the two approaches are symmetrical. That is, the meta-rhetorical studies can provide a needed theoretical framework for the historical/textual studies, and the historical/textual studies can provide a concrete grounding for meta-rhetorical speculation. At any rate, the union of these two approaches offers a convenient strategy for reviewing the literature as a coherent whole. And in the following pages, I have attempted to isolate some of the leading tendencies in the meta-rhetorical literature and explicate them by reference to historical/textual studies that have appeared recently in the journals. The fit between the two categories is not always perfect; at times, I have not been able to find historical essays that respond to the issues raised in the more purely theoretical literature, and in some cases, I have had to interpret the historical essays in a rather loose fashion. Consequently, the argument may sometimes oversimplify matters, but oversimplification seemed necessary in order to preserve coherence.

Rhetoric as Epistemic

If there is any unifying thread running through the recent literature, it is a heightened interest in the relationship between rhetoric and epistemology. Moreover, this interest regularly expresses itself in terms that re-arrange the conventional modern distinctions between knowledge and communication. Witness the following quotations from essays on a variety of different subjects: "At any given moment, what we know to exist in the world is a product of an evolving set of human agreements."[2] " . . . It seems safe to conclude that there is a new rhetoric, grounded not in the quest to make truth effective, but rather in the quest to evoke truth *via* rhetoric."[3] " . . . Rhetoric can no longer be seen simply as a means of persuasion. It becomes instead the medium in which selves grow."[4] "While rhetoric may be defined in many ways and on many levels, it is in the deepest and most fundamental sense the *advocacy of realities*."[5] "In many circumstances one can 'know' only through engagement in rhetorical activity."[6] The terminology changes somewhat as we move from one of these quotations to another, but the basic point is consistent. All of these authors, and others who could be cited, agree that rhetoric is a serious philosophical subject that involves not only the transmission, but also the generation, of knowledge. In other words, there appears to be an emerging consensus in support of Scott's view that rhetoric is epistemic.[7]

Furthermore, there is a growing tendency to assert that an epistemic view of rhetoric signifies a major break in the modern rhetorical tradition. One author goes so far as to identify a "postmodern" rhetoric.[8] This assertion marks our first issue: Does the epistemic view constitute such a radical departure from the recent past that we are entitled to distinguish between a modern and a postmodern approach to theory?[9] In order to deal with this issue, I propose to summarize the findings of a number of historical studies on modern rhetoric and compare them with the central tenets of the epistemic view. Specifically, we shall look at Jamieson's comparative study of Pascal and Descartes,[10] McKerrow's essay on Whately,"[11] and Hostettler's analysis of Saintsbury.[12]

Jamieson draws a sharp contrast between the views of Descartes and Pascal on rhetoric. Descartes abandons rhetoric as a respectable intellectual enterprise, since he regards his geometric *méthode* not only as the proper means of conducting an inquiry, but also as the most effective mode of persuasion. He, therefore, subsumes persuasion, insofar as it can be studied rationally, within the confines of demonstrative logic. Pascal assumes a less rigid stance, since he believes that rational appeals to the understanding cannot maintain absolute control over the will. He, therefore, rejects Descartes' assumption that persuasion can be reduced to demonstration and constructs a rhetoric that is "enthymematic, audience-based, psychologically oriented. . . ."[13]

Pascal, then, salvages a place for rhetoric within the system of the arts, but he certainly does not grant it epistemic status. Subscribing to a psychology that separates the will from the understanding, Pascal does not allow for the active integration of cognition and affect. From his perspective, rhetoric works its effects through appeals to pleasures and emotions governed by the volitional faculty, and such appeals have no bearing on the understanding, the faculty that yields rational knowledge. Rhetoric has the power to influence decisions, but not the power to generate or advance knowledge. Pascal's recognition of the importance of rhetoric, then, does not imply an enlargement of the Cartesian conception of rationality. It is merely a concession to the rational imperfections of the soul.

Ray McKerrow's recent essay on Whately provides a second case study in modern rhetorical epistemology. In analyzing the Whitely/Campbell debate concerning the merits of deduction, McKerrow notes that Whately makes a crucial distinction between investigation and argument. Investigation, Whately contends, is a matter of inductive inquiry, and its function is to ascertain the truth or probable truth of propositions. Argument, on the other hand, is deductive, and it deals with the interrelationships among propositions already known. Consequently, evidentiary knowledge falls outside the province of rhetoric and logic, the two arts of argumentation. Whately makes this point succinctly in one of his early writings: "It is not the design of *argument* to make any progress, except in effecting conviction, nor to gain new truths, but merely to *expand* and *unfold* what is, as it were, wrapt up in the truths you set out with. . . ."[14] And despite his differences with Campbell on the value of syllogistic logic, Whately's rhetorical epistemology is thoroughly consistent with eighteenth century thought. Like Campbell and Priestley before him, Whately reduces "rhetoric to a purely managerial or supervisory science—a science which assumes responsibility for communication only after the substance of the message has been derived and its general purpose and direction determined."[15]

In one sense, then, Whately simply reiterates the eighteenth century presumption that communication does not generate knowledge. But his position on the matter is particularly telling, since he is the most practical of the modern rhetoricians. Surely, it is significant that such a practical theorist and such a skilled advocate does not allow the contact of minds in an argument to count as a possible source for new knowledge. For Whately, intersubjective agreement is not a valid ground for knowledge.

Finally, we may turn to George Saintsbury's *A History of Literary Taste in Europe,* a massive three volume work published at the turn of the century. As Hostettler notes, the work presents a radical form of the belletristic view of rhetoric. Saintsbury holds that "rhetoric's *only* function was to be, and always should have been, literary criticism."[16] And since literary art, in Saintsbury's scheme of things, exists purely for the sake of art, rhetoric assumes a narrowly conceived aesthetic function. It has nothing to do with ethics, or social history, or even persuasion. It deals exclusively with the treatment of a subject, not with the subject itself. Thus, Saintsbury effects a complete separation between rhetoric and knowing.

This brief survey certainly does not amount to a definitive statement about the epistemological presumptions of modern rhetorical theory. There were certain eccentric figures on the modern landscape who foreshadowed the epistemic approach to the art. Vico was surely one such exception and following Wilkie, we might also include Marx.[17] Nevertheless, it is safe to say that the positions we have just reviewed represent the mainstream of opinion in the post-Cartesian era. Rhetoric was variously collapsed into demonstrative logic, revived as a mode of dealing with the irrational aspects of the psyche, confined within the aesthetics of style, and redeemed as a way of transmitting truths obtained from other disciplines. But it was almost never regarded as a method of inquiry or a vehicle for enlarging knowledge. The evidence, then, supports the assertion that in viewing rhetoric as epistemic, we are making a radical break from the modern tradition.

More important, perhaps, this historical analysis may help us acquire an operational definition of the epistemic view of rhetoric. We are in a better position to understand what the concept is after we have understood what it is not. To put the point in another way, the epistemic approach achieves greater clarity when it is limited by reference to well-known theories of rhetoric that fall outside its purview. At any rate, we have isolated some basic assumptions that militate against an epistemic conception of rhetoric: an unlimited faith in the power of pure reason, a willingness to separate cognitive and affective processes, a refusal to grant intersubjectivity (i.e. audience agreement) as a criterion for knowledge, and a disinterest in the way that the contact of minds alters the shape of knowledge. It requires no great act of imagination to change these statements into their contraries and thereby derive a preliminary list of the characteristics of an epistemic rhetoric. But, at best, the list would be partial, and, at worst, it might lead us into philosophical bi-ways that distract our attention from the central question. Negative definitions can take us only so far, and sooner or later, we have to face up to the problem of dealing with the concept on its own terms.

The problem deserves more disciplined treatment than it has received in the recent literature. Since the epistemic view is revolutionary in the context of modern thought, we lack a stable vocabulary in which to attempt to define it, and since it is also an extraordinarily complex notion, it invites attention at a multitude of different levels. Under the circumstances, scrupulous caution seems advisable. At the same time, however, the connection between rhetoric and knowing has had an exhilarating effect on rhetoricians who have suffered through long years of abuse from positivists, idealists, intuitionists, and other pure thinkers who occupy the higher levels of the academic totem pole. Hence the tendency to welcome the new concept with greedy enthusiasm and to attempt to gulp it down whole.

A careful reading of the literature reveals at least four different senses in which we may construe rhetoric as epistemic. Although all four are sometimes wrapped around each other in the same essay, it seems the better part of discipline to attack them separately. Each of these four approaches is complex in itself and therefore difficult to describe in a phrase. Nevertheless, let me make this tentative distinction among them: (i) Rhetoric is epistemic because it allows us to know how particular objects and events relate to fixed, abstract principles. (ii) Rhetoric is epistemic because it represents an active, social form of thinking that allows us to gain knowledge both of particulars and of principles in respect to practical matters. (iii) Rhetoric is epistemic since it can serve a meta-logical function that helps us to secure knowledge of the first principles of theoretical disciplines. (iv) Rhetoric is epistemic since knowledge itself is a rhetorical construct.

(i) The first of these senses represents that weakest claim that rhetoric can make to epistemic status. Scott outlines the nature of this claim in this way:

> Even those who take the position that there must be some unified hierarchy of stable standards in order to achieve decent individual and social lives will agree that such standards must be applied in specific sets of circumstances. Few will argue that in practice, at least, applications are seldom, if ever, possible in such a way that the standards are engaged without discomfort. . . . The existence of some set of circumstances in the guise of a case to be settled seems to suggest rather strongly the human participation of relating standards to particular, concrete events.[18]

In this instance, rhetoric imparts knowledge by clarifying the relationship between a problematic particular and a fixed, absolute standard of truth. Since the status of the particular is uncertain before the occurrence of the rhetorical event, we can say that the transaction creates new knowledge. Furthermore. since the relationship between the particular and the abstract standard remains logically problematic, we must conclude that the knowledge is sanctioned by an intersubjective consensus stemming from the interaction between the rhetor and his audience. And for this reason, we can call this knowledge "rhetorical." Thus, even in this weak sense of the concept, rhetoric is epistemic, because it has the capacity to locate concrete events within the ambit of stable principles.

(ii) The second sense of the epistemic view of rhetoric entails a more fluid conception of the relationship between particulars and abstract standards. Advocates of this position argue that inter-subjective agreement requires an interaction between particular experiences and the general categories for judging experience. Consequently, they conceive of an autonomous form of knowledge based on social consensus in which rhetoric plays a decisive role.

This form of knowing can be called "social knowledge." As Farrell defines this term, it comprises "conceptions of symbolic relationships among problems, persons, interests, and actions, which imply (when accepted) certain notions of preferable public behavior."[19] At every point, the characteristics of social knowledge correspond closely with the function of rhetoric. Such knowledge is essentially symbolic; it must be adjusted to the interests of those involved in a decision; it is validated by intersubjective agreement, and it is active in character. This last point is clarified in terms of a simple contrast: "Whereas technical or specialized knowledge is actualized through its perceived correspondence to the external world, social knowledge is actualized through the decision and action of the audience."[20]

The active quality of social knowledge explains how it operates to integrate particular events and general principles simultaneously within the context of a rhetorical transaction. Since social knowledge is intersubjective, it does have some claim to objectivity. Yet, such knowledge can never be reduced to the clear order and precision of a scientific system. The categories of social knowledge are not fixed. They are transitive, indeterminate, and potential.[21] Consequently, social knowledge only works in reference to specific problems that demand action on the part of a specific group of people. In general, the values of the group are sufficiently well-established to provide a general frame of reference for attacking the problem. But there is almost always a significant margin of ambiguity about how to construe these values, about which values are relevant, and about which have priority. This ambiguity is resolved on a case by case basis in terms of a deliberation about some specific problem. Thus, when we conceive of rhetoric as an instrument of social knowledge, we must conclude that rhetorical discourse influences both the perception of the situation and the conception of the abstract standards that apply to it.

In her essay on Aristotle's theory of epideictic, Oravec shows how this process might work. Objecting to interpretations that render the epideictic experience as pure observation, Oravec argues that the epideictic audience is required to make two sorts of judgments. First, the audience renders an aesthetic judgment about the skill of the speaker, about his command of the techniques of art. Second, and more important for our purposes, the audience judges whether the speaker has succeeded in achieving his goal. But to make a decision on this matter, the audience must consider the plausibility of the message; it must decide whether the object under consideration really deserves praise or blame. As Oravec describes it, the decision engages the auditor in an active process that has important epistemic consequence:

> Finally, the insight created by the presentation is not only a criterion of audience judgment, it also produces understanding and comprehension in the audience. The listeners learn the significance of their experience by witnessing the application of common values to familiar objects. The praiseworthy object, if represented with accuracy, may become a standard for practical action. . . . Thus the rhetor receives common values and experiences from his audience and, by reshaping them in artistic language, returns these experiences heightened and renewed. The process of "observation" which begins with perception and functions through judgment finally ends in heightened appreciation and intellectual insight.[22]

Epideictic rhetoric, then, influences the general standards of social knowledge. On one level, the rhetor may use the particular object or person as a vehicle for establishing or attacking abstract values. In such instances, one can appreciate the force of Oravec's comment about the object becoming a standard for practical action. The object serves as a model or anti-model and thus as a synechdochal representative of an abstract virtue or vice. On a more subtle level, interaction between the object and the value may alter the auditor's conception of the value. The process is most easily explained by analogy to the interaction that occurs between the elements of a metaphor. When we encounter a metaphor, normally we are aware only of the way that the vehicle affects our understanding of the tenor. But, as Richards has demonstrated, some energy always flows back in the other direction.[23] (Thus, if someone says, "Smith is a lion," we regard the metaphor as a description of Smith. Nevertheless, our attitude toward Smith may have a subtle, often unconscious, influence on our attitude toward lions.) Likewise, even when an epideictic orator assumes stable values and concentrates on evaluating the particular object, the juxtaposition between the object and the values may alter the values themselves. For example, let us suppose that an orator delivers an extremely skillful encomium on Richard Nixon, basing his argument on Nixon's diligence. The desired reaction is to change the auditor's attitude toward Nixon. Yet, intentions not withstanding, the speech might cause the auditors to reduce the value they attach to diligence as a standard for judging a man's character.

In sum, we have now reviewed two senses in which we may regard rhetoric as epistemic. We have found that rhetoric may make a weak claim to epistemic status because of the power of persuasive discourse to alter our perception of a specific object within a fixed scheme of general standards. Or rhetoric may make a stronger claim based on a theory of active knowledge in which objects and standards interact during the course of the rhetorical transaction.

(iii) The third approach to this concept moves us into the domain of theoretical knowledge. Rhetoric, in this sense, constitutes a method for deciding between alternative conceptions of reality. More specifically, advocates of this position view rhetoric as a kind of metalogic. It functions to secure the first premises of science and speculative philosophy by overcoming the limitations in formal systems of argument.

Scientific and logical demonstrations progress from the known to the unknown according to a fixed system of entailments. That is, they resolve problematic issues by deriving consequences from what is already known. When we examine this process carefully, we can trace the progression of proofs back to first principles that are themselves unproven and unproveable according to the rules of the discipline.[24] Consequently, logical and scientific systems are limited by the character of the assumptions that set them in motion.

For the most part, these basic assumptions are either unrecognized or unquestioned. Nevertheless, there are certain crisis situations in which rival "paradigms" interpret the material of the same discipline in different ways (i.e., present different views of reality). If both systems exhibit internal coherence, then there is no purely formal means of demonstrating the superiority of one over the other.[25] This is true because the rival theories differ in respect to first premises which cannot be demonstrated. Given these conditions, we can resolve the conflict only by resorting to a mode of argument that is more flexible than formal logic. This line of reasoning has encouraged recent authors to assert that rhetorical argumentation has a legitimate place in science.[26] It is also one of the reasons that Perelman advocates a rhetorical approach to ethical theory.[27]

Precisely how does rhetoric discharge this meta-logical function? No one has yet offered a direct and detailed answer to this question, but several interesting suggestions emerge from the recent literature. Holmberg, for example, advocates a return to an original and pure form of rhetoric.[28] In this guise, rhetoric is functionally distinct from dialectic. Dialectic, Holmberg argues, seeks correction to truth and therefore assumes that there is a single, correct view of reality. Pure rhetoric, on the other hand, assumes a pluralistic view, and it attempts to balance and harmonize different conceptions of the real. This attempt, we might add, seems especially necessary when we seek to assess competing philosophical and scientific paradigms.

Grassi offers a second and quite different approach. He distinguishes between a temporal, unconnected, and imagistic form of speech, and the rational, sequential, and ordered speech of scientific logic. The former puts us in direct emotional contact with the first principles of reality. But this type of speech lacks the power to explain itself to an audience. The exclusively rational speech of science has the virtue of clarity, but in itself it cannot put us in contact with first principles. The problem, then, is to bridge the gap, and Grassi assigns this function to rhetoric.[29]

Perelman's concept of presence suggests another possible approach to our problem. On first inspection, the possibility may seem remote, since Perelman carefully avoids epistemological issues when he discusses the elements of argumentation. Moreover he asserts that his concept of presence applies only to the technical analysis of rational argumentation, and he denies that it has any connection with a theory of knowledge.[30] Nevertheless, Karon has argued persuasively that the *New Rhetoric* implies an epistemology, and that presence is a crucial part of it.[31] Her argument leads to some interesting speculations about the function of rhetoric in determining the first principles of theoretical knowledge.

For Perelman, presence is a matter of focusing the attention on certain elements in a situation to the exclusion of others. This power to direct the attention, in effect, determines what is relevant in an argumentative situation and what should receive priority. Presence, therefore, becomes "a means by which reality is constructed and consequently a vehicle for transposing a phenomenon from the realm of the contingent to the realm of the absolute."[32] More specifically, Karon maintains that presence affects knowledge through its capacity to influence our apprehension of consensus relative to a premise.[33]

In order to interpret Karon's argument, we must understand Perelman's conception of how the rhetorician obtains his premises. Since he believes that all argumentation is relative to the audience addressed, Perelman holds that the rhetor must draw his premises from points of agreement within a given audience. In constructing the discourse, however, the rhetor does not confront an actual audience, and he must, therefore, construct an audience and assume points of agreement. This construct may be very abstract. In fact, the rhetor may conceive of an audience composed of all rational men, a universal audience. At this level, we enter into the realm of selecting first principles for the interpretation of reality.

But on what basis can we construct the universal audience? How do we obtain a sense of the premises that will win its assent? The answer, Karon argues, is that the universal audience is a construct created by the speaker's notion of reason, and the source of this construct is largely dependent on presence. That is, a premise will appear acceptable to all rational men to the extent that it is present in the mind of the thinker. As the presence of an idea increases, other ideas are forced out of attention, and we become more secure in asserting the universal rationality of the idea. Hence, presence plays an indispensible role in determining what is real.

Karon adds that this analysis exposes a problem in Perelman's system. Although Perelman rejects the Cartesian dichotomy between internal and external experience, the source of reality for him appears to be an internal sense of what is externally binding. The universal audience is the source of reality, but it proves to be a radically subjective construct.[34] But one must exercise some caution at this point. In Descartes, the force and clarity of the idea in the thinker's mind represents the end-point of the epistemological process. In Perelman, however, it is only the starting-point. Premises derived from the conception of the universal audience must be tested against actual, particular audiences.[35] Thus, our theoretical knowledge is constantly in flux, always in a state of dialectical tension between our subjective concept of reason and the inter-subjective agreements of an actual audience. It is precisely this tension that allows us to develop a rhetorical approach to the basic premises of theoretical knowledge.[36]

(iv) We come now to the final and boldest claim for the epistemic status of rhetoric. In considering this version of the concept, we no longer view rhetoric as epistemic, but rather view epistemology as rhetorical. The basic tenets of this position are similar to those advanced by Farrell, Scott, and the other advocates of the social knowledge theory. These theorists, however, claim only that rhetoric is one among the many ways of knowing. On the other hand, this final sense of the epistemic view entails the claim that knowledge itself is a rhetorical construct. I should add that this position is only incipient in the current literature. Nevertheless, several authors have at least flirted with it, and it is an idea that bears watching.

The best way to approach the rhetoric as knowledge concept is to understand that it explicitly reverses the basic terms of positivistic philosophy. The positivists, seeking to achieve mechanical objectivity, collapsed the symbolic into the empirical. The function of language was simply to present an accurate report of the events that occurred in the real world. The theory of rhetoric as knowledge, to borrow a phrase from Brummet, collapses the tunnel at the other end.[37] The empirical is subordinated to the symbolic. Or, to be a bit more accurate, reality is regarded as fundamentally symbolic, and thus language itself becomes the primary unit of empirical knowledge. Furthermore, since language is inherently valuative, all aspects of human life, even the hard sciences, are pervaded by value. Thus, Walter Weimer writes:

> This conception of rhetoric emphasizes the intrinsic valuational or ethical dimension inherent in all scientific activity. Knowing and valuing are inseparable. . . . In the past both scientists and rhetoricians accepted, seemingly as revealed truth, the idea that science and logic are value-free in contrast to properly rhetorical concerns (where values were grudgingly accepted). Methodologists of science have known otherwise for some time. Many have emphasized that the growth of knowledge and the practice of research, since they are embedded in pragmatic action, entail ethical and valuational considerations at (literally) every step. Knowing, doing, and valuing can and must be reunited. Insofar as all involve the argumentative function, rhetoric is the domain in which unification must occur.[38]

All in all, the complete version of this rhetoric as knowledge position involves two claims: (1) the symbolic and normative aspects of knowledge are prior to the objective and mechanical, and (2) the rhetorical function is the dominant aspect of the symbolic process.

The elevation of the symbolic over the literal is most forcefully developed in the works of Kenneth Burke. In his recent debate with Howell, Burke summarizes this point of view rather clearly.[39] Burke asserts that the central issue in his thought is "a total distinction between the realms of (symbolic) action and (nonsymbolic) motion." Furthermore, while "action is not reducible to motion," Burke holds that symbolic action encompasses sheer motion. In other words, the symbolic forms of drama apply not only to literature, but also to the construction of reality: "I began to see how my defining literary form in terms of 'expectations' could be extended to an empirical notion of 'reality' itself as a structure of expectations, plus the further step whereby our views of the future involve a set of (right or wrong) expectations."[40]

Burke, however, does not place rhetoric at the apex of the symbolic process. He recognizes it only as one of several dimensions of symbolic action. (In his most recent essay, he divides the symbolic into five components: poetic, rhetorical, logical, scientific, and philosophical.[41] While all five work with the same instruments on the same objects, they differ in respect to function.) Thus, Burke's thought leads to a symbolic, though not a strictly rhetorical, view of knowledge. If we are to obtain a clear statement of the epistemological autonomy of rhetoric, we must move far to the other side of the "modern" period, to the classical origins of rhetorical theory.

For some time, scholars in Speech-Communication have recognized the relevance of the doctrine of Gorgias of Leontini to the issues of contemporary rhetorical theory. Richard Enos' essay, "The Epistemology of Gorgias' Rhetoric: A Re-examination," is the latest in a series of essays devoted to this theme.[42] Enos rightly stresses the close connection between Gorgias epistemology and his rhetoric. (In fact, the two seem inseparable.) Denying the possibility of certain and immutible knowledge, Gorgias holds that our view of reality is based exclusively on opinion. We know what we know on the basis of encounters with actual situations as they are defined by the perceptual screen of language. The antithetical power of language creates the illusion of reality by framing our responses in terms of simple oppositions. Language provides concrete models and anti-models that allow us to make sense of the world. Furthermore, as its antithetical structure suggests, language itself operates through conflict and is therefore fundamentally persuasive in character. Consequently, the rhetor commands the whole field of epistemology:

> Since all human inquiry moves within the realm of opinion, where deception is easy, all persuasion (philosophic, 'scientific', legal or other) is a result of the force of eloquence rather than of rational insight. . . . If men *knew,* there would be a great difference between deception and truth. As it is, we can only distinguish between successful and unconvincing, persuasive and fruitless arguments.[43]

Our epistemological tour of the current rhetorical literature is now complete. We have moved from the "modern" views of Descartes, Pascal, and Whately, to the "postmodern" epistemic view, and, by only a slight departure from the main road, we have ended by returning to antiquity. Surely, it is significant that the thinking of Gorgias, rather than Plato or Aristotle, provided the point of entry into antiquity. Even in the absence of other evidence, this fact should alert us to the profound changes occasioned by granting rhetoric an epistemic status. The epistemic view, in any of its forms, alters the assumptive grounds of modern rhetorical theory, and it thereby reopens some basic questions about the nature of rhetorical theory. The two most prominent of these issues relate to the ethics of rhetoric and the proper scope of the art. And we must now turn our attention to these issues.

Epistemic Rhetoric and the Problem Of Values

The epistemic view of rhetoric leads to a number of serious ethical problems. Since the view is implicitly relativistic, its advocates are open to the charge that they are undermining the grounds for rational decision-making. Scott is well aware of the charge, and he replies to it on two levels. First, he argues that the "objectivist" alternative has problems of its own. The evidence shows that this position encourages fanaticism, intolerance, and an abrogation of responsibility in making decisions. Second, he points out that epistemic rhetoric is inter-subjective, not subjective. Since it is based on the standard of communal assent, the epistemic view encourages cooperation and saves us from solipsism. In general, then, Scott seems to accept rhetorical relativism as a fact of epistemological life, and argues that its effects are not debilitating. In fact, it encourages such desirable goals as tolerance, mutual respect, and responsibility.[44]

Nevertheless, this general defense is not acceptable to everyone. Although fanatics may often distort objective philosophy, intersubjective relativism also contains the seeds of its own corruption, since it is likely to degenerate into demagoguery. Consequently, it is not surprising that a number of scholars have attempted to qualify and purify rhetorical relativism. Some have placed specific ethical limitations on epistemic rhetoric; others have attempted to balance the intersubjective criterion against the more stable criterion of self-evident truth, and still others have sought to limit the range of intersubjectivity by acknowledging the objective force of public issues. Each of these positions deserves separate treatment.

In his essay, "Rhetoric as a 'Way of Knowing': An Attenuation of the Epistemological Claims of the 'New Rhetoric'," Cherwitz makes a direct attempt to bring the epistemic view under the control of ethical guidelines.[45] Cherwitz agrees with Scott that rhetoric has an epistemic function and with Brummett that rhetoric involves the advocacy of reality. Yet, he is not willing to let the mere fact of intersubjective consensus define the nature of rhetorical truth. Instead, he argues that "the speech act must . . . meet certain criteria before it can be considered as truth creative."[46] The criteria are: (1) Rhetoric "must be viewed as an activity of

correction, wherein the clash of contradictory ideas exposes error and yields truth."
(2) Participants "must be afforded an equal amount of control and initiative
regarding lines of influence," and (3) the rhetoric must function "as an enterprise
in person-risking and person building."[47] These qualifications are extraordinarily
broad, and I leave the reader to his own devices in interpreting and assessing them.

It is clear, however, that Cherwitz has done much more than "attenuate" Scott's
conception of an epistemic rhetoric. He has, in fact, shifted the ground of the
concept from a description of rhetorical practice to a prescription about how rhetoric
ought to proceed. Scott claims that rhetoric is epistemic because rhetoric-in-action
yields inter-subjective knowledge. He then defends this position ethically by
justifying the rationality of intersubjective agreement as a standard of truth.
Cherwitz, however, defines epistemic rhetoric in terms of certain ethical standards;
rhetorical acts that do not measure up to these standards are by definition
epistemologically insignificant.

Obviously, Cherwitz' view is not acceptable at the descriptive level. We can cite
a long list of rhetorical discourses deficient in respect to one or more of Cherwitz'
criteria that have succeeded in affecting public consensus. But this slight confusion
does not vitiate the main force of Cherwitz' argument. For once in the literature,
we encounter a rather clear issue: Should the term epistemic refer solely to the effect
of rhetorical discourse in promoting inter-subjective agreement, or should it also
refer to the quality of the discourse as judged against standards derived from social
philosophy?

The two remaining positions develop a more subtle approach that balances the
relative standard of intersubjective agreement against a more stable mode of
knowledge. We have already glanced at one of these approaches, Scult's analysis
of the universal audience, but it seems useful to review his argument again in the
present context.[48] Scult maintains that Perelman seeks to achieve an epistemological
middle-ground between the closed systems of formal logic and the open field of
scepticism. He effects this compromise through his conception of the interaction
between the universal audience and particular audiences. The speaker obtains his
concept of truth through his construction of the universal audience. But he must
test this subjective construct against some particular audience. Arguments, therefore, are validated by gaining the adherence of both the universal and the particular
audience. Since the particular audience is not constant, since it is always shifting
in composition and ideology, the rhetorician can never gain final validation for his
argument. He cannot achieve absolute, unshakeable truth. Yet, his commitment to
the process furthers the cause of knowledge, and the interaction between the two
audiences rectifies the problem involved in dealing with either one separately. The
rhetorician is saved from sophistic argument *ad populum* because his own sense of
rationality guides the selection of arguments. And he is saved from pure subjectiv-
ism since he must admit his arguments to the scrutiny of an actual audience.

The final position uses the concepts of situation and issue as external criteria for
limiting the range of intersubjectivity. In an essay that combines Bitzer's concept
of the rhetorical situation with a relativistic epistemology, Hunsaker and Smith
indicate how these constraints might work.[49] Following Bitzer, they maintain that

rhetorical discourse is grounded in a situation. The situation, in turn, guides the perception and formation of issues, and the issues determine the character of the rhetorical response. This process, however, is not mechanical or deterministic, since subjective and intersubjective factors intrude at every point. Both the situation and the issues that apply to it reflect the social and personal biases of those involved in the deliberation.

Nevertheless, there are certain limits on the construction that the speaker can impose on the situation, and certain conventions that restrict his license to interpret the issues. In respect to situation, Hunsaker and Smith argue: "Just as a block of wood precludes certain possibilities, such as a bronze statue, while allowing others, so the rhetorical situation, as first actuality, precludes certain issues from arising while allowing others."[50] Thus, the objective character of the situation as an event in the external world has some influence in delimiting the rhetorical transaction. In respect to issues, Hunsaker and Smith note that they are actualized in terms of subjective perceptions, but " . . . because cognitive and affective experiences are not completely private, but to some extent shared through common experience and communication, there exists a common core of perception. . . . It is within the realm of commonality of perception that rhetorical issues arise."[51] The perception of an issue, therefore, depends upon those relatively stable aspects of intersubjective agreement that constitute norms and traditions. In sum, the objective nature of the situation limits the possible selection of issues, and relatively fixed conventions exert a degree of control over the perception and formulation of issues.

Hunsaker and Smith's essay is a descriptive analysis of issue formation. It is not a study in the ethics of rhetoric and should not be construed as such. Nevertheless, the connection between external constraints and relativism suggests a possible approach to the ethics of rhetoric within the context of the epistemic view. If we believe that issues frame the rhetorical act, then we might carefully study the nature of issues in order to determine points of psychological and logical regularity. Of course, these regularities largely reflect socially determined norms, but it is always possible to convert the norm into the normative. In this way, we might be able to construct relatively stable points of reference for the conduct of arguments verified by intersubjective agreement.

J. Michael Sproule's essay on Whately's theory of presumption offers an interesting point of departure for speculation on this matter.[52] Sproule contends that Whately's theory of presumption is not entirely logical or legal. Rather, Whately believes that presumption also encompasses the psychological reaction of an audience to an issue. The rhetor, then, must adjust his argumentation to both an assigned and a psychological burden of proof. When these two aspects of presumption are juxtaposed, it is apparent that certain consistencies emerge in the direction of psychological response to an issue. For example, although audiences normally hold a presumption in favor of the *status quo,* the introduction of a novel idea may turn the presumption in the other direction. Or, again, deference to an authority may create a psychological presumption that overwhelms the logically assigned burden of proof. Thus, we have a logical norm and certain norms of psychological reaction that move in a contrary direction. If we abandon Whately's faculty psychology in favor of a broader view of rationality, we might next ask under what circumstances the psychological reaction constitutes a legitimate violation of the logical norm.

More generally, the notion of presumption may help us stabilize the concept of intersubjectivity. For example, Edward Hawkins, a contemporary and friend of Whately's, argues that there should be an initial disposition to accept "that side of an argument where the first presumption of truth appears." This rule applies, for example, in any case where an "uninterrupted tradition brings with it a reasonable *presumption* in its behalf."[53] Translated into the terms of an epistemic rhetorician, Hawkins' argument might be rendered this way: An arguer ought to respect intersubjectively certified traditions, agreements, and conventions, especially when they have survived over a long period of time. Where such agreements exist, the arguer ought to accept their truth unless he has good reason to doubt them. Stated in this way, the doctrine of presumption bears a striking resemblance to Wayne Booth's "post-modern" rhetoric of assent.[54] Both concepts reverse the terms of the scepticism implicit in modern dogma, since they hold that we should presume the truth of well-established traditions unless there is compelling evidence to the contrary. Viewed in this light, the inter-subjective approach to rhetoric not only respects the norms of thought, but it can also draw from them normative standards for the conduct of argument.

The Scope of Rhetoric

The attempt to define the limits of rhetoric constitutes one of the oldest and most persistent problems in the Speech Communication literature. Traditionally, the issue has centered on the distinction between rhetoric and poetic, and two rather clear positions have emerged. The first argues that the two arts deal with different types of objects. Rhetoric, in this view, applies to discourses that are literal in character and persuasive in intent, whereas poetic applies to discourses that are figurative and fictional. The second position distinguishes between the two on the basis of function. The rhetorical function in language is instrumental, designed to "produce effects 'beyond' the act."[55] The poetic function, on the other hand, is consummatory, designed to exercise "symbolic action in and for itself. . . ."[56] Rhetoric and poetic, therefore, represent two complimentary dimensions in discourse. They usually co-exist in the same discourse, and no clear line can be drawn between "rhetorical" literature and "poetic" literature.

During the past decade controversy over this issue abated. But the colloquy between Burke and Howell in the February 1976 issue of the *Quarterly Journal of Speech* has renewed the debate. Burke, of course, argues in favor of the functional approach, while Howell defends the distinction between the literature of literal statement and the literature of fiction.[57]

The consensus view in recent scholarship supports Burke's side of the issue.[58] This alignment is virtually mandated by the prominence of the epistemic theory of rhetoric, since that theory requires a functional approach to the art. Nevertheless, even as the contemporary emphasis on function and process ends the rhetoric/poetic controversy, it raises new and equally pressing issues about the limits of rhetoric. When we define rhetoric functionally, we immediately encounter questions about the range of application of the rhetorical function. Does it apply to scientific as well as axiological deliberations? Does it apply to theoretical as well as practical issues? Is this function so broad that it embraces all forms of argumentative discourse? Or should we follow the views of the ancient theorists who generally limit the function of rhetoric to practical deliberations about civic business?

In general, contemporary theorists expand the scope of rhetoric well beyond the boundaries established by the classical authorities. Thus, although Perelman restricts the application of rhetoric to the humanities and social sciences, he regards it as relevant to abstract philosophy as well as to public debate.[59] Grassi is even more emphatic about the philosophical character of rhetoric. He argues that rhetoric is not properly a "technique of exterior persuasion," but rather "the speech which is the basis of rational thought."[60] And a number of theorists, Weimer, Wander, Overington, and Finocchiaro among them, argue that rhetoric functions in an important way in scientific argument.[61] Some of them, Weimer most notably, go so far as to argue that science is fundamentally a rhetorical transaction.

There is, however, one important essay that manifests sympathy for the more restricted claims of the classical tradition. In fact, Farrell begins his essay, "Knowledge, Consensus, and Rhetorical Theory," with praise for Aristotle's conception of the relationship between rhetoric and "a generally accepted body of knowledge pertaining to matters of public concern."[62] He proceeds to make a sharp and rather Aristotelian distinction between active and theoretical knowledge, and he restricts rhetoric to the domain of active knowledge. Finally, he asserts that rhetoric has a definite substance:

> Having considered several distinguishing rhetorical characteristics of social knowledge, it should now be apparent that rhetoric, whatever its own attributed status is not purely a formalistic enterprise. There is something which this art is about. That 'something' is a kind of knowledge which is attributed, audience-dependent, potential in state, generative, and normative in implication.[63]

It appears that Farrell has not only limited the scope of rhetoric, but that he has also resolved the old process/substance dichotomy in favor of substance and thereby dissociated himself from those who entertain a purely functional or process view of the art. That is, having defined a subject-matter for rhetoric, it follows that Farrell should delimit the art in terms of a certain class of objects. His argument, however, subtly circumvents this issue, since it turns out that the substance of rhetoric is social knowledge, and social knowledge is itself a process. In the manner of Abelard, Farrell answers the question of substance both affirmatively and negatively, and thus he can define rhetoric as functional without sacrificing the logical right to restrict its area of operation. In short, rhetoric is functional, but it only functions in cases where social knowledge is engaged.

This position, as I interpret it, involves a synthesis of the classical and the more expansive contemporary views of the scope of rhetoric. On the one hand, Farrell reaffirms the classical conception of the function of the art; rhetoric is still an active faculty that bears on practical matters of social consequence. On the other hand, he does not limit the operation of this faculty to civic business as it is conducted in law courts, political assemblies, and public ceremonials. Instead, he expands the concept of social knowledge to the point that it might apply in any situation involving the deliberations of a group. Accordingly, one can justify the extension of rhetoric beyond its classical boundaries, but only insofar as the classical function of the art applies to discourses that fall outside the realm of normal public business.

Conclusion

The most consistent feature of the recent theoretical literature is the repetition of such key terms as "epistemic function," "intersubjective truth," "active knowledge," and "social consensus." These terms are closely related, and taken together, they reveal a certain consistency in the direction of recent thought. In general, the literature moves toward a revisionist theory of the epistemological status of rhetoric that rejects the modern dichotomy between communication and knowledge as it embraces the humanist conception of rhetoric as a way of knowing. The common goal, then, is to establish an epistemic base for the study of rhetoric. But this is a difficult goal, and despite the effort expended in pursuing it, the main features of the epistemic position are still opaque. We have yet to clarify the different levels of meaning that attach themselves to the epistemic view; we do not fully understand how it bears on the traditional issues of the discipline, and even when we have formulated issues, the analysis has failed to progress beyond the most primitive stages. Thus, although it is safe to say that rhetorical theory is changing, we have only a vague notion of what the change will bring.

In some measure, this lack of clarity results from problems inherent in any attempt to redefine the presumptions of a well-established academic tradition. Nevertheless, these unavoidable problems are compounded by the most serious defect in the literature—the void in the conceptual space between the specificity of the historical/textual studies and the grand abstractions of the meta-rhetorical essays. The literature tells us something about the history of rhetorical theory. It tells us a great deal about how we might identify the first principles of a new theory. But there is virtual silence about the middle level issues that form the content of a theory.[64] Thus, the literature leaves us in a state of limbo; we have a past and a future, but no present.

The problem may be set in context by means of comparison. A number of teachers of English composition also call themselves rhetoricians, and they have produced a body of literature that we can follow in such journals as *College English* and *College Composition and Communication*. This literature has its abstract moments. One can find grand speculations on a scale to satisfy the readership of the *Quarterly Journal of Speech* or *Philosophy and Rhetoric.* Nevertheless, beneath the level of meta-theory, there is a rather clear assumption about the common purpose of the enterprise. Almost everyone in the discipline centers his inquiry on the problem of how to teach students to write good English prose. And this common purpose translates itself into such issues as these: How does one find arguments to support a thesis? What is the best way to organize the main components of an essay? How does word order affect the meaning of a sentence? These issues are theoretical in character, but they also have practical ramifications, and consequently they offer a tangible ground for applying the results of meta-rhetorical speculation.

In turning to the Speech Communication literature one finds no counter-part to this stability of purpose or this commitment to middle-level theory. What practical issues are affected by our meta-theories? The answer clearly does not come from pedagogy, since the literature maintains strict silence about speech composition.[65] The history of public address is another possibility, and the abstract discussion of the relationship between theory and criticism continues. As a practical matter, however, the link between the two has yet to be made.[66] In fact, then, our meta-rhetorical speculation is autotelic. It does not have an outlet for application, and as a result, our theoretical literature stutters at the level of pure abstraction. Ironically, however, this same literature keeps insisting that rhetoric is a practical discipline, that it operates mainly in the context of concrete problems, and that it calls for decisions leading to action.

In a recent review article, Littlejohn notes that "the tremendous growth in research and theory has created an information overload making integration and synthesis very difficult."[67] The normal response to this problem is to search for a macro-theory that can serve as a magic thread leading us out of the conceptual maze into a position of theoretical clarity. Although rhetorical theorists cannot be accused of contributing to the information overload, they have joined enthusiastically the search for Ariadne's thread. The effort has given us a vague sense of direction, but it has done little to enhance our theoretical knowledge of persuasive communication. And until we have done more research and theory, it is difficult to understand how we can achieve a viable synthesis at the meta-theoretical level. Perhaps there is a magic thread, but I doubt that we can find it before we have explored the labyrinth more carefully and learned much more about its conceptual twists and turns.

Notes

1. The decline in the number of these short survey articles reflects the increasing maturity of scholarship in the history of rhetoric. Such essays obviously are unnecessary when the scholarship has advanced past the preliminary stages. Most of the recent essays of this type deal with the Middle Ages, a period for which we still lack comprehensive knowledge of the primary sources. See: James Bliese, "The Study of Rhetoric in the Twelfth Century," *Quarterly Journal of Speech,* 63 (Dec., 1977), 364–383, Lu'e M. Reinsma, "Rhetoric in England: The Age of Aelfric, 970–1020," *Communication Monographs,* 44 (Nov., 1977), 390–403, and John H. Timmis III, "Christian Rhetoric and the Western Church Fathers," *Central States Speech Journal,* 27 (Winter, 1976), 280–284.

2. Philip C. Wander, "The Rhetoric of Science." *Western Journal of Speech Communication,* 40 (Fall, 1976), 226.

3. Richard Cherwitz, "Rhetoric as a 'Way of Knowing: An Attenuation of the Epistemological Claims of the "New Rhetoric'," *Southern Speech Communication Journal,* 42 (Spring, 1977), 219.

4. Elaine Ognibene, *Review of Wayne Booth, Modern Dogma and the Rhetoric of Assent* and *A Rhetoric of Irony, Southern Speech Communication Journal,* 42 (Fall, 1976), 84.

5. Barry Brummett, "Some Implications of 'Process' on 'Intersubjectivity': Postmodern Rhetoric," *Philosophy and Rhetoric,* 9 (Winter, 1976), 31,

6. Walter Weimer, "Science as a Rhetorical Transaction: Toward a Nonjustificational Conception of Rhetoric," *Philosophy and Rhetoric,* 10 (Winter, 1977), 19, quoting an unpublished paper by Carroll C. Arnold.

7. See Robert L. Scott's essay, "On Viewing Rhetoric as Epistemic," *Central States Speech Journal,* 18 (Feb., 1967), 9–16, and its sequal, "On Viewing Rhetoric as Epistemic: Ten Years Later," *Central States Speech Journal,* 27 (Winter, 1976), 258–266. I use Scott's "epistemic" as the central term in this essay.

8. Brummett, 21.

9. For the purposes of this essay, modern is defined as post-Cartesian.

10. Kathleen M. Jamieson, "Pascal vs. Descartes: A Clash over Rhetoric in the Seventeenth Century," *Communication Monographs,* 43 (March, 1976), 44–50.

11. Ray E. McKerrow, "Campbell and Whately on the Utility of Syllogistic Logic," *Western Journal of Speech Communication,* 40 (Winter, 1976), 3–13.

12. Gordon F. Hostettler, "George Saintsbury's View of Rhetoric," *Western Journal of Speech Communication,* 41 (Fall, 1977), 210–220.

13. Jamieson, 50.

14. McKerrow, p. 9, quoting from an unpublished manuscript by Whately.

15. Douglas Ehninger, in the introduction to his edition of Whately's *Elements of Rhetoric* (Carbondale and Edwardsville: Southern Illinois University Press, 1963), p. xxvii.

16. Hostettler, 220.

17. For Vico, see Vincent Bevilacqua, "Vico 'Process' and the nature of Rhetorical Investigation: An Epistemological Perspective," *Philosophy and Rhetoric,* 7 (Summer, 1974), 166–174. For Marx, see Richard Wilkie, "Karl Marx on Rhetoric," *Philosophy and Rhetoric,* 9 (Fall, 1976), 232–246. It should also be noted that the epistemic view has clear and strong antecedents in pre-modern rhetorical theory. The concept of rhetoric as a way of knowing is carried through a humanistic tradition beginning with the early Greek sophists, continuing with Isocrates and Cicero, and extending into the thought of the Renaissance humanists. For a summary of this tradition see Nancy S. Struever, *The Language of History in the Renaissance: Rhetoric and Historical Consciousness in Florentine Humanism* (Princeton, New Jersey: Princeton University Press, 1970), pp. 5–39.

18. Scott, 265.

19. Thomas B. Farrell, "Knowledge, Consensus, and Rhetorical Theory," *Quarterly Journal of Speech,* 62 (Feb., 1976), 4.

20. Farrell, 4.

21. See Farrell, 9.

22. Christine Oravec, "Observation in Aritotle's Theory of Epideictic," *Philosophy and Rhetoric,* 9 (Summer, 1976), 171–172.

23. For an analysis of this interaction, see William J. Jordan and W. Clifton Adams, "I. A. Richard's Concept of Tenor-Vehicle Interaction," *Central States Speech Journal,* 27 (Summer, 1976), 136–137.

24. See Ernesto Grassi, "Rhetoric and Philosophy," *Philosophy and Rhetoric,* 9 (Fall, 1976), 200–201.

25. Cf. Edwin Black's concept of "argumentative synthesis," in *Rhetorical Criticism: A Study in Method* (New York: Macmillan, 1965), pp. 168–176. Black argues that if two opposing syntheses are equally coherent, then style determines which one will be most persuasive, pp. 174–175.

26. See the essays by Weimar and Wander, as well as Michael A. Overington. "The Scientific Community as Audience: Toward a Rhetorical Analysis of Science," *Philosophy and Rhetoric,* 10 (Summer, 1977), 143–63, and Mario Finocchiaro, "Logic and Rhetoric in Lavoissier's Sealed Note: Toward a Rhetoric of Science." *Philosophy and Rhetoric,* 10 (Spring, 1977), 111–122.

27. *The New Rhetoric: A Treatise on Argumentation,* trans. by John Wilkinson and Purcell Weaver (Notre Dame and London: University of Notre Dame Press, 1969), pp. 1–10.

28. Carl B. Holmberg, "Dialectical Rhetoric and Rhetorical Rhetoric," *Philosophy and Rhetoric,* 10 (Fall, 1977), 232–43.

29. Grassi, *Passim*. This is a very condensed and simplified version of Grassi's argument. His essay demands, and rewards, close reading.

30. Perelman, p. 119, and see also Louise A. Karon, "Presence in the *New Rhetoric*," *Philosophy and Rhetoric*, 9 (Spring, 1976), 97.

31. Karon, 97–101.

32. Karon, 97.

33. Karon, 106–110.

34. S. M. Halloran, "Tradition and Theory in Rhetoric," *Quarterly Journal of Speech*, 62 (Oct., 1976), 240, argues a similar point.

35. For a more complete version of this argument, see Allan Scult, "Perelman's Universal: One Perspective," *Central States Speech Journal*, 27 (Fall, 1976), 176–180.

36. One should note, however, that Perelman's system applies only to the humanities, since he makes no claims about a rhetoric of science.

37. Brummett, 28.

38. Weimer, 13.

39. "The Party Line," *Quarterly Journal of Speech*, 62 (Feb., 1976) 62–68.

40. Burke, 65. In a delightful essay that uses a Burkean method to analyze Burke, Laura Crowell clarifies the way that symbolic action establishes reality. Symbolic action allows us to discriminate and classify situations, to change them by linguistic encompassment (i.e., by naming and renaming them), to confront and control uncertainty, to bring matters to completion, and to realize and embody the whimsicality of the whole symbolic process. See "Three Sheers for Kenneth Burke," *Quarterly Journal of Speech*, 63 (April, 1977), 152–167.

41. Burke, 66.

42. Richard Leo Enos, "The Epistemology of Gorgias Rhetoric: A Re-Examination," *Southern Speech Communication Journal*, 38 (Fall, 1972), 27–38, and Richard A. Engnell, "Implications for Communication of the Rhetorical Epistemology of Gorgias of Leontine," *Western Speech* (Summer, 1973), 175–184.

43. L. Versényi, *Socratic Humanism* (New Haven, Conn.: Yale University Press, 1963), pp. 47–48.

44. Scott, 263–266.

45. See above, note 3.

46. Cherwitz, 217.

47. Cherwitz, 217–219.

48. See above, note 34.

49. David M. Hunsaker and Craig R. Smith, "The Nature of Issues: A Constructive Approach to Situational Rhetoric," *Western Journal of Speech Communication*, 40 (Spring, 1976), 144–155.

50. Hunsaker and Smith, 146.

51. Hunsaker and Smith, 148.

52. J. Michael Sproule, "The Psychological Burden of Proof: On the Evolutionary Development of Richard Whately's Theory of Presumption," *Communication Monographs*, 43 (June, 1976), 115–129.

53. Sproule, 124.

54. *Modern Dogma and the Rhetoric of Assent* (Chicago and London: The University of Chicago Press, 1974), esp. pp. 87–140.

55. Burke, 66.

56. Burke, 66.

57. Wilbur Samuel Howell, "The Two Party Line: A Reply to Kenneth Burke," *Quarterly Journal of Speech*, 62 (Feb., 1976), 69–77.

58. For a dissenting view, however, see Hostettler, 220.

59. Perelman, p. 6.

60. Grassi, 202.

61. See above, note 25.

62. Farrell, 1.

63. Farrell, 11.

64. In fact, only two articles in the literature I reviewed directly attacked a limited theoretical issue. See George P. Boss, "Essential Attributes of the Concept of Charisma," *Southern Speech Communication Journal*, 41 (Spring, 1976), 300–313, and David A. Kaufer, "Irony and Rhetorical Strategy," *Philosophy and Rhetoric*, 10 (Spring, 1977), 90–110. Kaufer's essay is a model of what might be accomplished by identifying and thinking through specific problems in theory.

65. I exaggerate only slightly. Of the essays that I read for this review, only one, Sproule's article on Whately, makes direct reference to pedagogy.

66. This assertion requires some qualification. A number of rhetorical critics have made good use of postmodern epistemology in specific studies. See, for example, Michael McGuire, "Mythic Rhetoric in *Mein Kampf:* A Structuralist Critique," *Quarterly Journal of Speech,* 63 (Feb., 1977), 1–13, Michael Mc Gee, "The Fall of Wellington: A Case Study of the Relationship Between Theory, Practice and Rhetoric in History," *Quarterly Journal of Speech,* 63 (Feb., 1977), 28–42, and Ernest G. Bormann, "Fetching Good Out of Evil: A Rhetorical Use of Calamity," *Quarterly Journal of Speech,* 63 (April, 1977), 130–39. This sort of approach, however, is relatively new and still in its formative stage.

67. Stephen W. Littlejohn, "Symbolic Interactionism as an Approach to the Study of Human Communication," *Quarterly Journal of Speech,* 63 (Feb., 1977), 84.

Hermeneutics and Rhetoric:
A Seen But Unobserved Relationship
by Michael J. Hyde and Craig R. Smith

Our purpose is to substantiate three claims: (1) that an important relationship existing between hermeneutics and rhetoric has been overlooked by communication scholars; (2) that the nature of this relationship, if elucidated, can clarify rhetoric's epistemic function; and (3) that such elucidation can provide important theoretical directives for rhetorical criticism.

The Relationship Between Hermeneutics and Rhetoric

The overlooked relationship between hermeneutics and rhetoric, ontological in nature, evolves from the "basic mode" of human "understanding"; in Heidegger's words this basic mode of understanding is an ontological (primordial) structure constituting the nature of human being (Dasein).[1] Thus, to observe and disclose the relationship between hermeneutics and rhetoric, one must describe it ontologically. Such an explication necessitates a phenomenological investigation: as Heidegger has shown, *"Only as phenomenology, is ontology possible."*[2] A phenomenological investigation of the relationship starts by showing what the basic mode of human understanding is and how it structures the experience of existential reality. This disclosure of understanding is itself a disclosure of the human experience of language; it entails showing how understanding is related to the ontological significations of "interpretation" and "meaning." This functional relationship—which Heidegger terms Dasein's "hermeneutical situation"—constitutes the

Reprinted from *The Quarterly Journal of Speech* 65 (1979), with permission of the National Communication Association.

"primordial signification" of hermeneutics. From the hermeneutical situation originates the primordial function of rhetoric. Later in this essay we shall further define
the hermeneutical situation and rhetoric's function in it, for it is the description of
the ontological relationship between the hermeneutical situation and rhetoric's
primordial function which is central to this study. At this point we mean only to
clarify the working premise of our investigation: The primordial function of
rhetoric is to "make-known" meaning both *to oneself and to others. Meaning is
derived by a human being in and through the interpretive understanding of reality.
Rhetoric is the process of making-known that meaning.*

By clarifying the ontological relationship between hermeneutics and rhetoric
one is able to observe from where the derivative and concrete (ontic) senses of the
terms originate; for the ontological relationship makes possible the derivative and
concrete senses. According to Schrag, "The ontological is not a separate realm 'off
by itself'; rather, it designates the structure of the concrete and hence is that which,
when it is disclosed, provides the concrete with its conceptual clarification."[3]
Furthermore, one is able to observe how the relationship is a primary condition for
the acquisition of any communicable knowledge. To date, such observation of the
relationship has not been made by communication scholars.

A Review

The use of hermeneutics to explore the diverse concerns of speech communication has been urged by various scholars,[4] but few seem to have seen the function of
rhetoric as it relates to hermeneutics. This is not to say that those who have
suggested what the function(s) of rhetoric might be, without discussing its relationship to hermeneutics, have misinformed their audiences. Many of these scholars,
although they have not explicated the relationship, must have "heard the call" of
the relationship given their informative discussions of the nature of rhetoric. For
example, Burke's claim that rhetoric "is rooted in an essential function of language
itself, . . . the use of language as a symbolic means of inducing cooperation in beings
that by nature respond to symbols,"[5] provides an important signpost that directs the
reader toward the ontological foundations of the term. Campbell used this signpost
in her discussion of "The Ontological Foundations of Rhetorical Theory," but her
claim that "rhetorical theorizing" from such a "symbolic perspective" provides "the
most productive and viable ontological basis from which to develop a complete and
coherent theory of rhetoric"[6] falls short of explicating *what* this ontological basis
is and *how* it is constituted.[7]

During the 1970 National Developmental Project on Rhetoric, the relationship
between hermeneutics and rhetoric was seen in various ways. McKeon, conceiving
hermeneutics in one of its derivative senses, suggested that it be used as a *method*
in developing rhetoric as an "architectonic productive art," that is, "an art of
structuring all principles and products of knowing, doing, and making."[8] Even
though he was not concerned with explicating the ontological relationship of the
terms, McKeon's correlation of hermeneutics, rhetoric, and knowing is suggestive.

Rosenfield's[9] argument that an authentic study of rhetoric must first and foremost be grounded in the "being" of human experience was indeed an attempt to have scholars understand rhetoric ontologically. Similarly, Johnstone encouraged an ontological understanding of rhetoric through a phenomenological investigation of "the role played by rhetoric in human life."[10]

Neither Rosenfield nor Johnstone explored rhetoric's relationship to hermeneutics, but their discussions of rhetoric in light of being (ontology) and phenomenology imply such a relationship. For, as both Ricoeur and Schrag have shown, phenomenological-ontological studies of the conditions of human experience presuppose a hermeneutic perspective.[11]

Deetz's phenomenological investigation of language presents an understanding of Heidegger's and Gadamer's hermeneutical approaches to the study of language.[12] Unfortunately, Deetz does not offer any specific observations on hermeneutics' relationship to rhetoric. Unlike Deetz, Holmberg does make an explicit and perceptive statement concerning the relationship. He contends that "hermeneutic is *the* rhetorical discipline since it is an articulating in order to manifest the morphic appearances of amorphic Being."[13] Holmberg's statement offers an important vision of the ontological relationship between hermeneutics and rhetoric. But this cryptic statement, even when placed in the context of his essay, is problematic; for Holmberg does not offer any clear explication of the relationship.

Communication scholars interested in rhetoric's epistemic function have generated discussions that lend focus to the relationship between hermeneutics and rhetoric. Of these scholars, Scott has been the most explicit. Drawing from the theory of philosophical hermeneutics as discussed by Gadamer, Scott concludes that "rhetoric must . . . be seen . . . as a human potentiality to understand the human condition."[14] Scott does not present an analysis of the ontological relationship between hermeneutics and rhetoric, although his conclusion is closely aligned with Gadamer's understanding of rhetoric's epistemic function as Gadamer relates it to the primordial signification of hermeneutics. But if rhetoric must be "seen" in the way that Scott suggests, is one not committed to make the seeing as clear as possible through an explication of what this seeing entails? Like Scott, we believe the commitment must be met.

Explication

Philosophical hermeneutics offers some of the most salient directives for explicating the relationship between hermeneutics and rhetoric. The contributions of Heidegger, Gadamer, and Ricoeur point to and show the relationship in ways that communication scholars still need to comprehend and investigate. For example, Heidegger suggests that Aristotle's analysis of the *pathé* in the *Rhetoric* can "be taken as the first systematic hermeneutic of the everydayness of Being with one another."[15] Although all three scholars are important, Gadamer's discussion of the relationship is the most explicit.

In his essay "On the Scope and Function of Hermeneutical Reflection," Gadamer establishes an important groundwork for conducting an inquiry into the ontological relationship of hermeneutics and rhetoric.[16] This groundwork takes shape in Gadamer's elucidation of the proposition that in both hermeneutics and rhetoric "theory is subsequent to that out of which it is abstracted, that is, to praxis."[17] What is meant here by "praxis" is human existence as it is actually "lived through" and experienced by individuals in its essential form, "the universal phenomenon of human linguisticality" (language). Following Heidegger's ontological conception of this universal phenomenon, Gadamer characterizes it as "understanding" (*Verstehen*). Understanding, defined ontologically, is the *universe of linguistic possibilities that history "projects" towards human beings* in their futural development. A person's understanding of existence always takes its experiential form from the linguistic possibilities present in a given culture's hermeneutical situation. As Gadamer puts it, "language is not only an object in our hands, it is the reservoir of tradition and the medium in and through which we exist and perceive our world."[18] For Gadamer, the Being of reality never happens "'behind the back' of language: . . . [it] happens precisely *within* language,"[19] within the hermeneutical situation of human experience. When actualized through the interpretive acts of thinking, speaking, and writing these linguistic possibilities mark out the developing historical-hermeneutical tradition and hence consciousness of human being. This interpretation of linguistic possibilities wherein Being is given an experiential and meaningful form as the historical-hermeneutical tradition of understanding is, for Gadamer, where the "fundamental function" of rhetoric shows itself.

Heidegger, like Gadamer, argues that the study of understanding in its experiential form is the "primary" task of philosophical hermeneutics. A hermeneutical investigation of this ontic mode of understanding enables one to elucidate the mode's ontological structure and thus approach a description of those conditions which found all human understanding.[20] Furthermore, one can show how and at what point in the development of these conditions rhetoric's fundamental function of making-known meaning in and through interpretive understanding manifests itself. According to Gadamer, rhetoric's fundamental function must be observed if one is to realize that rhetoric is not primarily a theory of forms, speeches, and persuasion; rather, it is the "practical mastery" that people have for making-known to others that which is understood.[21] Observing the ontological relationship between hermeneutics and rhetoric is possible, then, only if one can make thematic (i.e., describe phenomenologically) the experiential form of understanding.

As noted above, the experiential form of understanding is linguistic by nature. To thematize understanding as it is experienced and developed is to describe the process of human linguisticality as it unfolds existentially. Hermeneutic phenomenologists perform this description ontologically by describing understanding as a process of interpretation and meaning. A discussion of this process is offered below.

The development of understanding is a function of how human beings "work out" the linguistic possibilities that constitute and are projected in understanding. An act of interpretation is structured by the understanding (i.e., those linguistic possibilities) that it, itself, is. The structure of understanding as it appears in and through interpretation has three fundamental and interdependent modes: a "fore-having," a "fore-sight," and a "fore-conception."[22] These three modes of under-standing constitute the ontological realm wherein all human comprehension arises. Heidegger designates this realm as the "hermeneutical situation" of human being. This "hermeneutical situation," as it takes the form of a given culture's fore-having, fore-sight, and fore-conception, defines the horizon of human consciousness within that culture.

The *fore-having* is the realm of linguistic possibilities that a culture makes available to its members "in advance" of any particular act of interpretation that may be performed by any member of the culture. An interpretation is therefore never a "presuppositionless apprehending" of experience; it is always conditioned by the understanding that constitutes the intersubjective domain of a person's culture wherein the interpretation originates. This intersubjective realm of under-standing, in turn, constitutes the parameters of rationality wherein the members of the culture learn to think and behave in ways that other members can sensibly comprehend. Intersubjective thought and behavior presuppose a fore-having. The intersubjectivity characterizing a given culture's way of life is determined by how understanding is appropriated and structured by the culture's members.

The *fore-sight* is an abstraction of the fore-having; it originates when members of a culture appropriate the culture's fore-having and, in so doing, formulate specific "points of view" which guide the interpretation of a certain object. Consequently, these points of view are also "in advance" of any particular act of interpretation; they are the orientations one brings to the scenes of interpretation and which allow one to make sense out of what one sees. For example, a "prejudice" is an ontic representation of what is here being designated ontologically as a point of view (the fore-sight of understanding). To quote Heidegger, "This fore-sight 'takes the first cut' out of what has been taken into our fore-having, and it does so with a view to a definite way in which this can be interpreted."[23]

The *fore-conception* is the way by which one structures the linguistic possibili-ties of one's fore-sight "in advance" of an act of interpretation. A categorical system that, for example, is used in conducting some scientific experiment or rhetorical analysis is an ontic example of fore-conception.

All interpretation operates within the "fore-structure" (fore-having, fore-sight, fore-conception) of understanding. For example, when a person reads and under-stands a book, interpretation is at work. Yet the interpretation contributes to understanding only insofar as what is interpreted has already been understood.[24] That is, the interpretation's potential for disclosing understanding is defined by those linguistic possibilities (fore-having) the reader possesses (fore-sight) and uses in a certain way (fore-conception) when comprehending the text. Thus, the reader's consciousness of the book's meaning functions within the reader's fore-structure. When a person's consciousness of the book's (or any other object's) meaning actualizes those linguistic possibilities of the fore-structure that heretofore re-mained in a potential or nonperformed state, the resulting interpretation, if accepted by the other members of the person's culture, shows itself as a creative experience. Here new linguistic possibilities are called into Being (made-known) and thus expand a culture's awareness of reality. The occurrence of scientific revolutions, wherein new scientific paradigms are created to explain the anomolies of existence, is an example of such creative experience.[25]

Given the above example on reading a book, it should be clear that our use of "consciousness" thoughout this paper is not Cartesian. The fallacy of the subject-object split, which Edmund Husserl showed in his *The Crisis of European Sciences and Transcendental Phenomenology,* is never adopted in works characterizing the phenomenological-hermeneutical movement. Within this movement, consciousness always is understood in its relation to a person's life-world (Husserl) or, more explicitly, in its relation to a person's hermeneutical situation and fore-structure. The role of consciousness within one's fore-structure is examined in greater detail later in this essay when we discuss how the ontological relationship between hermeneutics and rhetoric has major implications for rhetorical criticism.

One can now begin to observe how understanding is developed by interpretation. As interpretation develops understanding, understanding shows itself in both a synchronic and diachronic form. Understanding is synchronic in that any particular act of understanding is a structuring of language at a specific moment in time; it becomes situation bound. Understanding is diachronic because once it is situated by interpretation it goes beyond the particular interpretation and forms the historical tradition moving language through time.[26] Taken together, the synchronic and diachronic dimensions of understanding (with their corresponding fore-structure) constitute the hermeneutical situation of any given culture and of human existence in general. The meaning of human existence, as it develops in and through interpretive understanding, always occurs within the hermeneutical situation.

Interpretation's development of understanding always is directed toward making understanding meaningful. Understanding becomes meaningful when interpretation shows it "as something." According to Heidegger, "The 'as' makes up the structure of the explicitness of something that is understood. It constitutes the interpretation."[27] For example, in the prereflective experiences of everyday existence, a person understands perceived entities by interpreting them, as a book, a picture, a car, and so on. This interpreting of "something as something" is an articulation of understanding by interpretation wherein the something is made-known and becomes meaningful.[28] (Here we caution that we are speaking ontologically. The articulation of understanding by interpretation is prior to any ontic performance of this articulation through speaking and/or writing.)

The meaning of something shows itself in and through the primordial "as" of interpretation. If all interpretation operates within the hermeneutical situation, then this primordial "as" is fundamentally hermeneutical.[29] The primordial signification of hermeneutics, i.e., the hermeneutical situation, finds its origin here—in the hermeneutical "as" that gives existence its experiential and meaningful form in and through interpretive understanding. If this is the primordial function of rhetoric, then this function of rhetoric can be related to hermeneutic's primordial signification. Rhetoric's ontological relationship with hermeneutics occurs when understanding becomes meaningful, when interpretation shows it "as something." This showing of understanding by interpretation, such that meaning is made-known, is rhetoric in the purest sense; it is how rhetoric originates as a fundamental condition of human existence. Ontologically speaking, *rhetoric shows itself in and through the various ways understanding is interpreted and made-known.* What the "as" of a perceived object is selected to be when a linguistic possibility (or possibilities) is actualized within a hermeneutical situation marks the presence of rhetoric. If the hermeneutical situation is the "reservior" of meaning, then *rhetoric is the selecting tool for making-known this meaning.* Hence, the making-known of meaning is dependent on the selective function of rhetoric. The ontological relationship between hermeneutics and rhetoric operates therefore in a dialectical manner: Without the hermeneutical situation there would be a meaningless void; without rhetoric the latent meaning housed in the hermeneutical situation could never be actualized. We are not saying here, however, that rhetoric's primordial function within the hermeneutical situation is synonymous with interpretive understanding. On the contrary, rhetoric functions as the *telos* of interpretive understanding; rhetoric is what situates and moves the hermeneutical situation in and through time. If the hermeneutical situation, being the primordial signification of hermeneutics, is constituted as the functional relationship of "understanding-interpretation-meaning," then rhetoric is the hyphen (-) binding the relationship.

Neither Heidegger nor Gadamer discusses the relationship between hermeneutics and rhetoric in this early stage of understanding's development. In fact, Heidegger, in his investigations of how understanding is made-known, never mentions rhetoric explicitly, though a careful reading of Gadamer's writings indicates Heidegger's concern for rhetoric. Gadamer does not discuss the relationship of hermeneutics to rhetoric until he investigates how understanding is made-known *between* people. Are we then in danger of misinterpreting the directives offered by both Heidegger and Gadamer? We think not. Given that both Heidegger and Gadamer stress the importance of observing how understanding is made-known through interpretation, and that Gadamer does see rhetoric as that which makes-known understanding between people, we believe our observations about rhetoric simply advance rhetoric to a deeper ontological stage. If Gadamer is going to discuss rhetoric's making-known function, then we submit, following Heidegger's investigation, *that this making-known function is operative before it is transformed into the interpersonal realm of communication.* Rhetoric's function shows itself originally in a person's thinking about existence, in a person's *intra*personal domain, wherein reality is brought first to the person's attention and where the person's practical mastery of understanding is a fundamental presupposition of interpersonal communication. Within this intrapersonal domain a person's thinking about existence is never isolated in a subjective void; rather, it always is conditioned by the existing hermeneutical situation such that what rhetoric determines an object's "as" to be is the result of the person's communication with the internalized other of that person's fore-structure.

Given this discovery of rhetoric at the intrapersonal level, one might ask how rhetoric's making-known function becomes operative at the interpersonal level. When something that is made-known through interpretive understanding is communicated by a person to others, the something shows itself as a "derivative mode" of the person's primordial interpretive understanding. Heidegger calls this derivative mode "assertion" and designates it as having three interdependent functions: (1) *"pointing out";* (2) *"predication"*; and (3) *"communication."*[30] When a person asserts an interpretive understanding of something, the something (e.g., "the steps") is pointed out by predicating it in a definite way (e.g., "were too steep") such that the person's interpretive understanding of this something can be communicated or "shared" with others. Taking these three functions together, Heidegger defines assertion as *"a pointing-out which gives something a definite character and which communicates."*[31]

Because assertion is a derivative mode of primordial interpretive understanding, it also operates within the fore-structure and within the hermeneutical situation. But the interpretive function of an assertion transforms the hermeneutical "as" into what Heidegger terms the "apophantical" "as." That is, the assertion communicates how a person relates to the something being talked or written about. For example, in the assertion "The steps were too steep," the something being talked about is not only "steps" but steps that are interpreted as being "too steep." Unless one can communicate how one relates to what is being pointed out and predicated, one's communication cannot be realized and shared.

What is it, then, that enhances the communicability of all discourse when such discourse takes the form of an assertion? For Heidegger, it is the "making-known" function of discourse which, when it shows itself in an assertion, derives its function from the primordial interpretive understanding wherein it first originated.[32] In its derivative form this making-known function is, according to Heidegger, the "way" discourse is expressed. All discourse that attempts to assert something is characterized by this making-known function. Whether it be the intonation of one who asserts "The steps were *too steep,"* the tempo of poetical discourse, or the technical sophistication of scientific discourse, all discourse that attempts to point out something in a definite way, so it can be communicated, possesses the making-known function of primordial interpretive understanding.

To summarize the discussion so far: we have described the ontological relationship between hermeneutics and rhetoric, a relationship that we argued has not been explicated in our literature. We have suggested that rhetoric's primordial function is the making-known of meaning in and through interpretive understanding and that such a function is in the strictest sense hermeneutical. We have argued that this function occurs at the deepest intrapersonal level and that in interpersonal contexts it is vital. In light of these findings, we now offer some observations concerning rhetoric's epistemic function.

Rhetoric's Epistemic Function

Rhetoric's relationship to hermeneutics reveals that rhetoric functions epistemologically in accordance with the hermeneutical situation. That is, rhetoric makes-known understanding both synchronically and diachronically. Synchronically, rhetoric functions to reify understanding; that is, it deposits understanding during moments in time and is constrained by a given culture's intersubjectivity. The synchronic nature of rhetoric's epistemic function thus restricts its "existential placement." Specifically, when people use rhetoric they use it in the immediacy of the present, of the now, wherein their verbal and nonverbal behavior become situationally bound to their culture's own understanding. But this synchronic depositing of understanding by rhetoric also takes a diachronic form as the understanding is sedimented. This sedimented understanding marks not only the historical growth of the culture's intersubjective knowledge, but also the historical growth of human knowledge in general. Hence, synchronic and diachronic understanding operate dialectically such that what is made-known constitutes simultaneously both a system of understanding and a structure of understanding—the historicity of human linguisticality.

In any act of understanding, rhetoric's synchronic and diachronic natures are present. When rhetoric functions synchronically to make-known meaning it draws from and adds to its diachronic nature; for rhetoric's epistemic function is always a "historical happening"; rhetoric never functions in a temporal void. Instead, it creates meaning by recreating the ever present yet potential historical meaning that is projected toward the present by past rhetorical-epistemological acts. One might say, therefore, that history is a growing succession of articulated "rhetorical visions"; or "Today's social reality is yesterday's rhetorical vision."[33]

When rhetoric's epistemic function manifests itself in ontic experience it constrains people to acquire knowledge filtered by their contextual interests. Contextual interests are a function of the hermeneutical situation. They designate the "conceptual points of view" that a person chooses to use within situations when the meaning of something, which is felt to be relevant to the situation, is interpreted and made-known. Here, "contextual" refers to the specific situation itself; "interests" refer to the conceptual points of view used to acquire knowledge. In any situation, the meaning of something is made-known by the interests that guide the interpretation. All practical knowledge is a product of such interests. According to Habermas, the failure to realize this essential relationship between "knowledge and human interests" makes impossible any accurate understanding of how knowledge is experienced and acquired.[34] Interests, however, are a product of a hermeneutical situation (context) that stimulates their occurrence for acquiring knowledge; they are a person's fore-sight and fore-conception. It follows then, that *all knowledge, when it is acquired, is contextual, a product of the hermeneutical situation, and therefore founded in rhetoric—the making-known of primordial interpretive understanding.*

Rhetorical Criticism
From The Hermeneutical Perspective

The rhetorical critic attempts to *interpret* and *re-create* past rhetorical phenomena by showing their meaning for the critic's own cultural situation. If rhetorical critics are to perform their criticism with accuracy and rigor, then the hermeneutical nature of their craft must be realized. In fact, rhetorical criticism might be what

Kockelmans describes as a "hermeneutic or interpretative social science."[35] An underlying assumption of hermeneutic social science suggests the similarity between it and rhetorical criticism: "No one is really interested in understanding something that is totally irrelevant for himself and the society in which he lives. Thus, after trying to understand a phenomenon in its historical origin and further development he must try to come to a view which states the meaning of all of this for his own situation."[36]

The ontological relationship between hermeneutics and rhetoric provides important directives for doing criticism. In this second section, we explore those directives and use some current theories of rhetorical criticism to demonstrate the change in perspective we are seeking. We begin by showing how an understanding of the notion of consciousness provides an important and appropriate foundation for illustrating how our observations concerning the ontological relationship between hermeneutics and rhetoric can be used in rhetorical criticism, thereby shedding light on its hermeneutical nature.

Earlier in this essay, we noted that a person's consciousness of any object's meaning operates within that person's cultural, hermeneutical situation. This fact of consciousness is important for rhetorical critics in that the conscious act of making-known an object's meaning in and through interpretation is rhetoric's fundamental epistemological function. Clearly, a rhetor is a rhetor because of the performance of such conscious (rhetorical) acts. The rhetorical critic's object of analysis is the collection of conscious acts. And when the rhetorical critic makes-known the meaning of this collection, the critic in turn performs a similar conscious act, thereby becoming a critic and rhetor in the same moment. Yet, what must be realized by both rhetors and critics is that what informs their conscious acts and makes these conscious acts a reality is the rhetor's and the critic's respective hermeneutical situations. Hence, the rhetorical critic's object of analysis must be more than the conscious acts of a speaker if such acts are to be understood clearly. Rhetorical critics must attempt to become cognizant of the rhetor's hermeneutical situation wherein the rhetor's discourse is a function of the rhetor's fore-structure. In turn, rhetorical critics must also be cognizant of their own hermeneutical situation so that what is said about the rhetorical phenomenon under investigation can be made-known to the intended audience in an understandable manner. When such communication is successful it reifies knowledge and becomes part of the epistemic foundation for auditor and speaker alike.

This problem of understanding past and present hermeneutical situations can be approached by realizing that the consciousness constituting any culture's hermeneutical situation exists, according to Goldmann, in two forms: actual and potential.[37] An explication of Goldmann's theory of consciousness, as it facilitates examination of the impact of the ontological relationship between hermeneutics and rhetoric on criticism, follows.

Goldmann defines "actual" consciousness as a result of cultural heritage, religion, life experiences, political attitude, and popular art. Actual consciousness would include contemporary values as applied in contemporary situations. Kenneth Burke's notion of scene and Lloyd Bitzer's notion of situation can be subsumed in

Goldmann's actual consciousness. In turn, actual consciousness is a large part of fore-having, fore-sight, and fore-conception. The linguistic possibilities of one's culture along with those abstracted by the individual to "make sense of" reality form the basis of actual consciousness. Obviously, rhetoric, to be effective, would need to be adapted to actual consciousness.

Goldmann uses the notion of actual consciousness to explain one of the tasks of the hermeneuticist; the lesson is instructive for rhetorical critics as well:

> [I]t is necessary not to read philosophers simply as surpassed historical facts which are studied to know what happened a hundred or a thousand years ago, but instead to actualize them. . . . It seems a bad actualization to say that all of Marxism and all our problems were already in Hegel, or to say that Hegel holds no interest and that our problems are essentially different. Actualizing a philosopher or a philosophical thought presupposes comprehending it as it was, with its different positive elements, its internal coherence, and its development within a social reality: beginning there, we can see how certain elements can still respond to our problems.[38]

Goldmann's formulation implies that the interpreter, whether historian or rhetorical critic, must actualize for an audience what is being interpreted. This requires analysis of the actual consciousness of the past context and the present audience. And such analysis requires an understanding of the past hermeneutical situation and the present hermeneutical situation so the actualization may be accomplished. Clearly, such actualizations, whether they be of speeches or philosophical tracts, reify again knowledge which then becomes a part of the epistemic foundation.

Goldmann goes on to develop a notion of "potential" consciousness. It is determined by the maximum possible awareness of an audience, the impact of the society's understanding of its historic destiny, and that society's highest achievements in the arts. Undoubtedly, the analysis of potential consciousness is difficult and complex. But an understanding of the particular audience's fore-having, fore-sight, and fore-conception would facilitate such analysis. When exploring potential consciousness, the hermeneuticist would examine linguistic possibilities as they shed light on potential awareness and spiritual growth.

Goldmann makes clear that most effective rhetor-leaders appeal to potential consciousness. His example is Lenin:

> Lenin explained that while a certain number of socialist slogans could be transmitted to the peasants, they could never be made to understand the advantages of large-scale cultivation or be convinced that they should renounce all claims to private ownership of land. Despite their loyalty to the Tsar, an information series tending to change their consciousness could be transmitted to them. But there was one message they could never be made to assimilate: that it would be better to work cooperatively than to possess land by personal right. To the indignation of many socialists . . . Lenin formulated a new and entirely unexpected slogan: the land to the peasants. This is a classic example of sociological analysis based on the concept of potential consciousness.[30]

The effective rhetor-leader, and for that matter the effective critic, adapts to both actual and potential consciousness, with the potential consciousness forming the horizon beyond which the rhetor or critic wishing to communicate dares not travel. For Goldmann, one gains an awareness of this horizon by forming a sensitivity to the historical praxis of one's intended audience.[40] In Lenin's instance, this awareness and sensitivity grew, in part, from his actual lived-experience in pre-revolutionary Russia. For the critic whose temporal distance from the object of study precludes such a lived-experience, the historical consciousness of the past must be sought in its surviving remnants, e.g., the written record, various art forms, or, if possible, in interview-conversations with those who did have a lived-experience.[41]

In the United States one of the best examples of an effective rhetor-leader is Daniel Webster. He seemed perfectly capable of adapting to actual consciousness, whether the consciousness of the spectators at Bunker Hill or the members of the Senate. At the same time, he was also able to lead those audiences by raising themes which were a part of their potential consciousness. In his two major speeches during the 1850 Compromise debates, Webster created an atmosphere of compromise because he was able to play on the common fears and aspirations of his auditors.[42] At the same time, those speeches address universal themes which are not only artistically developed but lead toward an increased loyalty to Union and other patriotic values.

To this point, we have argued that notions of consciousness are important to rhetorical criticism and can provide structures which allow a re-entry into hermeneutical situations. Although some critics hint at the use of consciousness and hermeneutics, they do not accomplish such analysis. That such analysis has not been done may help explain why certain problems persist in our literature.

The controversy between those defining rhetorical criticism as the study of immediate effect and those arguing for more enduring criticism is a case in point. Black, for example, claims that certain works should serve as "touchstones" for our theoretical and pedagogical efforts.[43] He also says that criticism "seeks as its end the understanding of man himself."[44] The major thrust of his book is that enduring criticism results from the criticism of enduring works.

But a serious problem arises when one asks how to determine what is enduring and why. Suppose that Chapman's Coatesville Address, Black's prime example, endures not because it is a "rhetorical touchstone" but because it has literary qualities that endure, or contains issues which are salient in the consciousness of contemporary audiences. In fact, Black admits as much himself.[45] But if it is poetics or issues which explain the enduring quality of a work, how can rhetorical criticism encompass it? Is not rhetoric defined as pragmatic communication, more concerned with contemporary audiences and specific questions than with universal audiences and general questions?[46] If one accepts these standard definitions, then Black's argument may collapse into a call for literary criticism of rhetorical discourse or an analysis limited to the contemporary consciousness and its perception of salient issues.

The same may be said of Bitzer's plea for the creation of a "*rhetorical* literature."[47] Bitzer claims that "situations . . . persist," and thus fitting responses to those situations recur.[48] The examples given, however, seem to belong more to the muses of poetic than to the province of rhetoric. They include the "Gettysburg Address,

Edmund Burke's Speech to the Electors of Bristol, and Socrates' Apology." Like Black, Bitzer argues that these examples speak to situations "which are in some measure universal."[49]

What Bitzer finds "universal" is the literary quality of the discourse. Lincoln, Burke, and Socrates were failures in the pragmatic and immediate sense. Hence the question: Why build a "rhetorical literature" out of rhetorical failures?

Several in our field have perceived this problem, and solved it by limiting their criticism to those works which prove effective in the immediate sense. Jones, for example, makes a cogent case for studying the gubernatorial rhetoric of Alfred E. Smith.[50] Smith's subjects are no longer of interest; he rarely addressed universal themes. And though he was original in language, his style is less than memorable. In other words, Jones criticizes exactly the kind of discourse Black and Bitzer would exclude from their respective libraries of rhetorical touchstones. But Jones implies that his work is more centered on rhetoric than theirs: "confinement of imaginative qualities to topical matters—thus limiting the philosophical and aesthetic reach—accounts for Smith's appeal in his day and for loss of that appeal in ours."[51] And one might argue, as Jones does by implication, that Edmund Burke's concern for universal themes and aesthetic beauty may account for his ineffectiveness in his day and his general praise in our own.

Black, Bitzer, and Jones pose a serious dilemma: If a speech endures, then it is likely to do so for the nonrhetorical qualities it possesses; if a speech succeeds, then it is likely to be so well adapted to its immediate audience that it cannot endure into another period. Goldmann's notions of consciousness provide a way out of this dilemma. A speaker constrained by actual consciousness might prove effective in the immediate, but not over time. A speaker who avoided actual consciousness and appealed only to potential consciousness would probably fail to achieve identification with his audience but might give a speech which endured. The reasons for this endurance open new vistas to critics. They include the possibility that the speech which appeals to the potential consciousness of its period might appeal to the actual consciousness in our own. Or it might be that in appealing to the potential consciousness of the audience the speaker took advantage of highly literate linguistic possibilities causing the speech to endure for stylistic reasons. Or in appealing to potential consciousness, a rhetor may touch upon what structuralists call "universal structures of the mind," which endure for all time. Clearly, the notion of potential consciousness relates to many diverse theories. Rhetorical critics need to understand this if their assessments are to actualize the rhetorical moment, reify it for a contemporary readership, and/or explain why it endures.

The views of Black, Bitzer, and Jones are easier to accommodate when their notions of audience are expanded to include the notion of consciousness as explicated by the hermeneutical perspective. Jones's assessment of Smith is concerned with Smith's adaptation to the actual consciousness of his audience. Such speeches as Richard Nixon's Checkers or William Jennings Bryan's Cross of Gold may have been so effective in the immediate sense because they were so well adapted to an actual consciousness. A rhetorical critic operating from the hermeneutical perspective might look to those speeches for values, attitudes, and appeals which would help form a picture of the actual consciousness of the time. In the process of bringing the speech alive in the present, the critic would need to investigate not only the hermeneutical situation out of which the discourse grew, and into which it was delivered, but the existent consciousness for which it must be reinterpreted.

Black's assessments are redeemed as rhetorical when seen as critiques of appeals to potential consciousness. In his piece on Chapman, Black himself comes close to making judgments based on a hermeneutical analysis of the available potential consciousness: "This dialogue has not ended, but still continues, and insofar as the model of the United States is increasingly influential in other parts of the world, the potential audience to this dialogue grows . . . Chapman's speech forces the auditor to perceive the event and to examine his own relationship to it; hence, the speech undermines the possibility of passive indifference."[52] What Black fails to ask is, why is indifference impossible? The answer lies in a deeper hermeneutical analysis of the consciousness to which Chapman appealed.

Like Chapman, Edmund Burke's appeal involved themes still relevant and certainly a part of the potential consciousness of his audience. Socrates may have been in the minority in Athens, but his argument was undoubtedly a part of the potential consciousness of his peers. Thus, if a rhetorical literature of their discourse is to be established, rhetorical critics must begin with a hermeneutical analysis of the available potential consciousness—inclusive of fore-sight, fore-having, and fore-conception of speaker and audience alike.

Finally, one could argue that the truly powerful address that ought to be included in any "rhetorical literature" or collection of "touchstones" is one that effectively appeals both to actual *and* potential consciousness. Black seems to sense this: "[S]peech shapes a perception . . . In functioning in this way, in conveying an experience that is unique for almost all its auditors and thus opening to them a new possibility for subsequent experience and creating in them a new potentiality for perceiving subsequent events, the speech shares . . . a quality of the supreme works of our literature."[53] Webster's Reply to Hayne, his speeches for Compromise in 1850, and his Eulogy to Adams and Jefferson possess this quality. They are a part of both actual and potential consciousness; they are both effective rhetoric and memorable literature—they realize the potential of the linguistic possibilities in each hermeneutical situation.

It should not be inferred from these remarks that critics should limit their criticisms to "successful" rhetoric. A critic studying Smith, or Chapman, or Burke would profit from understanding each consciousness addressed even if the rhetor did not. Webster endures because he is stylistically and ideationally attractive in the present time as well as in his own. The critic's task is to actualize him for the present audience. Criticism from the hermeneutical perspective would result in an understanding of consciousness in Webster's period and in the present. And, one might add, if the criticism is to be as enduring as the rhetoric examined, it should appeal to the potential consciousness of its readers. In short, the rhetorical critic's task is at least as difficult as that of the most successful rhetor.

The implications of this injunction are significant. First, the literary qualities in speeches which Black and Bitzer admire may result from the need to elevate language to appeal to potential consciousness. The linguistic possibilities available to a speaker wishing to address the potential consciousness may be stylistically more varied than the linguistic possibilities available for appeals to the actual consciousness. Such a hypothesis adds a new dimension to assessments of style in language. If different emphasis in style results from appeals to different consciousnesses, then the critic may have a useful way of talking about a speaker's intended audience. The difference between Nixon's Checkers speech and his First Inaugural is a case in point. In the former, he adapted to the actual consciousness in a style laden with emotional appeal, innuendo, and jargon. In the Inaugural, he appealed to potential consciousness in elevated language, consistent metaphor, and universal themes.

Second, what is true for style may be true for other rhetorical strategies. Argumentation, credibility, organization, and so on need to be reexamined in relation to the consciousness towards which they are directed or tend. Such analysis would broaden significantly the range and sophistication of rhetorical judgments. The critic may desire to determine what linguistic possibilities were available to the speaker at the time of invention, to the audience at the time of reception, and to the critic and the critic's audience at the time of assessment. In other words, the ontological relationship between rhetoric and hermeneutics deepens the meaning of the traditional definition of rhetoric—finding in any given situation the available means of persuasion.

Third, synchronic understanding is exhibited by both rhetor and critic when they address their audiences. The language they employ, the linguistic possibilities they play upon, are fixed at a specific moment in time and become situation bound. Webster's 1850 Compromise addresses are constrained in their moment of utterance, just as Black's critique of Chapman's address is fixed in its context. And yet each discourse is diachronic in several senses. Webster's interpretation of events and arguments, and Black's interpretation of Chapman's rhetoric, contribute to the history of ideas. They build for posterity an understanding of the consciousness focused upon at the time. They reify for contemporary culture the milieu of past cultures.

Thus, their understanding is both synchronic and diachronic, and thereby helps to reconstruct a hermeneutical situation with its corresponding fore-structure. This reconstruction of the past made relevant for the present is the ultimate task of the rhetorical critic. It constitutes the most important contribution a critic can make to human understanding.

Conclusion

Once consciousness is analyzed as part of audience analysis, the critic is "taken back" to the hermeneutical situation where structures exist for the examination of presuppositions in the form of linguistic possibilities. The speaker invents rhetoric in accordance with the speaker's hermeneutical situation and in adaptation to that of the audience. The more the critic knows about the speaker's and the audience's fore-having, foresight, and fore-conception, the better the critic will be able to understand, assess, and reify as knowledge the rhetorical transaction.

If rhetoric is the *telos* of interpretation, then rhetoric is essential to understanding. It functions quite early in the process of understanding by bringing to bear the linguistic possibilities appropriated by the individual. Each act of interpretation, each "making sense of," is a product of the fore-structure of that individual. The fore-structure precludes a presuppositionless interpretation of phenomena. Thus, all interpretation in a sense is rhetorical; all hermeneutics is rhetorical. Since interpretation makes understanding possible, and since interpretation is rhetorical, rhetoric underlies knowledge even at the intrapersonal level.

Clearly, our theory places rhetoric at a crucial place in ontology and epistomology. Once this placement is accepted, rhetoric becomes an existential structure, a defining characteristic, and a determinant of the individual's consciousness. Intrapersonally, rhetoric functions to accomplish the primordial interpretation in the hermeneutical situation. Interpersonally, rhetoric functions as a derivative mode of primordial interpretation; it thereby accomplishes a further making-known, a further adaptation to consciousness. As a derivative mode, it allows the individual to assert: to point out, to predicate, and to communicate. More than that, throughout the process of understanding and making-known, rhetoric functions to reify knowledge.

All this is to say that rhetoric is far more inherent, far more pervasive, and far more instrumental in the epistemic function than most scholars have supposed. Once the proper place of rhetoric is recognized, theories of communication, and particularly rhetorical criticism, will become deeper, more important, and more enduring.

Notes

1. Martin Heidegger. *Being and Time*, tr. John Macquarrie and Edward Robinson (New York: Harper & Row, 1962), p. 182.
2. Ibid., p. 60.
3. Calvin O. Schrag. *Existence and Freedom: Towards an Ontology of Human Finitude* (Evanston: Northwestern Univ. Press, 1961), p. 32. For example, when one talks about hermeneutics as a "method," or about "rhetorical situations," one is using the terms in a derivative and concrete sense.
4. For examples, see Sloan's and Campbell's book review essays: Thomas O. Sloan. "Hermeneutics: The Interpreter's House Revisited." *Quarterly Journal of Speech*, 57 (1971), 102–07, and John Angus Campbell, "Hans-Georg Gadamer's *Truth and Method*," Quarterly Journal of Speech, 64 (1978), 101–09. Also see Leonard C. Hawes, "Toward a Hermeneutic Phenomenology of Communication," *Communication Quarterly*, 25, No. 3 (1977), 30–41; Jesse G. Delia and Lawrence Grossberg, "Interpretation and Evidence," *Western Journal of Speech Communication*, 41 (1977), 32–42; Thomas M. Seebohm, "The Problem of Hermeneutics in Recent Anglo-American Literature: Part I," *Philosophy and Rhetoric*, 10 (1977), 180–98, and "Part II." *Philosophy and Rhetoric*, 10 (1977), 263–75; and John Stewart, "Foundations of Dialogic Communication," *Quarterly Journal of Speech*, 64 (1978), 183–201.
5. Kenneth Burke, *A Rhetoric of Motives* (New York: Prentice-Hall, 1952), p. 43. (Italics are Burke's.)

6. Karlyn Kohrs Campbell, "The Ontological Foundations of Rhetorical Theory," *Philosophy & Rhetoric*, 3 (1970), 106.

7. Cf. Heidegger, p. 206, where he argues that the ontological basis of language cannot be determined adequately by investigating it from the perspective of "symbolic form."

8. Richard McKeon, "The Uses of Rhetoric in a Technological Age: Architectonic Productive Arts," in *The Prospect of Rhetoric*, ed. Lloyd F. Bitzer and Edwin Black (Englewood Cliffs, N.J.: Prentice-Hall, 1971), p. 45.

9. Lawrence W. Rosenfield, "An Autopsy of the Rhetorical Tradition," in *The Prospect of Rhetoric*, pp. 64–77.

10. Henry W. Johnstone, Jr., "Some Trends in Rhetorical Theory," in *The Prospect of Rhetoric*, p. 84. Johnstone's actual investigations of rhetoric's role in human life can be found in his *The Problem of the Self* (University Park: The Pennsylvania State Univ. Press, 1970), esp. pp. 116–31; and in Maurice Natanson and Henry W. Johnstone, Jr., eds., *Philosophy, Rhetoric, and Argumentation* (University Park: The Pennsylvania State Univ. Press, 1965).

11. Paul Ricoeur, "Phenomenology and Hermeneutics," *???Nous*, 9 (1975), 85–102; and Schrag, esp. pp. 15–20.

12. Stanley Deetz, "Words without Things: Toward a Social Phenomenology of Language," *Quarterly Journal of Speech*, 59 (1973), 40–51; also, see his "Conceptualizing Human Understanding: Gadamer's Hermeneutics and American Communication Studies," *Communication Quarterly*, 26, No. 2 (1978), 12–23.

13. Carl B. Holmberg, "Rhetoric as Lifestyle and World Faculty, an Extemporalizing Prolegomenon for Any Contemporary Rhetorical Criticism," *Philosophy & Rhetoric*, 8 (1975), 245.

14. Robert L. Scott, "On Viewing Rhetoric as Epistemic: Ten Years Later," *Central States Speech Journal*, 27 (1976), 266. Scott's earlier essay is "On Viewing Rhetoric as Epistemic," *Central States Speech Journal*, 18 (1967), 9–17. Important investigations of rhetoric's epistemic function also have been offered by Thomas B. Farrell. "Knowledge, Consensus, and Rhetorical Theory," *Quarterly Journal of Speech*, 62 (1976), 1–14; Barry Brummett, "Some Implications of 'Process' or 'Intersubjectivity': Postmodern Rhetoric." *Philosophy & Rhetoric*, 9 (1976), 21–51; Richard Cherwitz, "Rhetoric as a 'Way of Knowing': An Attenuation of the Epistemological Claims of the 'New Rhetoric'," *Southern Speech Communication Journal*, 42 (Spring 1977), 207–19; and James W. Hikins, "The Epistemological Relevance of Intrapersonal Rhetoric," *Southern Speech Communication Journal*, 42 (Spring 1977), 220–27.

15. Heidegger, p. 178.

16. Hans-Georg Gadamer, "On the Scope and Function of Hermeneutical Reflection," trans. G. B. Hess and R. E. Palmer, in his *Philosophical Hermeneutics*, ed. David E. Linge (Berkeley: Univ. of California Press, 1976), pp. 18–43.

17. Ibid., p. 21.

18. Ibid., p. 29.

19. Ibid., p. 35. A detailed discussion of Gadamer's position is found in the third part ("The Ontological Shift of Hermeneutics Guided by Language") of his magnum opus, *Truth and Method*, 2nd ed., 1965, ed. Garrett Barden and John Cumming (New York: Seabury, 1975), pp. 343–447.

20. Bubner correctly points out that "Hermeneutic reflection finds itself involved in the very conditions of understanding it is out to demonstrate." See Rüdiger Bubner, "Is Transcendental Hermeneutics Possible?," in *Essays on Explanation and Understanding*, ed. Juha Manninen and Raimo Tuomela (Boston: Reidel, 1976), p. 70. Hermeneutics, therefore, is forced to raise a transcendental claim given its "self-referentiality."

21. Gadamer, "On the Scope and Function of Hermeneutical Reflection," p. 20. Gadamer's insistence that the making-known function of rhetoric is an interpersonal experience will be examined later in this essay. Here, however, a point of clarification is needed. When Gadamer discusses the function of rhetoric and its relationship to hermeneutics, he does not use the term "making-known" explicitly. Heidegger must be credited with stressing the term's importance in hermeneutical experience; his employment of the term, as it complements the thrust of our paper, is shown later. Although Gadamer's well-known allegiance to Heidegger does not in and of itself give us the license to argue that Gadamer's conception of rhetoric implies its making-known function, we believe that relevant passages in Gadamer's writings support our contention. For example, see his *Truth and Method*, p. 345; "On the Scope and Function of Hermeneutical Reflection," p. 24; "Semantics and Hermeneutics," trans. P. Christopher Smith, in Philosophical Hermeneutics, pp. 85, 87. In these instances, Gadamer's claims

about rhetoric, language, and the "experience" and "application" of meaning strongly suggest rhetoric's making-known function.

22. See Heidegger, pp. 188–95.

23. Ibid., p. 191.

24. This seeming paradoxical relationship between interpretation and understanding is commonly called the "hermeneutic circle." According to Heidegger, *"if we see this circle as a vicious one and look out for ways of avoiding it, even if we just 'sense' it as an inevitable imperfection, then the act of understanding has been misunderstood from the ground up."* Maintaining that this circle designates "the most primordial kind of knowing," Heidegger argues that "What is decisive is not to get out of the circle but to come into it in the right way." See Heidegger, pp. 194 and 195.

25. This interpretation may serve to ground Kuhn's explanation of the occurrence of scientific revolutions. Cf. Thomas S. Kuhn. *The Structure of Scientific Revolutions,* 2nd ed. (Chicago: The Univ. of Chicago Press, 1970).

26. Our characterization of understanding as synchronic and diachronic is based on directives offered by Ricoeur in his hermeneutic phenomenology of language and meaning. See Paul Ricoeur, *The Conflict of Interpretations, Essays in Hermeneutics,* ed. Don Ihde (Evanston: Northwestern Univ. Press, 1974), esp. pp. 27–96; and Paul Ricoeur, *Interpretation Theory: Discourse and the Surplus of Meaning* (Fort Worth: Texas Christian Univ. Press, 1976).

27. Heidegger, p. 189.

28. Ibid., p. 193.

29. Ibid., p. 201; also see p. 62.

30. Ibid., pp. 196–99.

31. Ibid., p. 199.

32. Ibid., pp. 55–62; 203–06.

33. Brummett, p. 31. Brummett's statement is based on his reading of Ernest G. Bormann, "Fantasy and Rhetorical Vision: The Rhetorical Criticism of Social Reality," *Quarterly Journal of Speech,* 58 (1972), 396–407.

34. Jürgen Habermas, *Knowledge and Human Interests,* tr. Jeremy J. Shapiro (Boston: Bacon, 1971), esp. pp. 161–317.

35. Joseph Kockelmans, "Toward An Interpretative or Hermeneutic Social Science," *Graduate Faculty Philosophy Journal, New School of Social Research,* 5, No. 1 (1975), 73–96.

36. Ibid., p. 86.

37. See Lucien Goldmann, *Cultural Creation in Modern Society,* trans. Bart Drake (St. Louis: Telos, 1976). Goldmann's work is derived from a tradition going back at least to Hegel. Hegel argued that every individual and every nation have a potential consciousness towards which reason inevitably leads them. Karl Marx added materialism to the formulation in his historicism. George Lukács, whom Goldmann cites extensively, refined "dialectical social science" for application in analysis of language. Although Goldmann's work is definitely Marxist in orientation, his discussion of hermeneutical problems in interpreting history closely coincides with the thrust of our paper and is thus appropriate for our purposes here. Also, see George Lukács, *History and Class Consciousness,* trans. Rodney Livingstone (London: Merlin, 1971).

38. Goldmann, pp. 108–09.

39. Ibid., p. 33.

40. See Lucien Goldmann, "Objective Possibility and Possible Consciousness," in his *Lukács and Heidegger, Towards a New Philosophy,* tr. William Q. Boelhower (London: Routledge and Kegan Paul, 1977), pp. 52–66. George Steiner explores the influence of Heidegger on Goldmann and Lukács in *Martin Heidegger* (New York: Viking, 1979), pp. 74–75 and 146–48.

41. For a discussion on the theory and praxis of such interview-conversations, see Michael J. Hyde, "Philosophical Hermeneutics and the Communicative Experience: The Paradigm of Oral History," in *Man & World,* forthcoming.

42. See Paul Arntson and Craig R. Smith, "The seventh of March Address: A Mediating Influence." *Southern Speech Communication Journal,* 40 (Spring 1975), 288–301.

43. Edwin Black, *Rhetorical Criticism: A Study in Method* (New York: Macmillian, 1965), p. 49. Black and Bitzer (see n. 47) are examined here for a number of reasons: First, their work is the most cited for reference from our field for use in rhetorical criticism; second, though other probes in the last ten years are interesting, they have yet to take hold as guides for the critic; third, on occasion Black and Bitzer come close to exhibiting a hermeneutic attitude in their writing. However, we encourage readers to

examine the work of more contemporary critics to observe if the hermeneutic perspective is employed. We could find no such studies.

44. Ibid., p. 9.
45. Ibid., p. 47. See, also, Norman R. Burdick, "The 'Coatesville Address': Crossroads of Rhetoric and Poetry," *Western Journal of Speech Communication,* 42 (1978), 73–82.
46. For example, see Hoyt H. Hudson, "Rhetoric and Poetry" in *Historical Studies of Rhetoric and Rhetoricians,* ed. Raymond F. Howes (Ithaca: Cornell Univ. Press, 1961), pp. 369–79; William Samuel Howell, "Aristotle and Horace on Rhetoric and Poetics," *Quarterly Journal of Speech,* 54 (1968), 325–39; Carroll C. Arnold, "Oral Rhetoric, Rhetoric, and Literature," *Philosophy & Rhetoric,* 1 (1968), pp. 191–210.
47. Lloyd F. Bitzer, "The Rhetorical Situation," *Philosophy & Rhetoric,* 1 (1968), 13.
48. Ibid.
49. Ibid.
50. James L. Jones, "Alfred E. Smith, Political Debater," *Quarterly Journal of Speech,* 54 (1968), 372.
51. Ibid.
52. Black, pp. 84 and 86.
53. Ibid., p. 89.

The "Ideograph":
A Link Between Rhetoric and Ideology
by Michael Calvin McGee

IN 1950, Kenneth Burke, apparently following Dewey, Mead, and Lippmann, announced his preference for the notion "philosophy of myth" to explain the phenomenon of "public" or "mass consciousness" rather than the then-prevalent concept "ideology."[1] As contemporary writers have pushed on toward developing this "symbolic" or "dramatistic" alternative, the concept "ideology" has atrophied. Many use the term innocently, almost as a synonym for "doctrine" or "dogma" in political organizations;[2] and others use the word in a hypostatized sense that obscures or flatly denies the fundamental connection between the concept and descriptions of mass consciousness.[3] The concept seems to have gone the way of the dodo and of the neo-Aristotelian critic: As Bormann has suggested, the very word is widely perceived as being encrusted with the "intellectual baggage" of orthodox Marxism.[4]

Objecting to the use or abuse of any technical term would, ordinarily, be a sign of excessive crabbiness. But in this instance conceptualizations of "philosophy of myth," "fantasy visions," and "political scenarios," coupled with continued eccentric and/or narrow usages of "ideology," cosmetically camouflage significant and unresolved problems. We are presented with a brute, undeniable phenomenon: Human beings in collectivity behave and think differently than human beings in isolation. The collectivity is said to "have a mind of its own" distinct from the individual qua individual. Writers in the tradition of Marx and Mannheim explain this difference by observing that the only possibility of "mind" lies in the individual qua individual, in the human organism itself. When one appears to "think" and "behave" collectively, therefore, one has been tricked, self-deluded,

Reprinted from *The Quarterly Journal of Speech* 66 (1980), with permission of the National Communication Association.

or manipulated into accepting the brute existence of such fantasies as "public mind" or "public opinion" or "public philosophy." Symbolists generally want to say that this trick is a "transcendence," a voluntary agreement to believe in and to participate in a "myth." Materialists maintain that the trick is an insidious, reified form of "lie," a self-perpetuating system of beliefs and interpretations foisted on all members of the community by the ruling class. Burke, with his emphasis on the individuals who are tricked, concerns himself more with the structure of "motive" than with the objective conditions that impinge on and restrict the individual's freedom to develop a political consciousness. Neo-Marxians, with focus on tricksters and the machinery of trickery, say that the essential question posed by the fact of society is one of locating precise descriptions of the dialectical tension between a "true" and a "false" consciousness, between reality and ideology.[5]

Though some of both sides of the controversy would have it otherwise, there is no *error* in either position. Both "myth" and "ideology" presuppose a fundamental falsity in the common metaphor which alleges the existence of a "social organism." "Ideology," however, assumes that the exposure of falsity is a moral act: Though we have never experienced a "true consciousness," it is nonetheless theoretically accessible to us, and, because of such accessibility, we are morally remiss if we do not discard the false and approach the true. The falsity presupposed by "myth," on the other hand, is amoral because it is a purely poetic phenomenon, legitimized by rule of the poet's license, a "suspension of disbelief." A symbolist who speaks of "myth" is typically at great pains to argue for a value-free approach to the object of study, an approach in which one denies that "myth" is a synonym for "lie" and treats it as a falsehood of a peculiarly redemptive nature. Materialists, on the other hand, seem to use the concept "ideology" expressly to warrant normative claims regarding the exploitation of the "proletarian class" by self-serving plunderers. No error is involved in the apparently contradictory conceptions because, fundamentally, materialists and symbolists pursue two different studies: The Marxian asks how the "givens" of a human environment impinge on the development of political consciousness; the symbolist asks how the human symbol-using, reality-creating potential impinges on material reality, ordering it normatively, "mythically."

Errors arise when one conceives "myth" and "ideology" to be contraries, alternative and incompatible theoretical descriptions of the same phenomenon. The materialists' neglect of language studies and the consequent inability of Marxian theory to explain socially constructed realities is well-publicized.[6] Less well-described is the symbolists' neglect of the non-symbolic environment and the consequent inability of symbolist theory to account for the impact of material phenomena on the construction of social reality.[7] I do not mean to denigrate in any way the research of scholars attempting to develop Burke's philosophy of myth; indeed, I have on occasion joined that endeavor. I do believe, however, that each of us has erred to the extent that we have conceived the rubrics of symbolism as an *alternative* rather than *supplemental* description of political consciousness. The assertion that "philosophy of myth" is an alternative to "ideology" begs the question Marx intended to pose. Marx was concerned with "power," with the capacity of an elite class to control the state's political, economic, and military establishment, to dominate the state's information systems and determine even the consciousness of large masses of people. He was politically committed to the cause of the proletariat: If a norm was preached by the upper classes, it was by virtue of that fact a baneful seduction; and if a member of the proletarian class was persuaded by such an argument, that person was possessed of an "ideology," victimized and exploited. Not surprisingly, symbolists criticize Marx for his politics, suggesting that his is a wonderfully convenient formula which mistakes commitment for "historically scientific truth." By conceiving poetic falsity, we rid ourselves of the delusion that interpretation is scientific, but we also bury the probability that the myths we study as an alternative are thrust upon us by the brute force of "power." While Marx overestimated "power" as a variable in describing political consciousness, Burke, Cassirer, Polanyi, and others do not want to discuss the capacity even of a "free" state to determine political consciousness.[8]

If we are to describe the trick-of-the-mind which deludes us into believing that we "think" with/through/for a "society" to which we "belong," we need a theoretical model which accounts for both "ideology" and "myth," a model which neither denies human capacity to control "power" through the manipulation of symbols nor begs Marx's essential questions regarding the influence of "power" on creating and maintaining political consciousness. I will argue here that such a model must begin with the concept "ideology" and proceed to link that notion directly with the interests of symbolism.

I will elaborate the following commitments and hypotheses: If a mass consciousness exists at all, it must be empirically "present," itself a thing obvious to those who participate in it, or, at least, empirically manifested in the language which communicates it. I agree with Marx that the problem of consciousness is fundamentally practical and normative, that it is concerned essentially with describing and evaluating the legitimacy of public motives. Such consciousness, I believe, is always false, not because we are programmed automatons and not because we have a propensity to structure political perceptions in poetically false "dramas" or "scenarios," but because "truth" in politics, no matter how firmly we believe, is always an illusion. The falsity of an ideology is specifically rhetorical, for the illusion of truth and falsity with regard to normative commitments is the product of persuasion.[9] Since the clearest access to persuasion (and hence to ideology) is through the discourse used to produce it, I will suggest that ideology in practice is a political language, preserved in rhetorical documents, with the capacity to dictate decision and control public belief and behavior. Further, the political language which manifests ideology seems characterized by slogans, a vocabulary of "ideographs" easily mistaken for the technical terminology of political philosophy. An analysis of ideographic usages in political rhetoric, I believe, reveals interpenetrating systems or "structures" of public motives. Such structures appear to be "diachronic" and "synchronic" patterns of political consciousness which have the capacity both to control "power" and to influence (if not determine) the shape and texture of each individual's "reality."

Hypothetical Characteristics of "Ideographs"

Marx's thesis suggests that an ideology determines mass belief and thus restricts the free emergence of political opinion. By this logic, the "freest" members of a community are those who belong to the "power" elite; yet the image of hooded puppeteers twisting and turning the masses at will is unconvincing if only because the elite seems itself imprisoned by the same false consciousness communicated to the polity at large. When we consider the impact of ideology on freedom, and of power on consciousness, we must be clear that ideology is transcendent, as much an influence on the belief and behavior of the ruler as on the ruled. Nothing *necessarily* restricts persons who wield the might of the state. Roosevelts and Carters are as free to indulge personal vanity with capricious uses of power as was Idi Amin, regardless of formal "checks and balances." The polity can punish tyrants and maniacs after the fact of their lunacy or tyranny (if the polity survives it), but, in practical terms, the only way to shape or soften power at the moment of its exercise is prior persuasion. Similarly, no matter what punishment we might imagine "power" visiting upon an ordinary citizen, nothing *necessarily* determines individual behavior and belief. A citizen may be punished for eccentricity or disobedience after the fact of a crime, but, at the moment when defiance is contemplated, the only way to combat the impulse to criminal behavior is prior persuasion. I am suggesting in other words, that social control in its essence is control over consciousness, the a priori influence that learned predispositions hold over human agents who play the roles of "power" and "people" in a given transaction.[10]

Because there is a lack of necessity in social control, it seems inappropriate to characterize agencies of control as "socializing" or "conditioning" media. No individual (least of all the elite who control the power of the state) is *forced* to submit in the same way that a conditioned dog is obliged to salivate or socialized children are required to speak English. Human beings are "conditioned," not directly to belief and behavior, but to a vocabulary of concepts that function as guides, warrants, reasons, or excuses for behavior and belief. When a claim is warranted by such terms as "law," "liberty," "tyranny," or "trial by jury," in other words, it is presumed that human beings will react predictably and autonomically. So it was that a majority of Americans were surprised, not when allegedly sane young men agreed to go halfway around the world to kill for God, country, apple pie, and no other particularly good reason, but, rather, when other young men displayed good common sense by moving to Montreal instead, thereby refusing to be conspicuous in a civil war which was none of their business. The end product of the state's insistence on some degree of conformity in behavior and belief, I suggest, is a *rhetoric* of control, a system of persuasion presumed to be effective on the whole community. We make a rhetoric of war to persuade us of war's necessity, but then forget that it is a rhetoric—and regard negative popular judgments of it as unpatriotic cowardice.

It is not remarkable to conceive social control as fundamentally rhetorical. In the past, however, rhetorical scholarship has regarded the rhetoric of control as a species of argumentation and thereby assumed that the fundamental unit of analysis in such rhetoric is an integrated set-series of propositions. This is, I believe, a mistake, an unwarranted abstraction: To argue is to test an affirmation or denial of claims; argument is the means of proving the truth of grammatical units, declarative sentences, that purport to be reliable signal representations of reality. Within the vocabulary of argumentation, the term "rule of law" makes no sense until it is made the subject or predicable of a proposition. If I say "The rule of law is a primary cultural value in the United States" or "Charles I was a cruel and capricious tyrant," I have asserted a testable claim that may be criticized with logically coordinated observations. When I say simply "the rule of law," however, my utterance cannot qualify logically as a claim. Yet I am conditioned to believe that "liberty" and "property" have an obvious meaning, a behaviorally directive self-evidence. Because I am taught to set such terms apart from my usual vocabulary, words used as agencies of social control may have an intrinsic force—and, if so, I may very well distort the key terms of social conflict, commitment, and control if I think of them as parts of a proposition rather than as basic units of analysis.

Though words only (and not claims), such terms as "property," "religion," "right of privacy," "freedom of speech," "rule of law," and "liberty" are more pregnant than propositions ever could be. They are the basic structural elements, the building blocks, of ideology. Thus they may be thought of as "ideographs," for, like Chinese symbols, they signify and "contain" a unique ideological commitment; further, they presumptuously suggest that each member of a community will see as a gestalt every complex nuance in them. What "rule of law" means is the series of propositions, all of them, that could be manufactured to justify a Whig/Liberal order. Ideographs are one-term sums of an orientation, the species of "God" or "Ultimate" term that will be used to symbolize the line of argument the meanest sort of individual *would* pursue, if that individual had the dialectical skills of philosophers, as a defense of a personal stake in and commitment to the society. Nor is one permitted to question the fundamental logic of ideographs: Everyone is conditioned to think of "the rule of law" as a *logical* commitment just as one is taught to think that "186,000 miles per second" is an accurate empirical description of the speed of light even though few can work the experiments or do the mathematics to prove it.[11]

The important fact about ideographs is that they exist in real discourse, functioning clearly and evidently as agents of political consciousness. They are not invented by observers; they come to be as a part of the real lives of the people whose motives they articulate. So, for example, "rule of law" is a more precise, objective motive than such observer-invented terms as "neurotic" or "paranoid style" or "*petit bourgeois.*"

Ideographs pose a methodological problem because of their very specificity: How do we generalize from a "rule of law" to a description of consciousness that comprehends not only "rule of law" but all other like motives as well? What do we describe with the concept "ideograph," and how do we actually go about doing the specific cultural analysis promised by conceptually linking rhetoric and ideology?

Though both come to virtually the same conclusion, the essential argument seems more careful and useful in Ortega's notion of "the etymological man" than in Burke's poetically-hidden concept of "the symbol-using animal" and "logology":

> Man, when he sets himself to speak, does so *because* he believes that he will be able to say what he thinks. Now, this is an illusion. Language is not up to that. It says, more or less, a part of what we think, and raises an impenetrable obstacle to the transmission of the rest. It serves quite well for mathematical statements and proofs. . . . But in proportion as conversation treats of more important, more human, more "real" subjects than these, its vagueness, clumsiness, and confusion steadily increase. Obedient to the inveterate prejudice that "talking leads to understanding," we speak and listen in such good faith that we end by misunderstanding one another far more than we would if we remained mute and set ourselves to divine each other. Nay, more: since our thought is in large measure dependent upon our language . . . it follows that thinking is talking with oneself and hence misunderstanding oneself at the imminent risk of getting oneself into a complete quandary.[12]

All this "talk" generates a series of "usages" which unite us, since we speak the same language, but, more significantly, such "talk" *separates* us from other human beings who do not accept our meanings, our intentions.[13] So, Ortega claims, the essential demarcation of whole nations is language usage: "This gigantic architecture of usages is, precisely, society."[14] And it is through usages that a particular citizen's sociality exists:

> A language, *speech*, is "what people say," it is the vast system of verbal usages established in a collectivity. The individual, the person, is from his birth submitted to the linguistic coercion that these usages represent. Hence the mother tongue is perhaps the most typical and clearest social phenomenon. With it "people" enter us, set up residence in us, making each an example of "people." Our mother tongue socializes our inmost being, and because of this fact every individual belongs, in the strongest sense of the word, to a society. He can flee from the society in which he was born and brought up, but in his flight the society inexorably accompanies him because he carries it within him. This is the true meaning that the statement "man is a social animal" can have.[15]

Ortega's reference, of course, is to language generally and not to a particular vocabulary within language. So he worked with the vocabulary of greeting to demonstrate the definitive quality of linguistic usages when conceiving "society."[16] His reasoning, however, invites specification, attention to the components of the "architecture" supposedly created by usages.

Insofar as usages both unite and separate human beings, it seems reasonable to suggest that the functions of uniting and separating would be represented by specific vocabularies, actual words or terms. With regard to political union and separation, such vocabularies would consist of ideographs. Such usages as "liberty" define a collectivity, i.e., the outer parameters of a society, because such terms either do not exist in other societies or do not have precisely similar meanings. So, in the United States, we claim a common belief in "equality," as do citizens of the Union of Soviet Socialist Republics; but "equality" is not the same word in its meaning or its usage. One can therefore precisely define the difference between the two communities, in part, by comparing the usage of definitive ideographs. We are, of course, still able to interact with the Soviets despite barriers of language and usage. The interaction is possible because of higher-order ideographs—"world peace," "detente," "spheres of influence," etc.—that permit temporary union.[17] And, in the other direction, it is also true that there are special interests within the United States separated one from the other precisely by disagreements regarding the identity, legitimacy, or definition of ideographs. So we are divided by usages into subgroups: Business and labor, Democrats and Republicans, Yankees and Southerners are *united* by the ideographs that represent the political entity "United States" and *separated* by a disagreement as to the practical meaning of such ideographs.

The concept "ideograph" is meant to be purely descriptive of an essentially social human condition. Unlike more general conceptions of "Ultimate" or "God" terms, attention is called to the social, rather than rational or ethical, functions of a particular vocabulary. This vocabulary is precisely a group of *words* and not a series of symbols representing ideals. Ortega clearly, methodically, distinguishes a usage (what we might call "social" or "material" thought) from an *idea* (what Ortega would call "pure thought"). He suggests, properly, that *language gets in the way of thinking,* separates us from "ideas" we may have which cannot be surely expressed, even to ourselves, in the usages which imprison us. So my "pure thought" about liberty, religion, and property is clouded, hindered, made irrelevant by the existence in history of the ideographs "Liberty, Religion, and Property."[18] Because these terms are definitive of the society we have inherited, they are *conditions* of the society into which each of us is born, material ideas which we must accept to "belong." They penalize us, in a sense, as much as they protect us, for they prohibit our appreciation of an alternative pattern of meaning in, for example, the Soviet Union or Brazil.

In effect, ideographs—language imperatives which hinder and perhaps make impossible "pure thought"—are bound within the culture which they define. We can *characterize* an ideograph, say what it has meant and does mean as a usage, and some of us may be able to achieve an imaginary state of withdrawal from community long enough to speculate as to what ideographs *ought* to mean in the best of possible worlds; but the very nature of language forces us to keep the two operations separate: So, for example, the "idea" of "liberty" may be the subject of philosophical speculation, but philosophers can never be *certain* that they themselves or their readers understand a "pure" meaning unpolluted by historical, ideographic usages.[19] Should we look strictly at material notions of "liberty," on the other hand, we distort our thinking by believing that a rationalization of a particular historical meaning is "pure," the truth of the matter.[20] Ideographs can *not* be used to establish or test truth, and vice versa, the truth, in ideal metaphysical senses, is a consideration irrelevant to accurate characterizations of such ideographs as "liberty." Indeed, if examples from recent history are a guide, the attempts to infuse usages with metaphysical meanings, or to confuse ideographs with the "pure" thought of philosophy, have resulted in the "nightmares" which Polanyi, for one, deplores.[21] The significance of ideographs is in their concrete history as usages, not in their alleged idea-content.

The Analysis of Ideographs

No one has ever seen an "equality" strutting up the driveway, so, if "equality" exists at all, it has meaning through its specific applications. In other words, we establish a meaning for "equality" by using the word as a description of a certain phenomenon; it has meaning only insofar as our description is acceptable, believable. If asked to make a case for "equality," that is to define the term, we are forced to make reference to its history by detailing the situations for which the word has been an appropriate description. Then, by comparisons over time, we establish an analog for the proposed present usage of the term. Earlier usages become precedent, touchstones for judging the propriety of the ideograph in a current circumstance. The meaning of "equality" does not rigidify because situations seeming to require its usage are never perfectly similar: As the situations vary, so the meaning of "equality" expands and contracts. The variations in meaning of "equality" are much less important, however, than the fundamental, categorical meaning, the "common denominator" of all situations for which "equality" has been the best and most descriptive term. The dynamism of "equality" is thus paramorphic, for even when the term changes its signification in particular circumstances, it retains a formal, categorical meaning, a constant reference to its history as an ideograph.

These earlier usages are vertically structured, related each to the other in a formal way, every time the society is called upon to judge whether a particular circumstance should be defined ideographically. So, for example, to protect ourselves from abuses of power, we have built into our political system an ideograph that is said to justify "impeaching" an errant leader: If the President has engaged in behaviors which can be described as "high crimes and misdemeanors," even that highest officer must be removed.

But what is meant by "high crimes and misdemeanors"? If Peter Rodino wishes to justify impeachment procedures against Richard Nixon in the Committee on the Judiciary of the House of Representatives, he must mine history for touchstones, precedents which give substance and an aura of precision to the ideograph "high crimes and misdemeanors." His search of the past concentrates on situations analogous to that which he is facing, situations involving actual or proposed "impeachment." The "rule of law" emerged as a contrary ideograph, and Rodino developed from the tension between "law" and "high crimes" an argument indicting Nixon. His proofs were historical, ranging from Magna Carta to Edmund Burke's impeachment of Warren Hastings. He was able to make the argument, therefore, only because he could organize a series of events, situationally similar, with an ideograph as the structuring principle. The structuring is "vertical" because of the element of *time;* that is, the deep meanings of "law" and "high crime" derive from knowledge of the way in which meanings have evolved over a period of time—awareness of the way an ideograph can be meaningful *now* is controlled in large part by what it meant *then.*[22]

All communities take pains to record and preserve the vertical structure of their ideographs. Formally, the body of nonstatutory "law" is little more than a literature recording ideographic usages in the "common law" and "case law."[23] So, too, historical dictionaries, such as the *O. E. D.,* detail etymologies for most of the Anglo-American ideographs. And any so-called "professional" history provides a record in detail of the events surrounding earlier usages of ideographs—indeed, the historian's eye is most usually attracted precisely to those situations involving ideographic applications.[24] The more significant record of vertical structures, however, lies in what might be called "popular" history. Such history consists in part of novels, films, plays, even songs; but the truly influential manifestation is grammar school history, the very first contact most have with their existence and experience as a part of a community.

To learn the meanings of the ideographs "freedom" and "patriotism," for example, most of us swallowed the tale of Patrick Henry's defiant speech to the Virginia House of Burgesses: "I know not what course others may take, but as for me, give me liberty or give me death!" These specific words, of course, were concocted by the historian William Wirt and not by Governor Henry. Wirt's intention was to provide a model for "the young men of Virginia," asking them to copy Henry's virtues and avoid his vices.[25] Fabricated events and words meant little, not because Wirt was uninterested in the truth of what really happened to Henry, but rather because what he wrote about was the definition of essential ideographs. His was a task of socialization, an exercise in epideictic rhetoric, providing the youth of his age (and of our own) with general knowledge of ideographic touchstones so that they might be able to make, or comprehend, judgments of public motives and of their own civic duty.

Though such labor tires the mind simply in imagining it, there is no trick in gleaning from public documents the entire vocabulary of ideographs that define a particular collectivity. The terms do not hide in discourse, nor is their "meaning" or function within an argument obscure: We might disagree metaphysically about "equality," and we might use the term differently in practical discourse, but I believe we can nearly always discover the functional meaning of the term by measure of its grammatic and pragmatic context.[26] Yet even a complete description of vertical ideographic structures leaves little but an exhaustive lexicon understood etymologically and diachronically—and no ideally precise explanation of how ideographs function *presently.*

If we find forty rhetorical situations in which "rule of law" has been an organizing term, we are left with little but the simple chronology of the situations as a device to structure the lot: Case One is distinct from Case Forty, and the meaning of the ideograph thus has contracted or expanded in the intervening time. But time is an irrelevant matter *in practice.* Chronological sequences are provided by analysts, and they properly reflect the concerns of theorists who try to describe what "rule of law" *may* mean, potentially, by laying out the history of what the term has meant. Such advocates as Rodino are not so scrupulous in research; they choose eight or nine of those forty cases to use as evidence in argument, ignore the rest, and impose a pattern of organization on the cases recommended (or forced) by the demands of a current situation. As Ortega argues with reference to language generally, key usages considered historically and diachronically are purely formal; yet in real discourse, and in public consciousness, they are *forces:*

> [A]ll that diachronism accomplishes is to reconstruct other comparative "presents" of the language as they existed in the past. All that it shows us, then, is changes; it enables us to witness one present being replaced by another, the succession of the static figures of the language, as the "film," with its motionless images, engenders the visual fiction of a movement. At best, it offers us a cinematic view of language, but not a *dynamic* understanding of how the changes were, and came to be, *made.* The changes are merely results of the making and unmaking process, they are the externality of language, and there is need for an internal conception of it in which we discover not resultant *forms* but the operating *forces* themselves.[27]

In Burke's terminology, describing a vertical ideographic structure yields a culture-specific and relatively precise "grammar" of one public motive. That motive is not captured, however, without attention to its "rhetoric."

Considered rhetorically, as *forces,* ideographs seem structured horizontally, for when people actually make use of them presently, such terms as "rule of law" clash with other ideographs ("principle of confidentiality" or "national security," for example), and in the conflict come to mean with reference to synchronic confrontations. So, for example, one would not ordinarily think of an inconsistency between "rule of law" and "principle of confidentiality." Vertical analysis of the two ideographs would probably reveal a consonant relationship based on genus and species: "Confidentiality" of certain conversations is a control on the behavior of government, a control that functions to maintain a "rule of law" and prevents "tyranny" by preserving a realm of privacy for the individual.

The "Watergate" conflict between Nixon and Congress, however, illustrates how that consonant relationship can be restructured, perhaps broken, in the context of a particular controversy: Congress asked, formally and legally, for certain of Nixon's documents. He refused, thereby creating the appearance of frustrating the imperative value "rule of law." He attempted to excuse himself by matching a second ideograph, "principle of confidentiality," against normal and usual meanings of "rule of law." Before a mass television audience Nixon argued that a President's conversations with advisers were entitled to the same privilege constitutionally accorded exchanges between priest and penitent, husband and wife, lawyer and client. No direct vertical precedent was available to support Nixon's usage. The argument asked public (and later jurisprudential) permission to expand the meaning of "confidentiality" and thereby to alter its relationship with the "rule of law," making what appeared to be an illegal act acceptable. Nixon's claims were epideictic and not deliberative or forensic; he magnified "confidentiality" by praising the ideograph as if it were a person, attempting to alter its "standing" among other ideographs, even as an individual's "standing" in the community changes through praise and blame.[28]

Synchronic structural changes in the relative standing of an ideograph are "horizontal" because of the presumed consonance of an ideology; that is, ideographs such as "rule of law" are meant to be taken together, as a working unit, with "public trust," "freedom of speech," "trial by jury," and any other slogan characteristic of the collective life. If all the ideographs used to justify a Whig/Liberal government were placed on a chart, they would form groups or clusters of words radiating from the slogans originally used to rationalize "popular sovereignty"—"religion," "liberty," and "property." Each term should be a connector, modifier, specifier, or contrary for those fundamental historical commitments, giving them a meaning and a unity easily mistaken for logic. Some terms would be enshrined in the Constitution, some in law, some merely in conventional usage; but all would be constitutive of "the people." Though new usages can enter the equation, the ideographs remain essentially unchanged. But when we engage idcological argument, when we cause ideographs to *do work* in explaining, justifying, or guiding policy in specific situations, the relationship of ideographs changes. A "rule of law," for example, is taken for granted, a simple connector betwcen "property" and "liberty," until a constitutional crisis inclines us to make it "come first." In Burke's vocabulary, it becomes the "title" or "god-term" of all ideographs, the center-sun about which every ideograph orbits. Sometimes circumstance forces us to sense that the structure is not consonant, as when awareness of racism exposes contradiction between "property" and "right to life" in the context of "open-housing" legislation. Sometimes officers of state, in the process of justifying particular uses of power, manufacture seeming inconsistency, as when Nixon pitted "confidentiality" against "rule of law." And sometimes an alien force frontally assaults the structure, as when Hitler campaigned against "decadent democracies." Such instances have the potential to change the structure of ideographs and hence the "present" ideology—in this sense, an ideology is dynamic and a *force,* always resilient, always keeping itself in some consonance and unity, but not always the *same* consonance and unity.[29]

In appearance, of course, characterizing ideological conflicts as synchronic *structural* dislocations is an unwarranted abstraction: An ideological argument could result simply from multiple usages of an ideograph. Superficially, for example, one might be inclined to describe the "bussing" controversy as a disagreement over the "best" meaning for "equality," one side opting for "equality" defined with reference to "access" to education and the other with reference to the goal, "being educated." An ideograph, however, is always understood in its relation to another; it is defined tautologically by using other terms in its cluster. If we accept that there are three or four or however many possible meanings for "equality," each with a currency and legitimacy, we distort the nature of the ideological dispute by ignoring the fact that "equality" is made meaningful, not within the clash of multiple usages, but rather in its relationship with "freedom." That is, "equality" defined by "access" alters the nature of "liberty" from the relationship of "equality" and "liberty" thought to exist when "equality" is defined as "being educated." One would not want to rule out the possibility that ideological disagreements, however rarely, could be simply semantic; but we are more likely to err if we assume the dispute to be semantic than if we look for the deeper structural dislocation which likely produced multiple usages as a disease produces symptoms. When an ideograph is at the center of a semantic dispute, I would suggest, the multiple usages will be either metaphysical or diachronic, purely speculative or historical, and in either event devoid of the force and currency of a synchronic ideological conflict.[30]

In the terms of this argument, two recognizable "ideologies" exist in any specific culture at one "moment." One "ideology" is a "grammar," a historically-defined diachronic structure of ideograph-meanings expanding and contracting from the birth of the society to its "present." Another "ideology" is a "rhetoric," a situationally-defined synchronic structure of ideograph clusters constantly reorganizing itself to accommodate specific circumstances while maintaining its fundamental consonance and unity. A division of this sort, of course, is but an analytic convenience for talking about two *dimensions* (vertical and horizontal) of a single phenomenon: No present ideology can be divorced from past commitments if only because the very words used to express present dislocations have a history that establishes the category of their meaning. And no diachronic ideology can be divorced from the "here-and-now" if only because its entire *raison d'être* consists in justifying the form and direction of collective behavior. Both of these structures must be understood and described before one can claim to have constructed a theoretically precise explanation of a society's ideology, of its repertoire of public motives.

Conclusion

One of the casualties of the current "pluralist" fad in social and political theory has been the old Marxian thesis that governing elites control the masses by creating, maintaining, and manipulating a mass consciousness suited to perpetuation of the existing order.[31] Though I agree that Marx probably overestimated the influence of an elite, it is difficult *not* to see a "dominant ideology" which seems to exercise decisive influence in political life. The question, of course, turns on finding a way accurately to define and to describe a dominant ideology. Theorists writing in the tradition of Dewey, Burke, and Cassirer have, in my judgment, come close to the mark; but because they are bothered by poetic metaphors, these symbolists never conceive their work as description of a mass consciousness. Even these writers, therefore, beg Marx's inescapable question regarding the impact of "power" on the way we think. I have argued here that the concepts "rhetoric" and "ideology" may be linked without poetic metaphors, and that the linkage should produce a description and an explanation of dominant ideology, of the relationship between the "power" of a state and the consciousness of its people.

The importance of symbolist constructs is their focus on *media* of consciousness, on the discourse that articulates and propagates common beliefs. "Rhetoric," "sociodrama," "myth," "fantasy vision," and "political scenario" are not important because of their *fiction,* their connection to poetic, but because of their *truth,* their links with the trick-of-the-mind that deludes individuals into believing that they "think" with/for/through a social organism. The truth of symbolist constructs, I have suggested, appears to lie in our claim to see a legitimate social reality in a vocabulary of complex, high-order abstractions that refer to and invoke a sense of "the people." By learning the meaning of ideographs, I have argued, everyone in society, even the "freest" of us, those who control the state, seem predisposed to structured mass responses. Such terms as "liberty," in other words, constitute by our very use of them in political discourse an ideology that governs or "dominates" our consciousness. In practice, therefore, ideology is a political language composed of slogan-like terms signifying collective commitment.

Such terms I have called "ideographs." A formal definition of "ideograph," derived from arguments made throughout this essay, would list the following characteristics: An ideograph is an ordinary-language term found in political dis-course. It is a high-order abstraction representing collective commitment to a particular but equivocal and ill-defined normative goal. It warrants the use of power, excuses behavior and belief which might otherwise be perceived as eccentric or antisocial, and guides behavior and belief into channels easily recognized by a community as acceptable and laudable. Ideographs such as "slavery" and "tyranny," however, may guide behavior and belief negatively by branding unacceptable behavior. And many ideographs ("liberty," for example) have a nonideographic usage, as in the sentence, "Since I resigned my position, I am at liberty to accept your offer." Ideographs are culture-bound, though some terms are used in different signification across cultures. Each member of the community is socialized, conditioned, to the vocabulary of ideographs as a prerequisite for "belonging" to the society. A degree of tolerance is usual, but people are expected to understand ideographs within a range of usage thought to be acceptable: The society will inflict penalties on those who use ideographs in heretical ways and on those who refuse to respond appropriately to claims on their behavior warranted through the agency of ideographs.

Though ideographs such as "liberty," "religion," and "property" often appear as technical terms in social philosophy, I have argued here that the ideology of a community is established by the usage of such terms in specifically rhetorical discourse, for such usages constitute excuses for specific beliefs and behaviors made by those who executed the history of which they were a part. The ideographs used in rhetorical discourse seem structured in two ways: In isolation, each ideograph has a history, an etymology, such that current meanings of the term are linked to past usages of it diachronically. The diachronic structure of an ideograph establishes the parameters, the category, of its meaning. All ideographs taken together, I suggest, are thought at any specific "moment" to be consonant, related one to another in such a way as to produce unity of commitment in a particular historical context. Each ideograph is thus connected to all others as brain cells are linked by synapses, synchronically in one context at one specific moment.

A complete description of an ideology, I have suggested, will consist of (1) the isolation of a society's ideographs, (2) the exposure and analysis of the diachronic structure of every ideograph, and (3) characterization of synchronic relationships among all the ideographs in a particular context. Such a description, I believe, would yield a theoretical framework with which to describe inter-penetrating material and symbolic environments: Insofar as we can explain the diachronic and synchronic tensions among ideographs, I suggest, we can also explain the tension between *any* "given" human environment ("objective reality") and any "projected" environments ("symbolic" or "social reality") latent in rhetorical discourse.

Notes

1. Kenneth Burke, A Rhetoric of Motives (New York: Prentice-Hall, 1950), pp. 197–203; John Dewey, *The Public and Its Problems* (New York: Henry Holt, 1927); George H. Mead, *Mind, Self, and Society* (Chicago: Univ. of Chicago Press, 1934); and Walter Lippmann, *Public Opinion* (1922; rpt. New York: Free Press, 1965).

Duncan groups the American symbolists by observing that European social theorists using "ideology" were concerned with "consciousness" (questions about the *apprehension* of society) while symbolists using poetic metaphors were concerned with a "philosophy of action" (questions about the way we do or ought *behave* in society). In rejecting the concept and theory of "ideology." Burke refused to consider the relationship between consciousness and action except as that relationship can be characterized with the agency of an a priori poetic metaphor, "dramatism." His thought and writing, like that of a poet, is therefore freed from truth criteria: Supposing his *form*, no "motive" outside the dramatistic terminology need be recognized or accounted for *in its particularly*. Though Burkeans are more guilty than Burke, I think even he tends to redefine motives rather than account for them, to cast self-confessions in "scenarios" rather than deal with them in specific. One might say of "dramatism" what Bacon alleged regarding the Aristotelian syllogism, that it is but a form which chases its tail, presuming in its metaphoric conception the truth of its descriptions. See Hugh Dalziel Duncan, *Symbols in Society* (New York: Oxford Univ. Press, 1968), pp. 12–14; Richard Dewey, "The Theatrical Analogy Reconsidered," *The American Sociologist,* 4 (1969), 307–11; and R. S. Perinbanayagam, "The Definition of the Situation: an Analysis of the Ethnomethodological and Dramaturgical View," *Sociological Quarterly,* 15 (1974), 521–41.

2. See, e.g., Arthur M. Schlesinger, Jr., "Ideology and Foreign Policy: The American Experience," in George Schwab, ed., *Ideology and Foreign Policy* (New York: Cyrco, 1978). pp. 124–32; and Randall L. Bytwerk, "Rhetorical Aspects of the Nazi Meeting: 1926–1933," *Quarterly Journal of Speech,* 61 (1975), 307–18.

3. See, e.g., William R. Brown, "Ideology as Communication Process," *Quarterly Journal of Speech,* 64 (1978), 123–40; and Jürgen Habermas, "Technology and Science as 'Ideology,'" in *Toward a Rational Society*, trans. Jeremy J. Shapiro (1968; Boston: Beacon, 1970), pp. 81–122.

4. Bormann's distrust of "ideology" was expressed in the context of an evaluation of his "fantasy theme" technique at the 1978 convention of the Speech Communication Association. See "Fantasy Theme Analysis: An Exploration and Assessment," S. C. A. 1978 Seminar Series, Audio-Tape Cassettes. For authoritative accounts of the various "encrustations," see George Lichtheim, "The Concept of Ideology," *History and Theory,* 4 (1964–65), 164–95; and Hans Barth, *Truth and Ideology*, trans. Frederic Lilge, 2nd ed. 1961 (Berkeley: Univ. of California Press, 1976).

5. See Kenneth Burke, *Permanence & Change*, 2nd ed. rev. (1954; rpt. Indianapolis: Bobbs-Merrill, 1965), pp. 19–36, 216–36; Karl Marx and Frederick Engels, *The German Ideology* (1847), trans. and ed. Clemens Dutt, W. Lough, and C. P. Magill, in *The Collected Works of Karl Marx and Frederick Engels*, 9+ vols. (Moscow: Progress Publishers, 1975–77+), 5:3–5, 23–93; Karl Mannheim, *Ideology and Utopia*, trans. Louis Wirth and Edward Shils (1929; rpt. New York: Harvest Books, 1952); and Martin Seliger, *The Marxist Conception of Ideology: A Critical Essay* (Cambridge: Cambridge Univ. Press, 1977).

My purpose here is to expose the issue between symbolists (generally) and materialists (particularly Marxians). This of course results in some oversimplification: With regard to the brute problem of describing "consciousness," at least two schools of thought are not here accounted for, Freudian psychiatry and American empirical psychology. Freudians are generally connected with the symbolist position I describe here, while most of the operational conceptions of American empirical psychology (especially social psychology) may fairly be associated with Marxian or neo-Marxian description. Moreover, I treat the terms "ideology" and "myth" as less ambiguous than their history as concepts would suggest. My usage of the terms, and the technical usefulness I portray, reflects my own conviction more than the sure and noncontroversial meaning of either "myth" or "ideology."

6. See, e.g., Willard A. Mullins, "Truth and Ideology: Reflections on Mannheim's Paradox," *History and Theory*, 18 (1979), 142–54; William H. Shaw, "'The Handmill Gives You the Feudal Lord': Marx's Technological Determinism," *History and Theory*, 18 (1979), 155–76; Jean-Paul Sartre, *Critique of Dialectical Reason*, trans. Alan Sheridan-Smith (1960; Eng. trans. London: NLB, 1976), pp. 95–121; and Jean-Paul Sartre, *Search for a Method*, trans. Hazel E. Barnes (1958; Eng. trans. New York: Vintage, 1968), pp. 35–84.

7. See W. G. Runciman, "Describing," *Mind*, 81 (1972), 372–88; Perinbanayagam; and Herbert W. Simons, Elizabeth Mechling, and Howard N. Schreier, "Mobilizing for Collective Action From the Bottom Up: The Rhetoric of Social Movements," unpub. MS., Temple Univ., pp. 48–59, in Carroll C. Arnold and John Waite Bowers, eds., *Handbook of Rhetorical and Communication Theory*.

8. Adolph Hitler, this century's archetype of absolute power—as well as absolute immorality—rose to dominance and maintained himself by putting into practice symbolist theories of social process. Hitler's mere existence forces one to question symbolist theories, asking whether "sociodramas" and "rhetorics" and "myths" are things to be studied scientifically or wild imaginings conjured up from the ether, devil-tools playing upon human weakness and superstition, and therefore things to be politically eradicated. In the face of Hitler, most symbolists adopted a high moral stance of righteous wrath, concentrating on the evil of the man while underplaying the tools he used to gain and keep power. But subtly they modified their logics: Burke is most sensitive to the problem, but in the end he does little more than demonstrate the moral polemical power of dramatistic methods of criticism, becoming the "critic" of his early and later years rather than the "historian" and "theorist" of his middle years. Cassirer's reaction is more extreme, backing away from the logical implications of the symbolist epistemology he argued for before Hitler, begging the problem of power by characterizing the state itself as nothing but a "myth" to be transcended. Hitler was an inspiration to Polanyi, causing him to take up epistemology as a vehicle to discredit social philosophy generally. In the process Polanyi became an unabashed ideological chauvinist of his adopted culture. See, resp., Kenneth Burke, "The Rhetoric of Hitler's 'Battle.'" in *The Philosophy of Literary Form*, 3rd ed. (Berkeley: Univ. of California Press, 1973), pp. 191–220, and cf. Kenneth Burke, Attitudes toward History (1937; 2nd ed. rev. rpt. Boston: Beacon, 1961), pp. 92–107; Ernst Cassirer, *The Philosophy of Symbolic Forms*, trans. Ralph Manheim (1923–29; Eng. trans. New Haven: Yale Univ. Press, 1953), 1:105–14; Ernst Cassirer, *The Myth of the State* (New Haven: Yale Univ. Press, 1946); Michael Polanyi, *The Logic of Liberty* (Chicago: Univ. of Chicago Press, 1951), pp. 93–110, 138–53; and Michael Polanyi, *Personal Knowledge: Towards a Post-Critical Philosophy* (1958; rpt. Chicago: Univ. of Chicago Press, 1962), pp. 69–131, 203–48, 299–324.

9. I am suggesting that the topic of "falsity" is necessary whenever one's conception of consciousness transcends the mind of a single individual. This is so because the transcendent consciousness, by its very conception, is a legitimizing agency, a means to warrant moral judgments (as in Perelman) or a means to create the fiction of verification when verification is logically impossible (as in Ziman and Brown). To fail to acknowledge the undeniable falsity of *any* description of mass or group consciousness is to create the illusion that one or another series of normative claims have an independent "facticity" about them. In my view Brown and Ziman are reckless with hypostatized "descriptions" of the consciousness of an intellectual elite, a "scientific community," which itself is in fact a creature of convention, in the specific terms of "description" a fiction of Ziman's and Brown's mind and a rhetorical vision for their readers. See Brown; Ch. Perelman and L. Olbrechts-Tyteca, *The New Rhetoric: A Treatise on Argumentation*, trans. John Wilkinson and Purcell Weaver (1958; Eng. trans. Notre Dame: Univ. of Notre Dame Press, 1969), pp. 31–35, 61–74; J. M. Ziman, *Public Knowledge: An Essay Concerning the Social Dimension of Science* (Cambridge: Cambridge Univ. Press, 1968), pp. 102–42; and contrast George Edward Moore, *Principia Ethica* (1903; rpt. Cambridge: Cambridge Univ. Press, 1965), esp. pp. 142–80; and Bruce E. Gronbeck, "From 'Is' to 'Ought': Alternative Strategies," *Central States Speech Journal*, 19 (1968), 31–39.

10. See Kenneth Burke, "A Dramatistic View of the Origins of Language and Postscripts on the Negative" in *Language as Symbolic Action* (Berkeley: Univ. of California Press, 1966), pp. 418–79, esp. pp. 453–63; Hannah Arendt, "What Is Authority?" in *Between Past and Future* (New York: Viking, 1968), pp. 91–141; Hannah Arendt, "Lying in Politics: Reflections on the Pentagon Papers," in *Crises of the*

Republic (New York: Harcourt Brace Jovanovich, 1972), pp. 1–47; Jürgen Habermas, "Hannah Arendt's Communications Concept of Power," *Social Research*, 44 (1977), 3–24; J. G. A. Pocock, *Politics, Language and Time* (New York: Atheneum, 1973), pp. 17–25, 202–32; and Robert E. Goodwin, "Laying Linguistic Traps," *Political Theory*, 5 (1977), 491–504.

11. See Kenneth Burke, *A Grammar of Motives* (New York: Prentice-Hall, 1945), pp. 43–46, 415–18; Burke, *Rhetoric*, pp. 275–76, 298–301; Ernst Cassirer, *Language and Myth*, trans. Susanne K. Langer (1946; Eng. trans. 1946; rpt. New York: Dover, 1953), pp. 62–83; Richard M. Weaver, The Ethics of Rhetoric (1953; rpt. Chicago: Gateway, 1970), pp. 211–32; and Rosalind Coward and John Ellis, *Language and Materialism* (London: Routledge & Kegan Paul, 1977), pp. 61–152.

12. José Ortega y Gasset, *Man and People*, trans. Willard R. Trask (New York: Norton, 1957), p. 245.

13. Ibid., pp. 192–221, 258–72.

14. Ibid., p. 221.

15. Ibid., p. 251.

16. Ibid., pp. 176–91.

17. See Murray Edelman, *Political Language* (New York: Academic Press, 1977), pp. 43–49, 141–55; Schwab, pp. 143–57; and Thomas M. Franck and Edward Weisband, Word Politics: *Verbal Strategy Among the Superpowers* (New York: Oxford Univ. Press, 1972), pp. 3–10, 96–113, 137–69.

18. Ortega y Gasset, *Man and People,* pp. 243–52. Further, contrast Ortega and Marx on the nature of "idea": José Ortega y Gasset, *The Modern Theme,* trans. James Cleugh (1931; rpt. New York: Harper, 1961), pp. 11–27; and Marx and Engels, pp. 27–37. See, also, Coward and Ellis, pp. 84–92, 122–35.

19. Ortega y Gasset, *Man and People,* pp. 57–71, 94–111, 139–91. Husserl's recognition of praxis and contradiction in his doctrine of "self-evidence" confirms Ortega's critique: Edmund Husserl, *Ideas: General Introduction to Pure Phenomenology,* trans. W. R. Boyce Gibson (1913; Eng. trans. 1931; rpt. London: Collier Macmillan, 1962), pp. 353–67. See, also, Schutz's and Luckmann's elaboration of the bases of Carneadean skepticism: Alfred Schutz and Thomas Luckmann, *The Structures of the Life-World,* trans. Richard M. Zaner and H. Tristram Engelhardt, Jr. (Evanston: Northwestern Univ. Press, 1973), pp. 182–229.

20. Michel Foucault, *The Archaeology of Knowledge,* trans. A. M. Sheridan Smith (1969; Eng. trans. New York: Pantheon, 1972), pp. 178–95; H. T. Wilson, *The American Ideology: Science, Technology and Organization as Modes of Rationality in Advanced Industrial Societies* (London: Routledge & Kegan Paul, 1977), pp. 231–53; and Roger Poole, *Towards Deep Subjectivity* (New York: Harper & Row, 1972), pp. 78–112.

21. Michael Polanyi and Harry Prosch, *Meaning* (Chicago: Univ. of Chicago Press, 1975), pp. 9, 22: "We have all learned to trace the collapse of freedom in the twentieth century to the writings of certain philosophers, particularly Marx, Nietzsche, and their common ancestors, Fichte and Hegel. But the story has yet to be told how we came to welcome as liberators the philosophies that were to destroy liberty.... We in the Anglo-American sphere have so far escaped the totalitarian nightmares of the right and left. But we are far from home safe. For we have done little, in our free intellectual endeavors, to uphold thought as an independent, self-governing force." Contrast this "personal knowledge" explanation with Max Horkheimer and Theodor W. Adorno, *Dialectic of Enlightenment,* trans. John Cumming (1944; Eng. trans. New York: Herder and Herder, 1972), pp. 255–56; and Jacques Ellul, *Propaganda: The Formation of Men's Attitudes,* trans. Konrad Kellen and Jean Lerner (1962; Eng. trans. New York: Vintage, 1973), pp. 52–61, 232–57.

22. See Peter Rodino's opening remarks in "Debate on Articles of Impeachment," U.S., Congress, House of Representatives, Committee on the Judiciary, 93rd Cong., 2nd sess., 24 July 1974, pp. 1–4.

The "vertical/horizontal" metaphor used here to describe the evident structure of ideographs should not be confused with Ellul's idea (pp. 79–84) of the structural effects of "Propaganda." Lasky's analysis of "the English ideology" represents the "vertical" description I have in mind: Melvin J. Lasky, *Utopia and Revolution* (Chicago: Univ. of Chicago Press, 1976), pp. 496–575.

23. See Edward H. Levi, *An Introduction to Legal Reasoning* (Chicago: Univ. of Chicago Press, 1948), esp. pp. 6–19, 41–74; Perelman and Tyteca, pp. 70–74, 101–02, 350–57; and Duncan, pp. 110–23, 130–40.

24. Collingwood suggests that the content or ultimate subject matter of history should consist of explaining such recurrent usages ("ideographs") as "freedom" and "progress": R. G. Collingwood, *The idea of History* (1946; rpt. London: Oxford Univ. Press, 1972), pp. 302–34. See, also, Herbert J. Muller, *The Uses of the Past* (New York: Oxford Univ. Press, 1952), pp. 37–38.

25. See William Wirt, *Sketches of the Life and Character of Patrick Henry,* 9th ed. (Philadelphia: Thomas Cowperthwait, 1839) dedication and pp. 417–43; Judy Hample, "The Textual and Cultural Authenticity

of Patrick Henry's 'Liberty or Death' Speech," *Quarterly Journal of Speech,* 63 (1977), 298–310; and Robert D. Meade, *Patrick Henry: Portrait in the Making* (New York: Lippincott, 1957), pp. 49–58.

26. At least two strategies (that is, two theoretical mechanisms) have the capacity to yield fairly precise descriptions of functional "meaning" within situational and textual contexts: See Hans-Georg Gadamer, *Philosophical Hermeneutics,* trans. David E. Linge (Berkeley: Univ. of California Press, 1976), pp. 59–94; and Umberto Eco, *A Theory of Semiotics* (Bloomington: Indiana Univ. Press, 1976), pp. 48–150, 276–313.

27. Ortega y Gasset, *Man and People,* p. 247. Cf. Ferdinand de Saussure, *Course in General Linguistics,* trans. Wade Baskin, ed. Charles Bally and Albert Sechehaye in collaboration with Albert Riedlinger (1915; Eng. trans. 1959; rpt. New York: McGraw-Hill, 1966), pp. 140–90, 218–21.

28. See Richard M. Nixon, "Address to the Nation on the Watergate Investigation," *Public Papers of the Presidents of the United States* (Washington, D.C.: U.S. Government Printing Office, 1975), Richard Nixon, 1973, pp. 691–98, 710–25. Lucas' analysis of "rhetoric and revolution" (though it is more "idea" than "terministically" conscious) represents the "horizontal" description I have in mind: Stephen E. Lucas, *Portents of Rebellion: Rhetoric and Revolution in Philadelphia, 1765–76* (Philadelphia: Temple Univ. Press, 1976).

29. See Jürgen Habermas, *Communication and the Evolution of Society,* trans. Thomas McCarthy (1976; Eng. trans. Boston: Beacon, 1979), pp. 1–68, 130–205.

30. See Foucault, pp. 149–65.

31. See Nicholas Abercrombie and Bryan S. Turner, "The Dominant Ideology Thesis," *British Journal of Sociology,* 29 (1978), 149–70.

Rhetorical Conversation, Time, and Moral Action
by Thomas S. Frentz

Quality, then, seems to have practically two meanings, and one of these is the more proper. The primary quality is the differentia of the essence, and of this quality in numbers is a part; for it is a differentia of essences, but either not of things that move or not of them *qua* moving. Secondly, there are the modifications of things that move, *qua* moving and the differentia of movements. Virtue and vice fall among these modifications; for they indicate differentia of the movement or activity, according to which things in motion act or are acted on well or badly; for that which can be moved or act in some way is good, and that which can do so in another—the contrary—way is vicious. Good and evil indicate quality especially in those which have purpose.

—Aristotle, *Metaphysics*

In ancient Greece, rhetoric was "a practical art . . . for cultivating and enacting practical reason in audiences with the potential for moral action."[1] Over the centuries, especially since the rise of science and the advent of positivism, rhetoric and morality became disjoined, leaving both adrift, depreciated, and vulnerable to redefinition in terms of the presuppositions of contemporary philosophies.[2] In the twentieth century, however, rhetoric and morality have enjoyed a renaissance of sorts. Writers as diverse as Thomas Kuhn, Chaïm Perelman, Jürgen Habermas, Hans-Georg Gadamer, Kenneth Burke, and Robert Pirsig—not to mention historians, linguists, classicists, philosophers, and speech communication scholars—have revived the ancient disciplines in a variety of ways. And yet, for many rhetorical scholars, one of the most intriguing works for reconstituting and re-uniting rhetoric and moral action, ironically, says nothing about rhetoric: Alasdair MacIntyre's *After Virtue.*[3] When tied to a classical conception of rhetoric and an actional

Reprinted from *The Quarterly Journal of Speech* 71 (1985), with permission of the National Communication Association.

conception of time, his work provides a ground for conceiving a paradigmatic form of human communication, what I will call *rhetorical conversation.*

To begin, we must first establish MacIntyre's position. He begins by noting a disturbing feature of contemporary moral arguments. Although public arguments appear in the guise of rationality, at base they derive from premises containing concepts (e.g., human rights and utility) divorced from the moral traditions which originally gave them meaning. Consequently, MacIntyre observes, there is no rational way to decide between competing moral positions and moral arguments become shrill and interminable.[4] The cause of this situation is that when moral philosophers rejected Aristotelian teleology, moral arguments could no longer be generated from impersonal premises concerning the optimal good for humankind, and their authoritative force could no longer be validated rationally.[5] For without a teleological conception of morality, all rational attempts to justify moral action culminate in some variant of "emotivism." Emotivism, MacIntyre tells us, grounds premises for moral action in the desires, preferences, and needs of the individual, values the ahistorical "autonomous moral agent" who is free to choose his or her moral actions, and views people as means to be manipulated as opposed to ends to be valued. The philosophical terminus of this liberal individualistic morality is Nietzsche's *Übermensch*—''the great man."[6]

To understand fully MacIntyre's alternative to emotivism, we must first recount Aristotle's moral position, because it is Aristotle to whom MacIntyre is most indebted. For Aristotle, morality entails a three-fold scheme in which practical reason and experience with political contingencies lead people from a present condition of moral happenstance to a future condition of moral excellence as persons approach their telos of happiness (*eudaimonia*). Practical reason and experience, the moral constituents of ethics, are guided by the virtues—e.g., courage, justice, truthfulness, friendship, and so on. Some virtues define a person's character and are acquired through habit (*hexis*), while others are intellectual and must be learned through instruction. As MacIntyre notes, "the immediate outcome of the exercise of a virtue is a choice which issues in right action."[7]

MacIntyre's account of moral action fuses Aristotle's teleological perspective with concepts whose root origins trace back to the Homeric epics and the mythology of pre-Socratic Greece.[8] The centerpiece of MacIntyre's moral perspective is a *practice,* which is:

> any coherent and complex form of socially established cooperative human activity through which goods internal to that form of activity are realized in the course of trying to achieve those standards of excellence which are appropriate to, and partially definitive of, that form of activity, with the result that human powers to achieve excellence, and human conceptions of the ends and goods involved, are systematically extended.[9]

If we unpack this highly compressed definition, several features stand out. First, a practice is a cooperative human activity engaged in by persons who conjointly value the goods intrinsic to the practice. Thus, to use MacIntyre's own example, throwing a football (an individual act) would not be a practice, while the game of football (a collective activity) would be.[10] Further, practices have internal goods which can only be achieved by participating in that practice. Internal goods, like the satisfaction derived by scoring in football, are sharply contrasted with external goods, like receiving money and prestige from playing the game.[11] Finally, practices are constituted and regulated by standards of excellence which participants in the practice must honor. It is through allegiance to and the possible extension of the standards of practices that the goods internal to those practices are themselves extended and improved.

Practices must be understood in relation to two additional concepts. The moral unity of an individual life MacIntyre identifies as a *narrative,* and it is while presenting the moral import of personal narratives that MacIntyre relies upon rhetoric's not-too-distant cousin in communication, the conversation: "For conversation . . . is the form of human transactions in general . . . I am presenting both conversations in particular and human actions in general as enacted narratives."[12] Conceptualizing an individual's life as a narrative allows an interpretation of a particular act as an instance of a story which gives moral continuity to the actor's life. If an individual's life is best understood as a narrative, a story in the process of being told, then the telos for humanity reflects the dramatic form of the Homeric epic—the quest.[13] The optimal end for humanity is neither the deification of human reason nor the stipulation of a transcendent God who commands moral obedience. Rather, MacIntyre's concept of telos is fluid and indeterminate; it is a telos of potential (*dynamis*), a nascent power to extend.[14]

Collectively constituted practices and personal narratives do not occur in a moral vacuum. Practices and narratives unfold in *moral traditions* which provide the cultural contexts for understanding moral action historically. Virtues such as courage, honesty, justice, and constancy bond practices, personal narratives, and moral traditions into a unified moral perspective. "The virtues find their point and purpose not only in sustaining those relationships necessary if the variety of goods internal to practices are to be achieved and not only in sustaining the [narrative] form of an individual life in which that individual may seek out his or her good as the good of his or her whole life, but also in sustaining those traditions which provide both practices and individual lives with their necessary historical context."[15]

This rather lengthy summary of MacIntyre's position has been undertaken because any assessment or extension of his framework must consider the complete perspective and not just constituents of it. What, then, are we to make of this work? Clearly, it is a most important treatise in moral philosophy. But, because MacIntyre's central concept of a practice is separated from an understanding of rhetoric, it is difficult to see how practices, as he conceives of them, could promote moral action.[16] Further, the concept of a narrative is oddly restricted to explaining the unity of an individual life.

If MacIntyre's moral posture is extended in a way which conjoins an Aristotelian sense of rhetoric with a temporal conception of narrative, we can derive a more adequate explanation of how rhetoric can affect moral action in contemporary society. In this essay, I will (1) argue that certain kinds of conversations are practices whose internal goods lead participants to recover their own potential as moral agents, (2) use the language-action paradigm to explain the distinctive narrative form of these conversations in relation to temporality, and finally (3) offer an extended exemplar of such a conversation—namely, the film *My Dinner with André.*

Rhetorical Conversations as Practices

By grounding practices in action (*praxis*), MacIntyre preserves the important Aristotelian notion that morality is less a form of knowing than of doing.[17] Practices include "arts, sciences, games, politics in the Aristotelian sense, the making and sustaining of family life."[18]

Although gaining the goods internal to a practice requires engaging in it in accordance with the virtues, not all goods internal to practices are directly relevant to moral action. For example, the goods MacIntyre finds internal to the practice of chess are "a particular kind of analytic skill, [and] strategic imagination and competitive intensity."[19] In like manner, one internal good of portrait painting in Western Europe from the late middle ages to the eighteenth century was the realization of how such portraits reveal the souls of their subjects.[20] Even in a period in which some teleological morality is embraced, it is difficult to see how "analytic skills" and "revealed souls" could directly influence moral action. And in modern society, which, as MacIntyre demonstrates so clearly, is sedimented in liberal individualism, most of the practices mentioned in *After Virtue* and their attendant internal goods seem woefully incapable of dislodging the sedimentation. Certain practices, then, seem more capable than others of facilitating moral tasks. Although MacIntyre does not identify those for us, Aristotle does.

In the context of the Greek *polis,* the possibility of an autonomous moral agent who exercised choice on the basis of personal preferences and desire would have been a moral aberration of the first order. For the Athenian statesperson, moral action occurred within a teleologically based moral tradition in which each act contributed to the cumulative narrative history of an individual's character as well as to the tradition in which the act was embedded. Against this backdrop, the central practice for honing practical reason and personal character to a moral sharpness was rhetoric.

Yet rhetoric, as Aristotle envisioned it, is often inadequate for confronting the moral dilemmas of modern societies. Where once agents could be presumed to share a common social knowledge from which moral action might emanate, that presumption has become all but untenable in an age of increased specialization and the concomitant proliferation of technical knowledge.[21] Moreover, the progressive separation of rhetorical audiences from advocates has largely eliminated the audience as the efficient cause of rhetoric—those who judge.[22] In its place, we often find a pre-packaged spectacle, which, when ingested by an apathetic public, creates the illusion of moral involvement in public decision-making.[23] But perhaps the most damaging blow to the classical rhetorical tradition is described by MacIntyre himself. For, as a practice which led to morally defensible action, Aristotelian rhetoric presupposed moral agents who possessed a sense of their own individual moral histories as well as an awareness of how particular choices extended the impersonal teleology of the Greek moral tradition. This presupposition is precisely what MacIntyre denies is possible in liberal individualistic conceptions of morality. Put somewhat differently, any contemporary approach to rhetoric which attempts to preserve the Aristotelian roots of the art must do so with the full realization that modern rhetorical advocates and audiences have lost their sense of individual moral coherence and a teleologically grounded moral tradition.

But the prospect for such a classical approach to rhetoric in modern times is not quite as bleak as the preceding account might suggest. To give some credence to this optimism, however, we will need to entertain the possibility that the form of such a rhetoric might differ significantly from its Aristotelian prototype and, further, that its functions might have to be more rudimentary than was the case for rhetoric in the classical tradition. I want to argue that in contemporary society the closest analogue to Aristotelian rhetoric is a special kind of conversation which I will call "rhetorical."[24] A rhetorical conversation is a narrative episode in which a conflict over opposing moral viewpoints re-unites the agents with their own moral histories, with the moral traditions of which they are a part, and—perhaps most important—with an awareness of the virtues.[25] As a practice, the goods internal to rhetorical conversations are an awareness of the moral unity of individual life and a sense of the quest for the ultimate good for self and humanity. Unlike MacIntyre's concept of practices, the goods internal to rhetorical conversations are themselves morally essential concepts which can be achieved only by acting in accordance with the virtues.

Before considering how rhetorical conversations promote moral action, it seems necessary to demonstrate that certain conversations—or parts of them—may assume a traditional rhetorical character. Recent inquiries into the relationship between rhetoric and conversation have revealed some basic similarities. For one, Thomas Farrell observes that both may derive from the same common origin—the poetic narrative of the Homeric epic.[26] For another, both conversation and rhetoric value relationships among interacting agents. For Aristotle, friendship was essential to insure that agents expressing opposing positions would not forget that the best political decisions demanded a cooperative spirit of fraternity in the face of controversy. On a very different level, conversational theorists also underscore how conversations affect the interpersonal relationships between or among participants.[27] To these commonalities, Farrell adds three conditions by which ordinary conversations assume rhetorical characteristics:

1) Cases where the content or expected direction of the conversation has been prepared in advance by at least one of the conversants.
2) Cases where the emergent status of the conversation, as a potentially complete unit of discourse, comes to rest upon the reflective and collaborative practical choices of the conversants themselves.
3) Cases where conversational discourse becomes disputational.[28]

I would add a fourth condition: cases where the conversational narrative structures time so that conversants experience past and future moral traditions—individual and impersonal—as an eternal present. I turn now to an elaboration of this fourth condition in relation to the language-action paradigm.[29]

Narrative Extension and the Temporal Present

Echoing the Homeric tradition, MacIntyre claims that individual acts become intelligible by placing them in personal narrative settings in which they are seen as interdependent parts of wholes. "We identify a particular action," he writes, "only by invoking two kinds of context, implicitly if not explicitly. We place the agent's intentions . . . in causal and temporal order with reference to their role in his or her history; and we also place them with reference to their role in the history of the setting or settings to which they belong."[30] Narratives are dramatic stories with beginnings, middles, and ends which give individual actions meaning, provide unity and self-definition to individual lives, and facilitate improvement of the impersonal good for humankind by showing the future as potential extensions of the present.

Some important rhetorical applications of narrative are provided in a recent essay by Walter R. Fisher.[31] He uses MacIntyre's notion of narrative as the basis for a paradigm for all human discourse which inevitably leads to moral action. Like MacIntyre, Fisher is distressed over the degenerate state of contemporary public moral argument. MacIntyre argues that there are no rational grounds for deciding between competing moral arguments, and when this is the case, Fisher observes, those "purveyors of ideological, bureaucratic, or technical arguments" often carry the day because of the privileged status of their roles in a hierarchical society and the presumed superiority of their attendant knowledge.[32]

It is clear that for MacIntyre and Fisher, narration is a pivotal construct in any modern teleological moral system. But it is also clear that very little has been said about how narrative structures—whether conversations, histories, or even full-blown paradigms—facilitate moral action. If narration is to fulfill its promise as a form of discourse which promotes moral action, the question of *how* must be addressed.

Some preliminary answers have been suggested by on-going work with the language-action paradigm.[33] Originally, the actional paradigm was a heuristic perspective on conversation designed to explain the structure and meaning of varied instances of interpersonal communication. The paradigm consists of three hierarchical layers of context. *Form of life contexts* are ranges of shared experience among agents—sometimes cultural, sometimes institutional, and sometimes interpersonal.[34] *Encounter contexts* are physical locations where social actors are mutually aware of each other's presence.[35] Finally, *episodic contexts*—those regions defined by conversations themselves—are rule conforming sequences of symbolic acts generated by two or more actors collectively oriented toward emergent goals.[36]

To explain how rhetorical conversation may lead toward moral action, we need to understand how such interactions affect conversants' experience of *time*. The central categories of the language-action paradigm were originally justified as contexts essential for understanding the meaning of symbolic acts. Yet these same constituents also function as more than analytic categories; they mark the ways in which time may be asserted, understood, even undermined, in the intentions and choices of actors. For example, we can easily recall conversations so involving that we thought they lasted a few minutes—only to discover that we had been engaged for hours. And the obverse is equally common; what we were sure was the drudgery of several eternal hours turned out to be only ten minutes by our watch. In both instances, we are faced with the complex interplay of communication and temporality.

As soon as we view our actional contexts as temporal modalities, however, we confront head-on the philosophical jungles involved in any reflective analysis of time. In part, this is because, as experienced directly, *time is pure change.* And because of that, temporality has become the Darth Vader for philosophical traditions whose ideological commitments lean toward permanence and universality. For when time becomes timeless, it ceases to be the phenomenon we set out to explain. For example, Cassirer notes that when Newton postulated "absolute time" as the foundation of his physics, he had created, in Kant's words, an "existing non-entity."[37] Of both realistic ontology and psychological empiricism, Cassirer concludes:

> neither things in themselves nor sensations in themselves explain the fundamental relation that confronts us in temporal consciousness. The succession of ideas is by no means synonymous with the representation of succession—nor is there any way of seeing how the latter might simply result from the former. For as long as the flow of representations is taken purely as an actual change, an objectively real process, it contains no consciousness of change as such of that mode in which time is posited as sequence and yet as unremitting present.[38]

If we are to understand how social actors experience time-as-change in rhetorical conversation, we shall have to seek assistance from those who preserve the transitory nature of the concept. Many of those thinkers turn out to be Christian theologians. As an exemplar of this tradition, Augustine observes that we always experience time in the present, but that the present is only knowable as a narrative which encapsulates both the past as memory and the future as expectation.[39] Centuries later, Paul Tillich makes the same point:

> The mystery is that we have a present; and even more, that we have our future also because we anticipate it in the present; and that we have our past also, because we remember it in the present. In the present, our future and our past are *ours*. . . . This is possible because every moment of time reaches into the eternal. . . . It is the eternal "now" which provides for us a temporal "now."[40]

For Augustine and Tillich, temporal consciousness means to experience the past, which was but is no more, and the future, which is not yet but will be, in the present, which is now. And the form of this temporal consciousness, as MacIntyre clearly recognizes, is narration. But not all narratives affect how we experience time in the same way, and if we are to understand how narration functions *vis-a-vis* rhetorical conversation, we will have to distinguish conversations which structure time as an emergent historical unity from conversations in which time is experienced as a linear sequence of temporal units. The distinction becomes clear in the different ways we experience time-in-conversation on the encounter and form of life levels of the language-action paradigm.

When we experience time on the encounter level, it is the quantitative cumulation of temporal units—seconds, minutes, hours, days. Ontically real, encounter time is the stuff that ages us, makes cars rust, and codifies nicely into the maxim, "The longer you live the older you get." Conversations in which agents experience time as encounter time are transitory and easily forgotten because the present is not extended into the past and future, is not an "eternal now," to use Tillich's phrase, but is rather a mere additive sequencing of chronological units. And when time in conversations is disconnected from past and future, a surrogate continuity can only be supplied by conventions and habitual choices. In the words of a particularly skilled phrase-maker, "when conversations are enacted simply to pass time, they become the time they are passing."[41] When we experience time on the encounter level, our temporal connection to past and future is limited to the spatio-temporal boundaries of the encounter context in which the episode occurs. But occasionally something unusual happens temporally, and it is to those instances that I now turn.

When conversations transcend encounter time, the participants experience time on the form of life level. As its name implies, form of life is an historical concept—fusing past and future in the present. When agents experience the temporal holism of a form of life all at once, in the consciousness of the present in an on-going conversation, they place themselves in a narrative context in which past and potential conversations are experienced as an historical unity emerging in the present—a unity whose evolving direction can be determined in part through cooperative action. By experiencing time in this way, agents are compelled to rediscover two preconditions to moral action: the unity of their individual lives as actors in a dramatic story, and the moral tradition within which the present narrative is being acted out.

Rhetorical conversations, then, manifest these features: The topic or content is morality. Conversants experience the tension of *agōn*—a contest between opposing moral systems. And most important, such conversations are narrative structures in which participants experience time-present as an extended form of life.[42] What we must now ask is whether rhetorical conversations actually occur in a moral universe which seems so alien to them. To answer affirmatively, we are led to an unusual place.

My Dinner With André

Conversations—rhetorical ones included—are difficult to pin down. No sooner are they enacted than they evaporate, leaving barely a trace of their existence. And so our task becomes doubly difficult—to find a permanent record of a particular type of conversation when permanent records of conversations in general demand planning and extreme care if the constituents of conversations (e.g., rules, strategies, etc.) are to function normally. Fortunately, a memorable rhetorical conversation has not only been preserved, but it also comes to us in the highly accessible form of a film entitled, *My Dinner With André*.[43] In a cinematic era of Jedi Knights, Valley girls, and Richard Gere, many people found *André* a rather tedious anachronism. After all, the action high-point of the film occurs when the head waiter brings Wally and André their main course. But like other superb films that did not exactly become box office smashes, *André* has already found a cult following of sorts, including diverse scholars in communication.[44] My purpose here, however, is to examine *André* as a paradigm example of a rhetorical conversation.

André is an unusual instance of a rhetorical conversation. André Gregory and Wallace Shawn did not simply have dinner at a New York restaurant in which their spontaneous remarks were filmed. Although the film creates the illusion that an emergent conversation has occurred, it is only an illusion. In reflecting on the incidents which led to the film, Shawn notes, "what if, instead of a play, we just did a very simple film, with lots of closeups, in which I would be talking with André? . . . And instead of just writing it myself out of my imagination, André and I would really talk for a while, and then my script would be based on our real conversations. . . . It wouldn't just be me! And the piece would say what he wanted it to say, as well as what I wanted it to say" (pp. 13–14). André seems even more aware of the potential impact of this theatrical conversation on film than Shawn: "It immediately struck me that the most necessary and appropriate piece that one *could* possibly do at this particular moment in history would be a piece about two friends sitting and talking to each other" (pp. 10–11).

On the surface, the film is an interesting hybrid. As a cinematic event, *André* exhibits a contemporary poetic form. In being premediated and scripted in accordance with the dictates and intentions of both Shawn and Gregory, the work has a pronounced rhetorical flavor. And yet, the exclusively conversational form of the plot harkens back, at least in structure, to matters more properly termed dialectical. I am not concerned with a "correct" labelling of the film—elements of each classical genre are readily apparent in the finished product. It is more important that the plot of *André* makes it rhetoric in conversational form, and that the two main characters play themselves.

As in the case with any richly textured discourse, *André* is far more than a blueprint of its observable action—of which there is very little. Still, some general overview seems warranted as a departure point. André and Wally work in the New York theater—Shawn as a playwright and part-time actor and Gregory as an award-winning director. Both are concerned with the theater's incapacity to present audiences with "reality" in a way that might change their lives. Both are also distressed with the quality of their own lives—although to different degrees and, as we discover, for different reasons. But each approaches their impending dinner with quite different expectations. For André, the dinner will afford an opportunity to share a series of "happenings" over the past several years with someone who was once a very close friend, but who—André correctly senses—has been avoiding him.

For Wally, the dinner promises to be a nightmare with a possible madman, who, allegedly, hallucinates regularly and has taken to chatting with plants; Wally's task is to survive. Their conversation, of course, transcends both sets of expectations. Plotted in encounter time, André shares his experiences, both agree on the degenerate quality of contemporary life, they disagree as to the role of the theater *vis-a-vis* the quality of life, and finally they confront one another's moral traditions and in the process learn something morally important.

As a prelude to our analysis, we note that Wally and André bring to their conversation incomplete moral selves. In his five years of travels, of living purely by his impulses, André has rediscovered a vital moral truth—that genuine living demands that we experience every moment to its fullest and that such living generates an interconnectedness with all people and all things. After recounting his experiences in Poland, André muses: "What I think I experienced was for the first time in my life to know what it means to be truly alive. . . . Now, that's very frightening, because with that comes an immediate awareness of death . . . because they go hand in hand . . . you know, that feeling of being connected with everything, means to also be connected with death" (p. 38). But in gaining some moral acuity through his experiences, André has lost other qualities. Principally, he has lost a sense of teleology, of purpose, of the moral life as a continual narrative quest in which the individual moves from a present moral condition toward something better.

Wally is an ideal moral counterpoint to André. Where André's international adventures in impulse have left him individually alive and vibrant, Wally's own existence has left him—as André himself might have put it—a lobotomized performer with no sense of the person behind the mask. Wally is not unreflective, however. On his way to meet André, he laments: "When I was ten years old I was rich, I was an aristocrat, riding around in taxis, surrounded by comfort, and all I thought about was art and music. Now I'm thirty-six, and all I think about is money" (p. 17). At this point, it is clear that while André has lost the teleological sense of moral tradition, Wally instinctually retains it. Well into their conversation, Wally tells André:

> You know . . . I think I do know what *really* disturbs me about the work that you've described, . . . if I've understood what you've been saying, it somehow seems that the whole point of the work that you did in those workshops . . . was to enable the people in the workshops, including yourself, to somehow sort of strip away every scrap of *purposefulness* from selected moments. And the point of it was so that you would then be able to experience somehow just *pure being*. . . . And I think I just simply object to that (pp. 103–104).

Despite his objection, Wally's sense of moral purpose has been perverted into making lists of errands to do and taking empty pleasure in doing them.

And so as they approach their evening together, Wally and André are oddly incomplete moral agents. Wally has some sense of tradition, but a crippled sense of self, while André is literally brimming over with "selfness," but has no idea what to do with it. But both are quite clear that *something* is wrong with their lives and that the theater—their vocation—seems ill-suited to address the malady—whatever it may be. With this preview, we turn now to the conversation itself.

It begins as a typical dialogue unfolding in encounter time. We do not experience that portion of the interaction directly. Rather, we are told about it by Wally: "So we talked for a while about my writing and my acting and about my girlfriend, Debby, and we talked about his wife, Chiquita, and his two children, Nicolas and Marina. Finally, I got around to asking him what he'd been up to in the last few years. He seemed a little reluctant to go into it, but that made me all the more anxious to know the story. I was sure I would feel very relaxed with him if only he'd tell his story. So I just kept asking, and finally he started to answer" (pp. 21–22). And when André begins to answer by telling his story, the conversation transcends encounter time and becomes a narrative grounded in form of life.

As a rhetorical conversation, the interaction has three phases, each conveniently correlated with a portion of the meal. The first phase begins with *hors d'oeuvres* and ends with the serving of the main course and is "André's story." The second begins with the entrée and concludes with the ordering of the after dinner drinks and involves "identification and conflict." The final phase starts with the after dinner drinks and ends with André paying the check. This phase, more subtle and complex than the preceding two, entails "moral closure."

"André's Story" is really a composite of five stories spanning several years of his life: (1) a theater workshop in Poland conducted with his friend and mentor, Jerzy Grotowski; (2) a trip to Tibet and an aborted plan to direct the *Little Prince* with a buddhist monk, Kozan, playing the lead role: (3) a brief trip to India: (4) a stay in the experimental Scottish community of Findhorn; and (5) a death and rebirth ritual conducted on Halloween at a friend's estate on Montauk, Long Island. André has shared these stories before—with other friends and acquaintances. This telling is different from previous versions because it is rhetorical. As such, André experiences two morally relevant insights, insights we may presume he did not encounter previously, or the dinner with Wally would not exhibit the ultimate moral import it had. André seems aware that these five adventures are not merely chronological sequences in encounter time, but rather a personal narrative which gives the past five years of his life moral continuity. It is significant that the Poland episode ends with his group christening André and re-naming him "Yendrush," and that the Montauk event symbolically kills André so that he may be born again—rather transparent evidence of the narrative force of the stories for André. But there is a more disquieting revelation as well. André seems increasingly aware of the incompleteness and even the potential for evil if his story were extended. In retrospectively examining the Polish workshop and his fascination with the *Little Prince,* André uses Nazi references as a means both of self criticism and as a ploy to coax the detached Wally to offer his own critical appraisal of André's story. When Wally does not respond, André intensifies the references and in so doing induces the reluctant Wally to enter the form of life narrative. After the entrée is served, both silently reflect on André experiences when André says:

Yes, you know, frankly, I'm sort of repelled by the whole story, if you really want to know I mean, who did I think I was? You know? I mean that's the story of some kind of spoiled princess. I mean, you know, who did I think I was, the Shah of Iran? I mean, you know, I wonder if people such as myself are not really Albert Speer, Wally. You know, Hitler's architect, Albert Speer. . . . Well, I've been thinking a lot about him recently. Because I think I am Speer. . . . Well, he was a very cultivated man, . . . so he thought the ordinary rules of life didn't apply to him. I mean, I would really like to be stripped and unmasked. I feel I deserve it. Because I really feel that everything I've done is horrific. Just horrific (pp. 57–58).

Once André rediscovers the unity of his life as a personal narrative, he also discovers that he will somehow be judged, held accountable, for the moral integrity of his life when he leaves it. And his fear is that he will not measure up in a narrative composed of "impulse living" (p. 58).

The second phase of the conversation begins as Wally leaves the detached context of encounter time by coming to his friend's defense. They share an intense interlude where both acknowledge that people in contemporary society have become mechanical automatons, persons who have lost the capacity to feel and who focus all their energy on accomplishing occupational goals. (We might note in passing that this precise view of humanity was offered by MacIntyre as the societal consequence of living in an age where morality is defined by liberal individualism.)[45] Ironically, Wally is diffidently unaware that he is one of the zombies himself. André's story may have left André raw and morally incomplete, but at least he knows it! Wally, on the other hand, has forgotten his story and in its place we find a craving for comfort, a distrust and fear of genuine emotion, and a life filled with the empty security of routine.

The confrontation begins innocently enough. Wally has just mentioned that sleeping under an electric blanket has subtly changed how he sleeps and even how he dreams (pp. 75–76). But André sees the blanket for what it is—a technological device designed to intensify comfort and anesthetize feeling:

Well, I wouldn't put an electric blanket on for anything, . . . turn on that electric blanket, and its like taking a tranquilizer, or it's like being lobotomized by watching television. I think you enter the dream world again. I mean, what does it do to us, Wally, to live in an environment where something as massive as the seasons and the cold and the winter don't in any way affect us? (pp. 76–77).

Wally's response, a defense actually, involves his occupation as a playwright. He admits that he succumbs to the dream world by valuing creature comforts in his personal life, but in his plays, he attempts to jar audiences to acknowledge the harsh reality around them. (p. 83) But André is relentless:

But, Wally, don't you see the dilemma? You're not taking into account the period we live in! I mean, of *course* that's what the theater *should* do. . . . But, Wally, the question is whether the theater now can do for an audience what Brecht tried to do or what Craig or Duse tried to do. . . . Because . . . I think people are so deeply asleep today that unless you're putting on those sort of superficial plays that help your audience sleep more comfortably, I think it's very hard to know what to do in the theater (pp. 84–85).

It is important to understand what André has done here. He has torn Wally loose from his moorings, and in so doing, has prepared both of them for a partial rediscovery of their roles in a moral tradition. Wally has conceded that his personal life is defined by creature comforts and habit. And now his vocation—often a surrogate tradition in a society governed by emotivism—has been challenged by someone who has intimate knowledge of it.

When backed against this wall, Wally strikes back and André is forced to admit some things too. After questioning André intensely over whether dropping out of society is necessary, Wally chides: "So I mean, is that our problem? Is that what you're saying? Are we just bored, spoiled children who've been lying in the bathtub all day, playing with their plastic duck, and now they're thinking. What can I do?" (p. 91). André's response places him squarely in the liberal individualist moral tradition, a tradition, MacIntyre tells us, which in one variant expresses a paranoid distrust of institutions which would suppress the freedom of the autonomous moral agent.[46] André says:

> Okay. Yes. We're bored now. We're all bored. But has it ever occurred to you, Wally, that the process which creates this boredom that we see in the world now may very well be a self-perpetuating unconscious form of brainwashing created by a world totalitarian government based on money? And that all of this is much more dangerous, really, than one thinks? And that it's not a question of individual survival, Wally, but that somebody who's bored is asleep? And somebody who's asleep will not say no (pp. 91–92).

And what is André's solution? How does the liberal individual confront this moral apocalypse? His solution seems even more detached and ethereal then his account of the problem.

> I keep thinking that we need a new language, a language of the heart, a language, as in the Polish forest, where language wasn't needed—some kind of language between people that is a new kind of poetry, that is the poetry of the dancing bee, that tells us where the honey is (p. 95).

André is wrong, of course, and both he and Wally know it. Moral action cannot be reinvented through a language of the heart. The heart itself must somehow be stirred from its moral slumbering and moved to a better place. And to do that, Wally must recover his own moral legacy and impart its significance to André.

It is unfortunate that as the final phase of the conversation begins, the audience may feel the emotional fatigue from what has transpired and, like André and Wally, be ready to sit back, relax, and enjoy some espresso and an Amaretto. But it is in this final phase that the disparate moral pieces of two lives become reassembled, and if we are not prepared for it, the moral closure is apt to slip by us quietly along with dessert.

Wally begins by sharing with André what he, Wally, "really thinks" of André's experiences and proclamations. Wally's thoughts are too long and complex to reproduce here in their entirety, but they contain two important clues to his own moral tradition (pp. 97–100). The first is Wally's genuine joy over the everyday continuities of life, those very same continuities which André's sees as unthinking habits that lead to ultimate passivity: "I mean . . . isn't it pleasant just to get up in the morning, and there's Chiquita, there are the children, the *Times* is delivered . . . why not lean back and just enjoy these details?" (p. 98). The second is his commitment to science. Wally's allegiance here is not to the naive belief that science will solve the world's problems. On the contrary, André and Wally believe that science is causing more problems than it is solving. (p. 103) But science is an undeniable force in an *evolving moral* universe. To deny that force, as André tries to do by becoming a slave to his impulses, is to deny a teleological morality and to float adrift in the uncharted seas of the encounter moment.

What is the moral heritage beneath Wally's impassioned comments? While no characterization would be uncontestable, the signs point toward Aristotelianism. The grounding of action in the practical world, the importance of familial ties and kinship to self identity, the exercise of practical reason and experience as the arbiters of action all point to the classical tradition. Subtly, André learns his Aristotelian lesson. "And I mean, as long as you're really alive inside, then of course there's no problem. I mean, you know, if you're living with someone in one little room, and there's a life going on between you and the person you're living with, well then, you know a whole adventure can be going on right in that room" (p. 106). Again, less hypothetically: "And when I allowed myself to consider the possibility of not spending the rest of my life with Chiquita, I realized that what I wanted most in life was to always be with her" (p. 108). And finally, as their conversation ends, André acknowledges the continual mystery of life even within the unending narrative in which each individual plays but a small part: "A baby holds your hands, and then suddenly there's this huge man lifting you off the ground, and then he's gone. Where's that son?" (pp. 112–13).

And what is learned? Wally rediscovers the wonderment of being alive as an individual and connected with all that surrounds him. "I rode home through the city streets. There wasn't a street—there wasn't a building—that wasn't connected to some memory in my mind" (p. 113). André realizes that self-awareness devoid of moral tradition has no purpose and that surrendering life to disconnected moments of "pure being" can lead to the fascistic horrors of Nazism which forever haunt his mind. André and Wally are re-united through a rhetorical conversation. They have rediscovered the constituents of a moral perspective each needed the other to supply. André imparted a sense of selfhood to Wally, while Wally gave André a renewed appreciation for a teleological tradition. The continuity of an individual life and a moral tradition are the goods internal to rhetorical conversations as practices and achievable only through enacting such conversations in accordance with the virtues of justice (the desserts each owe the other), courage (to risk one's self for the other), and honesty (to be truthful beyond all else).

Implications

The continuing work with the language-action paradigm reveals increasing similarities between rhetoric and conversation. Aristotle began the *Rhetoric* with the claim that rhetoric was the counterpart of dialectic; both were general methods for dealing with probabilities in the political realm of praxis.[47] To those initial similarities, Farrell has added others.[48] We may now add one, perhaps two, more. If the argument and extended example presented here specify the function of rhetorical conversations, then moral action—in its most general sense—would seem to be the telos of both public rhetoric and its conversational analogues. But, if MacIntyre is correct that moral premises in modern times take root in individual desires, then no common moral grounds (except desires—which are indefinitely variable) bond reasons together and no collectively deliberated moral decisions can be expected as a matter of course. Thus, I suggested with guarded optimism that the best we might hope from rhetorical conversations is that agents might become united with the necessary *preconditions* to moral action in the Aristotelian tradition.

Rhetoric and conversation may also be linked to temporal experience. I argued that rhetorical conversations are narratives in that conversants experience time-present as a narrative extension into the past and future forms of life in which they enact multiple stories simultaneously—their own, others, and those of their respective moral traditions. It is this protracted temporal experience which reunites agents with the moral goods internal to rhetorical conversations. We might now ask whether the temporal experience of time-present as extended forms of life is found in more traditional rhetorical artifacts. For if it is, it might provide additional clues to the suasory impact others find in public moral argument reconceptualized as narrative.

Our account of rhetorical conversations and moral action would not be complete without commenting—retrospectively—on the work that most centrally stimulated this effort. I refer, of course, to *After Virtue*. MacIntyre is quite clear that if the telos of humanity is not impersonal in nature, the resultant moral system will ultimately be reducible to some variant of emotivism when scrutinized rationally. But can MacIntyre's own impersonal ultimate good for humanity withstand the very test he devises? MacIntyre's telos is clearly set forth: "We have then arrived at a provisional conclusion about the good life for man: the good life for man is the life spent in seeking for the good life for man, and the virtues necessary for the seeking are those which will enable us to understand what more and what else the good life for man is."[49] But in defining the ultimate good for humanity as an indeterminant future condition which we constantly expand even as we search for it, MacIntyre commits himself to a humanism which contains the seeds of a collective emotivism. For if the ultimate good for humanity can only be created by cooperative human action, then this impersonal telos is also, in the final analysis, grounded in the collective wills, needs, and desires of human agents. If practices are cooperative human activities, then their internal goods must be rooted in human action. And if the virtues are set forth by human agents—whether Aristotle, Jane Austin, or MacIntyre himself—then they too are determined by humanity. And if the question were asked, which moral ends, which practices, or which virtues are best, the ultimate grounds for responding, I fear, would be the very grounds MacIntyre strives so diligently to avoid—the collective wills of the group or community in which moral action takes place. As long as the ultimate good *for humanity* is something which can be exclusively defined, changed, and acted upon *by humanity,* the moral philosophy which results will turn out to be another form of an emotivist moral system.

I believe MacIntyre has fallen prey to the same trap he argues has ensnared other modern moral philosophers. Throughout his work, MacIntyre claims that most contemporary moral philosophers try to construct coherent moral systems from concepts which represent ahistorical fragments of antithetical moral traditions.[50] If MacIntyre's own position suffers the same fate as those he so successfully indicts, perhaps he too is working with concepts from competing moral traditions. In fact, this turns out to be the case.

At the outset, I suggested that MacIntyre's moral philosophy contains concepts from two quite different moral traditions. The concepts of "the virtues," "practices," and "practical reason" are clearly Aristotelian. But the concepts of "narration," "quest," and "historical unity," while surely discussed in the Aristotelian corpus, are more centrally remnants of an older moral tradition we might call pre-Socratic, or more simply, Homeric. When concepts from one tradition are dislodged from their heritage and placed in another tradition, there is always the danger that the original meanings of the displaced concepts will have been lost. Two such concepts are "quest" and "teleology" and we must ask how their respective meanings changed as they assumed new roles within MacIntyre's moral system.

The answer is a complex one. For Aristotle, the ultimate telos for humankind is happiness, and the pursuit of happiness is "an activity of the soul and consists in actions performed in conjunction with the rational element."[51] MacIntyre rejects this view because "Aristotle's teleology presupposed his metaphysical biology" which has been shown to be untenable.[52] While rejecting Aristotle's animism, MacIntyre preserves a teleology by recasting it in Homeric terms, as a narrative quest. What MacIntyre fails to see is that a narrative quest in the Homeric tradition is inextricably linked to a supernatural telos—the desires and actions of the gods, as memorialized in poetry. As narrative quests, Homeric poetry presents the stories of the gods (*nomoi* or "custom laws") as normative models of the stories humans should live if their lives are to be characterized by *aretē*—overall excellence.[53] By divorcing the narrative quest from the gods, MacIntyre has changed its meaning and, in so doing, created a moral fiction of his own. When he then grafts that fiction onto a teleological tree, itself having been pruned of its theological impulse in the form of Aristotelian animism, the resultant bush does not exactly burn with moral authority. For when the telos for humanity is a quest plus humanly derived moral concepts, all that can follow is a humanly grounded morality, and those are at base emotivist, no matter how persistent the protests to the contrary.

Is there any way to construct a teleological morality that transcends emotivism and still preserves the classical system? Any satisfactory answer would be well beyond the scope of this work. We can, however, sketch one direction an answer might take. Suppose the concept of the narrative quest were re-united with "the gods." Such a move is not as radical as it might appear. In fact, if history is conceptualized as a narrative quest, then some sense of spirit is necessary if that quest is to be meaningful. As Ken Wilber notes, "If we assume that history has some sort of *meaning*, then we must also assume that it points to something *other* than itself, which is to say, something other than individual men and women. . . . Nothing can stay long removed from God, nor long divorced from that Ground of Being outside of which nothing exists, and history . . . is the story of men and women's love affair with the Divine."[54] This sense of human history evolving in concert with the gods epitomizes the teleology of the Homeric tradition. In such a system, practices and their attendant virtues would be vehicles for gaining access to the moral truths of the gods. The narrative unity of an individual's life and the historical unity of moral traditions would be narrative quests in the fullest Homeric sense, quests for universal moral truths.

This Homeric teleology would enrich our understanding of the classical rhetorical tradition by reaffirming aspects of the tradition which have long been neglected. For example, if moral truths are transcendent, they must comprise *archai* or first moral principles. Moral *archai* capture relationships between the universal and the particular, between the gods and humankind. According to Giambattista Vico, one central function of rhetoric is to set forth these *archai:* "This requires that rhetoric be understood as a science of narration which can comprehend the particulars of the human world in terms of necessity. Narration must tell us the story of the human world as the necessary sequence of the ideal eternal history. Narration and necessity are joined."[55] What is good in any given case is based upon moral principles which link the stories of the gods to the emergent narrative of human history.

But how are moral *archai* discovered? Writing of *archai* in the theoretical sciences, Aristotle concludes: "there will be no scientific knowledge of the primary premises, and since except intuition nothing can be truer than scientific knowledge, it will be intuition that apprehends the primary premises. . . ."[56] Moral *archai,* like their theoretical counterparts, are discoverable only through intuition, and intuition, Vico tells us, is grounded in the inventional facet of memory called *ingegno* or ingenuity.[57] *Ingegno* is the capacity to see immediately and directly a rationship between a moral problem in the human world and a solution in the spiritual world—what Vico refers to as "ideal eternal history."[58]

Although moral *archai* are discovered through *ingegno,* they are most clearly expressed through metaphor. As the grounds of moral argument, *archai* exhibit an imaginative quality neither reducible to nor derivable from rational argument. Extending the Homeric tradition through Vico, Ernesto Grassi captures well the expressive quality of this metaphorical discourse: "The *true rhetorical speech* . . . springs from the *archai* [and is] nondeducible, moving, and indicative, due to its original images. The original speech is that of the wise man, of the *sophos,* who is not only *epistetai,* but who with insight leads, guides, and attracts."[59] And so the initial vision of rhetoric which emerges from the Homeric tradition is quite unAristotelian with its emphasis upon moral *archai,* ingenious invention, and metaphorical expression.

But there is great danger if we stop here. For if moral action entails the unreflective acceptance of the advocacy of a rhetor who claims to have been to the mountaintop and received "the Truth," we are surely faced with a rhetoric having little to do with morality and the virtues. For every Moses, history sadly records a

hundred Hitlers and the tragic consequences of uncritically following false proph-
ets. Perhaps Aristotle's greatest legacy to the classical tradition was his insistence
that practical reason, *phronēsis*, should be the final arbiter of moral action. Whereas
the Homeric tradition allows us to recover the imagistic nature of moral insight, it
is the classical heritage which reminds us that the muse must be broken, interrupted,
and reflectively examined if the ensuing action is to be rationally justified.[60] But
who initiates the interruption? We may take a clue from Farrell's careful reading
of Aristotle's *Rhetoric*. Farrell notes that for Aristotle, the end of rhetoric is not the
production of persuasive discourse, but rather the enactment of moral choice
"through the adjudication of a reasoning and competent audience. . . . "[61] The
rhetorical audience is entrusted with the responsibility of critically assessing the
genuineness of the original vision, and is—as such—the ultimate guardian of moral
action.

   We have perhaps extended this fragment further than its speculative nature
would warrant. My point is to suggest that if we reunite the Homeric concepts of
narration, quest, and the universal moral truth of the gods with the Aristotelian
concepts of the classical rhetorical tradition, we may well gain a deeper understanding of the tradition and share MacIntyre's enthusiasm—however
guarded—for the potential of that tradition for dealing with contemporary moral
problems.

Notes

1. Thomas B. Farrell, "The Tradition of Rhetoric and the Philosophy of Communication," *Communication,*
     7 (1983), 152.
2. Farrell, p. 151.
3. Alasdair MacIntyre, *After Virtue* (Notre Dame, IN: University of Notre Dame Press, 1981).
4. MacIntyre, pp. 6–11.
5. MacIntyre, pp. 49–53.
6. MacIntyre, pp. 239–40.
7. MacIntyre, p. 140.
8. In commenting on the narrative structure of individual lives which makes their actions intelligible,
     MacIntyre writes: "Hence,there is no way to give us an understanding of any society, including our
     own, except through the stock of stories which constitute its initial dramatic resources. Mythology, in
     this original sense, is at the heart of things." p. 201.
9. MacIntyre, p. 175.
10. MacIntyre, p. 175.
11. MacIntyre, pp. 175–76.
12. MacIntyre, p. 197.
13. MacIntyre, p. 204.
14. Farrell makes much the same point in arguing that Aristotle saw virtue in the *Rhetoric* as "a powerful
     capacity awaiting propitious enactment." p. 165.
15. MacIntyre, p. 207.
16. I could discover only minimal uses of "rhetoric" in *After Virtue* and all support the claim made here.
     For example, on p. 69, MacIntyre qualifies his indictment of emotivist morality by noting that "the
     major protagonists of the distinctively modern moral causes of the modern world . . . offer a rhetoric
     which serves to conceal behind the masks of morality what are in fact the preferences of arbitrary will
     and desire is not of course an original claim." Again on p. 235, in a rare tip-of-the-hat to Marx,
     MacIntyre credits Marx with recognizing that fragmented social concepts "are used at one and the

same time to express rival and incompatible social ideals and policies *and* to furnish us with a pluralist political rhetoric whose function is to conceal the depth of our conflict." These usages, as well as the others, reveal the negativism common to naive contemporary nontechnical uses of rhetoric.

17. Aristotle, *Eudemian Ethics,* trans. J. Solomon, in *The Works of Aristotle,* ed. W. E. Ross (London: Oxford University Press, 1915), I, 5, 1216b.

18. MacIntyre, p. 175.

19. MacIntyre, pp. 175–76.

20. MacIntyre, p. 176.

21. For an account of the changes in the type of knowledge which underlies rhetoric, see Thomas B. Farrell, "Knowledge, Consensus, and Rhetorical Theory," Quarterly Journal of Speech, 62 (1976), 1–15; Thomas B. Farrell and G. Thomas Goodnight, "Accidental Rhetoric: Root Metaphors of Three Mile Island," *Communication Monographs,* 48 (1981), 271–300.

22. Farrell, "The Tradition," p. 161.

23. There are numerous elaborations of this claim, each with slightly different colorations. The two most germane to this essay are, Daniel J. Boorstin, *The Image* (New York: Atheneum, 1962), especially pp. 9–12; Thomas B. Farrell, "The Forms of Social Knowledge: Praxis and Spectacle," paper presented at the Speech Communication Association Convention, San Francisco, California, December, 1976.

24. Two caveats are necessary. First, "persuasion" is not a necessary condition for conversations to be rhetorical, because persuasion occurs in all conversations to some extent. Second, rhetorical conversations occur very rarely—as we should expect in a society dominated by emotivism.

25. Rhetorical conversations share some features with what others have called "dialogic communication." See, for example, Richard J. Bernstein, *Beyond Objectivism and Relativism: Science, Hermeneutics, and Praxis* (Philadelphia: University of Pennsylvania Press, 1983); Richard L. Johannesen, "The Emerging Concept of Communication as Dialogue," *Quarterly Journal of Speech,* 57 (1971), 373–82; John Stewart, "Foundations of Dialogic Communication," *Quarterly Journal of Speech,* 64 (1978), 183–201.

26. Thomas B. Farrell, "Aspects of Coherence in Conversation and Rhetoric," in *Conversational Coherence: Studies in Form and Strategy,* ed. Robert Craig and Karen Tracey (Berkeley, CA: Sage Publications, Inc., 1983), pp. 259–85.

27. The "content-relationship" distinction permeates most modern treatments of interpersonal communication. One of the earliest statements of the distinction is Paul J. Watzlawick, J. H. Bevin, and Don D. Jackson, *Pragmatics of Human Communication* (New York: W. W. Norton, 1967).

28. Farrell, "Aspects," p. 271.

29. See, for example, Thomas S. Frentz and Thomas B. Farrell, "Language-Action: A Paradigm for Communication," *Quarterly Journal of Speech,* 62 (1976), 333–49; Thomas B. Farrell and Thomas S. Frentz, "Communication and Meaning: A Language-Action Synthesis," *Philosophy and Rhetoric,* 12 (1979), 215–55; and Thomas S. Frentz and Thomas B. Farrell, "Discourse, Coherence, and Episodic Duration," paper presented at the Western Speech Communication Convention, Denver, Colorado, February, 1981.

30. MacIntyre, p. 194. It is interesting to note that MacIntyre's entire discussion of the intelligibility of human action in terms of contexts parallels quite closely the language-action approach to meaning in communication. See, for example, Frentz and Farrell, "Language-Action;" Farrell and Frentz, "Communication and Meaning;" and Frentz and Farrell, "Discourse."

31. Walter R. Fisher, "Narration as a Human Communication Paradigm: The Case of Public Moral Argument," *Communication Monographs,* 51 (1984), 1–22.

32. Fisher, p. 11.

33. Frentz and Farrell, "Discourse."

34. Frentz and Farrell, "Language-Action," pp. 334–35.

35. Frentz and Farrell, "Language-Action," pp. 335–36.

36. Frentz and Farrell, "Language-Action," p. 336.

37. Ernst Cassirer, *The Philosophy of Symbolic Forms* (New Haven, CN: Yale University Press, 1957), III, p. 163.

38. Cassirer, p. 173.

39. St. Augustine, *Confessions,* trans. Rex Warner (New York: Mentor-Omega Books, 1963), p. 273.

40. Paul Tillich, *The Eternal Now* (New York: Charles Scribner's Sons, 1963), pp. 130–31.

41. My compliments to Thomas Farrell for this aphorism in a personal letter long gone but not forgotten.

42. I am not implying that only rhetorical conversations restructure the experience of time on the form of life level. Clearly, many conversations I would not identify as "rhetorical" perform this temporal

function. Intense discussions about important relationships, philosophical issues, or even the Green Bay Packers, can result in the participants experiencing time as an extended narrative through discourse. I am claiming that experiencing time as an extended present is a necessary, but not sufficient, condition for a conversation being rhetorical.

43. Subsequent references to the film will cite pages from the screenplay by Wallace Shawn and André Gregory, *My Dinner With André* (New York: Grove Press, Inc., 1981).

44. The Mass Communication Interest Group co-sponsored a program with the Language Behavior Interest Group to explore different approaches to *André* at the Western Speech Communication Association's regional convention in Seattle, Washington, February 18–21, 1984.

45. MacIntyre, pp. 22–34.

46. MacIntyre, p. 33.

47. Aristotle, *Rhetoric,* trans. W. Rhys Roberts, I, 1, 1354a.

48. Farrell, "Aspects."

49. MacIntyre, p. 204.

50. MacIntyre, pp. 1–5.

51. Aristotle, *Nicomachean Ethics,* trans. Martin Ostwald, I, 7, 1098a.

52. MacIntyre, p. 152.

53. See Eric A. Haylock, *Preface to Plato* (New York: Grosset And Dunlap, 1967), pp. 61–86.

54. Ken Wilber, *Up From Eden: A Transpersonal View of Human Evolution* (Boulder, CO: Shambhala Publications, Inc., 1981), p. 1.

55. Donald Phillip Verene, *Vico's Science of Imagination* (Ithaca, New York: Cornell University Press, 1981), p. 165.

56. Aristotle, *Posterior Analytics,* trans. G. R. G. Mure, in *The Basic Works of Aristotle,* ed. Richard McKeon (New York: Random House, 1941). II, 19, 100b. It is true that for Aristotle, dialectic can critically assess first principles to ascertain their casual efficacy and thereby their degree of belief (*pistis*), but the initial *discovery* of *archai,* is a matter for intuition and not dialectic.

57. Verene, p. 105.

58. Verene, pp. 65–95.

59. Ernesto Grassi, *Rhetoric As Philosophy* (University Park, PA: The Pennsylvania State University Press, 1980), p. 32.

60. Havelock, pp. 208–209.

61. Farrell, "The Tradition," p. 165.

Genre as Social Action
by Carolyn R. Miller

Although rhetorical criticism has recently provided a profusion of claims that certain discourses constitute a distinctive class, or genre, rhetorical theory has not provided firm guidance on what constitutes a genre. For example, rhetorical genres have been defined by similarities in strategies or forms in the discourses,[1] by similarities in audience,[2] by similarities in modes of thinking,[3] by similarities in rhetorical situations.[4] The diversity among these definitions presents both theorists and critics with a problem.

While this problem is created by rhetoricians who have done work in genre theory or criticism, another problem is raised by some who do not believe rhetoricians should do such work at all. John H. Patton and Thomas M. Conley have argued that genre criticism requires too much critical distance between the text and the reader and thus leads to assessments that are not fully responsible. Genre criticism, they contend, invites reductionism, rules, formalism. Patton believes that such analysis results in "critical determinism of the worst sort,"[5] and Conley that it leads to "tiresome and useless taxonomies."[6]

The urge to classify is fundamental, and although it involves the difficulties that Patton and Conley point out, classification is necessary to language and learning. The variety of critical approaches referred to above indicates the many ways one might classify discourse, but if the term "genre" is to mean anything theoretically or critically useful, it cannot refer to just any category or kind of discourse. One concern in rhetorical theory, then, is to make of rhetorical genre a stable classifying concept; another is to ensure that the concept is rhetorically sound.

In this essay, I will address both of these concerns, the first by developing a perspective on genre that relies on areas of agreement in previous work and connects those areas to corroborating material; the second concern I will address

Reprinted from *The Quarterly Journal of Speech* 70 (1984), with permission of the National Communication Association.

by proposing how an understanding of genre can help account for the way we encounter, interpret, react to, and create particular texts. My effort will elaborate the approach taken by Karlyn Kohrs Campbell and Kathleen Hall Jamieson and support their position that genre study is valuable not because it might permit the creation of some kind of taxonomy, but because it emphasizes some social and historical aspects of rhetoric that other perspectives do not.[7] I will be arguing that a rhetorically sound definition of genre must be centered not on the substance or the form of discourse but on the action it is used to accomplish. To do so, I will examine the connection between genre and recurrent situation and the way in which genre can be said to represent typified rhetorical action. My analysis will also show how hierarchical models of communication can help illuminate the nature and structure of such rhetorical action.

Classifying Discourse

A collection of discourses may be sorted into classes in more than one way, as Jackson Harrell and Wil A. Linkugel note in their discussion of genre.[8] Because a classification sorts items on the basis of some set of similarities, the principle used for selecting similarities can tell us much about the classification. A classification of discourse will be rhetorically sound if it contributes to an understanding of how discourse works—that is, if it reflects the rhetorical experience of the people who create and interpret the discourse. As Northrop Frye remarks, "The study of genres has to be founded on the study of convention."[9] A useful principle of classification for discourse, then, should have some basis in the conventions of rhetorical practice, including the ways actual rhetors and audiences have of comprehending the discourse they use.

The semiotic framework provides a way to characterize the principles used to classify discourse, according to whether the defining principle is based in rhetorical substance (semantics), form (syntactics), or the rhetorical action the discourse performs (pragmatics). A classifying principle based in rhetorical action seems most clearly to reflect rhetorical practice (especially since, as I will suggest later, action encompasses both substance and form). And if genre represents action, it must involve situation and motive, because human action, whether symbolic or otherwise, is interpretable only against a context of situation and through the attributing of motives.

"Motive" and "situation" are Kenneth Burke's terms, of course, and Campbell and Jamieson's discussion of genre leans on them implicitly, particularly the latter: "A genre," they write, "does not consist merely of a series of acts in which certain rhetorical forms recur. . . . Instead, a genre is composed of a constellation of recognizable forms bound together by an internal dynamic" (p. 21). The dynamic "fuses" substantive, stylistic, and situational characteristics. The fusion has the character of a rhetorical "response" to situational "demands" perceived by the rhetor. This definition, they maintain, "reflects Burke's view of rhetorical acts as strategies to encompass situations."[10]

Their explanation of genre also reflects Lloyd F. Bitzer's formulation of the relationship between situation and discourse, perhaps more than it does Burke's.[11] In Bitzer's definition of rhetorical situation as a "complex of persons, events, objects, and relations" presenting an "exigence" that can be allayed through the mediation of discourse, he establishes the demand-response vocabulary that Campbell and Jamieson adopt. Furthermore, he essentially points the way to genre study, although he does not use the term himself, in observing that situations recur: "From day to day, year to year, comparable situations occur, prompting comparable responses." The comparable responses, or recurring forms, become a tradition which then "tends to function as a constraint upon any new response in the form" (p. 13). Thus, inaugurals, eulogies, courtroom speeches, and the like have conventional forms because they arise in situations with similar structures and elements and because rhetors respond in similar ways, having learned from precedent what is appropriate and what effects their actions are likely to have on other people.

Campbell and Jamieson's approach to genre is also fundamentally Aristotelian. In each of the three kinds of rhetoric Aristotle described—deliberative, forensic, and epideictic—we find a situation-based fusion of form and substance. Each has its characteristic substance: the elements (exhortation and dissuasion, accusation and defense, praise and blame) and aims (expedience, justice, honor). Each has its appropriate forms (time or tense, proofs, and style). These fusions of substance and form are grounded in the specific situations calling for extended discourse in ancient Greece, including the audiences that were qualified to participate and the types of judgments they were called upon to make. The three kinds of rhetoric seem to be quite distinct, the various aspects of each to be part of a rational whole. It is likely that an internal "dynamic" of the sort Campbell and Jamieson postulate was at the center of each of these three original genres. (I will comment later on the current status of the Aristotelian genres.)

Two features of this approach are of interest at this point. First, Campbell and Jamieson's discussion yields a method of classification that meets the requirement of relevance to rhetorical practice. Since "rhetorical forms that establish genres are stylistic and substantive responses to perceived situational demands," a genre becomes a complex of formal and substantive features that create a particular effect in a given situation (p. 19). Genre, in this way, becomes more than a formal entity; it becomes pragmatic, fully rhetorical, a point of connection between intention and effect, an aspect of social action. This approach is different in an important way from those of Frye and Edwin Black, to which it is indebted. Although both begin by tying genre to situation, Frye with the "radical of presentation" (a kind of schematic rhetorical situation) and Black with the rhetorical "transaction" (emphasizing audience effects), they base their critical analyses on form: strategies, diction, linguistic elements. For them, situation serves primarily to locate a genre; it does not contribute to its character as rhetorical action.

The second feature of interest in Campbell and Jamieson's method is that they proceed inductively, as critics. They do not attempt to provide a framework that will predict or limit the genres that might be identified. Their interest is less in providing a taxonomic system than in explaining certain aspects of the way social reality evolves: "The critic who classifies a rhetorical artifact as generically akin to a class of similar artifacts has identified an undercurrent of history rather than comprehended an act isolated in time" (p. 26). The result is that the set of genres is an open class, with new members evolving, old ones decaying.[12]

In contrast to Campbell and Jamieson's approach is that of Harrell and Linkugel, who proceed deductively, as theorists. Their discussion illustrates one of the risks of theory, that it lends itself to the development of a closed set, usually consisting of few members—a neat taxonomic system that does not reflect rhetorical practice so much as an *a priori* principle. Harrell and Linkugel begin with a definition that seems similar to that of Campbell and Jamieson: "rhetorical genres stem from *organizing principles* found in *recurring situations* that generate discourse characterized by a family of *common factors*" (pp. 263–4). The "common factors" account for substantive and formal similarities among discourses of the same type, and the "organizing principles," defined as "assumptions that crystallize the central features of a type of discourse," seem not unlike the "internal dynamic" of Campbell and Jamieson (p. 264). However, Harrell and Linkugel make of the organizing principle not a dynamic resulting from the interaction of situation and forms but a theoretical premise, unrelated to situation. The organizing principles are based on fundamental "modes of thinking," each of which yields a principle of classification: *de facto,* structural, motivational, and archetypal. The organizing principles, in fact, do not distinguish classes of discourse; they distinguish methods of classifying discourse. The structural principle yields classes based on formal similarities, the motivational yields classes based on pragmatic similarities, and the archetypal yields classes based probably on substantive similarities; the *de facto* principle apparently yields an unsystematic classification. Harrell and Linkugel suggest, however, that the motivational principle will yield more "productive" generic groups because it better accounts for the interaction between rhetor and situation (in this respect, it seems to be the only principle that adheres to their original definition). To define motivational genres, they adopt Walter R. Fisher's formulation of four primary "motive states" defined in terms of the possible effects of discourse upon the life of an idea or ideology (affirmation, reaffirmation, purification, and subversion). Fisher's discussion relies on the Burkean conception that motives are found within or created by situations and that situations are perceived in terms of motives.[13]

In his own discussion of genre theory, Fisher presents four levels of genre constitution.[14] The most general level distinguishes rhetoric from other types of discourse; the second level includes classifications within rhetoric, including (among other possibilities) the four motives; the third contains the rhetorical forms that are commonly identified as genres (eulogies, apologies, nominating speeches, etc.); and the fourth consists of categories described in terms of style. Fisher's characterization is similar to Harrell and Linkugel's spectrum, for the four levels of generality require four different principles of classification.

Both of these discussions of genre are useful as ways of accounting for the variety of genre claims that have been made—indeed, they succeed better as classifications of genre criticism than as classifications of discourse. But as theories of genre they have two shortcomings. First, neither presents a single, clearly defined principle of classification that could promote critical agreement and theoretical clarity. The clearest principles that are presented lead to closed classifications, which sacrifice the diversity and dynamism of rhetorical practice to some theoretical *a priori*. And second, neither of these discussions grounds genre in situated rhetorical action. The closest approach is Fisher's four motives, but these operate at a level of abstraction that is too high to represent the practical rhetorical experience of those who use genres. That is, the description of motives in terms of the possible effects of discourse on ideas does not reflect the way human motivation is engaged by particular rhetorical situations. The four motives describe more about human nature than they do about rhetorical practice. And yet, the Burkean relationship between motive and situation that Fisher invokes is promising because it clearly requires an action-based (pragmatic) principle of classification. What is lacking is a connection between the motives and the kind of experience represented by Fisher's third level and by Harrell and Linkugel's *de facto* classification.

Scholars in other fields have been interested in classifying discourse, for both pedagogical and theoretical reasons, and these classifications have occasionally been adopted by rhetoricians as the equivalents of genres. But most of these systems can be dismissed here on the same points: either the classes do not represent rhetorical action or the system is not open. In the fields of literature and composition, classifications are commonly based upon formal rather than pragmatic elements. Rene Wellek and Austin Warren, for example, classify literary genres on both outer form (specific meter or structure) and inner form (attitude, tone, purpose, as revealed in textual details).[15] In the field of composition, Cleanth Brooks and Warren (following Alexander Bain and a long textbook tradition) describe a closed, formal system based nominally on intention but described according to form: exposition, argumentation, description, narration.[16] James L. Kinneavy has classified discourse on the basis of "aim," an apparently pragmatic basis, but he also arrives at a closed system with four members: expressive, persuasive, literary, and referential discourse.[17] Aim is determined by which of the four components of a communication model a discourse "focuses" on: sender, receiver, code, or reality. This scheme suggests a substantive rather than a pragmatic classification.[18] Linguists have also wrestled with the problem of classifying discourse, but their efforts have produced systems that are mostly formal.[19]

In sum, what I am proposing so far is that in rhetoric the term "genre" be limited to a particular type of discourse classification, a classification based in rhetorical practice and consequently open rather than closed and organized around situated actions (that is, pragmatic, rather than syntactic or semantic). I do not mean to suggest that there is only one way (or one fruitful way) to classify discourse. Classifications and distinctions based on form and substance have told us much about sentimentalism, women's liberation, and doctrinal movements, for example.[20] But we do not gain much by calling all such classes "genres." The classification I am advocating is, in effect, ethnomethodological: it seeks to explicate the knowledge that practice creates. This approach insists that the "de facto" genres, the types we have names for in everyday language, tell us something theoretically important about discourse. To consider as potential genres such homely discourse as the letter of recommendation, the user manual, the progress report, the ransom note, the lecture, and the white paper, as well as the eulogy, the apologia, the inaugural, the public proceeding, and the sermon, is not to trivialize the study of genres; it is to take seriously the rhetoric in which we are immersed and the situations in which we find ourselves.

The problems that remain in defining rhetorical genre become somewhat more specific than those so far considered. First is the problem of clarifying the relationship between rhetoric and its context of situation; this is central to understanding genre as rhetorical action. Second is the problem of understanding the way in which a genre "fuses" (in Campbell and Jamieson's term) situational with formal and substantive textures. And third is the problem of locating genre on a hierarchical scale of generalizations about language use, in effect, of choosing among Fisher's four levels.

Recurrent Rhetorical Situations

Although Burke and Bitzer have both used the term "rhetorical situation," Bitzer's work brought a specific version into prominence in rhetorical theory.[21] One crucial difference between the two is Burke's use of *motive* and Bitzer's of *exigence* as the focus of situation. Although the two concepts are related, there is a tension between them that requires resolution before the relation of genre to situation can be clear. Burke's emphasis is on human action, whereas Bitzer's appears to be on *reaction*. In particular, Bitzer's use of demand-response language has made it possible to conceive of exigence as an external cause of discourse and situation as deterministic, interpretations that have been widely discussed.[22] Because these interpretations create problems for genre theory, a reconceptualization of exigence is necessary if genre is to be understood as social action.

Bitzer, Alan Brinton, and Patton all emphasize the ontological status of situations as real, objective, historical events.[23] All three describe situation as consisting of two sorts of components: Patton refers to the external and internal components, Brinton to objective and subjective, and Bitzer, in a later essay, to the factual and interest components of exigence.[24] All three regard the first term as fundamental, as the real part of situation, and the second as a perceptual screen. Patton believes, for instance, that objective phenomena serve as the basis for assessing the "accuracy" of perception. Brinton concludes that the factual component *is* the exigence and that consequently there may be "absolute" exigences. Bitzer also describes exigence as being independent of human awareness: "If drinking water contains a very high level of mercury, then surely an exigence exists even though no one is aware of the factual condition" (''Functional Communication,'' p. 31). For him, exigence can be synonymous with danger.[25] An account of the relationship between rhetoric and situation that thus empowers external, objective elements of situation is a theory that, in Kenneth Burke's terms, features scene above any other source of motive. Such a theory he characterized as "materialist" in a prophetic passage in *The Grammar of Motives:* "with materialism," says Burke, "the circumference of scene is so narrowed as to involve the reduction of action to motion."[26] Much of the debate regarding situational theory has concerned ways of mitigating the materialist interpretation of it.

What is particularly important about rhetorical situations for a theory of genres is that they recur, as Bitzer originally noted, but in order to understand recurrence, it is necessary to reject the materialist tendencies in situational theory. Campbell and Jamieson observe that in rhetoric "the existence of the recurrent provides insight into the human condition" (p. 27); in the materialist account, the recurrent would lead instead to scientific generalizations. Recurrence is implied by our understanding of situations as somehow "comparable," "similar," or "analogous" to other situations, but, as Robert A. Stebbins notes, "objective situations are unique"—they cannot recur.[27] What recurs cannot be a material configuration of objects, events, and people, nor can it be a subjective configuration, a "perception," for these, too, are unique from moment to moment and person to person. Recurrence is an intersubjective phenomenon, a social occurrence, and cannot be understood on materialist terms.[28]

Situations are social constructs that are the result, not of "perception," but of "definition." Because human action is based on and guided by meaning, not by material causes, at the center of action is a process of interpretation. Before we can act, we must interpret the indeterminate material environment; we define, or "determine," a situation. It is possible to arrive at common determinations of material states of affairs that may have many possible interpretations because, as Alfred Schutz has argued, our "stock of knowledge" is based upon types: "We can . . . imagine a type to be like a line of demarcation which runs between the determinations explicated on the basis of the 'hitherto existing' relevance structures . . . and the . . . unlimited possibilities for the determination of experience."[29] In other words, our stock of knowledge is useful only insofar as it can be brought to bear upon new experience: the new is made familiar through the recognition of relevant similarities; those similarities become constituted as a type. A new type is formed from typifications already on hand when they are not adequate to determine a new situation. If a new typification proves continually useful for mastering states of affairs, it enters the stock of knowledge and its application becomes routine. Although types evolve in this way, most of our stock of knowledge is quite stable. Schutz notes that because types are created and shared through communication, they come to reside in language:

> Whatever is typically relevant for the individual was for the most part already typically relevant for his predecessors and has consequently deposited its semantic equivalent in the language. In short, the language can be construed as the sedimentation of typical experiential schemata which are typically relevant in a society (p. 234).

Schutz's account of types is useful to a theory of rhetorical genres because it shows the importance of classification to human action. It is through the process of typification that we create recurrence, analogies, similarities. What recurs is not a material situation (a real, objective, factual event) but our construal of a type. The typified situation, including typifications of participants, underlies typification in rhetoric. Successful communication would require that the participants share common types; this is possible insofar as types are socially created (or biologically innate).

The linguist M. A. K. Halliday provides a corroborating perspective on situation types: "the apparently infinite number of different possible situations represents in reality a very much smaller number of general *types* of situations, which we can describe in such terms as 'players instructing novice in a game,' 'mother reading bedtime story to child,' 'customer ordering goods over the telephone,' 'teacher guiding pupils,' 'discussion of a poem,' and the like."[30] Typification is possible, here again, because situation "is not an inventory of ongoing sights and sounds but a semiotic structure" (p. 122). Moreover, the situation type is the developmental basis for meaning. In his work on the development of language in the child, Halliday finds that the child first learns a restricted set of functions that language can accomplish: "The child's uses of language are interpretable as generalized situation types; the meanings that he can express are referable to specific social contexts."[31] These original, limited uses of language expand as the child encounters and conceives a wide variety of social contexts, and "the adult has indefinitely many uses of language" ("Learning to Mean," p. 253). Systematizing or classifying the uses of adult language would, therefore, be difficult, according to Halliday: "the nearest we can come to that is some concept of situation type" (*Language as Social Semiotic,* p. 46).

If rhetorical situation is not material and objective, but a social construct, or semiotic structure, how are we to understand exigence, which is at the core of situation? Exigence must be located in the social world, neither in a private perception nor in material circumstance. It cannot be broken into two components without destroying it as a rhetorical and social phenomenon. Exigence is a form of social knowledge—a mutual construing of objects, events, interests, and purposes that not only links them but also makes them what they are: an objectified social need. This is quite different from Bitzer's characterization of exigence as a "defect" or danger. Conversely, although exigence provides the rhetor with a sense of rhetorical purpose, it is clearly not the same as the rhetor's intention, for that can be ill-formed, dissembling, or at odds with what the situation conventionally supports. The exigence provides the rhetor with a socially recognizable way to make his or her intentions known. It provides an occasion, and thus a form, for making public our private versions of things.

Bitzer argues that when Gerald Ford pardoned former President Nixon, Ford saw the exigence as "protection of the national interest, which would be harmed if Watergate were not put behind us as quickly as possible," while other citizens saw the exigence as seeing justice done ("Functional Communication," p. 30). The exigence, however, was what served as the grounds for Ford's doing anything at all—the need to establish a relationship with the previous administration, an exigence with unusual constraints in this case and one that could engage any of several particular *intentions.*

Exigence must be seen neither as a cause of rhetorical action nor as intention, but as social motive. To comprehend an exigence is to have a motive. Except in a primitive sense, our motives are not private or idiosyncratic; they are products of our socialization, as Burke makes clear: "Motives are distinctly linguistic products. We discern situational patterns by means of the particular vocabulary of the cultural group into which we are born."[32] Schutz says much the same thing: "Typified patterns of the Others' behavior become in turn motives of my own actions."[33] Exigence is a set of particular social patterns and expectations that provides a socially objectified motive for addressing danger, ignorance, separateness. It is an understanding of social need in which I know how to take an interest, in which one can intend to participate. By "defining" a material circumstance as a particular situation type, I find a way to engage my intentions in it in a socially recognizable and interpretable way. As Burke put it, "motives are shorthand terms for situations" (*Permanence and Change,* p. 29).

Herbert Blumer observed that "the preponderant portion of social action in a human society, particularly in a settled society, exists in the form of recurrent patterns of joint action."[34] Here is a rationale for the study of rhetorical genres. To base a classification of discourse upon recurrent situation or, more specifically, upon exigence understood as social motive, is to base it upon the typical joint rhetorical actions available at a given point in history and culture. Studying the typical uses of rhetoric, and the forms that it takes in those uses, tells us less about the art of individual rhetors or the excellence of particular texts than it does about the character of a culture or an historical period. For example, David Kaufer makes a telling point about classical Greek rhetoric when he observes that the "number of definable types of rhetorical situations in Classical culture appears both curiously small and stable."[35] The three Aristotelian genres signal a particular and limited role for rhetoric, according to Kaufer, but a very important one: maintaining "the normal functions of the state."

By contrast, Burke observes that in an age of "marked instability" such as ours, typical patterns are not widely shared and hence the matter of motivation is "liquid" (*Permanence and Change,* pp. 32–33). We may not know our own motives, we cannot name them, what recurs for me does not for someone else; with a wealth of stimuli and a dearth of shared knowledge, we hardly know how to engage each other in discourse. We have many and confused intentions, but few effective orientation centers for joint action. This may be why the whole matter of genre has become problematic.

Hierarchical Theories of Meaning

If we understand genres as typified rhetorical actions based in recurrent situations, we must conclude that members of a genre are discourses that are complete, in the sense that they are circumscribed by a relatively complete shift in rhetorical situation. Thus, we should recognize a lecture or a eulogy or a technical manual or a public proceeding by our determination of the typified rhetorical situation. But this does not go very far toward indicating how the genre works as rhetorical action, how we come to understand the generic meaning of "eulogy" as fitting to the social exigence that a death produces. The "generic fusion" that Campbell and Jamieson predicate of substantive, stylistic, and situational elements is, in their view, the key to understanding the meaningfulness or "significance" of a genre. Again using semiotic terminology, it is possible to explicate this "fusion" and to specify how it is central to a theory of meaning.

A particular kind of fusion of substance and form is essential to symbolic meaning. Substance, considered as the semantic value of discourse, constitutes the aspects of common experience that are being symbolized. Burke maintains that substance is drawn from our "acting-together," which gives us "common sensations, concepts, images, ideas, attitudes."[36] Form is perceived as the ways in which substance is symbolized. Campbell and Jamieson adopt Burke's understanding of form as "an arousing and fulfillment of desires. A work has form in so far as one part of it leads a reader to anticipate another part, to be gratified by the sequence."[37] Form shapes the response of the reader or listener to substance by providing instruction, so to speak, about how to perceive and interpret; this guidance disposes the audience to anticipate, to be gratified, to respond in a certain way. Seen thus, form becomes a kind of meta-information, with both semantic value (as information) and syntactic (or formal) value. Form and substance thus bear a hierarchical relationship to each other.

This hierarchical relationship is implicit in speech-act theory, where meaning, according to John Searle, has two elements: an utterance or proposition and the action it is used to perform, indicated as illocutionary force.[38] But such meaning-as-action exists only within a larger interpretive context. Stephen Toulmin explains how Wittgenstein described context:

> Any expression owes its linguistic meaning (Wittgenstein taught) to having been given a standard rule-governed use or uses, in the context of such activities [language-games]. Language-games in turn, however, must be understood in their own broader contexts; and for those contexts Wittgenstein introduced the phrase "forms of life."[39]

This description suggests that context is a third hierarchical level to meaning, encompassing both substance and form and enabling interpretation of the action resulting from their fusion.

But since context itself is hierarchical, as Toulmin emphasizes, we can think of form, substance, and context as relative, not absolute; they occur at many levels on a hierarchy of meaning. When form and substance are fused at one level, they acquire semantic value which is then subject to formalizing at a higher level. At one level, for example, the semantic values of a string of words and their syntactic relationships in a sentence acquire meaning (pragmatic value as action) when together they serve as substance for the higher-level form of the speech act. In turn, this combination of substance and form acquires meaning when it serves as substance for the still higher-level form imposed by, say, a language-game. Thus, form at one level becomes an aspect of substance at a higher level (this is what makes form "significant"), although it is still analyzable as form at the lower level. Figure 1 diagrams this kind of progression. It is through this hierarchical combination of form and substance that symbolic structures take on pragmatic force and become interpretable actions; when fused, the substantive and formal components can acquire meaning in context. A complex hierarchy of such relationships is necessary for constructing meaning.

Two recent communication models instantiate this hierarchical principle in remarkably similar ways; together, they suggest a connection between rhetorical genre and the hierarchical fusion of form and substance. One model, developed by Thomas S. Frentz and Thomas B. Farrell, is grounded specifically in action theory and makes explicit use of the rules approach to communication. The "paradigm" they propose consists of three "hierarchically structured constructs": context, episodes, and symbolic acts. Context "specifies the criteria for interpreting both the meaningfulness and propriety of any communicative event."[40] It consists of two hierarchical levels—form of life and encounters. "Form of life," Wittgenstein's term, is used by Frentz and Farrell to refer to the cultural patterns, both linguistic and nonlinguistic, that give significance to actions, both linguistic and nonlinguistic. Encounters, the second level of context, "particularize form of life through rules of propriety" (p. 335); they are "points of contact" in concrete locations, providing the specific situational dimension to context. The second level of the hierarchy is the episode, a "rule-conforming sequence of symbolic acts generated by two or more actors who are collectively oriented toward emergent goals" (p. 336). And the third and lowest level of the model is the symbolic act, the "component" of the episode. Symbolic acts are "verbal and/or nonverbal utterances which express intentionality" (p. 340), characterized in much the way Searle describes speech acts.

Another hierarchical model of communication, proposed by W. Barnett Pearce and Forrest Conklin, addresses the problem of interpreting nonliteral meanings in conversation.[41] Pearce's earlier work found that conversational coherence requires

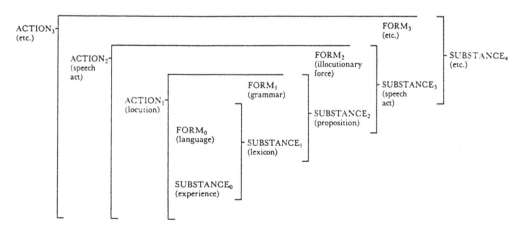

FIG. 8.1. Hierarchical relationships of substance, form, and meaning-as-action. The combination of form and substance at one level becomes an action (has meaning) at a higher level when that combination itself acquires form. Each action is interpretable against the context provided by actions at higher levels.

"coordinated management of meaning" among participants and that such coordination is accomplished through rules. In the later model, each level of meaning provides a context for constituents at lower levels by means of rule-governed relationships. The model consists of five levels in all: archetypes, episodes, speech acts, propositions (grammatical utterances), and the stream of behavior that must be interpreted. Archetypes are "those fundamental logical operations or symbolic reasoning procedures which persons use to detect or generate patterns in the sequence of events." These are based on the common physiology that human beings share and in the common physical properties of the world they live in (p. 78). Episodes are "sequences of messages which have a starting and a stopping point and an internal structure"; these patterned sequences provide the context for speech acts. The hierarchical levels are connected by sets of rules that coordinate cognitive movement between them. Between the top two levels are rules of symbolic identification; between the second two are rules of sociation; between the third and fourth are rules of communication; and between the last two, rules of information processing.

These two hierarchical schemes are persuasive, in part because of their comprehensiveness, in part because of their similarities, and in part because of their consistency with other social and psychological theory.[42] Although neither one has anything explicit to say about rhetorical genre, they provide a background for understanding genre as meaningful action that is rule governed (which is to say interpretable by means of conventions).[43]

Sharon D. Downey, moreover, has provided a rule-based explication of genre that is consistent with these two schemes; she defines genre as "a classification of rhetorical discourses whose recurrent constitutive and regulative rules are similar in distinction and pattern."[44] In the terms I have been using, her explanation maintains that it is constitutive rules that tell us how to fuse form and substance to make meaning and regulative rules that tell us how the fusion itself is to be interpreted within its context. For example, conventions of form and substance combine according to constitutive rules to create the typified rhetorical action of the eulogy; in addition, the action is interpretable under regulative rules provided by larger contexts, like religion or public affairs. Seen this way, the rhetorical genre is clearly analogous to the levels of meaning of the two communication models.

Figure 2 proposes a hierarchy similar to these models but including genre. Genre appears at a level of complete discourse types based on recurrent situations; genres are provided interpretive context by form-of-life patterns and are constituted by intermediate forms or strategies, analogous to the dialogic episode. Because communication must rest on experience, the lowest level must be that in which symbolizing takes place. Beyond symbols, experience is idiosyncratic and incommunicable. At the other extreme, we can envision universal experience, or the biological-psychological nature of the human species, Burke's "universal" rhetorical situation (*Rhetoric,* p. 146). Burke, in fact, offers a range of motives that spans both extremes of the hierarchy:

Proposed Hierarchy	Frentz and Farrell's Hierarchy	Pearce and Conklin's Hierarchy
Human Nature		Archetype
Culture		
Form of Life	Form of Life	
Genre	Encounter	
Episode or Strategy	Episode	Episode
Speech Act	Symbolic Act	Speech Act
Locution		Proposition
Language		
Experience		Behavior

FIG. 8.2. Proposed hierarchy of meaning, incorporating genre, compared with those of Frentz and Farrell and of Pearce and Conklin. Note the relationship of the four lowest levels in the proposed hierarchy to Figure 1; the higher levels would extend that figure beyond three levels of action.

Each man's motivation is unique, since his situation is unique, which is particularly obvious when you recall that his situation also reflects the unique sequence of his past. However, for all this uniqueness of the individual, there are motives and relationships generic to all mankind—and these are intrinsic to human agents as a class (*Grammar,* pp. 103–4).

At the level of the locution or speech act, idiosyncratic motives (or what I earlier called intentions) predominate. At the level of human nature (or archetypes) motives of the sort that Fisher describes have their force. But at the level of the genre, motive becomes a conventionalized social purpose, or exigence, within the recurrent situation. In constructing discourse, we deal with purposes at several levels, not just one. We learn to adopt social motives as ways of satisfying private intentions through rhetorical action. This is how recurring situations seem to "invite" discourse of a particular type.

The exact number of hierarchical levels of meaning may not be determinable with any precision, and it may be that different kinds of communication emphasize different levels. Because monologue and dialogue pose different problems, for example, they probably operate with differing hierarchical structures. In dialogue, because the audience tends to be small and constraints managed through interactive coordination, personal intentions manifest themselves more easily. Such interaction requires elaboration of the rule structure at the lower levels of the hierarchy, to guide turn-taking, implicature, and management of multiple intentions. In monologue, personal intentions must be accommodated to public exigences—because the audience is larger, the opportunity for complex statement is greater, and constraints are less easily managed; more elaborate rule structures at the upper end of the hierarchy, at the level of whole discourses, are therefore necessary for both formulation and interpretation.

As Herbert W. Simons observed, one of the important problems raised by recent genre theory is that "genres 'exist' at various levels of abstraction, from the very broad to the very specific" (p. 36). Indeed, the classifications of Fisher and of Harrell and Linkugel illustrated this problem. But if we define genre by its association with recurrent rhetorical situations, the exact hierarchical level at which the abstraction called genre occurs will be determined by our sense of recurrence of rhetorical situations; this will vary from culture to culture, according to the typifications available. Thus, the term "genre" might under differing circumstances be applied to the class of all public addresses in a society, to the class of all inaugural speeches, or to the class of all American presidential inaugurals.

It is worth noting, in addition, that there are two kinds of hierarchies to which genre may be seen to belong, and it is helpful to keep them distinct. One kind arranges single discourses into classes and the classes into broader classes; this is the kind to which Simons refers. The other arranges constituents into units and units into larger wholes (words, sentences, speech acts, texts, etc.), in the manner of the hierarchies in Figure 2.[45] Genre is hierarchical in both senses, but the second has more to do with its rhetorical significance, that is, the way it works as a source of meaning.

Implications

The understanding of rhetorical genre that I am advocating is based in rhetorical practice, in the conventions of discourse that a society establishes as ways of "acting together." It does not lend itself to taxonomy, for genres change, evolve, and decay; the number of genres current in any society is indeterminate and depends upon the complexity and diversity of the society. The particular features of this under-standing of genre are these:

1. Genre refers to a conventional category of discourse based in large-scale typification of rhetorical action; as action, it acquires meaning from situation and from the social context in which that situation arose.
2. As meaningful action, genre is interpretable by means of rules; genre rules occur at a relatively high level on a hierarchy of rules for symbolic interaction.
3. Genre is distinct from form: form is the more general term used at all levels of the hierarchy. Genre is a form at one particular level that is a fusion of lower-level forms and characteristic substance.
4. Genre serves as the substance of forms at higher levels; as recurrent patterns of language use, genres help constitute the substance of our cultural life.
5. A genre is a rhetorical means for mediating private intentions and social exigence; it motivates by connecting the private with the public, the singular with the recurrent.

Although this perspective on genre is not precise enough to permit quantification of formal features or elucidation of a complete hierarchy of rules, it can provide guidance in the evaluation of genre claims. Specifically, it suggests that a collection of discourses (or a potential collection) may fail to constitute a genre in three major ways. First, there may fail to be significant substantive or formal similarities at the lower levels of the hierarchy. Genre claims are rarely made without this kind of first-line evidence, however. Second, there may be inadequate consideration of all the elements in recurrent rhetorical situations. A genre claim may be based on similarities only in exigence or only in audience, etc. This type of claim is sometimes made about particularly novel or subtle combinations of forms by which a rhetor addresses a situation. In such a case, however, the rhetorical situation will be differently construed by rhetor and audience. The discourse constitutes an adaptation of form and substance to a private purpose, not a public exigence; the particular fusion achieved is based not on all the recurrent aspects of situation but on the unique ones. Ronald H. Carpenter's study of the historical jeremiad makes such a claim, based on evidence that three works "share salient formal characteristics."[46] But these works, rather, adapt the genre of historical essay to personal goals: they do not constitute another genre, because the motive that makes the discourse a social action is shared only for the historical essay, not for the jeremiad.

Another more general failure of this second sort is the attempt to use the Aristotelian types to identify contemporary genres. Although developed from recurrent situations in ancient Greece, these original genres do not describe complete situation-types that recur today—they are too general. Michael Halloran has suggested, for instance, that the public proceeding is a specialized and elaborated descendant of the epideictic genre; his analysis shows the public proceeding to be based in a recurrent situation (with several variants) and to involve elements of all three Aristotelian genres. For us, epideictic serves not as a single genre but as a form of life—a celebratory (or reaffirmative) arena of social life in which situation-types develop. The original genres also persist as constituent strategies of contemporary genres. Jamieson and Campbell's recent discussion of the rhetorical hybrid develops this point by noting the ways critics have found the three original genres permeating each other in practice and by offering an extended critique of several hybrids in recent American political rhetoric. The hybrid—a transient combination of forms based in a nonrecurrent (or not yet recurrent) situation—is itself not a genre but the adaptation of a genre to "the idiosyncratic needs of a particular situation, institution, and rhetor" (p. 157). In their analysis of the deliberative eulogy, it is clear that hybridization occurs not between genres but between subforms, on the level of what I have called strategies: in their examples of the eulogies of Robert Kennedy, "eulogistic [generic] requirements predominate and deliberative appeals [strategies] are subordinate" (p. 150).

The third way a genre claim may fail is if there is no pragmatic component, no way to understand the genre as a social action. In a study of Environmental Impact Statements during their first five years, I concluded that this clearly defined class of documents did not constitute a rhetorical genre because it did not achieve a rational fusion of elements—in spite of obvious similarities in form and substance, and in spite of a recurring rhetorical situation that was, in fact, defined by law.[47] These documents had no coherent pragmatic force for two reasons: first, the cultural forms in which they were embedded provided conflicting interpretive contexts; and second, there was no satisfactory fusion of substance and form that could serve as substance to higher-level forms and contexts. For example, the probabilistic judgments that are the substance of environmental science conflicted with the formal requirements of objectivity and quantification; further, the patterns of thinking in the context of administrative bureaucracies created a set of values at variance with the environmental values invoked by the legislation requiring impact statements. Overall, the imperfect fusion of scientific, legal, and administrative elements prevented interpretation of the documents as meaningful rhetorical action. This conclusion was, of course, substantiated by the legal and administrative problems the early impact statements created and their frequent criticism in industry, government, and the environmental movement.

What are the implications of the absence of a genre on the meaning-hierarchy? To say that a genre does not exist is not to imply that there are no interpretive rules at that level on the hierarchy. It means that the rules do not form a normative whole that we can consider a cultural artifact, that is, a representation of reasoning and purposes characteristic of the culture. The class of discourses is just a class of discourses; the set of rules is just a set of rules. But further, the absence of a normative whole at that level poses problems of certain kinds. It means that the interpreter must have a strong understanding of forms at both higher and lower levels, in order to bridge the gap at the level of genre. Similarly, in reading written discourse, we must base inferences about probable speech acts on strongly delineated propositions, at the level below, and strategies or episodes, at the level above.

The perspective on genres proposed here has implications not only for criticism and theory, but also for rhetorical education. It suggests that what we learn when we learn a genre is not just a pattern of forms or even a method of achieving our own ends. We learn, more importantly, what ends we may have: we learn that we may eulogize, apologize, recommend one person to another, instruct customers on behalf of a manufacturer, take on an official role, account for progress in achieving goals. We learn to understand better the situations in which we find ourselves and the potentials for failure and success in acting together. As a recurrent, significant action, a genre embodies an aspect of cultural rationality. For the critic, genres can serve both as an index to cultural patterns and as tools for exploring the achievements of particular speakers and writers; for the student, genres serve as keys to understanding how to participate in the actions of a community.

Notes

1. Edwin Black, *Rhetorical Criticism: A Study in Method* (Madison: University of Wisconsin Press, 1978); Karlyn Kohrs Campbell, "The Rhetoric of Women's Liberation: An Oxymoron," *Quarterly Journal of Speech,* 59 (1973), 74–86; Roderick P. Hart, "The Rhetoric of the True Believer," *Speech Monographs,* 38 (1971), 249–61; Richard D. Raum and James S. Measell, "Wallace and His Ways: A Study of the Rhetorical Genre of Polarization," *Central States Speech Journal,* 25 (1974), 28–35.
2. G. P. Mohrmann and Michael C. Leff, "Lincoln at Cooper Union: A Rationale for Neo-Classical Criticism," *Quarterly Journal of Speech,* 60 (1974), 459–67.
3. Bruce Gronbeck, "Celluloid Rhetoric: On Genres of Documentary," in *Form and Genre: Shaping Rhetorical Action,* ed. Karlyn Kohrs Campbell and Kathleen Hall Jamieson (Falls Church, VA: Speech Communication Association, 1978), pp. 139–61; Raymond S. Rodgers, "Generic Tendencies in Majority and Non-Majority Supreme Court Opinions: The Case of Justice Douglas," *Communication Quarterly,* 30 (1982), 232–36.
4. B. L. Ware and Wil A. Linkugel, "They Spoke in Defense of Themselves: On the Generic Criticism of Apologia," *Quarterly Journal of Speech,* 59 (1973), 273–83; Michael Halloran, "Doing Public

Business in Public," in Campbell and Jamieson, pp. 118–38; Theodore Otto Windt, Jr., "The Diatribe: Last Resort for Protest," *Quarterly Journal of Speech,* 58 (1972), 1—14.

5. John H. Patton, "Generic Criticism: Typology at an Inflated Price," *Rhetoric Society Quarterly,* 6 (1976), 5.

6. Thomas M. Conley, "Ancient Rhetoric and Modern Genre Criticism," *Communication Quarterly,* 27 (1979), 53; see also his review of Campbell and Jamieson in *Communication Quarterly,* 26 (1978), 71–75.

7. Karlyn Kohrs Campbell and Kathleen Hall Jamieson, "Form and Genre in Rhetorical Criticism: An Introduction," in Campbell and Jamieson, pp. 9–32. Further references to this essay will be made in the text.

8. Jackson Harrell and Wil A. Linkugel, "On Rhetorical Genre: An Organizing Perspective," *Philosophy and Rhetoric,* 11 (1978), 262–81; their essay, like this one, is motivated by the belief that rhetorical criticism suffers from the lack of a good theory of genres. Further references to this essay will be made in the text.

9. Northrop Frye, *Anatomy of Criticism* (Princeton: Princeton University Press, 1957), esp. pp. 243–51; and Black, ch. 5.

10. Kathleen Hall Jamieson and Karlyn Kohrs Campbell, "Rhetorical Hybrids: Fusions of Generic Elements," *Quarterly Journal of Speech,* 68 (1982), 146.

11. Lloyd F. Bitzer, "The Rhetorical Situation," *Philosophy and Rhetoric,* 1 (1968), 1–14.

12. It should be noted that this type of induction is different from that advocated by Herbert Simons (" 'Genrealizing' About Rhetoric: A Scientific Approach," in Campbell and Jamieson, pp. 33–50). Although Simons defines a genre is the fusion of forms *exemplified by* a text or texts; the genre represents "not only . . . what has recurred but . . . what may recur" (p. 24).

13. Walter R. Fisher, "A Motive View of Communication," *Quarterly Journal of Speech,* 56 (1970), 131–39.

14. Walter R. Fisher, "Genre: Concepts and Applications in Rhetorical Criticism," *Western Journal of Speech Communication* 44 (1980), 288–99.

15. Rene Wellek and Austin Warren, *Theory of Literature,* 3rd ed. (New York: Harcourt Brace Jovanovich, 1977), pp. 226–37.

16. Cleanth Brooks and Robert Penn Warren, *Modern Rhetoric,* 4th ed. (New York: Harcourt Brace Jovanovich, 1979), p. 40. This system is adapted from George Campbell's classification of the ends of speaking; see Robert J. Connors, "The Rise and Fall of the Modes of Discourse," *College Composition and Communication,* 32 (1981), 444–55.

17. James L. Kinneavy, *A Theory of Discourse: The Aims of Discourse* (Englewood Cliffs, NJ: Prentice-Hall, 1971).

18. "The language process seems to be capable of focusing attention on one of its own components as primary in a given situation" (p. 59). The fundamental problem in Kinneavy's system is the confusion of "aim" with "use": "The different uses of language are . . . a matter of which element of the [language] process dominates" (p. 38). See Walter H. Beale, "On the Classification of Discourse Performances," *Rhetoric Society Quarterly,* 7 (1977), 31–40, for a more complete critique of Kinneavy's work.

19. See the work of Teun A. van Dijk: *Text and Context: Explorations in the Semantics and Pragmatics of Discourse* (New York: Longman, 1977) and *Macrostructures* (Hillsdale, NJ: Lawrence Erlbaum, 1980). For a classification based on M. A. K. Halliday's work in sociolinguistics, see John Frow, "Discourse Genres," *Journal of Literary Semantics,* 9 (1980),73–81.

20. See Edwin Black, "The Sentimental Style as Escapism, or The Devil with Daniel Webster," in Campbell and Jamieson, pp. 75–86, and the essays by Campbell and Hart, cited earlier.

21. See Burke's "The Rhetorical Situation," in *Communication: Ethical and Moral Issues,* ed. Lee Thayer (New York: Gordon and Breach, 1973), pp. 263–75.

22. See Richard Vatz, "The Myth of the Rhetorical Situation," *Philosophy and Rhetoric,* 6 (1973), 154–61; Scott Consigny, "Rhetoric and its Situations," *Philosophy and Rhetoric,* 7 (1974), 175–86; and the exchanges among Philip K. Tompkins, Patton, Vatz, and Bitzer in the "Forum," *Quarterly Journal of Speech,* 66 (1980), 85–93 and 67 (1981), 93–101.

23. Alan Brinton, "Situation in the Theory of Rhetoric," *Philosophy and Rhetoric,* 14 (1981), 234–47; and John H. Patton, "Causation and Creativity in Rhetorical Situations: Distinctions and Implications," *Quarterly Journal of Speech,* 65 (1979), 5.

24. Lloyd F. Bitzer, "Functional Communication: A Situational Perspective," in *Rhetoric in Transition,* ed. Eugene E. White (University Park, PA: Pennsylvania State University Press, 1980).

25. In an earlier statement, Bitzer seemed aware of the problem into which this example of the drinking water leads him. In the 1980 "Forum," he wrote, "exigences are not 'objective' in the sense of being

simply factual; nor are exigences wholly independent of human apprehension" (p. 90). Robert Scott points out that "Bitzer's insistence throughout on *reality* and not *sociality* is no accident in the fashion of terms" ("Intentionality in the Rhetorical Process," in White, p. 57). He suggests a revaluation of the situational theory to recognize the intentionality of beings who act within a social reality.

26. Kenneth Burke, *A Grammar of Motives* (Berkeley: University of California Press, 1969), p.131. Materialism is not an exhaustive characterization of Bitzer's discussion of situation. In "Functional Communication," especially, there are strong elements of pragmatism, which Burke characterizes as the featuring of agency, and to the extent that Bitzer features the capacity of the rhetorical act to effect change, his work illustrates what Burke calls realism. In contrast, Vatz's emphasis on the creative power of the rhetor corresponds to the featuring of agent, which Burke characterizes as idealism.

27. Robert A. Stebbins, "A Theory of the Definition of the Situation," *Canadian Review of Sociology and Anthropology,* 4 (1967), 154; see also J. Robert Cox, "Argument and the Definition of the Situation," *Central States Speech Journal,* 32 (1981), 197–205.

28. As Bruce Gronbeck has observed, in a theory of communication based on social facts, "the idea of 'cause' almost disappears." "Qualitative Communication Theory and Rhetorical Studies in the 1980s," *Central States Speech Journal,* 32 (1981), 253.

29. Alfred Schutz and Thomas Luckmann, *The Structures of the Life-World,* trans. Richard M. Zaner and H. Tristram Engelhardt, Jr. (Evanston, IL: Northwestern University Press, 1973), p. 231.

30. M. A. K. Halliday, *Language as Social Semiotic. The Social Interpretation of Language and Meaning* (Baltimore: University Park Press, 1978), p. 29.

31. M. A. K. Halliday, "Learning to Mean," in *Children and Language,* ed. Sinclair Rogers (Oxford University Press, 1975), p. 255.

32. Kenneth Burke, *Permanance and Change* (Indianapolis, IN: Bobbs-Merrill, 1965), p. 35. Fisher's discussion of motives builds upon this same theme in Burke's work.

33. Alfred Schutz, *Collected Papers 1: The Problem of Social Reality,* ed. Maurice Natanson (The Hague: Martinus Nijhoff, 1971) p. 60.

34. Herbert Blumer, "Symbolic Interaction" in *Interdisciplinary Approaches to Human Communication,* ed. R. W. Budd and B. D. Rubens (Rochelle Park, NJ: Hayden, 1979), 148.

35. David Kaufer, "Point of View in Rhetorical Situations: Classical and Romantic Contrasts and Contemporary Implications," *Quarterly Journal of Speech,* 65 (1979), 176.

36. Kenneth Burke, *A Rhetoric of Motives* (Berkeley: University of California Press, 1969), p. 21.

37. Kenneth Burke, *Counter-Statement* (Berkeley: University of California Press, 1968), p. 124.

38. John Searle, *Speech Acts: An Essay on the Philosophy of Language* (London: Cambridge University Press, 1969), pp. 16–17.

39. Stephen Toulmin, "Concepts and the Exploration of Human Behavior," in *Human Action: Conceptual and Empirical Issues,* ed. Theodore Mischel (New York: Academic Press, 1969), pp. 73–74. Recent literary theory similarly emphasizes the impossibility of interpreting a work outside of a context or framework of expectations; see, for example, Stanley Fish, "Normal Circumstances, Literal Language, Direct Speech Acts, the Ordinary, the Everyday, the Obvious, What Goes Without Saying, and Other Special Cases," *Critical Inquiry,* 4 (1978), 625–44; Walter Benn Michaels, "Against Formalism: The Autonomous Text in Legal and Literary Interpretation," *Poetics Today,* 1 (1979), 23–34; Jonathan Culler, *Structuralist Poetics* (Ithaca, NY: Cornell University Press, 1975), esp. pp. 113–39.

40. Thomas S. Frentz and Thomas B. Farrell, "Language-Action: A Paradigm for Communication," *Quarterly Journal of Speech,* 62 (1976), 334.

41. W. Barnett Pearce and Forrest Conklin, "A Model of Hierarchical Meanings in Coherent Conversation and a Study of Indirect Responses," *Communication Monographs,* 46 (1979), 76–87.

42. Van Dijk, for example, says that the tasks involved in language, perception, complex planning, and action "cannot possibly be accounted for at the level of linear processing of micro-information, but . . . hierarchical rules and categories and the formation of macro-structures are necessary" (*Text and Context,* cited above, note 19, p. 159).

43. A likely reason for this failure to connect is that the hierarchical models and the study of genres come from different research traditions. Genre has been useful in discussions of literary art, written rhetoric, and public address, all of which are forms of monologue. The hierarchical models draw from work in interpersonal communication, which relies on dialogue. It seems reasonable to suppose that monologue and dialogue do not "mean" in different ways and that a hierarchy of rules and interpretative contexts might be as applicable to monologue as to dialogue. The constituents of each model do not preclude such an assumption, being for the most part terms common to rhetorical analysis.

44. Sharon D. Downey, "The Evolution of Rhetorical Genres," paper presented at the Speech Communication Association, Louisville, Kentucky, 1982. An important difference between her discussion and mine is that Downey does not distinguish between form and action.

45. In this type of hierarchy, once can deal either with instances or with types. John Searle has proposed a classification of speech-act types, but these types could not be further clustered into text types—that would mix the two kinds of hierarchies ("A Taxonomy of Illocutionary Acts," in *Language, Mind and Knowledge,* ed. Keith Gunderson, Minnesota Studies in the Philosophy of Science, vol. VII [Minneapolis: University of Minnesota Press, 1975], pp. 344–69).

46. Ronald Carpenter, "The Historical Jeremiad as Rhetorical Genre," in Campbell and Jamieson, pp. 105–17.

47. Carolyn R. Miller, "Environmental Impact Statements and Rhetorical Genres: An Application of Rhetorical Theory to Technical Communication," Diss. Rensselaer Polytechnic Institute, 1980.

The Die is Cast:
Topical and Ontological Dimensions
of the *Locus* of the Irreparable
by J. Robert Cox

Whether the results of it be good or evil, the irreparable event is a source of terror for man. . . . [1]

Thucydides reports that when the isle of Melos refused to surrender, Athenian envoys warned its magistrates: "Think over the matter . . . and reflect once and again that it is for your country that you are consulting, that you have not more than one, and that upon this one deliberation depends its prosperity or ruin." When the Melians still refused, the Athenians pressed their siege and subsequently put to death all adult males and sold the women and children of Melos for slaves.[2]

The argument by the Athenian envoys illustrates the use of a rhetorical commonplace derived from the irreparable nature of choice or action. Claims that a decision cannot be repeated or that its consequences may cause an irreplaceable loss are invoked at strategic moments in almost every aspect of our personal and public lives. The consent form for federally-funded sterilization operations includes this prominent statement: "I UNDERSTAND THAT THE STERILIZATION MUST BE CONSIDERED PERMANENT AND NOT REVERSIBLE. I HAVE DECIDED THAT I DO NOT WANT TO BECOME PREGNANT, BEAR CHILDREN OR FATHER CHILDREN."[3] Similar concerns underlie our discussion of abortion, capital punishment, environmental hazards, and even commercial advertising ("Final Closeout! Prices Will Never Be This Low Again!").

Reprinted from *The Quarterly Journal of Speech* 68 (1982), with permission of the National Communication Association.

The sense of caution aroused by a forewarning of the irreparable poses two questions for the rhetorical scholar: What is the basis for this strong evocation? And, what implications does this commonplace have for social judgment? In what follows, I intend to elaborate Perelman and Olbrechts-Tyteca's treatment of the *locus* of the irreparable as one of several "lines of argument relating to the preferable,"[4] and, second, to ground this account in Heidegger's general interpretation of human existence as *Ek-sistenz*—"the standing beyond oneself."[5] In the final section I will trace certain strategic and ethical implications that a forewarning of an irreparable occurrence has for individual and collective decision-making.

The Irreparable and Loci Communes

Perelman and Olbrechts-Tyteca observe that agreement upon common values often yields a divergence of opinion as soon as we move from general to specific references. Thus, our discussion of liberty, justice, or truth must be accompanied by an attempt to interpret and define these values in the particular contexts of judgment. In doing this, we resort to ideas regarding what is desirable, good, or preferable. Such common conceptions, *loci communes*, function as the constitutive principles of our discourse, i.e., as the bases for our interpretation of general values in situated moments of decision and action.

Though indebted to Aristotle's description of the common topics, the authors of *The New Rhetoric: A Treatise on Argumentation* insist their conception differs in two respects: First, identification of particular classes of *loci* is not tied to any metaphysical system; and, second, they refer only to *loci* of the preferable—"premises of a general nature that can serve as the bases for values and hierarchies."[6] Aside from these differences, however, Perelman and Olbrechts-Tyteca claim that arguments relating to the preferable are not unlike the subjects Aristotle treats under the heading "accident" in *Topics* III, 116a–119a. There the dialectical problem is whether one of two things is better or more worthy of choice than the other.[7] Aristotle explains: "[T]he inquiry we are making concerns . . . things that are nearly related and about which we commonly discuss for which of the two we ought rather to vote, because we do not see any advantage on either side as compared with the other. Clearly, then, in such cases *if we can show a single advantage, or more than one, our judgment will record our assent that whichever side happens to have the advantage is the more desirable*".[8]

Much of Book III provides a description of the principles by which a judgment of advantage can be made. Although not listing a topic of the irreparable per se, for example, he advises the dialectician to judge by the destructions, losses, or contraries of things: "for a thing whose loss or whose contrary is more objectionable is itself more desirable."[9]

In a similar fashion, Perelman and Olbrechts-Tyteca set forth a series of premises useful in establishing an object, act, or situation as having greater value than something else. They classify these principles under six general headings: *loci* of quantity, quality, order, the existing, essence, and the person. As part of this topical arrangement, then, the *locus* of the irreparable becomes a principle for securing agreement with an audience concerning a value or hierarchy of values.

In a sense, of course, all choice is irreparable: We can never experience precisely the same moment again. And the loss of certain things, though irreplaceable, may be of little or no consequence in themselves. For Perelman and Olbrechts-Tyteca, however, this *locus* gains importance when considered in light of the dialectical question Aristotle poses: How can we decide between two referents which seem to be of equal value, or demonstrate the advantage of one which is believed initially to have lesser value than another? The *locus* of the irreparable assists the rhetor in discovering arguments that accentuate the value or hierarchical ordering of one referent vis-a-vis another referent.

Specifically, Perelman and Olbrechts-Tyteca suggest the basis for the attention of the irreparable is linked to *loci* of quality: the unique or exceptional, a contrapuntal emphasis to what is usual, customary, or easily replaceable in human experience. "To be irreparable, an action must be one that cannot be repeated: it acquires a value by the very fact of being considered under this aspect."[10] The *locus* of the irreparable is a way of organizing our perceptions of a situation involving decision or action; its use calls attention to the *unique* and *precarious* nature of some object or state of affairs, and stresses the *timeliness* of our relationship to it.

Uniqueness

The object or act which qualifies as irreparable is necessarily unique. Human life and aspects of experience and the environment which cannot be restored, if "lost," are seen in their singularity—as distinct, original, rare, or exceptional. Such topical equations are often voiced explicitly: In its March/April 1981 newsletter, for example, the Nature Conservancy announced plans to safeguard a portion of "the *unique and priceless* riverine woodlands and streams that comprise the heart of the Deep South." Failure to act, the newsletter stressed, would lead to irreparable loss: "Gone with these forests will be the rich variety of flora and fauna they support. The Florida panther, the swallow-tailed kite, the green pitcher plant, and the untold number of less familiar plant and animal species *will have disappeared forever.*"[11] In this case, the irreparable acquires significance by being linked to that which is unique, for the "unique cannot be priced, and its value is increased by the very fact that it cannot be estimated."[12]

Loss of the unique is even more poignant when juxtaposed against the usual, the ordinary, the vulgar, that which is fungible or interchangeable.[13] This dialectic is quite explicit, for instance, in the appeal of the Center for Environmental Education for protection of the ocean's whales: "Why are these magnificent animals being killed? To produce mink food, fertilizer, cosmetics and lubricating oil." Thus, that which is exceptional—"these awesome, highly-intelligent marine mammals"—is sacrificed for the ordinary and the common. Is this practice necessary? "Although there are cheap, plentiful substitutes for all these products, the needless slaughter continues."[14]

Much of the potency of arguments regarding the irreparable derives from the value of what is unique or singular, and from the contrast between that and some fungible alternative.

Precariousness

Since what is unique (singular) may be lost, its constancy is open to challenge—its very existence, precarious. It is principally in terms of this quality that Perelman and Olbrechts-Tyteca define the irreparable: "as a limit, which accentuates the *locus* of the precarious. . . . "[15] That which is precarious, in turn, gains significance from its contrast with *loci* of quantity, with what is plentiful, permanent, or enduring. For, "as we know, anything that is threatened acquires great value: *Carpe diem.*"[16]

There is, nevertheless, some ambiguity in the identification of the irreparable with the *locus* of the precarious. For the urge to "enjoy the day" invites a sense of inevitability—an absence of choice or ability to affect the future. In this sense, precariousness refers to what is transitory, fleeting, or ephemeral, e.g., a special season, encounter, or state of affairs which cannot intrinsically be sustained; even with our intervention, its special status cannot be preserved or its existence lengthened. "Loss" is inevitable. Yet, the association which Perelman and Olbrechts-Tyteca seem to draw between the irreparable and human choice supposes that that which is threatened *need not be lost if one acts as the rhetor requests.*

This second sense of precariousness is captured in references to what is (1) fragile and (2) established, stable, or secure, but threatened by radical intrusion. That which is fragile requires protection or an agent's active intervention to ensure its continued existence. Perelman and Olbrechts-Tyteca illustrate this sense in citing the peroration of St. Vincent de Paul's appeal to women patrons for support of the orphans under his protection: "You have been their mothers by grace since the time when their mothers by nature abandoned them. Consider now whether you too wish to abandon them forever . . . ; their life and death are in your hands. . . . If you continue to give them your charitable care, they will live; but I tell you before God, they will all be dead tomorrow if you forsake them."[17]

Second, the established, stable, or secure may itself be threatened by disease, accident, or the actions of a powerful agent. The identification of the irreparable with this sense of precariousness incorporates a wide range of references—from capital punishment (human life), abortion and sterilization (reproductive processes), to whaling and clear-cutting of rain forests (natural resources).

An act, object, or condition gains value in our eyes when it is seen in any one of the foregoing senses—as transitory, fragile, or as secure but now threatened by radical action. The precarious becomes identified with the *locus* of the irreparable, however, when that which is threatened *need not be lost,* when choice is possible. The irreparable is offered as a defining limit to the precarious, for if choice is foresaken what is "lost" cannot be restored. "Extinction," declares the Center for Environmental Education, "is the ultimate crime against nature. Extinction means forever."[18]

Timeliness

Our experience with precarious reality places value upon the timeliness of choice or action. Though Perelman and Olbrechts-Tyteca do not associate this quality with the irreparable, timeliness seems both a natural and logical outcome of its claims. In *The New Rhetoric* the *locus* of timeliness is derived from Aristotle's discussion of transitory existence. The authors observe, "by making value dependent upon a transitory state of affairs, we lay stress on the precariousness of this value and, at the same time, increase the store set on it while it lasts."[19]

With regard to claims of finality, however, timeliness assumes other dimensions: in the caution evoked in contemplating an irreparable consequence, and in the urgency of action that is required to save something rare and irreplaceable. In the first instance, caution is elicited when one's own actions may be cause for an irreparable occurrence, as in a juror's vote where the death penalty is mandatory upon conviction for a capital offense. A similar concern also arises in what might broadly be termed *decisions of renunciation,* e.g., the decisions facing the potential expatriate, kidney donor, or person considering surgical sterilization. For the value of what we may normally take for granted is accentuated by images of death, denial, separation, or loss. In other cases, urgency of choice and action occurs when what we perceive as fragile or essential to our well-being is threatened; hence, we act to forestall or oppose forces that would do irreparable harm, to save what is exceptional. It is this dimension of timeliness which the Democratic National Committee draws upon in attacking the policies of U.S. Secretary of the Interior James Watt: "*Because* the destruction to our environment cannot be undone. . . . *Because* our fragile wilderness areas once desecrated by senseless development are lost forever. . . . *Because* the insensitive, dangerous, and irreversible decisions by Secretary Watt will devastate the air we must breathe, the water we must drink, the soil we must live upon . . . *we, as a nation, must act immediately to stop the senseless waste.*"[20] If allowed to go unchecked, the Secretary's policies will do irreparable damage to the nation's natural resources. Thus, action is "timely": "Therefore, the Democratic National Committee is immediately forming a special fund—unique in our 132-year history—to make certain that Mr. Watt and the special interests he represents are stopped from irrevocably ruining our lands, water, and wildlife."[21]

Approached from the viewpoint of its topical associations, the *locus* of the irreparable functions in a *nomos*-building capacity, i.e., as a principle governing our interpretation of experience. A speaker's claim of irreparableness helps to structure a situation in which an auditor perceives X as being of heightened value. Such a claim assumes: (1) X is a referent whose quality is considered vis-a-vis some other referent (usually "not-X"); (2) X is *unique* (exceptional, rare, or original); further, (3) X's status is *precarious,* threatened by some agent's actions or because its survival cannot be assured without our intervention; thus (4) choice or action regarding X is *timely.* In relation to these attributions, then, the *locus* of the irreparable presents itself as a defining limit: Its rhetorical appeal occurs as a *forewarning,* an opportunity to act in appropriate ways before it is too late. Once "lost," X cannot be restored, the consequence of choice being irreversible, final.

Beyond these topical dimensions, there seems to be a more fundamental dimension which assigns value to X. For the notion of an irreparable act anticipates some state that is *subsequent* to the act, *a-time-when* choice cannot be repeated or X restored. The value we assign to the irreparable, in other words, presupposes our experience of time and our valuing of an object or act in this dimension.

Time and The Irreparable

Perelman and Olbrechts-Tyteca themselves suggest that temporality comprises a basis for the value of the irreparable. They link this dimension specifically to *loci* of quantity: "the infinity of time which will elapse after the irreparable has been done or established, the certitude that the effects, whether or not they were wanted, will continue indefinitely."[22] They do not, however, develop this idea further in *The New Rhetoric*. This is unfortunate because the topical traits of "length" and "duration" capture only part of our experience of time. We can also regard time as an ontological dimension, as a necessary condition for our forming any judgments of value at all.

From an ontological perspective, the appeal of the irreparable emerges from the interaction between our perception of time—especially future time—and human meaning. For, in temporalizing, we structure our existence in relation to certain ends—in relation to purposes which are realizable *within* time. We experience time as "opportunity" as in the Greek *kairos,* "the knife edge of chance, a choice point of fortune."[23]

Heidegger develops this idea more fully in *Being and Time* in his general interpretation of human existence as *Eksistenz*—literally, the "standing beyond oneself." The meaning of our experience is rooted, not in a succession of particular Nows, but in a field or temporal spread of Future-Present-Past. Heidegger calls this basic temporality "*ecstases*" for in experiencing the Present we are already "standing outside" of it.[24] The unifying thread in this temporal field is *future* time; it is our anticipation of future (potentiality-for-Being) which constitutes and informs our present understanding.

Within this structuring framework of time, we are able to establish our lives meaningfully; we can entertain hope, make plans, act, or organize projects. "Project" (*Entwurf*) is a central word in Heidegger's ontology. Barrett explains: "Not only do we plan specific projects for today or tomorrow, but our life as a whole is a project in the sense that we are perpetually thrown-ahead-of-ourselves-toward-the-future."[25] Our experience of the future, then, is more than mere foretelling of what will occur; it is, in Cassirer's words, *an imperative of human life:* "to think of the future and to live in the future is a necessary part of [our] nature."[26]

This fact, nevertheless, confronts us with an existential dilemma: The symbolic capacity which allows us to "stand beyond" ourselves also brings us face to face with our finitude. As humans, we know that in the future we will die. Such knowledge, in turn, emphasizes the precarious investment of our existence: accident or disease may strike unexpectedly; the death of a friend or loved one wrenches from us a vital part of ourselves.

Loss, separation, and death, then, transform our experience of time. We experience the future as closed. When this happens, time becomes threatening; the future becomes a source of anxiety and dread. The human dilemma is inescapable: Whether in turning away or in resolving to face the future, we risk irreparable loss. In turning from the future as a way of reducing anxiety, we choose an "inauthentic" existence.[27] Yet, in forming projects, in opening ourselves to the future, we expose ourselves to the possibilities of suffering and loss, including our own death.

Thus, knowledge of the irreparable is rooted in *self*-knowledge, in an awareness of our own end—the absence of human possibility and of Being itself. "Madness and death," Camus reminds readers in *The Myth of Sisyphus,* "are [our] irreparables."[28] *Death* is the archetypal symbol of the irreparable event. In mythology, religion, and art, images of death effectively embody both the topical qualities and experience of time which an irreparable act evokes. One who has "died" spiritually, for example, suffers a radical severance or separation from God—the negation of the "wholly other" (*ganz endere*).[29]

Unlike religious promises of grace (restoration), the irreparable does not offer hope. That which is "fallen" cannot be undone, its effects lasting an infinity of time. Such a conception of time, Eliade suggests, separates us from the sacred. "*By its very nature sacred time is reversible* in the sense that . . . it is *a primordial mythical time made present.*"[30] Sacred time is "indefinitely recoverable, indefinitely repeatable;" it does not "pass," "does not constitute an irreversible duration."[31] By contrast, an irreparable event constitutes not only radical severence—an altered state or condition—but also the ceaseless experiencing of its consequence. It is perhaps this "fall" into temporality that prompts Perelman and Olbrechts-Tyteca to observe: "Whether the results of it be good or evil, the irreparable event is a source of terror for man."[32]

Because we "stand beyond" ourselves in time, we recoil at its loss; to lose the opportunity for meaningful choice is to lose something vital in ourselves. By calling upon such powerful psycho-emotional sources, the *locus* of the irreparable creates what Solomon terms an "effective rhetorical vision." Such visions "(and those least amenable to logical refutation)," she suggests, "draw from a reservoir of myth, a complex of psychic and cultural associations of enormous nonrational persuasion."[33]

Strategic and Ethical Implications

A rhetor's claim that an act is irreparable has both strategic and ethical implications for human deliberation and decision-making. When choice cannot be repeated or its consequences later reversed, actors may adapt in ways that depart from ordinary decision processes. Such *strategic* adaptations include: (1) an expansion of the time frame in which choices are considered, (2) heightened information-seeking, (3) invocation of a minimum condition rule, and, ironically, (4) the warranting of extraordinary measures. In addition, actors confront an ethical responsibility for informed choice when doing that which cannot be undone later.

Strategic Implications

An Expanded Time Frame. The portrayal of a possible alternative as irreparable fundamentally alters the time frame which informs actors' deliberation. For the basis of this *locus,* Perelman and Olbrechts-Tyteca remind us, derives *inter alia* from "the infinity of time which will elapse after the irreparable has been done or established. . . . "[34] Alternative courses of action, conceived as tentative or temporary measures, must now be considered in terms of long-term, permanent effects.

A focus upon the irreversible effects of an act specifically renders inappropriate a strategy of incremental decision-making. Such a strategy concentrates only upon marginal differences among alternatives. The effects of a decision are adjusted in a series of incremental, exploratory, and remedial moves. Thus, an actor need not be "right" on any one move: "If his move fails or is attended by unanticipated adverse consequences, he assumes that someone's (perhaps even his own) next move will take care of the resulting problem."[35] Neither long-term consequences nor the future per se plays much of a role in those adjustments. If, however, an actor is persuaded that a projected consequence will be irreparable, he or she cannot then assume there will be a "next move;" for the effect—whether or not it was wanted—cannot be undone. This expanded "scene" (in Burke's vocabulary) imbues an individual's act with qualities of permanence, finality.

Heightened Information-Seeking. The irrevocability of certain decisions increases actors' need to be accurate, correct, or right in their actions. For, should things turn out to be other than expected, the decision cannot be undone or its consequences set aside. In such circumstances, we would expect that actors would seek more information (and more accurate information) about the possible outcomes of alternative courses of action before making their decision. Based on their conflict model of decision-making, Janis and Mann hypothesize that such actors are more likely to become open-minded, less inclined to selective exposure, and less biased in assimilating the information to which they are exposed.[36] Mann and Taylor have reported some experimental evidence supporting this hypothesis. When forewarnings were provided that their decisions (involving preferences among art prints) would be irrevocable, subjects took longer to decide and engaged in more "vigilant" patterns of information processing.[37] Such findings seem to underscore the importance of actors' *talk:* though their decision cannot be undone once actually implemented, actors' verbal projections of a course of action and its consequences are revocable—their imagining of what may happen can be revised as different alternatives are contemplated.

Where increased information-seeking does not offer a sufficient basis for action, the decision-makers may postpone choice or act in a way that does not unduly restrict choice at a later time. Such are the alternatives facing a physician who, after trying to discern the preference of a terminally ill patient, must decide whether procedures serving only to artifically prolong life should be ended. "In some cases we don't have enough information," concedes a physician with University Hospitals of Cleveland. "If we don't know what the patient's life was like, we have to be supportive *because not being supportive is irrevocable.*"[38]

A Minimum Condition Rule. If the consequences of a course of action cannot later be reversed, a decision-maker may be inclined to invoke a strategy of risk-avoidance. Such a strategy differs from usual conceptions of maximizing one's values or utility. In the latter situation, the decision-maker accepts the possibility of negative outcomes on any one occasion on the expectation of a greater return "over time."

In severe-risk situations, however, an individual or society may not be able to "lose" even once; hence, Blackstone's dictum that it is better that ten guilty individuals should go free than one innocent person be convicted. A pleading of irreparable consequences in such cases presents a minimum condition for choosing: *a course of action whose consequences turn out to be "unacceptable" must be remediable.* Such a method closely resembes Savage's criterion of "regret" or minimization of the maximum likely harm (*minimax*)[39] and Lee's rule for lexicographic ordering of preference dimensions. The latter requires that the bases for evaluating the outcomes of a decision be ranked in importance. Preference among alternative courses of action, Lee explains, "is determined by the utility magnitudes for *the most important dimension alone.*"[40] Similarly, adoption of a minimum condition rule requires that prospective actions be evaluated against a threshold criterion: that the capacity to "undo" consequences that are unacceptable be preserved. Alternatives satisfying this criterion would then be evaluated along other, subordinate dimensions to arrive at a final decision.

Opponents of high-risk courses of action thus have available a *locus* that is grounded in a fundamental presumption of society: the preservation of future choice. The West Virginia Highlands Conservancy found this to be appropriate source of arguments in opposing the U.S. Office of Surface Mining's proposal to allow coal mining in environmentally sensitive areas: "The line of argument which in theory would be most effective in compelling a designation of unsuitability would concentrate on the likelihood of irreversible damage from mine subsidence, landslides, destruction of endangered plant and animal species, and loss of habitat for native trout, black bear and other species."[41]

Strategically, the invocation of a minimum condition rule allows actors to subsume other potentially conflicting values in the "remediable" alternatives. Such seems to be the intention in some environmentalists' plea: "Preserving land and water resources today still allows for development at some future time. Uncontrolled development now leaves few options for the future."[42] In other words, if X, then never Y; however (if the minimum condition rule is invoked), if Y, then, if necessary, X. A *Washington Post* editorial develops this line of reasoning in support of the Alaskan Lands Act. To allow exploitation of energy and timber resources in disputed wilderness areas would irreparably damage critical wildlife habitats and other wilderness qualities: if X (resource exploitation), then the loss of Y (original habitat/ecosystem). But, the *Post* pointed out, "the wilderness designation should not be regarded as totally irreversible. Its purpose is to preserve for the future as much unspoiled acreage as the nation can now afford. . . . Surely future members of Congress will not believe themselves unable to open the range . . . if the time comes when the resources they contain are needed desperately."[43] Pleadings in support of remediable action are especially likely to succeed if the "*X*" option is characterized as fungible or easily substituted for, e.g., energy resources can be located elsewhere, or alternative sources such as solar or conservation can be utilized.

Warrant for Extraordinary Measures. Because the irreparable lasts "an infinity of time," actors may feel justified in going to extreme lengths to block or forestall the loss of something rare, precious, or unique. On the other hand, one may find comfort in claims of finality, in the acceptance of the inevitable. Hence, an actor may knowingly undertake irreparable measures or declare his or her decision to be irrevocable in an attempt to ensure the occurrence of a desired outcome. In either event, the *locus* of the irreparable may be said to warrant "extraordinary" measures—actions which go beyond the usual, customary, or what most people would approve.

The former occasion arises when an actor invokes the minimum condition rule. Logically, the rule may be satisfied in either of two ways: (1) suitable modification or abandonment of alternatives posing irreparable damage, or, failing this, (2) radical intervention—the adoption of action designed to prevent the consequences of such alternatives from occurring. Because the minimum condition rule is a *minimum* condition—else the unique (priceless) lost, the "unacceptable" allowed—actors may undertake extraordinary measures. In recent times, these have included: obstructing nuclear weapons facilities, resisting the draft, firebombing an abortion clinic, or kidnapping of sons and daughters whom parents believe have been brainwashed by religious cults. In announcing her decision to "refuse to pay Internal Revenue [sic] that 32 percent of my taxes which the budget applies to current military expenditures," the writer of a letter-to-the-editor of a local newspaper explains: "There may still be time to choose between life and death on this planet earth of ours."[44] Certainly, in the minds of the individuals involved, each of these interventions poses less danger than loss of what is irreparable. "After all," such a person may reason, "what else have I if 'all' is lost?"

Warrant for extraordinary action can also occur under very different circumstances. A paradigm case is Caesar's action, in 49 B.C., in leading his favorite Thirteenth Legion across the Rubicon, the stream forming the frontier between Gaul and Italy. Suetonius reports him as saying *Iacta est alea*—"the die is cast."[45] Caesar was now openly committed in his opposition to the Roman Senate and Pompey's armies. In taking an irrevocable step (as Caesar in crossing the Rubicon), one is committed, in a sense, *to seeing the act through.* Such a commitment removes (or alleges to have removed) any further choice: "We have no alternative but to do *X*" (continue toward Rome), "now that the alternative for doing not-*X* has been passed over."

The commitment of what can be called the Rubicon Ploy is of course a *social*—not logical—commitment. For choice is seldom literally between *X* and not-*X;* one may choose to do *R, S,* or some other action depending upon social and physical constraints. Nevertheless, the announcement that a decision is irrevocable tends to imbue action associated with it with a certain presumption. We feel compelled by what is inevitable, by what seems foreordained. In classical oratory this aspect of the irreparable underlies much of what Demosthenes says about resisting Philip. In *On the Crown,* he tells his audience: "The only choice, and the necessary choice, left to you was justly to oppose all his unjust actions against you."[46]

Demosthenes' use of this commonplace illustrates the phenomenon of actors' *post*-decisional bolstering of their behavior. This need to rationalize actions that cannot now be undone is vividly displayed in what Childs terms the "exile mentality" of some refugees. Such individuals feel compelled to picture what is happening in their former homelands as worse than it is *"to justify their departure and the renunciation of their birthright."*[47]

Thus, individuals may find warrant for extraordinary measures in both the fear and consolation of finality, of that which cannot be undone or changed.

Ethical Implications

Somewhat more complex questions arise when we turn to the ethical implications of irrevocable decisions: Is it unwise, irrational, or wrong to do knowingly that which cannot be undone?

In one sense, the commission of an irreparable action presupposes what the act's consequences deny—the possibility of further choice. This consideration implies that a presumption exists in favor of remediable alternatives. Nevertheless, the fact that its consequences will be permanent does not in itself render all irreparable action unethical; for an individual or society may pursue other ends whose utility presumably is greater than that which may be damaged or lost as a result. And each may find assurance in customs, practices, or rituals whose forms are unchanging or which provide a sense of permanence.

Ideally, then, ethical considerations should take into account the irreversibility—the finality—of a decision's consequences while not *a priori* ruling these consequences "unacceptable." At a minimum a decision to undertake an irreparable course of action should be an *informed* choice. Increasingly, the concept of informed choice serves as a guide when individuals must routinely undertake or counsel irreparable actions: voting, jury deliberation, regulatory permit-granting, marriage or problem pregnancy counseling. The Hastings Center's Institute of Society, Ethics, and the Life Sciences raises this consideration specifically in regard to sterilization. It notes that while technology alone seldom determines the ethics of a biomedical procedure, "the virtually irreversible nature of surgical sterilization makes the choice a more drastic one than it might be otherwise."[48] Ethically, what must be preserved in such circumstances is, not any "right to procreate" per se, but an individual's right "to control her or his own body and to decide, in a fully informed and conscious way, what sorts of interventions may be made into bodily processes, including the biological capacity to procreate."[49]

But what must a choice include to be "fully informed?" In guidelines governing jury decision-making, research using human subjects, and sterilization, the following factors seem to be recognized: (1) Awareness of any irreversible consequences of a contemplated course of action; (2) Evaluation of alternatives to this course (if any), including knowledge of the potential consequences of each course; (3) Sufficient time in which to consider each of the above and to arrive at a decision; and (4) Absence of coercive factors, i.e., that the resulting decision be voluntary.[50]

Obviously, requirements for informed choice work best in instances of individual decision-making where both time and access to relevant information are readily available. Federal regulations for surgical sterilization, for example, require a mandatory 30-day waiting period between the date of informed consent and the actual operation. The purpose of this waiting period is to ensure, insofar as possible, that "the individual reflects carefully on the consequences of the proposed sterilization and makes a decision that he or she will not later regret, since the procedure must be considered irreversible."[51]

When pressures for a decision mount, however, actors may find it more difficult to fulfill the requirements for fully informed choice. Or, as members of a strongly cohesive group, individual actors may feel less responsible for—or more invulnerable to—possible adverse consequences of their actions.[52] To the degree actors restrict the time frame informing their choices or fail to evaluate alternative courses of action, their potential for error and disappointment grows. Thus, requisites for informed choice and the constraints of time and resource limitations pose a dilemma: At what stage should deliberation be suspended and a decision made? The answer may tell us much about an individual or group's confidence (rightly or wrongly) in its capacity to affect the future.

Conclusion

What then is the value of the foregoing analysis for the rhetorical scholar? Elsewhere I have suggested Perelman and Olbrechts-Tyteca's conception of *loci communes* makes several important contributions to critical methodology.[53] Understanding of the topical and ontological bases of the *locus* of the irreparable adds, I believe, further support for this view.

Such understanding, in particular, reveals two important aspects of social judgment: First, occurrence of this commonplace in discourse points the critic to key "objects of agreement" shared by members of a group or culture.[54] In characterizing choice as irrevocable, a rhetor also signifies what he or she believes an audience values as unique, exceptional, rare, or original. Such claims "encompass," in Burke's terminology, certain types of situations in the sense that they "name their structure and outstanding ingredients, and name them in a way that contains an attitude toward them."[55]

Second, rhetorical occurrences of the irreparable may offer some understanding of the ways a culture views its own future. The critic, for example, may ask: What are the deliberative occasions in which actors knowingly undertake an irrevocable action? What do such actors count as "good reasons" for the acceptance of irreplaceable loss? And what sense does a culture generally have of its own efficacy? Does it believe that it possesses the authority or necessary resources to affect those aspects of the future upon which its well-being rests?

Perhaps we shall find rhetorical uses of the irreparable only in a culture that is confident of its ability to address the future. A culture as much as an individual "stands beyond" itself in time, in its ability to act in the future. Without this confidence, the irreparable has little power to persuade. Indeed, in a culture for which the future is closed, the foretelling of loss does not function in a *rhetorical* sense at all. It is not an impetus for action, but only the fatalistic announcement of forces over which it has no control.

Notes

1. Ch. Perelman and L. Olbrechts-Tyteca, *The New Rhetoric: A Treatise on Argumentation,* trans. John Wilkinson and Purcell Weaver (Notre Dame: University of Notre Dame Press, 1971), p. 92.
2. *The Complete Writings of Thucydides: The Peloponesian War,* trans. R. Crawley (New York: The Modern Library, 1934), p. 336.
3. Rosalind Pollack Petchesky, "Reproduction, Ethics, and Public Policy: The Federal Sterilization Regulations," *The Hastings Center Report,* 9 (1979), 34.
4. Perelman and Olbrechts-Tyteca, p. 66. Recent discussions of commonplaces and the problem of invention include: Manual Bilsky, McCrea Hazlett, Robert E. Streeter, and Richard M. Weaver. "Looking for an Argument," *College English,* 14 (1953), 210–216; John F. Wilson and Carroll C. Arnold, *Public Speaking as a Liberal Art,* 2nd ed. (Boston: Allyn and Bacon, 1968), p. 115; Karl R. Wallace, *"Topoi* and the Problem of Invention," *Quarterly Journal of Speech,* 58 (1972), 387–395; and Ralph T. Eubanks, "Axiological Issues in Rhetorical Inquiry," *Southern Speech Communication Journal,* 44 (1978), 11–24. Eubanks outlines eight values (health, creativity, wisdom, love, freedom, justice, courage, and order) which define the demands of the "right" and the "good."
5. William Barrett, "The Flow of Time," in *The Philosophy of Time,* ed. Richard M. Gale (Garden City, N.Y.: Anchor, 1967), p. 356.
6. Perelman and Olbrechts-Tyteca, p. 84.
7. Aristotle does not explicitly define what he means by a topic. De Pater suggests that he is actually using the term in two senses: (1) as a formula or rule for conducting an argument, and (2) as a principle upon which the formula is founded. Walter de Pater, "La Fonction du lieu et de l'instrument dans les Topiques," in *Aristotle on Dialetic. Proceedings of the Third Symposium Aristotelicum,* ed. G. E. L. Owen (Oxford: Clarendon Press, 1968), p. 165.
8. Aristotle, *Topica and De Sophistica Elenchis,* trans. W. A. Pickard-Cambridge, in *The Works of Aristotle,* ed. W. A. Ross (Oxford: Oxford University Press, 1928). I. 116a 4–13. Emphasis added.
9. Aristotle, *Topica,* 117b 6–7. In this and other topics in Book III, Aristotle uses "topic" to refer to a principle, rather than a formula. For further discussion, see Eleanore Stump, "Dialectic and Aristotle's Topics," in *Boethius's De topicis differentiis,* trans. E. Stump (Ithaca: Cornell University Press, 1978), p. 169.
10. Perelman and Olbrechts-Tyteca, p. 92.
11. William D. Blair, Jr., "The Conservancy's Richard King Mellon Grant: GREAT EXPECTATIONS," *The Nature Conservancy News,* 31 (March/April 1981), 5. Emphasis added.
12. Perelman and Olbrechts-Tyteca, p. 90.
13. Perelman and Olbrechts-Tyteca, p. 90.
14. "Will the Whales Survive?" Letter received from the Center for Environmental Education, 17 July 1980.
15. Perelman and Olbrechts-Tyteca, p. 91.
16. Perelman and Olbrechts-Tyteca, p. 91.

17. Cited in A. Baron, *De la Rhétorique ou de la composition oratoire et Littéraire,* 4th ed. (Brussels and Liège, Belgium: Libraries polytechniques de Deaq, 1879), quoted in Perelman and Olbrechts-Tyteca. p. 91.

18. "Will the Whales Survive?"

19. Perelman and Olbrechts-Tyteca, p. 91. Aristotle observes: "everything is more desirable at the season when it is of greater consequence; e.g., freedom from pain in old age more than in youth: for it is of greater consequences in old age." *Topica,* III, 117a 26–29.

20. Letter received from Cecil D. Andrus for the Democratic National Committee, 27 October 1981.

21. Letter from Cecil D. Andrus.

22. Perelman and Olbrechts-Tyteca, p. 92.

23. John Cohen, "Time in Psychology," in *Time in Science and Philosophy,* ed. Jiri Zeman (New York: Elsevier, 1971), p. 163.

24. Martin Heidegger, *Being and Time,* trans. John Macquairie and Edward Robinson (New York: Harper and Row, 1962), p. 377, n. 2.

25. Barrett, p. 361.

26. Ernst Cassirer, *An Essay on Man: An Introduction to a Philosophy of Human Culture* (New Haven: Yale University Press, 1962), pp. 55, 53.

27. Commenting on Heidegger's use of this term, Barrett states: "The inauthentic individual, . . . cowering before his own possibilities, lets time slip away and experiences it only as a passive flow of his being," p. 362.

In their study of the relationship between death anxiety in elderly persons and future time orientation, Bascue and Lawrence report that "the elderly may turn away from the future as a way of controlling death anxiety." L. O. Bascue and R. E. Lawrence, "A Study of Subjective Time and Death Anxiety in the Elderly," *Omega Journal of Death and Dying,* 8 (1977), 81.

28. Albert Camus, *The Myth of Sisyphus and Other Essays,* trans. Justin O'Brien (New York: Vintage, 1955), p. 47.

29. Rudolf Otto, *Das Heilige* (Breslau, 1917), cited in Mircea Eliade, *The Sacred and the Profane: The Nature of Religion* (New York: Harvest, 1959), p. 9.

30. Eliade, p. 68.

31. Eliade, p. 69.

32. Perelman and Olbrechts-Tyteca, p. 92.

33. Martha Solomon, "The 'Positive Woman's' Journey: A Mythic Analysis of the Rhetoric of STOP-ERA," *Quarterly Journal of Speech,* 65 (1979), 263.

34. Perelman and Olbrechts-Tyteca, p. 92.

35. David Braybrooke and Charles E. Lundblom, *A Strategy of Decision: Policy Evaluation of a Social Process* (New York: The Free Press, 1963), p. 123.

36. Irving L. Janis and Leon Mann, *Decision Making: A Psychological Analysis of Conflict, Choice, and Commitment* (New York: The Free Press, 1977), p. 302.

37. L. Mann and V. A. Taylor, "The Effects of Commitment and Choice Difficulty on Pre-Decisional Processes," *Journal of Social Psychology,* 82 (1970), 225.

38. Matt Clark, Mariana Goshall, and Dan Shapiro, "When Doctors Play God," *Newsweek,* August 31, 1981, p. 51. Emphasis added.

39. Leonard J. Savage, "The Theory of Statistical Decision," *Journal of the American Statistical Association,* 46 (1951), 55–67.

40. Wayne Lee, *Decision Theory and Human Behavior* (New York: Wiley, 1971), pp. 98–99. Emphasis added.

41. Bard Montgomery, "'Blatant Errors,' Ignored Issues . . . ," *The Highlands Voice,* March 1981, p. 5. Emphasis added.

42. Peter Stoler, "The Trouble with Watt," *Time,* May 11, 1981, p. 51. This also appears to be the rationale for the choice of a naval blockade in the 1962 Cuban missile crisis. Secretary of Defense Robert McNamara, in particular, argued a blockade constituted "limited pressure" which left the U.S. still in control of events. Such an option allowed contingency adjustments and, importantly, did not foreclose stronger measures should the blockade have failed. Robert Kennedy, *Thirteen Days: A Memoir of the Cuban Missle Crisis* (New York: New American Library, 1969), p. 34.

43. "Saving the Best of Alaska," *The Washington Post,* July 21, 1980, p. A18.

44. "U.S. Citizens Must Resist Trend Toward Violence," *Chapel Hill Newspaper,* August 3, 1980, sec. C, p. 3.

45. Gaius Suctonius Tranquillus, *The Twelve Caesars,* trans. Robert Graves (London: Penquin, 1957), p. 27.

46. *Demosthenes' On the Crown,* ed. James J. Murphy with trans. by John J. Keaney (New York: Random, 1967), p. 73.

47. Robert P. Newman and Dale R. Newman, *Evidence* (Boston: Houghton Mifflin, 1969), p. 63. See, Marquis Childs, "Behind the Errors on Cuban Invasion," *The Washington Post,* April 26, 1961, p. A18. Emphasis added.

48. Petchesky, p. 29.

49. Petchesky, p. 29.

50. Partially because of past abuses with surgical sterilization, similar criteria have been promulgated as a condition for federal funding of agencies performing such operations. Petchesky notes: "Not only must the person be given information about 'available alternative methods of family planning and birth control,' a complete explanation of the procedure to be used and all of its known risks and benefits, and explicit notice of its irreversibility, but this information must be provided orally, in the person's preferred language, and in a mode accessible to blind, deaf, or otherwise handicapped individuals." (p. 33)

51. *The Federal Registrar,* 43: 217 (Nov. 8, 1978), p. 52151, cited in Petchesky, p. 33.

52. Wallach et. al. suggests that selection of risky options results from the tendency of groups to engage in a "process of diffusion or spreading of responsibility as a result of knowing that one's decisions are being made jointly with others rather than alone," M. A. Wallach, N. Kogan, and D. J. Biem, "Group Influences on Individual Risk Taking," *Journal of Abnormal and Social Psychology,* 65 (1962), 85. Cline and Cline report recent experimental support for this "diffusion-of-responsibility" theory; see, Rebecca J. Cline and Timothy R. Cline, "A Structural Analysis of Risky-Shift and Cautious Shift Discussions: The Diffusion-of-Responsibility Theory," *Communication Quarterly,* 28 (Fall 1980), 26–36, See also, Irvin L. Janis, *Victims of Groupthink* (Boston: Houghton Mifflin, 1972): "An important symptom of groupthink is the illusion of being invulnerable to the main dangers that might arise from a risky action in which the group is strongly tempted to engage. Essentially, the notion is that 'if our leader and everyone else in our group decides that it is okay, the plan is bound to succeed. Even if it is quite risky, luck will be on our side'" (p. 36).

53. J. Robert Cox, "*Loci Communes* and Thoreau's Arguments for Wilderness in 'Walking' (1851)," *Southern Speech Communication Journal,* 46 (1980), 1–16.

54. Perelman and Olbrechts-Tyteca, p. 67.

55. Kenneth Burke, *The Philosophy of Literary Form,* 3rd ed. (Berkeley: University of California Press, 1973), p. 1.

Rhetoric and Its Double:
Reflections on the Rhetorical Turn
in the Human Sciences
by Dilip Parameshwar Gaonkar

The Flight From "Mere" Rhetoric

Rhetoric cannot escape itself. Rhetoric cannot escape its "mereness," or to use the fashionable vocabulary of our time (here I am alluding to Derridean deconstruction), it cannot escape its status as a "supplement." Yet this simple fact that there is no exit for rhetoric, nor an exit from rhetoric, escapes many friends of rhetoric. Rhetoric cannot efface itself to become its traditional counterpart, dialectic, as Perelman and Valesio would have it.[1] Nor can it recast itself, as Grassi proposes, as the seat of primordial poetic utterance, which apprehends and articulates "the first principles" on which the rational speech of philosophy, in turn, depends.[2] Nor can rhetoric be equated with a hermeneutics of suspicion, as the linguistically inclined followers of Marx, Nietzsche, and Freud would suggest.

To be sure, rhetoric stands in a historically fluctuating relationship with other disciplines, especially those formal disciples which are its neighbors. To a certain measure, its identity and its fortunes are linked to those fluctuating affiliations. For that reason, Roland Barthes; tells us that "rhetoric must always be read in the structural interplay with its neighbors (Grammar, Logic, Poetics, Philosophy): it is the play of the system, not each of its parts in itself, which is historically significant."[3] Sometimes its systemic proximity to one of the neighbors is so great and compelling that one is prone to overlook its distinctive character and its essential difference. If such a misreading of rhetoric happened but occasionally, it would be understandable.

Reprinted from Herbert Simons (ed.) *The Rhetorical Turn: Invention and persuasion in the Conduct of Inquiry* (Chicago: U of Chicago Press, 1990). Reproduced by permission of the publisher.

However, when scholars repeatedly fail to distinguish rhetoric from its neighbors, and do so even in a period marked by a renewed and self-conscious interest in rhetoric, it is reasonable to suspect that something more than an accident is involved. The tenacity of this error, if error it is, should give us pause and prompt us to review this impulse (this habit of the mind) which urges us to make rhetoric into something other than itself.

What is involved in these misreadings, in my opinion, is simply a "flight from rhetoric," or to be more precise, a flight from "mere" rhetoric—that is, rhetoric conceived as a "supplement." What's so frightening, you may ask, that one should seek to flee from "mere" rhetoric in so deliberate a manner?

Once rhetoric is conceived as a "supplement," it becomes a formal, hence an empty discipline. It is without substance, without a secure set of referents, or to put it mundanely, it has no subject matter of its own. To be sure, one can take the general and recurrent lines of arguments (topics) and certain structural/functional resources of language (tropes and figures) as the special province or the subject matter of rhetoric. But this does not resolve the difficulty. Such a view, it seems to me, while recognizing rhetoric as a mode of practical reasoning and discourse production does so precisely in terms of its formal character as a language art. Thus deprived of substance, rhetoric stands in a parasitic relationship vis-a-vis substantive disciplines such as ethics and politics. Sometimes this "parasite" becomes so deeply entangled with the affairs of an alien body, especially the "body politic," it forgets its own nature and purpose and pretends to be a substantive entity. Perhaps this is what Aristotle had in mind when he said, "It thus appears that rhetoric is an offshoot of dialectic and also of ethical studies. Ethical studies may fairly be called political: and for this reason rhetoric masquerades as political science, and the professors of it as political experts."[4] For much the same reason, Plato reached a more severe judgment and dismissed rhetoric as a counterfeit art (*Gorgias,* 464–65).

Brian Vickers, a distinguished contemporary champion of rhetoric, notes that rhetoric, having no subject matter of its own, functions a bit like a "service industry," and thereby gets into territorial disputes with other disciplines.[5] The very fact that rhetoric is without a domicile is seen as profoundly threatening to the integrity of substantive disciplines. The territorial disputes between two substantive disciplines, say, law and sociology, are far less acrimonious than when rhetoric enters the picture and attempts to transform and use the materials characteristic of either of those two disciplines. Here I am reminded of Cicero's characterization of Marc Antony as a "homeless" transgressor in the *Fourth Philippic.* According to Cicero, one could negotiate with an enemy on some "settled principle" so long as he has "a republic, a senate house, a treasury, harmonious and united citizens" which he hopes to protect and promote. But Antony, says Cicero, "is attacking your republic, but has none himself; is eager to destroy the Senate, . . . but has no public council himself; he has exhausted your treasury, and has none of his own. For how can a man be supported by the unanimity of the citizens, who has no city at all?"[6] If we substitute rhetoric for Antony, we have an apt image for the kind of danger rhetoric represents to the established disciplines. Rhetoric can spring up any time, from within or without, to pollute and possess what is not its own for the sake of temporary advantage and gratification. Thus, rhetoric is seen as a nomadic discipline that threatens the integrity of the republic of knowledge itself. Why would anyone want to admit such a discipline to the council of learning when it refuses to abide by the academic rules of property and propriety?

Such is the impulse of an empty discipline to become substantive, to become something other than itself. It is as if rhetoric were in search of its other, the substantive other, who, when found, would fill out its formal emptiness. But this other which is to provide rhetoric with a grounding, relieve it from that epistemic anxiety with which it has been burdened since Plato, will always elude us. Perhaps this is the fatal game which animates rhetoric and keeps it going.

The flight from "mere" rhetoric consists of a double movement which, in my view, regulates, shapes, and determines the self-image of rhetoric. This double movement simultaneously propels rhetoric on a vertical axis downward into its past to find itself a suitable history and on a horizontal axis sideways to situate itself within the discursive practices of special "substantive" sciences, especially the human sciences. Rhetoric moves diachronically to discover for itself an alternative historical tradition that will free it from its supplementary status, and it moves synchronically to find itself in the discursive body (textuality) of other disciplines that will confirm its "presence."

These two movements motivated by their distaste for "mere rhetoric" direct us to flee from it, especially if we are serious about this business of rehabilitating rhetoric as "the once and future queen of the human sciences."[7] They play on our disciplinary "lures" and anxieties (which are predictably many), and urge us to make rhetoric into something other than itself.

This double movement in the contemporary self-understanding of rhetoric is not necessarily fully "articulated." Nor is it an entirely "implicit" and subterranean movement which I am somehow magically bringing to light. If this movement is partially "invisible," its invisibility is not due to its obscure presence but to what Alfred Schutz calls its "taken-for-granted" character.[8]

As you may have inferred from my characterization of this double movement as a "lure," I regard it as fundamentally problematic and possibly destructive of rhetoric as a vocation. However, I am not here to reject it but to contest it. In fact, this double movement is not something which can be either accepted or rejected, for it is one of the "essentially contested" features of our discipline.[9]

The First Movement: The Supplementary Tradition

The idea that rhetoric is no more than a "supplement" makes its initial appearance in the fabled encounter between the Older Sophists and the Platonic Socrates, the first site of the so-called quarrel between rhetoric and philosophy. Naturally, there are several strands to this quarrel between rhetoric and philosophy, but both historically and in our own time much of the dispute concerns the epistemic status of rhetoric.[10] The idea that rhetoric is no more than a "supplement" has its origin in the articulation of this question.

The question in its simplest form is this: Does rhetoric, the art of discovering available means of persuasion in a given case (Aristotle), have anything to do with the generation of knowledge? If not, as Socrates, Plato, and Aristotle appear to have assumed, then we may ask, as Heidegger asked of poets: *What are rhetoricians for?*

The Aristotelian compromise on this question, which sets into motion the "supplementary" tradition in rhetoric, is well known. For Aristotle, among other things, rhetoric makes knowledge more readily comprehensible and acceptable in the domain of civic discourse. That is, rhetoric cannot generate knowledge but is useful, possibly indispensable, for the transmission of knowledge discovered by philosophy and the special substantive sciences. Rhetoric, to use a term popularized by Jacques Derrida, is a supplement to knowledge, much as writing is a supplement to speech.[11]

The placing of Aristotle within the supplementary tradition is somewhat problematic. In the Aristotelian scheme, while demonstrative (apodictic) reasoning belongs to the domain of the necessary, rhetoric and dialectic operate within the domain of the contingent and the probable. Further, neither rhetoric nor dialectic "is a science that deals with the nature of any definite subject, but they are merely faculties of furnishing arguments."[12] Rhetoric, in other words, is a general art consisting not of knowledge about substantive fields but a flexible system of formal and prudential devices—topics, tropes and figures, inferential schemes, probabilities, prudential rules, and so on.[13] At the same time, however, this general art is functionally implicated in managing and transforming common opinion for persuasive ends. This functional link to common opinion, according to Leff, prevents rhetoric from becoming a purely formal discipline, and its practical applications extend to the whole field of human affairs.[14] Moreover, the functional aspect of rhetoric is particularly decisive in the civic arena when citizens have to make judgments on issues without recourse to the special sciences to guide their deliberation.[15] This unresolved tension between the formal and the functional dimensions of rhetoric threatens its identity in two distinct but contradictory ways. On the one hand, rhetoric cannot posit a substantive identity because it has no subject matter of its own; on the other hand, its functional involvement with *doxa* threatens its formal identity by what Ricoeur calls an "overburdening of content."[16] Thus, rhetoric is simultaneously empty of subject matter and overburdened with content.

It is against this background one has to negotiate the question as to whether rhetoric has an epistemic function. The centrality of "invention" in the rhetorical tradition as a whole hints at a generative rather than a purely managerial and transmissive function for rhetoric. Yet a closer examination reveals that the aim of rhetorical inquiry is quite different from that of dialectical inquiry. A distinction introduced by Kenneth Burke is particularly useful in this context. Burke, following Aristotle, recognizes that both dialectic and rhetoric begin their inquiry with a critique of common opinion in the realm of the contingent and the probable. But the two critiques have different ends. Although the dialectical critique occurs in the scenic order of truth with a view toward transcending the conflict intrinsic to opinion, the rhetorical critique occurs in the moral order of action with a view toward managing and transforming conflicting opinions in accordance with the exigencies of a given situation. Hence rhetoric, unlike dialectic, is not constitutive of general truth and propositions but of specific beliefs, attitudes, and actions.[17]

Roland Barthes arrives at a similar conclusion regarding Aristotle's treatment of the passions. What Aristotle offers in his *Rhetoric,* according to Barthes, is a "projected" psychology: a psychology as everyone imagines it—not "what is in the mind" of the public, but what the public believes others "have in mind." In Barthes' view, Aristotle's innovative treatment of the passions (in contrast to the technographers who preceded him) lies precisely in his decision to view them *"in their banality"* and to classify "the passions not according to what they are, but according to what they are believed to be: he does not describe them scientifically, but seeks out arguments which can be used with respect to the public's ideas about passion."[18] Rhetorical psychology is therefore quite the opposite of a reductive psychology that would try to see is *behind* what people say and attempt to reduce anger, for instance, to *something else,* something hidden. For Aristotle, public opinion is the first and last datum; he has no hermeneutic notion (of decipherment): anger is what every one thinks about anger, passion is never anything but what people say it is.[19]

Rhetoric thus puts together a disparate set of materials and insights originating in common opinion and popular understanding by recourse to a flexible system of formal devices on an ad hoc basis. Despite its generality as a formal system, rhetoric is marked by a radical particularity in its practices and products. Thus, unless one is prepared to collapse the distinction between knowledge and belief, understanding and action, it seems unreasonable to invoke the authority of Aristotle to claim that rhetoric has an epistemic function.

At any rate, according to the "supplementary" tradition, the quarrel between sophistic rhetoric and Platonic philosophy, as mediated by Aristotle, was decided in favor of the latter. Rhetoric was pushed into the margins of philosophy and the special sciences, and there it was forced to function as a *supplement to knowledge.* The subsequent history of rhetoric is the history of a supplement, living in the margins of philosophy, periodically attempting to widen that margin, as in the case of Cicero and the Renaissance Humanists, or to deepen the dignity of supplementary function, as in the case of St. Augustine.[20] On the whole, however, it is not a history of violent opposition and rebellion against philosophy, but one of accommodation, adjustment, and redefinition.

This tradition of the *supplement* has led many students of rhetoric into a conceptual impasse, as illustrated by John Quincy Adams, the first holder of the Boylston Professorship of Rhetoric at Harvard. In a lecture given in 1806, he declares that rhetoric "which has exhausted the genius of Aristotle, Cicero, and Quintilian, can neither require nor admit much additional illustration. To select, combine, and apply their precepts, is the only duty left for their followers of all succeeding times, and to obtain a perfect familiarity with their instructions is to arrive at the mastery of the art."[21] The same frame of mind prompted the English scholar J. E. C. Welldon in 1886 to praise Aristotle's *Rhetoric* "as being perhaps a solitary instance of a book which not only begins a science, but completes it."[22] Such is the praise heaped on a text (an incomplete set of lecture notes to be precise) that, whatever its genius, stands profoundly divided against itself. This is the extent to which rhetoric had been emasculated within the rubric of a "supplementary" tradition by the end of the nineteenth century.

Understandably, the revived interest in rhetoric in this century is marked by a desire to break free from such a conceptual impasse. The tale of twentieth-century rhetoric, at least in its theoretical speculations, if not in its critical practice, can be read as a revolt against the "supplementary" tradition.

The Sophistic Tradition

This escape from "mere" rhetoric takes many forms and employs many strategies. One way to escape from the conceptual impasse brought about by the "supplementary tradition" is to revive its historical opponent, the sophistic tradition. The rehabilitation of the older sophists that began in the early part of the nineteenth century under the sponsorship of Hegel in Germany and Grote in England has gained considerable momentum in this century. Their name, if not their work, is prominent in the current revival of rhetoric.[23] A return to their skeptical outlook on the "language-ridden" world of human culture is regarded as central to any serious attempt at reviving rhetoric. This revival of the sophistic tradition consists of two related sets of moves, the philosophical and the historical.

The philosophical move in restoring the sophistic tradition to its former glory requires one to de-center the epistemic question. Instead of asking whether rhetoric can generate knowledge, a more fundamental (ontological) question is pushed to the center: How is rhetoric possible?[24] This Kantian type of question refers to the ultimate grounds of rhetoric. In response to this question, two unavoidable human characteristics are offered as the ultimate grounds of rhetoric. First, to use a phrase of Kenneth Burke, humans are symbol-using (misusing) creatures. Second, to use a phrase of Hannah Arendt, life is given to humans under "the condition of plurality."[25] From these two ultimate grounds, one can derive, in turn (as de Man and Todorov do), two distinct but related concepts of rhetoric.[26] They are rhetoric as persuasion and rhetoric as trope. Although the dimension of plurality, marked by "unity in division" (Burke), imposes on humans the necessity of persuasion, the tropological dimension of language makes them susceptible to persuasion. The basic strategy here is to derive in a global fashion the inevitability of rhetoric from our social relations as they are mediated by language. This strategy clearly favors certain theories of language and social relations over others. For instance, while the theory that views language as a transparent medium for the communication of things and ideas is clearly unacceptable, the thesis that social reality, among other things, is linguistically constructed and legitimated is enthusiastically endorsed.[27] The main difficulty with this strategy, with rare exceptions, is that it operates at an extremely high level of generality and almost equates rhetoric with language use and sociability. As a result, this philosophical strategy is disconnected from the sense of rhetoric as a local phenomenon which is so central to the human experience of rhetoric as a material force.[28]

The historical move is far more intriguing. The return to the sophists requires a reconstitution of the history of rhetoric. One cannot traverse 2500 years back to the origins of rhetoric without acknowledging the intervening steps. According to this reconstituted history, there are not one but two histories of rhetoric—a manifest history and a hidden history. And they are dominated by two different traditions—the manifest history by the "supplementary" tradition, and the hidden history by the sophistic tradition.

The manifest history begins predictably enough with the older sophists and their celebrated quarrel with the Platonic Socrates; it moves through Aristotle, Isocrates, Cicero, Quintilian, and St. Augustine in the classical world, and then through the Middle Ages and the Renaissance and the eighteenth century neoclassical rhetoric and the Scottish School. This is the official history of Boethius, Alcuin, George of Trebizond, Agricola, Ramus, Bacon, Fenelon, Lawson, Campbell, and Blair, which finally culminates in Bishop Whately's *Elements of Rhetoric*. This is the history of rhetoric conceived as a "supplement," a history of obscure places, unfamiliar names, and forgotten texts.

The other history of rhetoric, its hidden history, also begins with the celebrated quarrel between the sophists and the Platonic Socrates, and moves indecisively alongside the manifest history until the end of the classical world; then, suddenly, it disappears, until it is *rediscovered* by Kenneth Burke. The "hidden" history places a somewhat different interpretation on the quarrel between sophistic rhetoric and Platonic philosophy. According to this version, the fabulous quarrel that held the Greek mind captive during the declining years of Periclean Enlightenment involved more than the competing claims of two skirmishing disciplines. Rather, it was a contest between two competing ways of life, *the vita activa* and *the vita contemplativa*. Their competing claims to civic attention is described vividly, but with a decided bias, in the Platonic dialogues, especially in the *Theaetetus* (172c–175e). Such a contest could not be settled in a single generation, even if that generation could produce so rare a phenomenon as Socrates. So it continues to engage our attention to this day in varying degrees of intensity. At any rate, for a variety of reasons, both political and intellectual, this competition for cultural hegemony ended in a defeat for the sophists, and they were promptly driven out of the cultural milieu by their philosophical detractors. Thereafter sophistry, insofar as it is a permanent opening for man, had to live an underground, subterranean existence. Later when Aristotle made the compensatory move towards rhetoric and granted it the status of a supplement, rhetoric and sophistic became divorced. While rhetoric, in its attenuated form as a "supplement," was allowed to live in the margins of philosophy, sophistic was "repressed." Thus, rhetoric continued to function as a supplement to philosophical knowledge, where it regulated certain discursive practices and products, but it could not function as a supplement to a sophistic *Weltanschauung* marked by ethical relativity and epistemic skepticism. In this managerial placement, style retained a legitimate interest for the art, but rhetoric seems incapable of generating its own grounding as a mode of persuasion. This partly explains why the theory of invention in rhetoric became moribund, but the theory of *lexis (eloqutio)* was endlessly refined and elaborated.

But what is "repressed" is not erased. It must resurface in various symptomatic forms. Besides, the natural affinity between rhetoric and sophistic would continually draw the two together. Hence, there follows a series of illicit relations and subterranean connections, which constitute the "hidden" history of rhetoric. In some sense, this is the "return of the repressed." And the most distinguished chronicler of this return is none other than Kenneth Burke.

In Burke's *A Rhetoric of Motives,* this proposed reconstruction of the "hidden" history of rhetoric was brilliantly outlined, if not filled out in detail. His initial project in this book was to extend the range of rhetoric, but that extension, as he quickly realized, required an historical grounding, which forced him to depart from the manifest history. He began "by showing how a rhetorical motive is often present where it is not usually recognized, or thought to belong":

> In part, we would but *rediscover* rhetorical elements that had become obscured when rhetoric as a term fell into disuse, and other specialized disciplines such as esthetics, anthropology, psychoanalysis, and sociology came to the fore (so that esthetics sought to outlaw rhetoric, while the other sciences we have mentioned took over, each in its own terms, the rich rhetorical elements that esthetics would ban).[29]

He continues:

> But besides this job of *reclamation,* we also seek to develop our subject beyond the traditional bounds of rhetoric. There is an intermediate area of expression that is not wholly deliberate, yet not wholly unconscious. It lies midway between aimless utterance and speech deliberately purposive.[30]

In order to analyze this rhetorical area, Burke has to shift from reliance on "persuasion" to "identification" as the key term of rhetoric:

> Particularly when we come upon such aspects of persuasion as are found in "mystification," courtship, and the "magic" of class relationships, the reader will see why the classical notion of clear persuasive intent is not an accurate fit for describing the ways in which the members of a group promote social cohesion by acting rhetorically upon themselves and one another.[31]

At this point, I am not interested in examining Burke's concept of identification, which has already received ample critical attention. What interests me is the implications of this shift from "persuasion" to "identification" for a history of rhetoric. Consider, for instance, the second part of the book, which bears the title: "Traditional Principles of Rhetoric." In the first few pages (49–84), Burke examines some classical texts by Aristotle, Cicero, Quintilian, and St. Augustine where "persuasion" is the key term. Then, on page 90, there occurs a "break," a "rupture," in the text, as Burke begins to move with "identification" as the key concept into what I would call the "hidden" history of rhetoric. Here the task of "reclamation" proper begins: Bentham's theory of fictions, Marx on "Mystification" (*The German Ideology*), Carlyle on "Mystery" (*Sartor Resartus*), Diderot on "Pantomime"

(*Neveu de Rameau*), De Gourmont on "Dissociation" (*La Dissociation des Idées*), Pascal on "Directing the Intention," Administrative Rhetoric in Machiavelli, Dante's *De Vulgari Eloquentia,* and so on. After a long underground existence, the sophistic tradition in rhetoric has been rediscovered, reclaimed, and reconstituted.

Here Burke, the "reclaimer," is in his "true form." While tracking down the implications of "persuasion" in classical texts, Burke is impatient, restrained, like a tiger in a cage, summarizing the formal/tropological principles laboriously catalogued by Cicero in a mere page or two, and then quickly moving on to something else, say, Longinus' *On the Sublime.* But once we come to Bentham's *Book of Fallacies,* a dazzling intellectual journey begins, a veritable *tour de force* through the corridors of the history of ideas, interweaving text upon text, in the same breath speaking of Pascal and Joyce. It is a consummate performance.

It is almost impossible not to be seduced by this other "hidden" history of rhetoric, as "reconstituted" by Burke, especially when he invites "other analysts" to join him in "the task of tracking down the ways in which the realm of sheerly worldly powers become endowed with attributes of 'secular divinity.'"[32]

Who can refuse such an invitation, especially someone about to embark on rhetoric as a vocation. If accepted, this invitation calls at one level for extending the range of rhetoric, which I find perfectly legitimate. But that extension, in turn, requires a "reinterpretation" of the history of rhetoric that is problematic, if not ill-conceived.

Such is the seductive tale of the two histories of rhetoric. There are, to be sure, many other tales about the birth, the rise, the decline, the fall and even the "death" of rhetoric. These tales have been constructed frequently by those who are not themselves, as I am not, full-fledged historians of rhetoric. They are clearly political tales, meant to account for the troubled relationship between rhetoric and other disciplines and culture in general. They are designed so as to legitimate its claim to renewed intellectual and cultural attention. Each putative revivalist of rhetoric has to tell a tale of its glorious origins, its civilizing effects, its unjustified suppression, and its eventual demise and dispersion. So the tale I have told above on behalf of Kenneth Burke (unauthorized, to be sure) is only one among many tales circulating among the current revivalists of rhetoric. As a revivalist tale it is only partly true. And this tale, like so many of the recent tales about the history of rhetoric, is epistemologically driven. It speaks as though the quarrel between Plato and the older sophists over the epistemic status of rhetoric continually and exclusively shaped its complex history. It fails to acknowledge that from late antiquity to the high Middle Ages, Latin rhetorical instruction was largely dominated by two manuals of what George Kennedy calls "technical rhetoric": *De Inventione* and *Rhetorica ad Herrennium.*[33] It completely overlooks the third tradition in rhetoric, the tradition of civic humanism that stretches from Protagoras through Isocrates and Cicero to the Renaissance humanists, and continues to manifest itself in the activities of great orators like Edmund Burke. But these errors, repeatedly corrected by the orthodox historians like Kennedy and Vickers, continue to remain occluded from a disciplinary consciousness obsessed with abstract epistemological questions.

My reservations are quite simple. The "lure" of the hidden history has led to a denigration of the manifest history of rhetoric. One simple fact attests to this. Despite all the talk about the "Revival of Rhetoric" and the coming of the "New Rhetoric" in this century, we have yet to produce a definitive history of rhetoric. As an intellectual enterprise, rhetoric cannot continue to be viable without an adequate understanding of its own history, even if that history is an uninspiring one, which I don't think it is. If there is one thing we can learn from Jacques Derrida, it is that the history of a supplement may be more interesting than the history of that which is in need of a supplement.

The Second Movement: The Rhetoric of Inquiry

The second horizontal movement that propels rhetoric to constantly reconfirm its "presence" in the discourse of other disciplines is fashionably characterized these days as the "rhetorical turn" in the human sciences, or as the Iowa School prefers to call it the "rhetoric of inquiry."

In this paper I am not primarily concerned, as the Iowa School avowedly is, with the discovery of rhetoric by the practitioners of human sciences and the consequences of that discovery for the discursive practices of their disciplines. What interests me at this moment is the impact of that discovery on the self-understanding of rhetoric itself. To be sure, I recognize that rhetoric and the human sciences interpenetrate one another in innumerable ways, and the evolving dialectic between the two has a long history. What I seek to problematize here is but a single aspect of that dialectic.

The "rhetorical turn" refers to the growing recognition of rhetoric in contemporary thought, especially among the special substantive sciences. It means that the special sciences are becoming increasingly rhetorically self-conscious. They are beginning to recognize that their discursive practices, both internal and external, contain an unavoidable rhetorical component. *Internal* here refers to those discursive practices that are internal to a specific scientific language community; *external* refers to the discursive practices of that scientific language community in respect to its dealings with other scientific (or nonscientific) language communities and the society in general. While the external dimension is sometimes noted, the work of the Iowa School clearly emphasizes the internal dimension.

The existing body of literature pertaining to the internal dimension of the rhetorical turn in contemporary thought can be further divided into two groups: the explicit rhetorical turn and the implicit rhetorical turn. By *explicit* rhetorical turn, I refer to those works that explicitly recognize the relevance of rhetoric for contemporary thought and where rhetoric is used as a critical and interpretive method. The works of the following scholars, including those generally identified as the new rhetoricians (Chaim Perelman, Kenneth Burke, Richard McKeon, I. A. Richards, and Richard Weaver), may be placed in this category: Wayne Booth, Paul de Man, Walter J. Ong, Ernesto Grassi, Paolo Valesio, Northrop Frye, Tzvetan Todorov, Harold Bloom, Hugh Dalziel Duncan.

Clearly, however, those authors are not equally enthusiastic about rhetoric. While some of them have written several books on rhetoric, others confine their observations on rhetoric to a mere essay or two. While some of them view rhetoric as a general theory of discourse (hence a metadiscipline), others simply admit the importance of rhetoric for the human sciences and employ it as a critical instrument in their analyses of literary and social texts; and there are those who simply scatter the word *rhetoric* carelessly through their texts. For instance, there is a renewed interest in rhetoric among the literary critics. But the nature and intensity of interest varies significantly. Thus, while Wayne Booth, operating from a distinctly humanistic perspective, concentrates on the argumentative dimension of literature, especially novels, Paul de Man, operating from a deconstructionist perspective, stresses the figural dimension of literary language.[34] Other critics, like Frye, Todorov, Mailoux, and Bloom, have paid varying degrees of attention to rhetoric, but as opposed to Booth and de Man, we could not properly entitle them "rhetorical critics."

Finally and perhaps most important, there are also texts that evince signs of an *implicit* rhetorical turn. These are texts whose authors, while relatively unaware of the rhetorical lexicon, seem to be groping for a vocabulary that could adequately characterize the tropological and suasory aspects of the discursive practices that remain occluded from disciplinary consciousness.

The list of authors and their texts that evince signs of such an implicit rhetorical turn is truly formidable: Thomas Kuhn's *The Structure of Scientific Revolutions,* Paul Feyerabend's *Against Method,* Steven Toulmin's *The Uses of Argument,* Lacan's *Ecrits,* Gadamer's *Truth and Method,* Foucault's *Archeology of Knowledge,* and Habermas's *Legitimation Crisis,* to name a few. These are the master texts of our time, and they are, we are told, bristling with rhetorical insights, even though they often are not consciously recognized.

Furthermore, on some accounts, whole "schools of thought" reveal a decisively rhetorical orientation. Here one might list the sociology of knowledge tradition (from Scheler to Berger and Luckmann), the symbolic interactionists, the dramatistic movement in anthropology and sociology (Geertz, Turner, and Goffman), and various philosophical positions that stress the role of language and language action (e.g., the "later" Wittgenstein and the "early" Heidegger, Austin, Searle, and other speech-act theorists). The contemporary intellectual landscape is, thus, replete with signs of an implicit rhetorical turn. With a bit of diligence and, of course, with requisite faith, anyone could read those signs and celebrate what they portend.

The *locus classicus* of this implicit rhetorical turn in contemporary thought is Kuhn's *The Structure of Scientific Revolutions.*[35] The reasons for the choice of this text are quite obvious. *First,* it examines the discursive practices of the hard sciences, such as physics and chemistry. *Second,* it brings to light the rhetorical aspect of discursive practices internal to the scientific language community. *Third,* Kuhn makes these profound observations without the slightest awareness of the rhetorical lexicon. *Fourth,* though unconscious of rhetoric, he makes a fairly radical claim for the primacy of rhetoric when he asserts that "paradigm shifts" in any scientific community are more like religious conversions than carefully considered and well-reasoned shifts in scientific practices. *Fifth,* he calls for a reexamination of the history of science from a sociological perspective. He rejects the textbook version of the history of science as an idealization which assumes that the growth of knowledge is a purely logical-rational enterprise. These aspects of Kuhn's work have made him into the very embodiment of the rhetorical turn. If the discourse of the physicists cannot detach itself from rhetoric, how can the chatter of lesser mortals, such as historians and sociologists, hope to emancipate itself from rhetoric?

In short, it appears that there is more to the "rhetorical turn" than the mundane explicit turn. Just as there are two histories of rhetoric, the manifest and the hidden, there are two rhetorical turns, the explicit and the implicit. The lure of the implicit rhetorical turn is infinitely greater than the reality of the explicit rhetorical turn. Although the explicit rhetorical turn is a result of practical necessity—a literary critic like Booth, for example, is unable to make sense of novelistic prose without recourse to a rhetorical vocabulary and rhetorical sensibilities—the implicit rhetorical turn is a largely theoretical and epistemological enterprise. If the explicit rhetorical turn is only a decade or two old, the implicit rhetorical turn is of more ancient vintage. Its roots can be traced all the way back to that celebrated quarrel between Platonic Socrates and the older sophists. If Kenneth Burke is the chronicler of the hidden history of rhetoric, Professors Nelson and Megill have undertaken to chronicle the story of the implicit rhetorical turn. Nelson and Megill, along with Donald McCloskey, are the leading figures in the Iowa School, which has done much to place claims of the rhetorical turn before the scholarly community.

The Nelson and Megill Myth

In a recent essay, Nelson and Megill set out to furnish the "rhetoric of inquiry" with what they call an "animating myth."[36] They write:

> Rather, we sketch the development of the field so far, focusing on how early contributors have regarded rhetoric and inquiry. This is not the history of rhetoric, science, or philosophy widely familiar to scholars of communication. It is instead an animating myth of the new field.[37]

They are, however, certain that "what begins as myth ends as history." A myth of this sort requires a set of precursors who were but dimly aware of what they were doing, that is, preparing the way for the progressive dismantling of a logic of inquiry which is to be replaced by a rhetoric of inquiry.

Nelson and Megill do, indeed, give us a myth, a good one at that. It is reminiscent of Protagoras's reply in Plato's dialogue of that name when Socrates asks him to identify what he does. Protagoras admits to being "a sophist and an educator' (317b). But he claims to practice an ancient art and not something new and fashionable as people assume. According to Protagoras, since sophistry seems to arouse, however unjustifiably, suspicion among people, those who practiced it before did not admit to being sophists. They adopted suitable disguises and worked under the cover of some other profession. Homer, Hesiod, and Simonides claimed to be poets, Orpheus and Musaeus claimed to be musicians, and Herodicus of Selymbria claimed to be a physician. In fact, however, they were all sophists (316d–e). But that strategy of concealment did not work. They were discovered for what they were, and their attempt to disguise their art excited even greater mistrust. So Protagoras freely admits to being a sophist and welcomes any opportunity to explain and defend his art, for only through constant public exposure can sophistry hope to overcome the undeserved fear and suspicion with which it is presently regarded.

However, the myth which Nelson and Megill want to weave for us cannot be a simple Protagorean tale of exposing one's timorous and somewhat inept precursors. For them, rhetoric, and by implication the rhetoric of inquiry, is a ubiquitous and unavoidable component in human belief and behavior. Since rhetoric always already exists, it cannot be simply discovered and enunciated. It has to be rediscovered and reconstituted. For that reason, it must be first repressed and made to disappear. If someone is going to be credited with recovering and recuperating rhetoric, then someone must be charged with its prior repression and dispersion."

The story of the progressive repression of the rhetoric of inquiry begins, predictably enough, in the seventeenth century with the birth of modern philosophy—with Descartes' quest for "clear and distinct ideas." In the quest for certainty, the "empiricist" Locke and the "idealist" Kant follow the "rationalist" Descartes. They embrace mathematics as the ideal model of conviction and "dream of dispelling disagreement through demonstration." Thus, rhetoric comes to be repressed. The repression is carried out through a series of dichotomies: truth vs. opinion, object vs. subject, conviction vs. persuasion, all of which valorize the logic of inquiry over rhetoric.

This repression also had political implications. According to Nelson and Megill,

> Plato denigrated opinion and rhetoric so as to celebrate truth and order at a time of Greek conflict and Athenian decline. Similarly, Aristotle subordinated mythos to logos and rhetoric to dialectic. In an era when radical disagreements racked the peace of Europe, Descartes wrote off rhetoric in favor of mathematical reason and Hobbes enslaved language to the sovereign. Later, Kant sought perpetual peace through pure and practical reason.[38]

The sole voice of dissent on behalf of rhetoric in the late seventeenth and early eighteenth century was Vico, who opposed Cartesianism with the same sort of vigor with which Isocrates had once opposed Platonism. According to Nelson and Megill, effective opposition to the hegemonic rule of modern philosophy over scholarly inquiry did not occur until the late nineteenth century, and it is Nietzsche who emerges as the leading *persona:* "One *implicitly* rhetorical challenge to the sovereignty that modern philosophy claims over scholarship actually begins with Nietzsche's assault on the subject/object dichotomy."[39] As the opposition gathered speed and momentum in the twentieth century the privileged set of dichotomies was challenged, undermined, and dissolved. The quest for certainty was questioned.

The fear of disagreement abated. The mathematic model of conviction began to yield to the discursive model of persuasion. Modern epistemology came to be seen as a source of, rather than a shield against, the philosophical anxiety about "skepticism, solipsism, and nihilism." This challenge to "the Cartesian foundations and Kantian principles of modern philosophy" followed from a series of internal discursive crises and tensions in philosophy and science. Nelson and Megill identify three such crises (but do not discuss them): the philosophical attack on foundationalism, the philosophical reconstruction of science, and, the rhetorical conception of epistemology. And they enumerate a list of twentieth-century thinkers (a now familiar litany from Dewey and Heidegger through McIntyre and Rorty) who recognize and grapple with these crises and thus, unwittingly, open the way to a rhetoric of inquiry.

All this intellectual ferment, Nelson and Megill conclude, leads to Iowa City in the 1980s where the logic of inquiry is officially transformed into a rhetoric. This transformation yields a good many benefits: We will escape from the clutches of "Western rationalism and its paradox of authoritarian liberation." As we begin to pay more attention to the actual reasoning that goes on in scholarly inquiry, we will learn to "recognize that rhetoric is reasonable and reason is rhetorical." As we begin to notice that scholarship is also a mode of communication addressed to an audience, we will learn to "insist that rhetoric is contextual and context is rhetorical."

Such, then, is the history of the implicit rhetorical turn. (Note that, of the writers cited in this history, only Perelman, Burke, Booth, and White make systematic use of a rhetorical lexicon in their studies.) Nelson and Megill are, indeed, worthy successors to Kenneth Burke. They do for the implicit rhetorical turn what Burke has done for the hidden history of rhetoric.

The Lure of The Implicit Rhetorical Turn

Once again, in my opinion, the lure of the implicit rhetorical turn will gradually overwhelm, if it has not done so already, the promise of the explicit rhetorical turn. The implicit rhetorical turn will have the same sort of psychological hold over our disciplinary imagination as the hidden history of rhetoric has had since the publication of Burke's *A Rhetoric of Motives*.

The reason for this is quite simple. The study of the explicit rhetorical turn is, in the long run, a tedious affair, which is only occasionally redeemed by critical excellence and achievement, while the pursuit of the implicit rhetorical turn is a boldly constitutive, well-nigh archeological, venture, which "lures" us to discover "traces" of rhetoric virtually everywhere. The explicit rhetorical turn suffers from sheer obviousness. Once it is recognized, as it ought to be, that the discourse of the human sciences contains an unavoidable rhetorical component, the task of analysis consists in making explicit the functioning of that component in the production and the reception of discourses. There are some brilliant instances of such critical analysis. In an excellent essay, Hexter unpacks the rhetoric of history in terms of the historian's habitual and distinctive use of quotations, footnotes, and statistics in writing history, and he shows how the rhetoric of history differs from the rhetoric of natural sciences.[40] The type of rhetorical analysis of historiography that Hexter offers is unlikely to unsettle the self-understanding of rhetoric. For Hexter has merely shown how the discourse of history cannot productively emulate the rhetoric of natural sciences; and, his explication of rhetorical elements in historiography is analogous to the explication of "manifest" rhetoric in any discursive practice. The model for unpacking the argumentative strategies and the play of stylistic devices is much the same in history as in oratory.

In contrast, the implicit rhetorical turn is engaged in a far more grandiose project. It is, in essence, a philosophical enterprise, or to be more precise, it is a critique of Western metaphysics that begins with Nietzsche and continues in the work of Heidegger and his deconstructive followers. It is preoccupied with the theme of the end of philosophy (modernism, or the end of modernism), and sees in rhetoric an alternative to the foundationalist epistemology. The implicit rhetorical turn is thus largely a product of an internal crisis in philosophy. Here rhetoric becomes entangled in the schemes of those who are attempting to articulate a counter-tradition in philosophy. And the story of rhetoric's initial suppression and the subsequent recuperation is read, in the Nelson and Megill version, in terms of an objectivist/subjectivist dichotomy that has fractured Western consciousness since the beginning of philosophical reflection. Nelson and Megill are quite correct in asserting that an objectivist epistemology is generally damaging to the fortunes of rhetoric, while a subjectivist/relativist epistemology is more encouraging to its growth. But this observation is so broad as to be banal and not easily translatable into concepts for use. Moreover, such an enlarged epistemological perspective makes the idea of rhetoric so thoroughly elastic as to incorporate anyone averse to objectivism and foundationalism. In short, while the explicit rhetorical turn is local in its application, the implicit rhetorical turn is global in its aspirations.

Thus, it is hardly surprising that Nelson and Megill's prospectus for the "rhetoric of inquiry" should end, not with a whimper but with a bang:

> Our world is a creature and a texture of rhetorics: of founding stories and sales talks, anecdotes and statistics, images and rhythms; of tales told in nursery, pledges of allegiance or revenge, symbols of success and failure, archetypes of action and character. Ours is a world of persuasive definitions, expressive explanations, and institutional narratives. It is replete with figures of truth, models of reality, tropes of argument, and metaphors of experience. In our world, scholarship is rhetorical.[41]

This is, alas, the fate of rhetoric. Like Blanche DuBois in Tennessee Williams's *A Streetcar Named Desire,* we, the rhetoricians, have always relied on "the kindness of strangers," but too much kindness could kill us. We are either dismissed out of hand, excommunicated, cast out from the realm of light and truth, or we are given the whole world all to ourselves and asked to preside over "the conversation of mankind."[42]

Such is Nelson and Megill's myth for the new field. But the myth calls for some finer interpretation. How important is this story of repression and the subsequent regeneration of rhetoric of inquiry in the development of modern philosophy from Descartes to Derrida? Even Nelson and Megill will not venture to place it on the center stage. There are, to be sure, some negative comments about rhetoric in Descartes, Locke, and Kant. On the whole, however, they and their philosophical followers simply ignored rhetoric. If their work had the effect of repressing a rhetoric of inquiry, which I admit that it did, it was a latent outcome rather than a manifest intent. It would be preposterous to imagine that Kant set out to write the three critiques in order to repress rhetoric or to obviate a rhetoric of inquiry. The motivation for his labor came from different sources. Similarly, the dismantling of the modernist dogma in this century by Heidegger, Dewey, Wittgenstein, and others was not motivated by a manifest desire to make space for a rhetoric of inquiry. (I am not trying to suggest here that the suffocation of the rhetoric of inquiry under the modernist dogma was not genuine and severe simply because it was latent. Perhaps, it was more insidious because of its latency.)

Nelson and Megill will probably disagree with me on this point. For them the repression and the subsequent regeneration of the rhetoric of inquiry in modern philosophy is a critical thread. For me, it is a sideshow. The fact that it is a sideshow does not make me apologetic about the place of rhetoric in the life of the mind. The fact that it is a sideshow is in keeping with the nature and function of rhetoric.[43]

In the long and enduring quarrel between rhetoric and philosophy, the latter has not always set out to undermine the former.[44] Rhetoric has often been trampled on accidentally in philosophy's quest for certainty or whatever else it is bent on pursuing at any given time. Historically, philosophers have not evinced a profound concern with rhetoric. There is a sort of narcissistic streak in philosophy, an overdetermination of its own self-sufficiency and autonomy, which keeps it from seriously entertaining the competing claims of rhetoric.

There was only one philosopher, in my opinion, who set out earnestly to repress rhetoric; and when he couldn't, he sought to and pretty much succeeded in emasculating it. That was Plato. There was only one orator/rhetorician who seriously attempted to reconcile the competing claims of rhetoric and philosophy and pretty much succeeded in uniting the competing claims of eloquence and wisdom in his own person. That was Cicero. We might add other names to either column in this list, but, even by a liberal standard, the list would not be long.

This brings me to the main point. Academically rhetoric has never been able to determine its own fortune. It lies embedded in the cultural practices of the time. It is always already there as a supplement, as an insert. Extract it from that to which it is a supplement or from that within which it is embedded, and it evaporates. It is present, to borrow a phrase from Lacan, only in "the discourse of the other." Ironically, the art of eloquence has no voice of its own within the academy. Pure persuasion is possible, as Kenneth Burke tells us, only in the furthest regions of religion and poetry where one hesitates, as in *Finnegans Wake,* between sound and sense.

The fortunes of rhetoric, more than any other discipline, turn on the roll of cultural dice. Rhetoric has good days and bad days, mostly bad days. This is one of the good days. If there is a myth about rhetoric, it is that of an outsider whose day of reckoning is deferred, time and again.

This is my counter-myth for an old discipline which constantly seeks to escape itself. If you had to choose between the two myths, I suspect Nelson and Megill would carry the day, despite my carping . . . At least, that is what my myth requires me to believe. After all, this is one of the good days for rhetoric.

Conclusion

Finally, what is the significance of the rhetorical turn in the self-understanding of rhetoric? At the sociological level, the rhetorical turn implies a renewed disciplinary legitimacy for rhetoric as an intellectual enterprise. If rhetoric is an unavoidable component in discourses as diverse as theoretical physics, economics, literary criticism, and psychoanalysis, then, the story of rhetoric is a tale well worth telling. However, this would also suggest that the "legitimacy" of a formal discipline, such as rhetoric, is relative to its measurable "presence" in the substantive disciplines. This could be problematic, because, if rhetoric requires a constant "reconfirmation" of its "presence" in the discourse of other disciplines, it would suggest that rhetoric is a supplement to those discourses rather than constitutive of them. To put it differently, one could argue that rhetoric is parasitic vis-a-vis the special discourses rather than productive of them in the way that a "rule" is productive of a series of rule-governed actions, or that the "deep structure" of a natural language is said to be productive of its "surface structure." I believe (and this is a provisional statement) that an adequate understanding of the rhetoric of the human sciences is possible only when we have an adequate grasp of the logic of supplementarity within which rhetoric is habitually caught.

At another level, the rhetorical turn sets up an expectation that there would be a renaissance in rhetoric in the near future—that rhetoric would regain its lost glory as "the queen of the human sciences" in our time, and that it would preside over other disciplines as the metascience of culture in the Isocratean sense. The anticipation of a rhetorical turn could, thus, revive and set in motion the dormant foundational aspirations characteristic of formal, hence empty, disciplines like rhetoric, dialectic, and hermeneutics. That is, one has to travel but a short psychological distance to make that fatal move from anticipating a rhetorical turn in contemporary thought to proclaiming rhetoric as the foundational discipline (obviously, in its capacity as the general theory of discourse) for the human sciences.

Before we become intoxicated with such visions of grandeur, we have to ascertain exactly what role, if any, rhetoric as an academic discipline has played in bringing about this rhetorical turn, other than recognizing and celebrating its alleged arrival. As I indicated earlier, Kuhn's *The Structure of Scientific Revolutions,* which is treated as the *locus classicus* of the rhetorical turn, is entirely innocent of rhetoric as a discipline. This innocence or ignorance of rhetoric is not uncommon among the writers and the texts cited earlier as participating in the implicit rhetorical turn.

Even among those who write self-consciously about rhetoric and its presence, and whose texts were cited earlier as constituting the explicit rhetorical turn, few are conscious of rhetoric as an academic discipline. As for the majority, if they acknowledge their debt to rhetoric, it is usually to some classical texts, especially to Aristotle's *Rhetoric;* among the moderns, it is invariably Kenneth Burke and occasionally Perelman, and rarely I. A. Richards. For these writers, contemporary rhetoric simply means the idiosyncratic works of Kenneth Burke. This is best exemplified in the work of sociologist Hugh Dalziel Duncan, who has systematically, albeit mechanically, sought to reinterpret social theory from a decidedly rhetorical perspective, but the rhetorical perspective here simply means a Burkian perspective.[45] For other American writers like Geertz, Goffman, and Hayden White, who are clearly conscious of rhetoric, Burke provides the only link between classical rhetoric and its contemporary possibilities. The continental writers like Lacan, Derrida, Ricoeur, Gennette, and Gadamer, whose texts bristle with rhetorical concepts and terms, are either entirely unaware of Burke's work or only marginally aware of it.

But on the whole, it is clear that rhetoricians have played but a limited role in bringing about this rhetorical turn. What concerns me here is not the sociological embarrassment resulting from the fact that we who celebrate this "rhetorical turn" in contemporary thought have contributed so little to its making. What does concern me is the fact that people like Kuhn and Toulmin were driven to make certain observations, which we characterize as marking a rhetorical turn in their respective thinking, by the internal logic (both synchronic and diachronic) of their own special discourses. They became, as it were, infected with a "rhetorical consciousness" by immersing themselves in their own special discourses and by tracing the discursive implications of their own distinctive theory and practice. It was not as if they were struggling for a vocabulary, absent in the ordinary language, that could articulate their "break" from the traditional discourse. The "break," or the "rupture," in the traditional discursive practices with which their names are associated neither occurred nor came to be articulated as a result of their sudden acquaintance with the rhetorical lexicon. Kuhn was not awakened from his dogmatic slumber after reading Aristotle or Burke, as Kant allegedly was after reading Hume.

To be sure, one could argue that it would have been easier for Kuhn to articulate his rhetorical insights had he been acquainted with the rhetorical tradition. This could serve as an argument for a greater dissemination of rhetorical lore in our culture, especially in the academy. But one could just as easily argue that in some situations a familiarity with the rhetorical lexicon could be a hindrance. Perhaps people like Kuhn do not really need a stylized rhetorical lexicon to recognize rhetoric; and their rhetorical insights are possibly richer, less labored, and more firmly grounded precisely because they are the insights of someone driven by the compulsions of a special discourse in search of a special knowledge, the knowledge of the world so to speak. The ordinary language which, as Cicero reminds us, is the language of rhetoric, is sufficiently versatile to meet the needs of a Kuhn or a Toulmin. If we follow this logic, then, it would appear that an institutionalized presence of rhetoric is neither necessary nor sufficient for the rhetorical turn.

Furthermore, it may be interesting to note that these fabled rhetorical turns occur in times of crisis. Clearly, Kuhn's theory about paradigm shifts, Habermas's thesis regarding the legitimation crisis in the modern welfare state, and Derrida's method of reading as a textual "deconstruction" refer to and have their origin in specific crisis situations, be they in scientific theory, social theory or literary theory. Perhaps it is during the discursive crises that a scientific language community becomes "rhetorically conscious." Further, we could argue that every special discourse and every scientific language community periodically goes through "rhetorical stages." And sometimes the general culture itself, passing through a general crisis, becomes rhetorically self-conscious. But with the passing of the crisis, the rhetorical consciousness once again erodes. That is, the emergence of a rhetorical consciousness is directly related to a crisis within a special discourse. That relation can be formulated as follows: A crisis, discursive or otherwise, makes rhetoric visible; that is, a crisis brings to the fore the incipient rhetorical consciousness. The sheer possibility of a rhetorical consciousness, the possibility that rhetoric is a permanent though unrealized opening for man, does not by itself induce a crisis, but it is something always waiting to be exploited when the crisis comes. In short, rhetoric is the medium and not the ground of discursive and cultural crises.

Notes

1. Chaim Perelman and L. Olbrechts-Tyteca, *The New Rhetoric: A Treatise on Argumentation,* trans. John Wilkinson and Purcell Weaver (Notre Dame, Ind.: University of Notre Dame Press, 1969); Paolo Valesio, *Novantiqua: Rhetoric as Contemporary Theory* (Bloomington, Ind.: Indiana University Press, 1980). For a tendency to subordinate rhetoric to dialectic, see Maurice Natanson, "The Limits of Rhetoric," *Quarterly Journal of Speech* 41 (1955): 133–39; Richard Weaver, "The *Phaedrus* and the Nature of Rhetoric," in his *The Ethics of Rhetoric* (Chicago: Henry Regnery Co., 1953), 3–26.
2. Ernesto Grassi, *Rhetoric as Philosophy: The Humanistic Tradition* (University Park, Pa.: The Pennsylvania University Press, 1980).
3. Roland Barthes, "The Old Rhetoric: An Aide-Memoire," in his *The Semiotic Challenge,* trans. Richard Howard (New York: Hill and Wang, 1988), 46.
4. Aristotle, *The Art of Rhetoric,* ed. and trans. Lane Cooper (New York: Appleton-Century-Croft, 1932), 9.
5. Brian Vickers, "Territorial Disputes: Philosophy versus Rhetoric," in *Rhetoric Revalued,* ed. Brian Vickers (Binghamton, N.Y.: Medieval and Renaissance Texts and Studies, 1982), 248.
6. Cicero, "Fourth Philippic," in *The World's Great Speeches,* 3d ed., ed. Lewis Copeland and Lawrence W. Lamm (New York: Dover Publications, 1973), 48.
7. This phrase—*alte und neue Konigin der Wissenschaften*—comes from Walter Jens, *Von Deutscher Rede* (Munich: Piper, 1969), and is cited by Chaim Perelman in *The Realm of Rhetoric,* trans. William Kluback (Notre Dame, Ind.: University of Notre Dame Press, 1982), 162.
8. Alfred Schutz, *The Phenomenology of the Social World,* trans. George Walsh and Frederick Lehnert (Evanston, Ill.: Northwestern University Press, 1967). Also see his *Collected Papers,* vol. 1, subtitled *The Problems of Social Reality,* ed. Maurice Natanson (The Hague: Martinus Nijhoff, 1971).
9. For a discussion of "essentially contested concepts," see W. B. Gallie, *Philosophy and the Historical Understanding* (New York: Schocken, 1964), 157–91.
10. For an excellent critical survey of the literature on this question in the speech communication journals, see Michael Leff, "In Search of Ariadne's Thread: A Review of the Recent Literature on Rhetorical Theory," this volume.
11. Jacques Derrida, *Of Grammatology,* trans. Gayatri Chakravorty Spivak (Baltimore: Johns Hopkins University Press, 1976). Also see "Plato's Pharmacy," in his *Dissemination,* trans. Barbara Johnson (Chicago: University of Chicago Press, 1981), 61–171.

12. Aristotle, *The "Art" of Rhetoric,* trans. John Henry Freese (Cambridge, Mass.: Harvard University Press [Loeb ed.], 1926), 19 (1856a).

13. Lloyd Bitzer, "Political Rhetoric," in *Handbook of Political Communication,* ed. Dan Nimmo and Keith Sanders (Beverly Hills: Sage Publications, 1981), 225–48.

14. Michael Leff, "The Habitation of Rhetoric," in *Argument and Critical Practices: Proceedings of the Fifth SCA/AFA Conference on Argumentation,* ed. Joseph Wenzel et al. (Annandale, Va: SCA Publications, 1987), 5.

15. Bitzer, "Political Rhetoric," 231.

16. Paul Ricoeur, *The Rule of Metaphor: Multidisciplinary Studies in the Creation of Meaning in Language,* trans. Robert Czerny with Kathleen McLaughlin and John Costello (Toronto: University of Toronto Press, 1976), 30.

17. Kenneth Burke, *A Rhetoric of Motives* (Berkeley: University of California Press, 1969, 1950), 54–55.

18. Barthes, "The Old Rhetoric," 73.

19. Ibid., 75.

20. Cicero, *De Oratore,* 2 vols., trans. E. W. Sutton (Cambridge, Mass.: Harvard University Press [Loeb ed.], 1942); Saint Augustine, *On Christian Doctrine,* trans. D. W. Robertson, Jr. (New York: Bobbs-Merrill, 1958). In Cicero's *De Oratore,* there are a number of references to rhetoric (the art or theory of oratory) as a supplement to inborn talent and correct practice based on imitation of suitable models. Cicero, while exalting the powers of the orator in a variety of ways, repeatedly observes that the art of oratory cannot produce the orator by itself without assistance from nature, which supplies talent, and practice, which deepens and perfects talent. The art itself, according to Cicero, plays but a minor role, and what is there to understand of the art can be obtained easily and quickly. Augustine is more explicit about the status of rhetoric as a supplement. In the fourth book of *De Doctrina Christiana,* rhetoric is clearly drawn into the orbit of hermeneutics as a supplement to elucidate what interpretation has uncovered of the sacred texts.

21. Cited in George A. Kennedy, *Classical Rhetoric and Its Christian and Secular Tradition from Ancient to Modern Times* (Chapel Hill: University of North Carolina Press, 1980), 240.

22. Cited by Lane Cooper, trans. and ed., in *The Rhetoric of Aristotle* (New York: Appleton-Century-Croft, 1932), xii.

23. For a general overview on the sophists in the light of the current revival of scholarly interest in them, see W. K. C. Guthrie, *The Sophists* (New York: Cambridge University Press, 1971), and G. B. Kerferd, *The Sophistic Movement* (New York: Cambridge University Press, 1981).

24. For an early attempt to articulate the ontological basis of rhetoric, see Karlyn K. Campbell "The Ontological Foundation of Rhetorical Theory," *Philosophy and Rhetoric* 3 (1970), 97–108.

25. Hannah Arendt, *The Human Condition* (New York: Anchor, 1958), 10.

26. Paul de Man, *Allegories of Reading* (New Haven, Conn.: Yale University Press, 1979), 103–31; Tzvetan Todorov, *Theories of the Symbol,* trans. Catherine Porter (Ithaca, N.Y.: Cornell University Press, 1982), 60–110.

27. For the most influential account of the "reality construction" thesis, see Peter L. Berger and Thomas Luckmann, *The Social Construction of Reality: A Treatise in the Sociology of Knowledge* (New York: Anchor Books, 1967, 1966).

28. For an account of rhetoric as a "material force," see Michael Calvin McGee, "A Materialist's Conception of Rhetoric," in *Explorations in Rhetoric: Studies in honor of Douglas Ehninger,* ed. R. E. McKerrow (Glenville, Ill.: Scott, Foresman, 1982), 23–49.

29. Burke, *A Rhetoric of Motives ,* xiii.

30. Ibid.

31. Ibid., xiv.

32. Kenneth Burke, *A Grammar of Motives and A Rhetoric of Motives* (New York: Meridian Books, 1962), 523.

33. Kennedy, *Classical Rhetoric,* 86–107.

34. Wayne C. Booth, *The Rhetoric of Fiction* (Chicago: University of Chicago Press, 1961, 1983); Paul de Man, *The Rhetoric of Romanticism* (New York: Columbia University Press, 1984).

35. Thomas S. Kuhn, *The Structure of Scientific Revolutions* (Chicago: University of Chicago Press, 1962, 1970).

36. John S. Nelson and Allan Megill, "Rhetoric of Inquiry: Projects and Prospects," *Quarterly Journal of Speech* 72 (1986), 20–37. McCloskey appears to share the views of Nelson and Megill on the prospects of a rhetoric of inquiry. This same essay, with minor modifications, appears as the introductory essay in the volume of papers from the Iowa conference held on 28–31 March 1984. See John S. Nelson,

Allan Megill, and Donald N. McCloskey, eds., *The Rhetoric of the Human Sciences: Language and Argument in Scholarship and Public Affairs* (Madison: The University of Wisconsin Press, 1987), 3–18.

37. Nelson and Megill, "Rhetoric of Inquiry," 20.

38. Ibid., 22–23.

39. Ibid., 24.

40. J. H. Hexter, "The Rhetoric of History," *History and Theory* 6 (1967), 1–14. For an expanded version of the same essay, see the chapter by the same title in his *Doing History* (Bloomington, Ind.: Indiana University Press, 1971), 15–76.

41. Nelson and Megill, "Rhetoric of Inquiry," 36.

42. This popular phrase among the proponents of the rhetorical turn was originally coined by Michael Oakeshott in "Poetry as a Voice in the Conversation of Mankind," in his *Experience and Its Modes* (1933), and reprinted in his *Rationalism in Politics* (New York: Methuen, 1962), 197–247.

43. On the "marginality" of rhetoric in the disciplinary contest for "status," see Robert Hariman, "Status, Marginality, and Rhetorical Theory," *Quarterly Journal of Speech* 72 (1986), 38–52.

44. The literature on the quarrel between philosophy and rhetoric is quite extensive. For both an historically and conceptually informed general view of the quarrel, see, Brian Vickers, *In Defense of Rhetoric* (Oxford: Clarendon Press, 1988), especially chs. 2 & 3, 83–213.

45. Hugh Dalziel Duncan, *Communication and Social Order* (New York: Oxford University Press, 1968, 1962).

Contested Histories of Rhetoric:
The Politics of Preservation,
Progress, and Change
by Carole Blair

New scholarship in the history of rhetorical theory increasingly gestures toward the need to revise or reform that field of inquiry. Critiques of historiographic assumptions and procedures have multiplied, and the problems they identify in traditional histories of rhetoric are legion.[1] These critical accounts have been global, cataloging multiple problems. Yet two common themes emerge in a number of these treatments: (1) that historiographic stances in histories of rhetoric contain embedded, but typically unacknowledged, presuppositions about history and/or rhetoric; and (2) that historians' assumption of these stances has culminated in partial historical accounts that mask their own partiality.

Put differently, histories of rhetoric are themselves rhetorical, but, ironically, they are "blind to [their] own rhetoric" (LaCapra, *History and Criticism* 17).[2] It is especially peculiar that rhetoricians, who have identified and explored rhetorics of various fields of inquiry, have neglected the rhetoricity of their own historical studies.[3] Blair and Kahl observe the diversity of inventional choices that historians of rhetorical theory make, and they argue that, "One who reads a history of rhetorical theory is not . . . merely absorbing enormous numbers of texts that have been condensed or re-presented by the historian. Rather one reads the historian's choices, reinscriptions and interventions, which constitute a particular reenactment of a conversation with the past of rhetorical theory. To the extent that we take the history of rhetoric seriously, we must take the historian's inventional choices as seriously" (148). They conclude that historians "have barely considered these

Reprinted from *The Quarterly Journal of Speech* 78 (1992), with permission of the National Communication Association.

choices at all" (148). Murphy suggests one result, that "there is no clear agreement on the principles which should govern the historiography of rhetoric. There are certainly problems enough" ("Historiography" 4).[4] Vitanza suggests another, that historians might "fall prey to . . . a form of *ideological terrorism*" in giving too little heed to their historical assumptions and methods (93).

My objective in this essay is to explore only one of the rhetorical problems of traditional histories, what Blair and Kahl describe as the organization of historical theories according to patterns of continuity and discontinuity. They suggest that, "Continuous histories present the field of rhetoric as a singular path of development or influence over time," while discontinuous history marks "major discontinuities and disruptions in the development of rhetorical theories and maps large synchronous blocs" of rhetorical theorizing (152). These patterns typically take the form of influence studies and systems histories. I will argue that these patterns of organization embody implicit rhetorical-political stances that work to defeat the principal goal of historical inquiry in rhetorical theory.

The suggestion that traditional historical practices have foreclosed the goals of rhetoric's disciplinary history is rather difficult to maintain, for historians have been diffident in describing their objectives. For the purposes of this discussion, however, I will take the primary goal of historical study of rhetorical theory to be the continued enrichment of our understanding of rhetoric. That seems unextraordinary; historians of rhetoric typically are rhetoricians, not historians. For rhetoricians, historical study should be directed toward deriving insight from the works of past thinkers who also were interested and/or engaged in rhetoric. Michael Leff concurs, suggesting that, "The most important function of the history of rhetoric is to guide our understanding of the nature of rhetoric itself; and this function does not easily divide into questions of past fact and future policy" ("Concrete Abstractions" 24). Enos goes further, arguing that the *presumption* of historical studies is that they "will provide evidence leading to greater knowledge of communication" (28).[5]

What is explicit in both Leff's and Enos' statements is a future orientation. Theoretical understanding of rhetorics of the past underwrites our capacity for further theorizing. Historical rhetorics provide material capable of appropriation and accommodation; they also contain aspects, components, and ways of thinking that may be altered or rejected, or that may even spur radical ways of retheorizing rhetoric. Implicit in these statements is the suggestion that the history of rhetorical theory can enhance the potential for future theorizing by elaborating the particularities of multiple historical views of rhetoric. Arguing against the idea that the availability of more views of rhetoric grounds broader understanding is difficult. Duhamel put the case clearly, if negatively, when he suggested that, "If histories of rhetoric are to be written after first postulating a definition of the concept and then re-examining the history of the assumed concept, the resulting inquiry would be the history not of rhetoric but of one conception of rhetoric" ("Function" 38).[6] The objective of historical studies of rhetoric, on this view, should be the continued and enhanced understanding of rhetoric.

Both influence and systems studies implicitly work to defeat this historical objective. The influence study embodies a politics of preservation; its practice sacralizes ancient rhetorical theory by treating later rhetorics as monuments to classical rhetoric. Influence studies typically treat ancient Greek and Roman works with an uncritical reverence; they treat later rhetorics as derivations or versions of ancient rhetoric, thus privileging the ancient writers. These histories frequently overlook, snub, or distort the writings of later thinkers, especially those that did not hold to the classical tradition. As a result, influence studies conceal the particularity of later views, even though such particularities might offer insights not available in earlier works. Moreover, in venerating originary works, these histories imply that future attempts to theorize rhetoric must either emulate and appropriate ancient doctrine or run the risk of being judged inadequate.[7]

Systems studies reflect a different politics, but with similar implications. This pluralist, progressive politics presents the history of rhetoric as a succession of paradigms that have given rise to present ways of theorizing. Systems studies treat historical rhetorics as relics of a primitive past that were *necessary* to the progress that produced the present state of knowledge. The systems approach is pluralist in that it admits of several systems or paradigms of rhetoric, in contrast to the more unitary view of the influence study which treats ancient rhetoric as a "preferred archetype from which all departures are greater or lesser aberrations" (Ehninger, "On Systems" 55). Although they are pluralist, systems studies are almost as reductive in character as their counterpart influence studies; they reduce the particularity of historical theories to the characterizing containers of three or four "systems." Moreover, in valuing the present state of knowledge as the culmination of a series of improvements in rhetorical theorizing, systems studies implicitly devalue attempts to rethink rhetoric outside of this privileged present.

Influence and systems may appear to be neutral models of temporality, dispositional devices used by historians of rhetoric to lend organizational coherence to their chronicles. In fact, they constitute competitive rhetorics of history with serious entailments for how we understand rhetoric's theoretical past and how we accommodate and situate future inquiry in rhetorical theory.[8] In illustrating the problems with influence and systems study of historical rhetorics, I hope to provoke further discussion of historiographic issues and to entertain the idea of an alternative historical practice.[9] Some possible directions for a "critical history" follow my discussion of influence and systems study.

Influence and the Politics of Preservation

A concentration upon the continuity of "the rhetorical tradition" is perhaps still the most pervasive theme in histories of rhetorical theory. Some studies, like Kennedy's *Classical Rhetoric,* are devoted exclusively to tracing the influences of early thinkers on later ones: "This book as a whole is an attempt to define classical rhetoric and its tradition by examining the various strands of thought which are woven together in different ways at different times" (3). Murphy's goal for his comprehensive history of the Middle Ages reflects this theme as well: "This book, then, provides the first comparative study of the various forms in which medieval writers continued the preceptive tradition. Whether applied to preaching, verse-writing, letter-writing, or other fields, it is clear that the basic preceptive assumption continues through the period from Saint Augustine to the revival of classical learning in the Renaissance" (*Rhetoric in the Middle Ages* ix).[10]

Even in historical studies not explicitly dedicated to this goal, influence is a ubiquitous theme. Tracing influence sometimes is even equated with the study of history.[11] This equation, in fact, appears to have become such a dictate of historical writing that historians have resorted to a number of questionable argumentative strategies to claim patterns of influence. They minimize the particular character of theories in order to maintain claims for influence, and they often overlook or ignore theories that do not fit the influence configuration. When historians do consider theories that do not align with a linear influence sequence, they treat these theories as aberrant. And, these historians frequently expend more space arguing for an influence pattern than they do exploring what the theorists said about rhetoric.

That historians sometimes minimize the particular nature of the historical texts they study to establish influence is illustrated in Conley's assessment of Kennedy's *Classical Rhetoric.* He suggests that, "If he passes over subjects like these [Byzantine thought, John of Salisbury, Ciceronianism in the Italian Renaissance] rather hastily, Kennedy seems determined to find classical influence where it can barely be glimpsed—in Locke and Hume, for instance" ("Kennedy" 207). Ward and Bitzer join Conley in noting this tendency in Kennedy's history. Ward observes that, "One is left to wonder . . . what the major novel insights of the Renaissance rhetorician actually were" ("Kennedy" 212). And Bitzer complains that, "[R]eaders particularly drawn to the modern or new rhetorics of the eighteenth and nineteenth centuries will be disappointed because Kennedy examines the moderns with far less than his usual detail and acumen. His focus on classical rhetoric and its fortunes perhaps led him to compress his coverage of modern rhetorics *not sufficiently exhibiting marks of classicism*" ("Kennedy" 213. Emphasis added). Here Bitzer notes not only the problem but also the conditions giving rise to it. He identifies the focus on classical rhetoric's influence as the cause of the problem.

This tendency to eclipse the historical materials themselves is not an accident of application in influence studies; it is inherent in the model of influence itself.[12] The historian who traces influences attempts to find in a theory only what has been said before. S/he tries to locate characteristics of a theory that render it similar to antecedent theories. In so doing, the historian is almost certain to pass over the unique features of a theoretical text, seeing in it only those characteristics that are reminiscent of an earlier theory.

Kennedy's work is not unique in this approach,[13] nor is Bitzer alone in accounting for the problems. Bevilacqua notes the same approach and consequences in Howell's treatment of eighteenth-century rhetoric:

> To measure the rhetorical modernity of Joseph Priestley, for example, by his seemingly unenthusiastic view of *topoi*, while largely disregarding Priestley's enthusiastic acceptance of Bacon's *inventio* and his particularly influential espousal of eighteenth-

century association psychology is *methodologically* to distort both the tenor and precept of Priestley's rhetoric. *It is in fact to characterize the new rhetoric in terms of essentially irrelevant concerns of the old rhetoric* . . . ("W. S. Howell" 345. Emphasis added)

Such observations as this point to a major problem of influence studies. In their attempt to locate temporal continuity among theories, writers of such works overlook vital aspects of theories or reduce them to adumbrations of their predecessors.

In cases in which influence is difficult to establish, historians still assert it, often to the point of minimizing documentary evidence. Seigel suggests that, "Although Petrarch seems never to have quoted Cicero's direct statements on the harmony of Peripatetic ethics with the tasks of the orator, *he must have felt the connection*" (56. Emphasis added). And Kennedy argues that:

The only surviving precedent for Quintilian's discussion of Greek authors is the work of Dionysius of Halicarnassus, *On Imitation.* Quintilian does not refer to this, though *he may have read it at some time* since Dionysius was well known to him (III,i,16). The parallels between what Dionysius says and Quintilian's chapter are great enough to suggest that we arc dealing with a recognized tradition, but not close enough to prove that Quintilian has copied Dionysius. (*Quintilian* 106–7. Emphasis added)[14]

These speculations, while not very enlightening, seem harmless in comparison to the practice of leaving entire theories out of a history to argue for a linear path of influence.

Seigel is the most explicit about overlooking theories that do not "fit" his general pattern of continuity. He admits "an element of the arbitrary in presenting this development only through the thinkers treated here; had other humanists been included, the line of evolution might have been less clear" (255–6).[15] In his admission, Seigel acknowledges that establishing influence is more important than understanding the theories. He has chosen to include in his study only those theorists who exemplify the line of influence for which he argues.

Even when an historian considers theories that depart from the influence of an antecedent source, s/he sometimes simply dismisses the later writer's modifications as wrongheaded or confused.[16] Kennedy calls critics of Ramus "perceptive" for noting "several features of Ramism which negate or even vitiate the principles on which classical rhetoric is based." He finds it less than surprising that a "reassertion of the fuller tradition of classical rhetoric soon emerged" as a response to Ramism (*Classical Rhetoric* 212). Howell suggested that Wilson "shows traces of confusion . . . particularly when he first explains what the legal state is" (*Logic and Rhetoric* 100). Howell grounded this claim by describing the "only" interpretation "justified by the *Rhetorica ad Herennium,* from which Wilson's classification of states is derived" (100n). Whether Kennedy's and Howell's assessments are legitimate judgments is irrelevant; the grounds are unacceptable. Extended to their logical conclusions, these premises would render all variations on earlier theories confused or wrong.

Perhaps the most problematic feature of influence studies, however, is the historian's focus on the influence of one thinker on another at the expense of what either of them said about rhetoric. For example, in discussing Priestley's rhetoric, Bevilacqua and Murphy spend more time identifying antecedent sources than exploring the entailments or value of those ideas. Others render judgments of theories on the grounds that they were influential. Warnick responds to the "discrepant" valuations of Rollin's *Traité des études* (45–7), by concluding that "its educational and critical theories influenced English belletristic rhetoricians" (65). Murphy uses the same standard of judgment, assessing Alcuin's work as "stillborn," on the grounds that "[i]ts influence was negligible . . . " (*Rhetoric in the Middle Ages* 81–2). The degree of influence a theory had in a later period is a facile and unworthy standard for judging its value, because it tells us little about what we or future theorists might learn from it. This standard focuses on a work's later appropriation rather than its theoretical value or substance.

Whether studying a pattern of influence is worthwhile or useful at all is worth considering. Historians become mired in questions and disputes over what or who influenced whom and how much, but the answers and resolutions often do not further theoretical understanding. The quality of argumentation that results is exemplified by Howell's insistence that John Milton was a Ramist:

> A recent interpreter of Milton's attitude toward Ramism, P. Albert Duhamel, argues that Milton "was never a Ramist except superficially," and uses as proof, among other considerations, the opening words of the quotation . . . where Milton promises to explain Ramism "except when I disagree." It is true that Milton like every other English Ramist disagrees in some particulars with Ramus's own logical doctrine. . . . But, it must always be remembered that Ramus had encouraged disagreement between himself and the scholastics. Moreover it must be insisted that, while Milton availed himself of opportunities to disagree with Ramus, he did not therefore become a superficial Ramist or covert Peripatetic. Had he wanted to write an Aristotelian logic, he would have modeled his work upon such neo-scholastic logics of his day as Bludedville's *The Arte of Logicke,* Smith's *Aditus ad Logican,* or Sanderson's *Logicae Artis Compendium. (Logic and Rhetoric* 216)[17]

Howell artificially dichotomized the possibilities open to Milton: if Milton was not a Ramist, than he would have had to be an Aristotelian. And if he were an Aristotelian he *would have* modeled his work on that of other neo-scholastics.[18] Additionally, Howell argued that Milton's disagreements with Ramus could be overlooked, for Ramus encouraged disagreement. On that premise, *anyone* might be classified a Ramist, no matter how much that individual's view differed from Ramus's.[19]

I do not mean to suggest that continuity or sequence among historical rhetoric is lacking or that either is unimportant. The temporal character of rhetoric's history is an interesting question, but certainly not more important for rhetoricians than the substantive character of historical rhetorics. In attempting to establish a case for a linear sequence of influence, these historians mask and/or distort the particularity of rhetorical theories, the *details* that make them theoretically significant.

These attempts to establish patterns of influence rely on unsound argumentative practices that mask the particularities of and differences among historical rhetorics. However, these problems should not be attributed to the ineptitude of historians. "Influence," apparently a neutral, organizational device *used by* historians, is a marker for a preservative politics that *dictates* the maintenance or continuity of tradition. To the extent that establishing influence is equated with writing history, this politics succeeds. This stance posits a privileged origin, a "golden age" of rhetorical theorizing that has been recovered and monumentalized in later works. The role of later works in the history of rhetoric is one of *memory;* they are treated as monuments to classical rhetoric, not as contributors to rhetorical thought. The later rhetorics reinforce the overwhelming significance and value of classical rhetoric in appropriating it and demonstrating its timelessness. Those rhetorical theories that depart from the classics or that cannot be contained within the influence pattern are devalued; they become symptoms of decadence, decline, or irrelevance in rhetorical theorizing.

Although this preservative politics usually is not fully articulated, traces of it surface in histories of rhetorical theory. Vickers is the most explicit about it: "In the study of rhetoric, as with all other disciplines, a narrow conception leads to narrow thinking, facile rejections, and hasty abandonment of the subject. Give rhetoric a trivial function and you trivialize it; *conceive of it as widely as it originally existed, and you may begin to do justice to it*" ("Rhetorical" 105. Emphasis added).[20] Vickers, in fact, finds rhetoric in need of a restorative "Defence," apparently because of its decline since ancient times. He argues that Aristotle's *Rhetoric* "remains the most penetrating analysis of speech in its full individual and social dimension" (*In Defence* 26).[21] In contrast to what he sees as the "fragmentation" of rhetoric in the Middle Ages, Vickers suggests that "Renaissance rhetoric got things back into the proper perspective" (*In Defence* 253), apparently because of its more classical orientation.[22] And he finds "in contemporary work on rhetoric, evidence of a progressive atrophy of the discipline" (*In Defence* 439). Vickers and others who subscribe to this view refuse innovation and difference.[23] Influence studies preserve classical rhetoric, valorize it, and if necessary defend it. Attempts to retheorize rhetoric are condemned as further evidence of departure or decline from ancient times. On this view, contemporary rhetoricians theorize at their own risk, for they may become a new chapter on rhetoric's continued decline.

While departures from ancient doctrine are scorned, those rhetorics that were influenced by the classics are trivialized as were monuments to the works they appropriated. Abbreviated examples of such trivialization abound. Fogarty described Cicero's "basic philosophy [as] Aristotelian" (16); Howell referred over and over to Whately as an Aristotelian or even a "convinced Aristotelian" (*Eighteenth-Century* 576, 708, 710, 712); Bevilacqua describes Campbell's theory as "basically classical" ("Philosophical Origins" 4); and Seigel describes Alcuin's work as "thoroughly Ciceronian" (180). Fogarty suggested that Melanchthon, Cox, and Sherry "did little but reorganize the traditional ideas of Aristotelian theory with the Ciceronian emphasis upon style" (18). Howell asserted that the "distinctive" characteristic of Wilson's theory was "that he followed Cicero ..." ("Ramus"

303–4). And Clarke went so far as to suggest that the lesser Latin rhetoricians "do not deserve to be read on their own account . . . " (139), in part because of their heavy reliance on prior sources (140). The trivialization of these "influenced" thinkers in these instances is clear; each merely reflected the earlier works they appropriated. The "influencing" theories are privileged at least implicitly, for they are portrayed as durable and as worthy of appropriation or emulation.

In all of these cases, a classical theorist or work, or classicism in general, is valorized. Others have noted historians' fervent admiration for and privilege of classical sources. Covino describes the history of rhetoric as "a series of footnotes to the Ancients" (45). McKeon argued that, since the Renaissance, the history of rhetoric has been "in part the monotonous enumeration of doctrines . . . repeated from Cicero or commentators of Cicero" ("Rhetoric" 121). Influence studies present the history of rhetoric as a linear series of appropriations of ancient Greek and Roman rhetoric; departures from the ancients are devalued. Influence studies, thus, are inherently preservative. They argue, at least implicitly, that the best theorizing has already occurred and that the most we can (or should) do is to revive, imitate, or resuscitate ancient work. Influence studies treat later rhetorical theories as variations or departures from earlier ones. They present classical rhetoric as the single coherent and systematic view, the single origin from which all later rhetorics derive, or as the prototype against which all later theories must be judged. The unique substance of later theories is circumscribed in these accounts, their rhetorics reduced to versions of, and thus monuments to, classical rhetoric. Any theoretical *difference* that they may have with ancient sources is sacrificed to the desire to maintain a linear, influential tradition.[24] But these differences are the potential source of theoretical significance and insight. Consideration of the substantive differences between Aristotle and theorist X would serve current and future understandings of rhetoric more than does the argument that theorist X's rhetoric was Aristotelian.

The single, residual vision of rhetoric from which current and future theorists might draw insight or from which they might depart, on the view of influence studies, is an ancient one. Moreover, that single vision, presented as it is in influence studies, implies a formidable challenge to anyone who would depart from it. In light of classical rhetoric's long and venerable history of preservation, any "new" rhetoric is suspect, or it is itself rendered as a marker of decline, reduced to a flawed or inadequate version of the tradition.

Systems and the Politics of Progress

Douglas Ehninger introduced the notion of historical "systems" of rhetorical theory as an alternative to "arid catalogues of names, dates and passages; a record of who said what, when, under the influence of which predecessors and with what effect on those who followed" ("Promise" 8). The purpose of his perspective was to consider multiple historical theories in terms of their own unique characteristics and their responses to the temporal contexts in which they were generated. Ehninger claimed that, "[T]he central task of the historian of rhetorical thought is to explore the nexus between theories of communication and the intellectual, cultural, and socio-political environments in which those theories arose and flourished" ("Promise" 6). Thus, in lieu of accepting the continuous, linear connections among rhetorical theories that characterize influences studies, Ehninger advocated the inscription of rhetorical theories within their own temporal contexts. These different contexts, he argued, gave rise to new, sometimes revolutionary, systems of theory production ("Colloquy" 452). By studying these theories as products of their own times and places, the historian would be able to describe various unified systems or groups of theories unique to various milieux.

Ehninger's systems view was self-consciously pluralistic in character:

> No matter how sound internally or how imposing architecturally a given system may be—no matter how much its ethical or aesthetic groundings may arouse our admiration—to regard it as a universally applicable paradigm is to overlook a fundamental fact concerning the very nature of rhetoric [its mutability through history].
>
> ... From this it follows that the continuing dialogue on the question, what is rhetoric? except as an academic exercise, is largely profitless. If there is no generic rhetoric which, like a Platonic idea, is lurking in the shadows awaiting him who shall have the acuteness to discern it, the search for a defining quality can only end in error or frustration. It would serve the cause of rhetorical studies in general, I think, if instead of continuing the dialogue we openly adopted the plural of the noun and spoke of the history or theory of "rhetorics." ("On Systems" 55)

He concluded that the result of considering rhetoric as a succession of systems would be a "healthy and much needed relativism" in historical studies, for the systems approach stresses "diversity rather than uniformity of the rhetorics of different times and places" ("On Systems" 55). This pluralism is attractive, especially when considered in contrast to the unifying tendencies of influence studies. It seems to underwrite an enhanced understanding of rhetoric and, thus, appears to hold potential for the projects of current and future theorizing.

Because of this pluralism, one can argue that systems histories are superior to influence studies. However, while systems histories admit of more heterogeneity among historical rhetorics, they are still reductive. Instead of compressing the particularities of rhetoric's history back into a singular origin as influence studies do, systems studies reduce those particularities to three or four "systems." They capture the history of rhetoric within standardized period divisions of intellectual history, raising the issues of whether these "systems" really are paradigmatic formulations of rhetoric and whether they capture the peculiarity or discreteness of rhetoric's history. Moreover, whole periods are dropped out of these histories, an indication of their reduction of rhetoric's multiplicity to mere plurality. Finally, systems studies are so encompassing that they mask the diversity they claim to reveal. Although recognizing differences *between* systems, these histories elaborate no differences *within* systems. Instead, they reduce the rhetorical theories contained in a system to a "dominant" or representative rhetoric of that system.

Ehninger's most prominent statement of his revised history, "On Systems of Rhetoric," identified "the three crucial eras in the development of Western rhetorical thought" (50). These systems—a "grammatical" ancient rhetoric, a "psychological" rhetoric of the late eighteenth century, and a "sociological" contemporary rhetoric—were his "case studies" ("On Systems" 50–4). In an earlier formulation, Ehninger had discussed four important rhetorics: a "grammatical" high classicism, an "aesthetic" Renaissance rhetoric, a "pragmatical" Enlightenment rhetoric, and a "social" contemporary rhetoric ("On Rhetoric" 243–6).

The later, more prominent of these statements, "On Systems of Rhetoric" is of principal concern here, for in it Ehninger addressed the issue of historiography directly.[25] However, for the moment, considering both accounts together is instructive, for Ehninger's earlier formulation in "On Rhetoric and Rhetorics" points to a problem in the second. Ehninger's reformulation of rhetoric's history, while a history of difference, was not necessarily a history of *systemic* difference. It was not so much a systematization of historical rhetorics as it was a discussion of differences among rhetorics in history. As a result, it is not a reliable statement about rhetoric's particular historicity or temporality. Ehninger's account treated rhetoric's history as reducible to standard periods posited by general intellectual history.

There is a distinction between studying rhetorical theories in different times and periodizing or systematizing rhetoric's history. The first option, studying rhetoric in different historical times, *assumes* that rhetoric has changed significantly over time. Its interest is not in locating points or loci of change or in establishing more and less significant differences among rhetorical theories; its objective is to notice difference.[26] The second option, periodizing or systematizing rhetoric's history, requires a focus on difference also. But it seeks out points of radical difference in order to isolate systemic epochs of theory production and the transformational changes that gave rise to new systems.

Ehninger's essay, "On Rhetoric and Rhetorics," clearly took the first of these routes. He sought there the "dominant traits which . . . rhetoric has exhibited in four important periods in its history" (242). His goal in that essay clearly was not to re-form historical studies of rhetoric. He situated his goal explicitly in contemporary "inquiries into the nature, function, and scope of rhetoric" (242).[27] While his point, that there are multiple rhetorics, not a singular one, clearly had implications for historical study, he did not pursue those implications.

Ehninger's "On Systems of Rhetoric" announced a much bolder objective: to address "rhetorical systems as systems" (49). Ehninger appears to have moved his focus from studying rhetoric in historical periods to periodizing or systematizing historical rhetorics. Despite the apparent change, Ehninger did not engage the kinds of issues necessary to establish his projected systems as systems. He neither located points of transformation among these groupings nor argued that the differences he found among them were significant enough to be systemic or paradigmatic ones.[28] He conflated the isolation of difference with the establishment of systematicity. Michael Leff is correct in identifying Ehninger's presumption that, "a certain set of dominant metarhetorical assumptions" characterizes each system ("On Systems"

1). But Ehninger's additional presumption was that those different metarhetorical assumptions were *the* differences that marked the boundaries of "*the* three crucial eras" of rhetorical theory production ("On Systems" 50). To date that remains an unsupported hypothesis.

Ehninger appears to have appropriated three standard period divisions of general intellectual history—classicism, the Enlightenment, and modernity—and advanced them as if they reflected rhetoric's past. But the division of rhetoric's particular history according to this general periodization scheme has never been defended. On its face, the premise that historical succession differs among fields of study is difficult to refute.[29] If the premise holds, these "systems" may well not be descriptive of the specific historicity or periodicity of rhetorical theory production. Without a case for their centrality, they can hold no claim to periodizing or "systematizing" the history of rhetoric specifically. Thus, they cannot serve as the definitive markers of continuity and change among historical rhetorics that their proponents claim they do. This lack of specificity is a problem in its own right, for it undermines the capacity for these systems to describe "the three crucial eras" in Western rhetorical thought (Ehninger, "On Systems" 50). More important, however, it suggests that "systems" cannot be posited simply on the grounds of difference.

That suggestion is given concrete form in the dispute over the "classical" versus "revolutionary" character of George Campbell's *Philosophy of Rhetoric*. McDermott and LaRusso both dispute Ehninger's claim that Campbell's view of rhetoric was a revolutionary one.[30] Both argue that Campbell's orientation was essentially classical in character and was situated within a continuous tradition.[31] Ehninger attempted to resolve the difficulty posed by this challenge:

> Because systems of rhetoric share in part or in whole the same substance, no matter how much they vary in form or purpose they have inescapable elements of commonality. Therefore, looked at from one point of view they are different rather than alike, while from another they are alike rather than different. It is, I suggest, a failure on the part of the disputants to make clear how they are viewing a rhetoric which lies at the basis of the wearisome controversy concerning the classical or non-classical orientation of the rhetorics of George Campbell or Kenneth Burke. In any event, by making their respective points of view clear, the parties to this argument almost certainly could narrow the area of dispute. ("On Systems" 56).

However, the suggestion that these parties to the argument clarify their criteria begged the question. The criteria for establishing a new or revolutionary system and for differentiating it from another were precisely the points of unclarity, and they resided in Ehninger's own arguments, specifically about Campbell and generally about systems.

In sum, "systems" of rhetoric represent only abstract categories that have no special descriptive suitability for the history of rhetoric. Their legitimacy as descriptive categories has not been established or even defended. That rhetorical theories have differed in times as distinct as the fourth century, B.C., the late eighteenth century, and the mid-twentieth century is not surprising, but that claim is all that the systems view has demonstrated conclusively. Proponents of the systems approach have masked the specificity of rhetoric's history under the gross temporal categories of intellectual history. Thus, systems studies are pluralistic, but they may well be arbitrary in their pluralism; they foreground three different rhetorical formulations, but the "systemic" character of those formulations is assumed.

If Ehninger's "systems" represent only rehearsals of the history of rhetoric under the guise of standard intellectual history, the problem is complicated further by those who appropriate or "confirm" his periodization scheme.[32] Some of these historians tend to reduce the entire history of rhetoric to three systems. Using Ehninger's three-system treatment in "On Systems of Rhetoric," Golden, Berquist, and Coleman treat medieval and Renaissance rhetoric as a transition between classical and Enlightenment rhetoric in their first two editions.[33] In their first edition, they suggest that, "Although medieval rhetoric is an appropriate topic for the research specialist, we do not perceive it as a body of literature whose creative importance rivals the three great rhetorics cited by Ehninger. Consequently we seek here only to provide a transition between the Romans and the Renaissance" (ix). Further on, they observe that, "despite innovations which occasionally altered its scope or emphasis, rhetoric at the close of the sixteenth century was still primarily an integral part of an old and cherished system dating back to Socrates, Plato, Aristotle, Cicero, and Quintilian" (1st ed. 53). In introducing their "bridge" section from classical to Enlightenment rhetoric in the second edition, they claim that "these theories [by medieval and Renaissance scholars], while relevant for a changing society, do not constitute a separate system that is unique and influential in its long range impact" (93). If medieval and Renaissance rhetoric have received inadequate attention, the neglect cannot be attributed exclusively to studies that use systems as their model of temporality. Nonetheless, clearly those who support systems study find it tempting to overlook these so-called "transitional" theories.

The same problem appears even more acute with respect to the nineteenth century; the systems model effectively eliminates consideration of that period. Although there is some discussion of nineteenth-century theories as addenda to the "psychological" system, comparatively little consideration has been given to this later period by systems study.[34] The systems approach again is not entirely at fault in overlooking the nineteenth century. Fogarty, for example, observes what most historians have taken as a truism: "With few exceptions of any moment in rhetorical theory, Whately was the last rhetorician until the nineteen-twenties" (20). The nineteenth century witnessed the fragmentation and diffusion throughout the curriculum of the study of rhetorical concepts. Theoretical concepts related to rhetoric were frequently studied under the sign of a different discipline like philosophy or political theory. Moreover, consideration of important European thinkers, like Friedrich Nietzsche and Karl Marx, was no doubt delayed by political as well as language barriers (Enos 36). However, the systems perspective reinforces the likelihood of overlooking nineteenth-century sources precisely because it was not a period of *systematic,* organized inquiry in rhetoric. That fact does not diminish the theoretical insight available from theorists of the period. The reduction of all rhetorical theories to the characteristics of three "dominant" models restricts our understanding of past rhetorics to those three formulations. In sum, systems studies may be pluralistic, but they demonstrate a severely restricted pluralism.

If examining what systems histories exclude is instructive, contemplating how they treat the historical materials that they do include is even more interesting. The particular character of individual rhetorical theories disappears within the broad "systems" that contain them. Ehninger admitted that the study of systems "submerges differences and details so as to call forth the common characteristics of rhetorical systems as organized wholes" ("On Systems" 50). For this reason, as McKerrow suggests, systems constructions are "vulnerable to the objection that . . . [they] hide more than they disclose about the theory in question" (6). He suggests further that, if one examines systems historiography with a view to uncovering specific details, the result will be disappointing" (6). Systems constitute such broad contextual units that details are vanquished in their construction. These "details," of course, are precisely the source of theoretical insight, but they disappear in the descriptions of systems.

To abstract the unity of a system from the differences among theories, Ehninger suggested that, "one must select from diverse possibilities the trends and emphases that are dominant" ("On Systems" 50). Notably missing from Ehninger's explanation are the warrants for identifying "dominant" trends and emphases. For example, in his analytic account of rhetorical theory in the late eighteenth century, Ehninger identified four patterns or "dominant trends": classicism, psychological-epistemological theories, elocutionism, and belletristic rhetoric ("Dominant Trends"). But in his account of systems, he apparently singled out the psychological-epistemological rhetorics as *more* dominant than the other three trends. The basis for determining this dominance is unstated. On his own terms, Ehninger's broad characterization of "the" eighteenth-century rhetorical system is highly reductive.[35]

The principal consequence is that particular theories of a period are given more prominence than others without justification. Whole periods of theory production are characterized in terms of composite accounts, reducing all different theoretical endeavors to trivial variations or to non-dominant, and therefore less significant, status. Thus, each system dismisses all but a single type of theory. Furthermore, there is no articulated justification for studying primarily the "dominant" theories, even if one were able to warrant his/her choices. Oravec argues that it is particularly dangerous to focus solely on "the dominant view of an era," for it makes "the emergence of alternative tendencies more difficult to comprehend" ("Democratic Critics" 420). These alternative theories may hold different, perhaps even more valuable, theoretical insight than the so-called "dominant" theories of an era. But systems histories, because they are internally reductive, deprive their readers of access to any theories except those that they designate as "dominant."

The issue of what constitutes a "dominant" theory in the systems account leads rather naturally to the question of politics. Perhaps the periods of intellectual history that systems studies feature *were* the major or exclusive, paradigmatic systems of theory production. That seems unlikely, given that they are never defended as such. Similarly, those rhetorics that systems histories advance as "dominant" may have been the most useful or insightful, but that case has not been made either. More probably, the periods and rhetorics that these studies have highlighted have been marked as a result of the progressive politics that pervades Ehninger's founding account of systems. If Ehninger elided the nineteenth century as well as the centuries between the Roman empire and the late 1800s, he may have done so in order to demonstrate progress in rhetoric's history.[36]

Ehninger presented the history of rhetoric as a continuous series of refinements or improvements upon theoretical doctrine.[37] This progressive politics suggests a privileged present that has come about by rejecting primitive, inadequate theories and replacing them with ever more advanced theoretical formulations. The role of the earlier, "primitive" theories, on the systems view, was one of *necessity;* their principal contributions were to serve as necessary conditions for present theorizing. These earlier versions of rhetoric are treated as quaint antiques rather than as contributors to rhetorical thought. They are valued only as historical relics, their crudity a contrast to the profundity of contemporary rhetorical theory. On this view, contemporary rhetoric has reached a pinnacle, surpassing its predecessors. The future of rhetorical theorizing, to be determined by whatever "need" may generate it, is greeted with an optimism generated by a faith in inevitable progress.

Ehninger was quite clear about this political stance.[38] He described the ancients' rhetorical theories as "hampered by the primitive psychology and epistemology with which they worked" ("On Systems" 51). As a result, he argued that, "[T]he classical writers tended either to scant or to present a patently naive account of the relation between the speech act and the mind of the listener" (51). But, the primitive and naive were replaced by the more sophisticated: "For as Locke and his successors among the British empiricists began to develop more sophisticated systems of psychology and epistemology, not only did the ancients' lack of attention to the message-mind relationship seem a more glaring deficiency, but many of the traditional assumptions concerning how men know or are persuaded no longer were acceptable" ("On Systems" 52). As a consequence of following the empiricists, it was to be "the major contribution of the 'new British rhetoric' of the late eighteenth century . . . that it corrected the major deficiency of the classical system ..." ("On Systems" 51–2).

Ehninger was not as critical of Enlightenment rhetoric as he was of the ancients, but he described it as "now largely dated," and criticized it for "too intense a preoccupation with one aspect of the communication spectrum" ("On Systems" 52). In addition, the eighteenth-century rhetorics were, on Ehninger's view, less concerned than they might (should?) have been with the roles practical discourse serves in society. He argued that, "in their preoccupation with the message-mind relationship the architects of the "new" rhetoric gave insufficient attention to another vital dimension of a complete and rounded theory of communication. And this is the role that practical discourse plays in society—the function it performs and should perform in promoting social cohesion and exercising social control" ("On Systems" 53). But again, that inadequate rhetoric would be replaced with the superior contemporary system, which *is* concerned with rhetoric's social character.

Ehninger expressed some concerns about particular issues in the "new and revolutionary" and "amazingly vital" contemporary system ("Colloquy" 452, 453).

His general assessment, however, was quite positive. He argued that rhetoric of the present "has provided a more comprehensive picture of the role which rhetorical forces play in promoting social cohesion and effecting social control" ("On Systems" 54). In fact, he discussed this "rhetoric dedicated to the promotion of healthy and productive human relations" in contrast to "the cultivation of the arts of persuasion" ("Colloquy" 449). In this contrast Ehninger found the real "progress" of contemporary rhetoric beyond the ancient and Enlightenment rhetorics:

> Through the long centuries in which man, upon the authority of Aristotle, was defined as a rational being—a being whose essence was assumed to lie in his ability to think and to reason abstractly—rhetoric as the art of symbolic inducement not only was adventitious to his nature, but hostile to it. To undertake to persuade—to seek to bend the beliefs or behavior of another to one's own will—was a dehumanizing process, for both of the parties concerned. By treating the persuadee not as a "person," but as a "thing" to be manipulated, the persuader also sacrificed his own claim to humanity.

> Today, by contrast, with man redefined as a symbolizing and therefore, by extension, a rhetorical creature, the cloud which for long has hovered over the entire rhetorical enterprise has been removed. . . . [T]he rhetorical transaction itself need no longer be regarded as something that dehumanizes the inducer no less than the induced. Instead, rhetoric becomes a respectable human enterprise, an activity to be understood and reckoned with rather than shunned. ("Colloquy" 452–3)

Contemporary rhetoric, on Ehninger's view, has so improved upon its historical predecessors that its historically disdained reputation has been restored to respectability.

Ehninger's case for progress was not only anecdotal or tied to the specific systems he delineated. He suggested that, "[T]hrough the ages, and despite occasional setbacks, rhetorics have constantly become both richer in content and more embracing in scope" ("On Systems" 57). Ehninger described this constant improvement in ways that suggest he viewed it as historical necessity. For example, he argued that the ancients' "grammatical" focus was "entirely understandable. Before the classical writers could consider the pragmatic or aesthetic aspects of speech making, they first *had to* determine what the act of speaking entailed and devise a grammar for talking about its parts and their relationships" ("On Systems" 51. Emphasis added). Ehninger's statement implied a natural order in which intellectual inquiry must proceed. He indicated here that the ancients could not have dealt with the concerns he saw as characteristic of the Renaissance (aesthetics) or the Enlightenment (pragmatics), because those were more "advanced" concerns that *necessitated* a preceding grammar. Similarly, Ehninger described contemporary rhetoric's focus on human understanding as "natural," in light of its rootedness in a context of tensions ranging from the interpersonal to the international ("On Systems" 53). And he suggested that the human, "*as we at last are able to see,*" is more than a creature of reason alone" ("Colloquy" 453. Emphasis added). Presumably contemporary rhetoricians' new-found vision is a direct and determined result of its myopic but "necessary" predecessors.

This theme of deterministic progress has entailments for future theorizing. Ehninger was unclear about what we might expect from such future endeavors, but he did provide his readers with an attitude toward them: "Perhaps the central lesson to be learned from an analysis of the rhetorics of various periods considered as systems is that while the final word on rhetorics never has and probably never will be said, there is reason for optimism concerning the future of rhetoric as a discipline—reason to believe that as man's knowledge grows and his attempts to talk about practical discourse in a coherent and consistent fashion improve, rhetorics ever will become more penetrating and more fruitful" ("On Systems" 57). This optimism, a normal corollary of any progress theme, is interestingly problematic. First, if progress is as inexorable as Ehninger held, then there seems little value in effort or intervention. Since a better, more advanced system of rhetoric appears to be inevitable, inertia should be as expedient as effort in achieving progress toward that end. Moreover, if rhetorical theories "arise out of a felt need and are shaped in part by the intellectual and social environment in which the need exists," as Ehninger maintained ("On Systems" 55), we need only wait for a new and better rhetoric until such time as a new felt need manifests itself.

Certainly Ehninger did not argue that attempts to re-theorize beyond the privileged present would be inexpedient, but his elaboration of necessity and progress suggests that view. When or how rhetorical theorists will identify a need sufficiently compelling to reconceptualize rhetoric is unclear. That they will do so and that their reconceptualization will represent progress are certain, on Ehninger's view. The attitude toward future theorizing forwarded by systems history, thus, is an odd configuration of optimism and caution. We may be sure that some rhetorical "system" of the future will be better than the present one. However, attempts to rethink rhetoric in the absence of an obviously compelling social or intellectual need might be premature and ultimately fail to achieve the progressive status of a "dominant" or systemic rhetoric. In short, while the progressive, pluralist stance of systems histories differs radically from the preservative, unitary politics of influence studies, they both advance attitudes of complacency and caution about change in rhetorical theorizing.

Conclusion:
Toward a Critical Historiography of Rhetoric

Histories of rhetorical theory are not neutral or objective reconstructions of facts. They are themselves rhetorical iterations, saturated with the impure representations, intrinsic interestedness, and general obstreperousness of any discourse. Historical discourse is not magically exempt from the inherent partisanship of language use. Nor is its practice devoid of choice. Historians make inventional/presentational choices that determine the kinds of histories they compose. These choices have shaped the ways in which we read the history of rhetoric and our own place in relation to that history.

The two views of history addressed here—influence and systems study—advance political rhetorics of significant consequence. The first grants almost complete intellectual authority to the ancients; and the other invests contemporary rhetoric with full sanction. These two conceptions of history account for Scott's recognition of the "Promethean role" attributed to Aristotle and Kenneth Burke (439). The influence seekers privilege classical authors, while the systematizers valorize contemporary thinkers. Both models in turn disenfranchise the current or future theorist of rhetoric by implication. On the one hand, the influence study's message is that everything worthy in our understanding of rhetoric is always already present in prior doctrine. Valuable "new" insight is unavailable for an historian can always find the "real" source of insight in an earlier work. Or retheorizing will be condemned as a departure from "the tradition." On the other hand, systems study forwards the smug historical necessity of "progress" that virtually guarantees "improvement" in our understanding, regardless of the quality or thoroughness of our efforts. Since the condition of history is its progress, our interventions will not alter its course for better or worse.

These views of rhetoric's history are unsatisfying, but not because they display the interestedness of a political program. An at least implicit politics inheres in any history.[39] Influence and systems study are problematic, because their politics are fundamentally in conflict with any program that sanctions current or future theorizing. While they implicitly devalue or discourage such effort, they also present radically circumscribed accounts of past theoretical work. Historians ignore some rhetorical theories altogether, present some as more "dominant" than others, find in theories what they think *ought* to be there on the basis of *or* in spite of the texts, and valorize theories on the tenuous grounds that they came first or last or that they were appropriated more or less. These practices deny to the reader all past theoretical insights that do not accord with the historian's program.

If past conceptions of rhetoric have any value for future rhetorical theorizing and if the enablement of current understanding and future theorizing are legitimate goals, this *kind* of partiality in history writing must be undone. Certainly no single historiography is the correct one; there is no simple or perfect solution to the problems identified here and in other critiques. So, a consensus among historians of rhetoric to practice a single alternative historiography is not the appropriate objective. At the same time, Skopec's suggestion, that historians simply use a variety of assumptions and methods in writing the history of rhetoric, is not an adequate solution either ("Systems Theory" 12). Diversity of method guarantees no resolution of these problems; multiple unsound assumptions and methods merely produce multiple inadequate histories. A "critical history" of the kind described by Nietzsche and later by Foucault is not the only solution, but it offers one remedy in keeping with the goals for history outlined here.[40] I would like to offer a series of four contrasts among influence, systems, and critical histories. The third member of each contrastive set—text, particularity, change, and criticism—signals an important characteristic or assumption of critical history. These characteristics are not exhaustive of critical history; they are the ones that respond most directly to the problems with influence and systems histories.[41] Critical history is advanced here in the interest of resolving the historiographic problems of influence and systems formulations; at the very least this discussion may foster consideration of other possible solutions.

Monument/Relic/Text. That historical rhetorics should be regarded as texts or instances of discourse seems obvious. Because they are written, they have the same degree of nuance and uniqueness as any written text.[42] Undoubtedly, some rhetorical theories are derivative, appropriating much, even most, of their contents from prior works. That, however, does not render them as mere markers or monuments to the works from which they borrow. Similarly, because some historical theories bear the clear mark of psychological, philosophical, or political programs that we might consider obsolete, they are not merely relics. Critical history treats historical events as texts rather than as monuments or relics. If historians of rhetoric were to attend to theories as texts rather than as monuments or relics, they might find that these theories contain insights that were not borrowed or even that they might take useful positions not sullied by obsolescence. Even if these texts contain nothing that is currently acceptable, they might tell us something about the rhetorical practices of their own times.[43] McGee suggestively implores us, for example, to "ask what Aristotle *saw* in ancient Greece" in addition to "what Aristotle *said* in Greek" (45. Emphasis in original).

Both McGee's specific admonition and the general notion of treating rhetorical theories as texts imply the corollary concern of context. Systems history, if it contributed nothing else, made an important and convincing case for studying historical rhetorics in relation to the contexts in which they were produced. However, much of what has counted as context in histories of rhetorical theory has been academic practice. Certainly rhetorical theories bear important and unique relationships to other fields of intellectual inquiry, but they are theories of rhetorical practice.[44] Influence studies tend to contextualize rhetorical theories within the limited arena of rhetorical theorizing. Systems history usually contextualizes rhetorical theories within the somewhat broader confines of academic inquiry. A critical history would add to those the context of rhetorical practices. The point is not to judge precept by application but to understand the multiple relations of theorizing text to theorized practice more fully.[45]

Singularity/Plurality/Particularity. The dangers of opting for a singular view of rhetoric in history are clear. The principal problem is that the reader of a history is deprived of exposure to all historical formulations of rhetoric that do not echo or emulate the single, privileged one. Pluralist historical writing overcomes that problem but only by degree. It affords the reader a glimpse of three or four different historical formulations of rhetoric, but only those. The problem with pluralism is that it is merely plural; it still overlooks the intricacies and complexities of the past in favor of "dominant" configurations. By contrast, critical history, which assumes particularity, opens the door to multiple rhetorics, on the grounds that all such formulations are significant in some way.[46]

The assumption of particularity demands that differences among historical texts be taken seriously. Even a theoretical formulation that "merely" reorganizes, translates, or redefines concepts from prior rhetorical theories constitutes a unique and potentially interesting statement. The particular organization of concepts in relation to one another, the particular terminological choices, and the particular modes of describing concepts certainly must be important to historians of rhetoric, at least in principle. Rhetoricians attend to these issues in other kinds of discourses; to overlook them or declare them to be insignificant in historical rhetorics is to ignore the obvious fact that historical theories of rhetoric are themselves texts, discursive formulations. Critical history shares with rhetoric the views that discursive choices make a difference and that such choices are frequently responsive to particular, practical circumstances. Thus, instead of attending to the continuity of a single tradition of rhetoric or of recognizing a few dominant rhetorics, critical history would regard rhetoric's past as a myriad of specific articulations of rhetoric, any of which might bear important insight, and all of which tell us something about the historical conditions in which they were articulated.

Preservation/Progress/Change. Enough has been said here about the problems of conceiving the history of rhetoric as essentially preservative or progressive. Both of these notions entail preconceived valuations of history, and historians often treat those valuations as if they were synonymous with historical succession. They obviously are not; they are rhetorical constructions imposed upon historical sequence by the historian. Critical history substitutes the underdetermined assumption of change for the heavily determined notions of preservation or progress. What any history should be is a recognition and account of change. Obviously, all changes are not equally significant nor do they follow a unitary pattern. Quite the contrary. Change is an "empty, abstract notion" in itself; it allows for multiple elaborations (Foucault, *Archaeology* 173). Rather than assuming that historical change is always preservative or continually progressive, critical history leaves the particular variety of change as an open question. This allows the historian to recognize and elaborate various types of relationships and forms of succession among historical texts and contexts. As Gordon Leff observes, "everything is not related to everything else such that, in finding the master relation, all the others fall into place" (169). Moreover, everything is not related to everything else *in the same ways.* Various kinds of relations among historical theories may be articulated, if the historian is not constrained to always see relationships as "influence" or "progress."

Sacralization/Optimism/Criticism. All historical writing renders judgments, at least implicitly. The fact that influence and systems study value particular theories is not itself problematic. That they value those theories unreflectively or for the purposes of sacralizing the great wisdom of ancient "origins" or of contemplating with optimism the "advanced" present is problematic. The value of a historical theory of rhetoric has little to do with its later appropriation or its anticipation of the present. As McGee suggests, a rhetorical theory can be judged legitimate "only when measured, directly and explicitly, against the objects it purportedly describes and explains" (26). A rhetorical theory's worth is its capacity to render rhetorical practices understandable. Although rhetorical theories are at least in part products of their own intellectual and social contexts, their value is not necessarily exhausted within those contexts. They may be *more* useful in accounting for the practices of their own times but that is a matter for judgment, not prejudice.

Because of its focus on particularity and difference, critical history also allows for comparative assessment of rhetorical theories. Judgments of the greater or lesser worth of rhetorical theories may be products of historical study, if those theories are considered in terms not only of a context of practices but also of other theories.[47] The comparison and contrast among theories can enable judgment, if the articulation of tensions among these theories results in mutual criticism.[48] Most important though, such judgments must be results, not assumptions, of critical history.

Such a critical stance toward rhetorical theories reorients historical study toward the future. The critical historian would assume that the final word on rhetoric was not spoken by the ancients; nor does the historically optimal rhetorical theory reside in the present or in one more step into the light of the future. Critical history abandons the complacency that attends attitudes of both sacralization and optimism. Its critical stance dislodges complacency by demonstrating that past and present formulations are neither perfect or necessary. It poses the question of history precisely for the purpose of prodding the future.

Deleuze's representation of Foucault's position marks such a critical relation among past, present, and future: "Thought thinks its own history (the past), but in order to free itself from what it thinks (the present), and be able finally to 'think otherwise' (the future)" (119). Foucault described his own work as "the endeavor to know how and to what extent it might be possible to think differently, instead of legitimating what is already known" (*Use* 9). For Nietzsche, a critical history represented a "powerful resolve for new life" (*On the Advantage* 21). It was not the only useful form of history in his view, but a tendency that would allow for reconceptualizing and rethinking: "[Man] must have the strength, and use it from time to time, to shatter and dissolve something to enable him to live: this he achieves by dragging it to the bar of judgment, interrogating it meticulously and finally condemning it; every past, however, is worth condemning . . . " (*On the Advantage* 21). The point of history, of course, is not solely to condemn the past; Nietzsche argued that the historical sense must *allow* for that by means of meticulous interrogation. If it does not, history is reduced to the operation of worshipful preservation, smug self aggrandizement, or blind optimism. Such views of history as Foucault's and Nietzsche's offer to the historian of rhetoric a way to conduct history without devaluing the potential for future theorizing. And they provide a stimulus for such future effort by critical juxtapositioning of past and present. As Foucault suggested, what is "demonstrated as the exotic charm of another system of thought, is the limitation of our own . . . " (*Order* xv).

A critical history is only one alternative to influence and systems study. But it promises at least in principle to better serve those interested not just in the history of rhetoric but also in rhetoric.[49] Although critical history demands a more focused, extensive, and sophisticated analysis of historical texts than has been typical in histories of rhetoric, our understanding of rhetoric and its history also might be more extensive and sophisticated as a result. As Murphy suggests, "Rhetoric as a universal human activity has naturally left its records in a wide variety of cultures and languages over thousands of years of civilization. Consequently our efforts to understand its complexity need to be as sophisticated as the subject itself" ("Historiography" 8).

Notes

1. Until very recently, there were astonishingly few treatments of goals and approaches in the history of rhetorical theory. As Blair and Kahl suggest, the notable exceptions were: Duhamel, "Function"; Ehninger, "On Systems"; and Scott. More recently, there has been activity in this area, but it has only begun to address the range of relevant issues. For examples, see: Anderson; Berlin; Blair, "Archaeological Critique"; Blair and Kahl; Brinton; Cahn; Covino; Jarratt; Michael C. Leff, "Concrete Abstractions"; Makus; McGee; McKerrow, "On Rhetorical Systems"; Murphy, "A Historian's Guide"; Murphy, "Historiography"; Octalog [James Berlin, Robert J. Connors, Sharon Crowley, Richard Leo Enos, Susan C. Jarratt, Nan Johnson, Jan Swearingen, and Victor J. Vitanza (Moderator James J. Murphy)]; Oravec, "The Democratic Critics"; Oravec, "Where Theory and Criticism Meet"; John Poulakos; Takis Poulakos; Schilb, "Differences"; Schilb, "History of Rhetoric"; Skopec, "Systems Theory"; and Vitanza.

2. Although LaCapra refers here to professional historians, the same is true of historians of rhetorical theory. See Berlin 50; and Vitanza 85.

3. Rhetorics of sciences and mathematics have been identified and discussed, as have rhetorics of human "sciences," e.g. anthropology, psychology, economics, philosophy, political science, history, theology, and law. See Nelson, Megill, and McCloskey; and Simons.

4. I disagree with Murphy in his assumption of a need for *agreement* on historiographic principles. At this point, it seems reasonable to suggest simply that historians of rhetoric *acquaint* themselves with the issues involved in composing histories. To ask for an early resolution or consensus may invite premature and simplistic decision in a field of extraordinarily complex issues. I *do* agree with Murphy's assessment that there are problems, but I believe they are a result not of lack of consensus but of lack of consideration.

5. Also see Clark, whose goal is to "expose the modern reader to the conflicting winds of ancient doctrine in the hope that he will be enabled better to understand and to evaluate modern discussions of the same problems in the teaching of rhetoric" (4).
   I do not mean to suggest that enhancement of our present and future states of understanding is the *only* goal of historical studies of rhetoric; but I concur with Leff, Enos, and Clark that it is the most important, even the presumptive, goal.
   McKeon implies the same position when he argues that, "Histories of rhetoric . . . throw little light on the principles or purposes by which present methods and uses of rhetoric might be evaluated or changed . . . " ("Uses" 1). Hauser seems to concur as well, in his complaint that historical research fails to abstract "any message that adds to an ongoing and developing theory" (269).

6. Duhamel illustrated his case for pursuing multiple and particular views of rhetoric by arguing that classical rhetoric cannot be taken as a monolith, that it is a multiplicity of theoretical stances.

7. Ehninger argued, for example, that, "The work of the classical rhetoricians in devising such a [rhetorical] grammar was admirable. So well, indeed, did they perform this task that even today any system of rhetoric which fails to encompass the basic terms and relationships which they isolated is properly regarded as incomplete" ("On Systems" 51). Although Ehninger's systems approach was a reaction against influence studies, this statement about classical rhetoric is much more attuned to the politics of influence studies than to systems study.

8. Influence and systems studies reflect historiographic tendencies of nineteenth-century philology and historicism respectively. Although there have been many versions of philology, it frequently was uncritical toward classical sources and sought to preserve or revive the "life" of those sources. As Lloyd-Jones suggests, "We have unfortunately no exact equivalent for the German term *Nachleben-*

studien. . . . [T]he term properly denotes the continuing life of the classics and the effect which they have continued to exercise upon the world" (*Blood* 9). Sandys described Niebuhr's view of the ancients: "[T]hey were to be read with reverence . . . with a resolve to assimilate their spirit" (80). Friedrich Ast's view was similar, according to Palmer: "[T]he study of philology . . . serves a 'pedagogical-ethical purpose': to become more like the Greeks" (76). Also see: Bengtson; Bleicher; Butler; Lloyd-Jones, Editor's Introduction; and McGann. Bengtson's book is a translation of the sixth edition of *Einführung in die Alte Geschichte.* Munich: C.H. Beck'sche Verlagsbuchhandlung, 1969.

Historicism, although a highly varied historiographic position, tended in some cases toward an unreflective elaboration of the "progress" of history. Mandelbaum suggests that, "[T]he nineteenth-century form of the doctrine of progress had emerged from an acceptance of historicism, and was widely taken to be one of its necessary corollaries" (370). He also describes the emphasis on "necessity" as the force of history (127). Mandelbaum's treatment of historicism is quite thorough. For other discussions of historicism and "progress" in historiography, see: Carr; Fischer; Meyerhoff; Nevins; and Popper.

The critical view that I have taken toward these two historiographies is similar to, but not identical with Nietzsche's and Foucault's critiques. See Nietzsche, "We Philologists"; Nietzsche, "On the Advantage"; and Foucault, "Nietzsche, Genealogy, History."

9. My procedure here is, by necessity, illustrative and inductive. The alternatives, to analyze the problems as they are exhibited by a single historical work, or to exemplify all of the problems by reference to multiple histories, would be far more problematic. The first would be to argue that the problems of one historical account inhere in all others of its type; the second would require a much longer and redundant exposition than is possible here.

10. The preceptive tradition is a continuation of classical rhetoric as exemplified in the works of Isocrates and Quintilian and in the *Rhetorica ad Herennium.*

11. See Bevilacqua, "Lord Kames' Theory," 324, 327; Bevilacqua and Murphy, xlvii–xlviii; Caplan, "A Late Medieval Tractate," 61–90; Caplan, "Four Senses," 282–90; Clark, 56–8; Murphy, *Rhetoric in the Middle Ages,* ix; and Ong, *Ramus* 8, 21, 63–4, 176–8, and 297.

Even Covino's otherwise revisionist history works to establish a continuity in the history of rhetoric. He argues that the "art of wondering" demonstrated in classical rhetorics was "*continued* by the revisionary figures . . . presented in this study" (122). For example , he suggests that, "[P]ostmodern criticism has reinvented the 'forgotten' rhetoric that DeQuincey mourns ..." (122).

12. For a discussion of "progressive continuity," see Jarratt, "Towards a Sophistic Historiography," 14–7.

13. Fogarty's conclusion about the rhetorical tradition demonstrates the same reductionism: "[T]he philosophy of rhetoric has not perceptibly changed since Aristotle" (21). Lunsford and Ede's goal also reflects the reductive bias. They attempt to attenuate the differences between classical and modern rhetorical theory.

14. Kennedy does point out unique features of Quintilian's work occasionally. And, when Kennedy speaks of the influences on Quintilian, he sometimes does acknowledge that Quintilian rearranged the materials he appropriated. The impact of those changes is not addressed, however.

15. Although Seigel's preferred pattern is "evolution" and not influence, he constructs this "evolution" as a series of thinkers influencing one another.

16. Conley notes this tendency sardonically in discussing the marked lack of influence of Aristotle in Byzantium: "Partisans of Aristotle will, of course, continue to be disappointed by the fortunes of that great philosopher in the East and perhaps continue to think of the scholars of Byzantium as narrow-minded and incompetent" ("Aristotle's *Rhetoric*" 43).

17. Howell's complaint is with the position taken by Duhamel in "Milton's Alleged Ramism."

18. Zappen notes the same problem with standard interpretations of Hobbes as a Ramist. Zappen concludes that, "Hobbes's rhetorical method defies strict classification as Aristotelian, Ramist, anti-Ramist, or counterreformist" (90).

19. The inference should not be made that I am defending Duhamel's position by questioning Howell. I do not regard Milton's degree of Ramism as very important.

20. Interestingly, while Vickers argues that we might do justice to rhetoric by conceiving it as *widely* as in its original manifestation, he apparently believes that rhetoric should not be viewed *more* broadly than it was in ancient times. He is concerned that studies of rhetorics of inquiry, for example, will "widen the meaning of rhetoric to the point of no return" (*In Defence* 439n).

21. Of course, Vickers is not alone in this assessment. Fogarty argued that. "Most students of Aristotle would admit that he made the greatest contribution to rhetoric up to our time. The 'Rhetorica' not only sums up the best of all the elements developed prior to his time but, together with his own and Plato's ideas, forms the best synthesis of any before or since" (12).

22. Kennedy's assessment of the Romans is similar. He suggests that his "basic theme is that the Romans imitated from the Greeks an art of persuasion which gradually developed into an art often more concerned with what I call the secondary characteristics of rhetoric: not persuasion, but style and artistic effect. But in the empire an effort was made by a number of writers to recover some of the power of persuasion ..." (*Art of Rhetoric* xv).

23. Another unfortunate consequence of a linear historiography of any kind is the tendency to mark a single "origin," excluding knowledge from other cultures. Kennedy, for example, describes ancient Greek rhetorical theory as "the universal and accepted doctrine of the civilized speaking world" (*Art of Persuasion* 13). Works like Bernal's *Black Athena* have called into question the notion that Western civilization is a product of Greek origin. Essays more specific to rhetorical histories that posit other cultures' rhetorics are: Abbott; Fox; Jensen; Oliver; and Rabinowitz.

24. Schilb's description of some historians' tendency, "to see particular texts merely as embodiments of some thesis about the past that they wish to flesh out" ("Differences" 34), is particularly appropriate as a description of these traditional histories.

25. In addition, "On Systems" had been the more appropriated and accessed of the two essays. It remains the principal source of "order" for the fourth edition of the popular text. *The Rhetoric of Western Thought,* by Golden, Berquist, and Coleman. And, it probably is not an exaggeration to suggest that most students encounter the history of rhetoric divided into systems or periods like those Ehninger described.

26. Barilli uses this approach explicitly, "following the chronological thread of history and the major cultural periods" (xi). His concern is not to systematize but to show differences among rhetorics of various periods in history. Thus, he covers the ancient Greeks, the ancient Romans, the Middle Ages, Renaissance humanism, early modernity, modernity, and what he calls a contemporary "revival" of rhetoric.

27. Ehninger was explicit in aiming this essay at the center of the contemporary discussion regarding rhetoric's character and its differentiation from poetic, noting the "divergent and incompatible views" forwarded by: Bryant; Bigelow; Howell, "Literature"; and Staub and Mohrmann ("On Rhetoric" 242n).

28. The term "paradigmatic," of course, suggests Kuhn's work. In fact, Skopec compares Ehninger's systems history to the work of both Kuhn and Foucault, who "emphasize the uniqueness of historical epochs and maintain that the purpose of historical studies is to understand the internal dynamic of intellectual processes as they functioned in their own context" ("Systems Theory" 10). Although Skopec's general characterization of Kuhn and Foucault is at least arguably accurate, the analogy with Ehninger's systems view is untenable. Both Kuhn and Foucault were interested in locating points of transformation. Both argued carefully to establish differences among paradigms or discursive formations as significant, transformational differences. And Foucault especially concerned himself with the very specific historicities of particular fields of discourse. Ehninger did none of those things. See Kuhn; and Foucault, *Archaeology.*

29. Gordon Leff points out that, "the criterion [to define an epoch] must vary according to what is being periodized" (147). Foucault concurred, arguing that historical study should undertake comparative, "regional" concerns rather than "symptomatalogical" studies (*Order* x), because each discursive field has its "own type of historicity" (*Archaeology* 165).

30. Although this exchange did not arise from Ehninger's "On Systems," but from his "George Campbell," it is predicated on the same problem. That is, Ehninger consistently evaded the question of what would constitute "the revolutionary" or the criteria for distinguishing one system from another.

31. That McDermott and LaRusso may have subscribed to the equally problematic preservative stance of influence studies in making their arguments does not ameliorate the argumentative problem for Ehninger.

32. The Golden, Berquist, and Coleman text appropriates Ehninger's "On Systems" explicitly. Scott suggests that his version of systems "supplements and in a sense confirms" Ehninger's (439). Skopec advances an additional "system," in part as a confirmation of Ehninger's approach ("Theory"). Golden, Berquist, and Coleman are of principal concern here, because they follow Ehninger. Both Scott and Skopec approach systems in different ways, and their approaches merit separate discussion. Their approaches share only in part the assumptions, and thus the problems, of Ehninger's.

33. They have included progressively more on these periods with new editions, but the treatment of the Middle Ages and the Renaissance remains quite limited. See Golden, Berquist, and Coleman, *The Rhetoric of Western Thought,* (first edition, 1976; second edition, 1978; and fourth edition, 1989).

34. Evidence is accumulating that suggests a serious error of omission regarding nineteenth-century rhetorical thought. Although systematic, disciplinary study of rhetoric did not flourish in this period,

thinkers in other fields explicitly addressed questions of interest to rhetoric. Exploration of these thinkers' works in rhetorical studies has only begun. And such study does not occur within a systems context. See for example: Anderson and King; Blair, "Friedrich Nietzsche's Lecture Notes"; Bormann; Braun; Brockriede, "Bentham's Philosophy"; Cherwitz and Hikins; Galati; Gilman, Blair, and Parent; Ijsseling; Lunsford; Lyne; McGuire; Shearer, "Alexander Bain"; and Trautman.

35. Ehninger described "pressures" resulting in the formation of these four trends, and these pressures are different in each case. Furthermore, it is clear that Ehninger did not view the three "less" dominant trends as primarily psychological in nature. See his "Dominant Trends."

36. Of course, this is impossible to claim conclusively. However, Ehninger did posit a clear, linear sequence of progress in his account. Moreover, he noted that rhetoric has had "occasional setbacks" in its historical progress, but he did not elaborate on what they were or when they occurred ("On Systems" 57). One is left to wonder if Ehninger saw "setbacks" in some of the periods he overlooked in his history. If that is so, it would certainly call the premise of progress into question.

37. See Anderson, who argues that these characteristics render Ehninger's systems approach a "Whig" history. He suggests that, in Ehninger's assumption of progress in history lies a devaluation of earlier systems and an unjustified valorization of later systems. He goes on to question Ehninger's labeling of classical rhetoric as merely "grammatical" and suggested that much of what systematizers see as a product of revolutionary theorizing in contemporary rhetoric was already present in classical rhetoric (19). Anderson's objections are important on two levels. First, they identify correctly the bias of continuous historical "progress" in Ehninger's view of systems. Second, they summarize the tension between the two temporal contextualizing models used in histories of rhetoric. Ehninger's progressivism is in stark contrast to Anderson's view, which is a variation of the influence model. Anderson finds traces of contemporary thought in an overidealized, origin—classical rhetoric. His stance is a reenactment in reverse of the influence study and its overenthusiastic imputation of omnificence to earlier writers.

38. That is not to suggest that he considered it "political." It is quite likely that he saw nothing interpretive, rhetorical, or political about considering history and progress as virtually synonymous. Working as he was within the confines of an essentially liberal modernist posture, progress could be taken as an *a priori*.

39. The goals that I have forwarded for the historical study of rhetoric also are politically charged, of course. They assume that historical study should serve the present, that rhetorical theories of the past are valuable because of their content as well as their relation to other theories and practices, and that writing the history of rhetoric is an activity principally about rhetoric and only secondarily about historical sequence.

40. Nietzsche discussed a critical history as one form of history in *On the Advantage*. While Foucault did not call his project a critical history, it is very close to Nietzsche's view of one. Foucault did describe his goal in *Birth of the Clinic* as critical: "The research that I am undertaking here therefore involves a project that is deliberately both historical and critical, in that it is concerned—outside all prescriptive intent—with determining the conditions of possibility of medical experience in modern times" (xix). His objective in that study was very much like those in his later historical writings as well. He referred to his project variously as "genealogy," "history of the present," and "history of systems of thought." The proximity of Nietzsche's and Foucault's stances is made most clear in Foucault's "Nietzsche, Genealogy, History."

41. Critical history, as described here, is a perspective and not itself a historiography. Thus, there is more than one type of critical history, which may vary in methods and middle-level assumptions.

42. Schilb describes the task of his "revisionary" project for history as "a sustained, even laborious confrontation with the intricacies of texts . . . " ("Differences" 32).

43. Michael Cahn's fine essay does precisely that. In fact, it goes one step further and discusses rhetorical instruction or precept as being itself rhetorical.

44. McGee makes this point powerfully, arguing that, "a 'rhetorical theory' should be related to practice as generalization to data" (45).

45. Conley, *Rhetoric:* Eagleton; and Ward, "Magic" all concern themselves with pragmatic contexts and rhetorical theorizing.

46. Paul Veyne puts the case clearly, when he suggests that, [F]or historical knowledge, it is enough for an event to have occurred for it to be worth knowing" (17). Foucault suggested that virtually any historical discourse is worth considering because, in its infinite specificity of text and context, it makes a unique statement. See Foucault, *Archaeology* 28.

47. Hauser suggests that a valuable history of rhetoric "must be comparative in nature" (256).

48. As Michael Leff suggests, "[I]n the resulting tension between the text from the past and our interests in the present, our conceptions of both past and present emerge in a new light" ("Concrete Abstractions" 24).

49. Willard makes this point in his review of Vickers ' *In Defence*. He suggests that, "Although [Vickers'] epilogue is entitled 'The Future of Rhetoric,' his concern is the future of historical studies in rhetoric. The reason for this is simple: Unlike Sidney and Shelley, Vickers does not profess the art he defends and is not much interested in those who do" (174).

Works Cited

Abbott, Don P. "The Ancient Word: Rhetoric in Aztec Culture." *Rhetorica* 3 (1987): 251–64.

Anderson, Floyd D. "On Systems of Rhetoric: A Response to 'Whig' Misreading." *Pennsylvania Speech Communication Annual* 38 (1982): 15–9.

Anderson, Floyd D., and Andrew A. King. "William Hazlitt and the Romantic Assault on the Commonplace." *Western Journal of Speech Communication* 45 (1981):317–26.

Backman, Mark, ed. *Rhetoric: Essays in Invention and Delivery*. [By Richard McKeon]. Woodbridge, CT: Ox Bow Press, 1987.

Barilli, Renato. *Rhetoric*. Trans. Giuliana Menozzi. Minneapolis: U of Minnesota P, 1989.

Bengtson, Hermann. *Introduction to Ancient History*. Trans. R.I. Frank and Frank D. Gilliard. Berkeley: U of California P, 1970.

Berlin, James. "Revisionary History: The Dialectical Method." *Pre/Text* 8 (1987): 47–61.

Bernal, Martin. *Black Athena: The Afro-Asiatic Roots of Classical Civilization*. London: Free Association Press, 1987.

Bevilacqua, Vincent M. "Lord Kames' Theory of Rhetoric." *Speech Monographs* 30 (1963): 309–27.

Bevilacqua, Vincent M. "Philosophical Origins of George Campbell's *Philosophy of Rhetoric.* " *Speech Monographs* 32 (1965): 1–12.

Bevilacqua, Vincent M. "W.S. Howell and the Relatives of Rhetoric." [Review essay] *Quarterly Journal of Speech* 58 (1972): 344–6.

Bevilacqua, Vincent M., and Richard Murphy. "Editors' Introduction." *A Course of Lectures on Oratory and Criticism*. By Joseph Priestley. Carbondale: Southern Illinois UP, 1965. ix–lviii.

Bigelow, Gordon E. "Distinguishing Rhetoric from Poetic Discourse." *Southern Speech Journal* 19 (1953): 83–97.

Bitzer, Lloyd F. "Kennedy on Modern Rhetorics." [Review essay] *Quarterly Journal of Speech* 67 (1981): 213–5.

Blair, Carole. "An Archaeological Critique of the History of Rhetorical Theory: Beyond Historical-Critical Dualism in the Analysis of Theoretical Discourse." Diss. The Pennsylvania State University, 1983.

Blair, Carole. "Friedrich Nietzsche's Lecture Notes on Rhetoric: A Translation." *Philosophy and Rhetoric* 16 (1983): 94–129.

Blair, Carole, and Mary L. Kahl. "Introduction: Revising the History of Rhetorical Theory." *Western Journal of Speech Communication* 54 (1990): 148–59.

Bletcher, Josef. *Contemporary Hermeneutics: Hermeneutics as Method, Philosophy, and Critique*. London: Routledge & Kegan Paul, 1980.

Bormann, Dennis R. "Adam Müller on the Dialogic Nature of Rhetoric." *Quarterly Journal of Speech* 66 (1980): 169–81.

Braun, John Elliott. "The Philosophical Roots of the Nineteenth-Century 'Repose' of Rhetoric. With Emphasis on the Idea of Communication in the Thought of Josiah Royce." Diss. University of Michigan. 1977.

Brinton, Alan. "The Outmoded Psychology of Aristotle's Rhetoric." *Western Journal of Speech Communication* 54 (1990): 204–18.

Brockriede, Wayne E. "Bentham's Philosophy of Rhetoric." *Speech Monographs* 23 (1956): 235–46.

Bryant, Donald C. "Rhetoric: Its Function and Its Scope." *Quarterly Journal of Speech* 39 (1953): 401–24.

Butler, Marilyn. "Against Tradition: The Case for a Particularized Historical Method." McGann, ed. 25–47.

Cahn, Michael. "Reading Rhetoric Rhetorically: Isocrates and the Marketing of Insight." *Rhetorica* 8 (1990): 103–18.

Campbell, George. *The Philosophy of Rhetoric.* Ed. Lloyd F. Bitzer. Carbondale: Southern Illinois UP, 1963. ix–xxxvii.

Caplan, Harry. "The Four Senses of Scriptural Interpretation and the Medieval Theory of Preaching." *Speculum* 4 (1929): 282–90.

Caplan, Harry. "A Late Medieval Tractate in Preaching." *Studies in Rhetoric and Public Speaking in Honor of J. S. Winans.* Ed. A.M. Drummond. New York: Century, 1925, 61–90.

Carr, Edward Hallett. *What is History?* New York: Vintage, 1961.

Cherwitz, Richard A., and James W. Hikins. "John Stuart Mill's *On Liberty:* Implications for the Epistemology of the New Rhetoric." *Quarterly Journal of Speech* 65 (1979): 12–24.

Clark, Donald Lemen. *Rhetoric in Greco-Roman Education.* New York: Columbia UP, 1957).

Clarke, M. L. *Rhetoric at Rome: A Historical Survey.* New York: Barnes and Noble, 1963.

Conley, Thomas M. "Aristotle's *Rhetoric* in Byzantium." *Rhetorica* 8 (1990): 29–44.

Conley, Thomas M. "Kennedy on the History of Rhetoric." [Review essay] *Quarterly Journal of Speech* 67 (1981): 206–9.

Conley, Thomas M. *Rhetoric in the European Tradition.* New York: Longman, 1990.

Covino, William A. *The Art of Wondering: A Revisionist Return to the History of Rhetoric.* Portsmouth, NH: Boynton/Cook, 1988.

Deleuze, Gilles, *Foucault.* Trans. and Ed. Sean Hand. Minneapolis: U of Minnesota P, 1986.

Duhamel, P. Albert. "The Function of Rhetoric as Effective Expression." *Journal of the History of Ideas* 10 (1949): 344–56. Rpt. in *The Province of Rhetoric.* Ed. Joseph Schwartz and John A. Rycenga. New York: Ronald Press, 1965. 36–48.

Duhamel, P. Albert. "Milton's Alleged Ramism." *Publications of the Modern Language Association* 67 (1952): 1035–53.

Eagleton, Terry. "A Small History of Rhetoric." In *Walter Bejamin, or Towards a Revolutionary Criticism.* London: Verso, 1981, 101–13.

Ehninger, Douglas. "Colloquy II: A Synoptic View of Systems of Western Rhetoric." *Quarterly Journal of Speech* 61 (1975): 448–53.

Ehninger, Douglas. "Dominant Trends in English Rhetorical Thought, 1750–1800." *Southern Speech Journal* 18 (1952): 3–12.

Ehninger, Douglas. "George Campbell and the Revolution in Inventional Theory." *Southern Speech Journal* 15 (1950): 270–6.

Ehninger, Douglas. "On Rhetoric and Rhetorics," *Western Speech* 31 (1967): 242–9.

Ehninger, Douglas. "On Systems of Rhetoric," *Philosophy and Rhetoric* 1 (1968): 131–44. Rpt. in *Contemporary Rhetoric: A Reader's Coursebook.* Ed. Douglas Ehninger. Glenview, IL: Scott, Foresman, 1972, 49–58.

Ehninger, Douglas. "The Promise of Rhetoric." *H TEXNH: Proceedings of the Speech Communication Association 1978 Doctoral Honors Seminar, "Research Methods and Topics for the History of Rhetoric."* Ed. Richard Leo Enos and William E. Wiethoff. Ann Arbor, MI: privately printed, 1978, 1–9.

Enos, Richard Leo. "The History of Rhetoric: The Reconceptualization of Progress." *Speech Communication in the 20th Century.* Ed. Thomas W. Benson. Carbondale: Southern Illinois UP, 1985, 28–40.

Fischer, David Hackett. *Historians' Fallacies: Toward a Logic of Historical Thought.* New York: Harper, 1970.

Fogarty, Daniel, S. J. *Roots for a New Rhetoric.* New York: Teachers College, Columbia University, 1959.

Foucault, Michel. *The Archaeology of Knowledge and The Discourse on Language.* Trans. A. M. Sheridan Smith. New York: Pantheon, 1972.

Foucault, Michel. *The Birth of the Clinic: An Archaeology of Medical Perception.* Trans. A.M. Sheridan Smith. New York: Vintage, 1975.

Foucault, Michel. "Nietzsche, Genealogy, History." In *Language, Counter-Memory, Practice: Selected Essays and Interviews.* Ed. Donald F. Bouchard. Trans. Donald F. Bouchard and Sherry Simon. Ithaca: Cornell UP, 1977. 139–64.

Foucault, Michel. *The Order of Things: An Archaeology of the Human Sciences.* Trans. Alan Sheridan. New York: Vintage, 1973.

Foucault, Michel. *The Use of Pleasure: Volume 2 of The History of Sexuality.* Trans. Robert Hurley. New York: Pantheon, 1985.

Fox, Michael V. "Ancient Egyptian Rhetorics." *Rhetorica* 1 (1983): 9–22.

Galati, Michael. "A Rhetoric for the Subjectivist in a World of Untruth: The Tasks and Strategies of Soren Kierkegaard." *Quarterly Journal of Speech* 55 (1969): 372–80.

Gilman, Sander L., Carole Blair, and David J. Parent, trans. and eds. *Friedrich Nietzsche on Rhetoric and Language.* New York: Oxford UP, 1989.

Golden, James L., Goodwin F. Berquist, and William E. Coleman. *The Rhetoric of Western Thought.* 1st ed. Dubuque, IA: Kendall/Hunt, 1976.

Golden, James L., Goodwin F. Berquist, and William E. Coleman. *The Rhetoric of Western Thought.* 2d ed Dubuque, IA: Kendall/Hunt, 1978.

Golden, James L., Goodwin F. Berquist, and William E. Coleman. *The Rhetoric of Western Thought.* 4th ed. Dubuque, IA: Kendall/Hunt, 1989.

Hauser, Gerard A. "Searching for a Bright Tomorrow: Graduate Education in Rhetoric During the 1980s." *Communication Education* 28 (1979): 259–70.

Howell, Wilbur Samuel. *Eighteenth-Century British Logic and Rhetoric.* Princeton: Princeton UP, 1971.

Howell, Wilbur Samuel. "Literature as an Enterprise in Communication." *QJS* 33 (1947): 417–26.

Howell, Wilbur Samuel. *Logic and Rhetoric in England, 1500–1700.* New York: Russell and Russell, 1961.

Howell, Wilbur Samuel. "Ramus and English Rhetoric: 1574–1681." *Quarterly Journal of Speech* 37 (1951): 299–310.

Ijsseling, Samuel. *Rhetoric and Philosophy in Conflict: An Historical Survey.* Trans. Paul Dunphy. The Hague: Martinuus Nijhoff, 1976.

Jarratt, Susan C. "Toward a Sophistic Historiography." *Pre/Text* 8 (1987): 9–26.

Jensen, J. Vernon. "Rhetorical Emphases of Taoism." *Rhetorica* 3 (1987): 219–29.

Kennedy, George A. *The Art of Persuasion in Greece.* Princeton UP, 1963.

Kennedy, George A. *The Art of Rhetoric in the Roman World.* Princeton: Princeton UP, 1972.

Kennedy, George A. *Classical Rhetoric and Its Christian and Secular Tradition from Ancient to Modern Times.* Chapel Hill: U of North Carolina P, 1980.

Kennedy, George A. *Quintilian.* New York: Twayne, 1969.

Kuhn, Thomas S. *The Structure of Scientific Revolutions.* 2d ed. Chicago: U of Chicago P, 1970.

LaCapra, Dominick. *History and Criticism.* Ithaca: Cornell UP, 1985.

LaCapra, Dominick. *Rethinking Intellectual History: Texts, Contexts, Language.* Ithaca: Cornell UP, 1983.

LaRusso, Dominic S. "Root or Branch? A Re-examination of Campbell's 'Rhetoric'." *Western Speech* 32 (1968): 85–91.

Leff, Gordon. *History and Social Theory.* University: U of Alabama P. 1969.

Leff, Michael C. "Concrete Abstractions: A Response to Anderson and Skopec." *Pennsylvania Speech Communication Annual* 38 (1982): 21–4.

Leff, Michael C. "On Systems of Rhetoric: A View From the Center of the Circle." Paper presented in the Special Seminar on "Systems and Beyond." Speech Communication Association convention. Minneapolis, MN. November 1978.

Lloyd-Jones, Hugh. *Blood for the Ghosts: Classical Influences in the Nineteenth and Twentieth Centuries.* London: Duckworth, 1982.

Lloyd-Jones, Hugh. Editor's Introduction. U. von Wilamowitz-Moellendorff. *History of Classical Scholarship.* Trans. Alan Harris. London: Duckworth, 1982. v–xxxii.

Lunsford, Andrea. "Alexander Bain's Contributions to Discourse Theory." *College English* 44 (1982): 290–301.

Lunsford, Andrea, and Lisa S. Ede. "On Distinctions Between Classical and Modern Rhetoric." *Essays on Classical Rhetoric and Modern Discourse.* Ed. Robert J. Connors, Lisa S. Ede, and Andrea Lunsford. Carbondale: Southern Illinois UP, 1984, 37–49.

Lyne, John R. "Rhetoric and Semiotic in C. S. Peirce." *Quarterly Journal of Speech* 66 (1980): 155–68.

Makus, Anne. "Rhetoric Then and Now: A Proposal for Integration." *Western Journal of Speech Communication* 54 (1990): 189–203.

Mandelbaum, Maurice. *History, Man, and Reason: A Study in Nineteenth-Century Thought.* Baltimore: Johns Hopkins UP, 1971.

McDermott, Douglas. "George Campbell and the Classical Tradition." *Quarterly Journal of Speech* 49 (1963): 403–9.

McGann, Jerome D. "Introduction: A Point of Reference." McGann, ed. 3–21.

McGann, Jerome D., ed. *Historical Studies and Literary Criticism.* Madison: U of Wisconsin P, 1985.

McGee, Michael Calvin. "A Materialist's Conception of Rhetoric." McKerrow, ed. 23–48.

McGuire, Michael. "The Ethics of Rhetoric: The Morality of Knowledge." *Southern Speech Communication Journal* 45 (1979): 133–48.

McKeon. "Rhetoric in the Middle Ages." *Speculum* 17 (1942): 1–32. Rpt. in Backman. 121–66.

McKeon, Richard. "The Uses of Rhetoric in a Technological Age: Architectonic Productive Arts." *The Prospect of Rhetoric.* Ed. Lloyd F. Bitzer and Edwin Black. Englewood Cliffs, NJ: Prentice-Hall, 1971. 44–63. Rpt. in Backman 1–24.

McKerrow, Ray E. "On Rhetorical Systems: A Symposium—Introduction." *Pennsylvania Speech Communication Annual* 38 (1982): 5–7.

McKerrow, Ray E., ed. *Explorations in Rhetoric: Studies in Honor of Douglas Ehninger.* Glenview, IL: Scott, Foresman, 1982.

Meyerhoff, Hans. "History and Philosophy: An Introduction." *The Philosophy of History in Our Time.* Ed. Hans Meyerhoff. Garden City, NY: Doubleday, 1959, 1–25.

Murphy, James J. "The A-Historian's Guide: Or, Ten Negative Commandments for the Historian of Rhetoric." *H TEXNH: Proceedings of the Speech Communication Association 1979 Doctoral Honors Seminar, "Research Methods and Topics for the History of Rhetoric."* Ed. Richard Leo Enos and William E. Wiethoff. Ann Arbor, MI: privately printed, 1978, 1–8.

Murphy, James J. "The Historiography of Rhetoric: Challenges and Opportunities." *Rhetorica* 1 (1983): 1–8.

Murphy, James J. *Rhetoric in the Middle Ages: A History of Rhetorical Theory from St. Augustine to the Renaissance.* Berkeley: U of California P, 1974.

Nelson, John S., Allan Megill, and Donald N. McCloskey, eds. *The Rhetoric of the Human Sciences: Language and Argument in Scholarship and Public Affairs.* Madison: U of Wisconsin P, 1987.

Nevins, Allan. *The Gateway to History.* Garden City, NY: Doubleday, 1962.

Nietzsche, Friedrich. *On the Advantage and Disadvantage of History for Life.* Trans. Peter Preuss. Indianapolis: Hackett, 1980.

Nietzsche, Friedrich. "We Philologists" [1874]. Trans. J.M. Kennedy. *The Complete Works of Friedrich Nietzsche.* Ed. Oscar Levy. Volume 8. Edinburgh: T.N. Foulis, 1911, 109–90.

Octalog. "The Politics of Historiography." *Rhetoric Review* 7 (1988): 5–49.

Oliver, Robert T. *Communication and Culture in Ancient India and China.* Syracuse: Syracuse UP, 1971.

Ong, Walter J., S.J. *Ramus, Method, and the Decay of Dialogue.* Cambridge, MA: Harvard UP, 1958.

Oravec, Christine. "The Democratic Critics: An Alternative American Rhetorical Tradition." *Rhetorica* 4 (1986): 395–121.

Oravec, Christine. "Where Theory and Criticism Meet: A Look at Contemporary Rhetorical Theory." *Western Journal of Speech Communication* 46 (1982): 56–71.

Palmer, Richard E. *Hermeneutics: Interpretation Theory in Schleiermacher, Dilthey, Heidegger, and Gadamer.* Evanston: Northwestern UP, 1969.

Popper, Karl. *The Poverty of Historicism.* London: Routledge & Kegan Paul, 1957.

Poulakos, John. "Hegel's Reception of the Sophists." *Western Journal of Speech Communication* 54 (1990): 160–71.

Poulakos, Takis. "Historiographies of the Tradition of Rhetoric: A Brief History of Classical Funeral Orations." *Western Journal of Speech Communication* 54 (1990): 172–88.

Rabinowitz, Isaac. "Pre-Modern Jewish Study of Rhetoric: An Introductory Bibliography." *Rhetorica* 3 (1985): 137–44.

Sandys, John Edwin. *A History of Classical Scholarship.* Volume 3. New York: Hafner, 1958.

Schilb, John. "Differences, Displacements, and Disruptions: Toward Revisionary Histories of Rhetoric." *Pre/Text* 8 (1987): 29–44.

Schilb, John. "The History of Rhetoric and the Rhetoric History." *Pre/Text* 7 (1986): 11–34.

Scott, Robert L. "Colloquy I: A Synoptic View of Systems of Western Rhetoric." *Quarterly Journal of Speech* 61 (1975): 439–47.

Seigel, Jerrold E. *Rhetoric and Philosophy in Renaissance Humanism: The Union of Eloquence and Wisdom, Petrarch to Valla.* Princeton: Princeton UP, 1968.

Shearer, Ned A. "Alexander Bain and the Genesis of Paragraph Theory." *Quarterly Journal of Speech* 58 (1972): 408–17.

Shearer, Ned A. "Psychology as a Foundation to Rhetoric: Alexander Bain and Association Psychology's Relation to Rhetorical Theory." *Western Speech* 35 (1971): 162–8.

Simons, Herbert W., ed. *Rhetoric in the Human Sciences.* London: Sage, 1989.

Skopec, Eric Wm. "Systems Theory as an Historiographic Perspective." *Pennsylvania Speech Communication Annual* 38 (1982): 9–13.

Skopec, Eric Wm. "The Theory of Expression in Selected Eighteenth-Century Rhetorics." McKerrow, ed. 119–36.

Staub, A. W., and Gerald P. Mohrmann. "Rhetoric and Poetic: A New Critique." *Southern Speech Journal* 28 (1962): 131–41.

Trautman, Frederick. "Communication in the Philosophy of Arthur Schopenhauer." *Southern Speech Communication Journal* 40 (1974): 142–57.

Veyne, Paul. *Writing History: Essay on Epistemology.* Trans. Mina Moore-Rinvolucri. Middleton, CT: Wesleyan UP, 1984.

Vickers, Brian. *In Defence of Rhetoric.* Oxford: Clarendon, 1988.

Vickers, Brian. "Rhetorical and anti-rhetorical tropes: On writing the history of *elocutio.*" *Comparative Criticism: A Yearbook.* Ed. E. S. Shaffer. 3 (1981): 105–32.

Vitanza, Victor J. "'Notes' Towards Historiographies of Rhetorics; or the Rhetorics of the Histories of Rhetorics: Traditional, Revisionary, and Sub/Versive." *Pre/text* 8 (1987): 63–125.

Ward, John O. "Kennedy on Medieval and Renaissance Rhetoric." [Review essay] *Quarterly Journal of Speech* 67 (1981): 209–13.

Ward, John O. "Magic and Rhetoric From Antiquity to the Renaissance: Some Ruminations." *Rhetorica* 6 (1988): 57–118.

Warnick, Barbara. "Charles Rollin's *Traité* and the Rhetorical Theories of Smith, Campbell, and Blair." *Rhetorica* 3 (1985): 45–65.

Willard, Thomas. Rev. of Brian Vickers, *In Defence of Rhetoric. Rhetoric Review* 8 (1989): 173–7.

Zappen, James P. "Aristotelian and Ramist Rhetoric in Thomas Hobbes's *Leviathan:* Pathos versus Ethos and Logos." *Rhetorica* 1 (1983): 65–91.

Bibliography

Articles

Aristotle. *Nicomachean Ethics*. Translated by M. Ostwald. Indianapolis: Bobbs-Merrill, 1962

Aristotle. *The Politics of Aristotle*. Edited and Translated by Ernest Barker. New York: Oxford University Press, 1968

Aristotle. *On Rhetoric: A Theory of Civic Discourse*. Translated by George A. Kennedy. New York: Oxford University Press, 1991.

Beiner, Ronald. *Political Judgment*. Chicaago: University of Chicago Press, 1983.

Bitzer, Lloyd. "Aristotle's Enthymeme Revisited," *Quarterly Journal of Speech*, 45, 1959.

Bitzer, Lloyd F. "The Rhetorical Situation." *Philosophy and Rhetoric*, 1, 1968.

Bitzer, Lloyd F. " Rhetoric and Public Knowledge." In D.M. Burks, ed. *Rhetoric, Philosophy and Literature: an Exploration*. West Lafayette: Purdue University Press, 1978.

Bitzer, Lloyd F. "Functional Communication: a Situational Perspective." In E. E. White, ed. *Rhetoric in transition: Studies in the Nature and Uses of Rhetoric*. University Park: Pennsylvania State University Press, 1980.

Black, Edwin. *Rhetorical Criticism: a Study in Method*. Madison: University of Wisconsin Press, 1968.

Booth, Wayne, *The Company We Keep: an Ethics of Fiction*. Berkeley: University of California Press, 1988.

Brooks, Cleanth and Warren, Robert Penn, *Modern Rhetoric*. New York: Harcourt Brace Jovanovich, 1979.

Burke, Kenneth. *A Grammar of Motives and a Rhetoric of Motives*. Cleveland: World Publishing, 1962.

Campbell, Karlyn Kohrs and Jamieson, Kathleen Hall, eds. *Form and Genre: Shaping Rhetorical Action*. Falls Church, VA: Speech Communication Association, 1978.

Cherwitz, Richard, "Rhetoric as a 'Way of Knowing': An Attenuation of the Epistomological Claims of the 'New Rhetoric'" *Southern Speech Communication Journal*, 42, 1976.

Cicero, Marcus Tullius. *De Oratore*. 2 vols. E. E. Sutton and H. Rackham, trans. Cambridge: Harvard University Press, 1979.

Cicero, Marcus Tullius. *Topica*. H.M. Hubbell, trans. Cambridge: Harvard University Press, 1949.

Conley, Thomas. *Rhetoric in the European Tradition*, New York: Longman, 1990.

Derrida, Jacques. *Dissemination*, Barbara Johnson, trans. Chicago: University of Chicago Press, 1981.

Dewey, John. *The Public and its Problems*. Chicago: Swallow Press, 1927.

Farrell, Thomas B. "Knowledge, Consensus, and Rhetorical Theory," *Quarterly Journal of Speech* , 62, 1976.

Farrell, Thomas B. "Validity and Rationality: the Rhetorical Constituents of Argumentative Form," *Journal of the American Forensics Association*, XIII, 1977.

Farrell, Thomas B. and Frentz, Thomas S., "Communication and Meaning: a Language-Action Synethesis," *Philosophy and Rhetoric*, XII, 1979.

Farrell, Thomas B. *Norms of Rhetorical Culture*. New Haven:Yale University Press, 1993 .

Fisher, Walter R. "A Motive View of Communication," *Quarterly Journal of Speech*, 56, 1970.

Fisher, Walter R. "Genre: Concepts and Applications in Rhetorical Criticism," *Western Journal of Speech Communication*, 44, 1980.

Fisher, *Human Communication as Narration: Toward a Philosophy of Reason, Value, and Action*. Columbia: University of South Carolina Press, 1987.

Fotheringham, Wallace C. *Perspectives on Persuasion*. Boston: Allyn and Bacon, Inc. 1966.

Garver, Eugene, *Aristotle's Rhetoric*: An Art of Character Chicago: University of Chicago Press,1994.

Grimaldi, William M. A. *Aristotle, Rhetoric I*: A Commentary. New York: Fordham University Press, 1980.

Gross, Alan G. and Keith, William M., eds. *Thetorical hermeneutics: Invention and Interpretation in the Age of Science*. Albany: State University of New York Press, 1997.

Harriman, Robert. "Status, Marginality, and Rhetorical Theory," *Quarterly Journal of Speech, 72,* 1986.

Harriman, Robert. *Political Style: the Artistry of Power.* Chicago: University of Chicago Press, 1995.

Howell, W. S. *Logic and Rhetoric in England, 1500-1700*. Princeton: Princeton University Press, 1956.

Johnstone, Henry. "The Relevance of Rhetoric to Philosophy and of Philosophy to Rhetoric," *The Quarterly Journal of Speech, 52*, 1966.

Johnstone Jr., Henry W. "Response," *Philosophy and Rhetoric, 20*, 1987.

Kahn, Victoria, *Rhetoric, Prudence and Skepticism in the Renaissance,* Ithaca, N.Y.: Cornell University press, 1985.

Kennedy, George A. *Classical Rhetoric and Its Christian and Secular Tradition from Ancient to Modern Times*. Chapel Hill: University of North Carolina Press, 1980.

Kinneavy, James L., *A Theory of Discourse: the Aims of Discourse*. Englewood Cliffs, NJ: Prentice-Hall, 1971.

Lanham, Richard. *The Electronic Word: Democracy, technology, and the Arts*, Chicago: University of Chicago Press, 1993

MacIntyre, Alasdair. *After Virtue*. Notre Dame: University of Notre Dame press, 1982.

McKeon, Richard, "Dialectic and Political Thought and Action," *Ethics*, 55, 1954.

McKeon, Richard, "The Uses of Rhetoric in a technological Age: Architectonic Productive Arts," *The Prospect of Rhetoric*, Lloyd F. Bitzer and Edwin Black (eds.), Englewood Cliffs, N.J.: Prentice-Hall, 1974.

Nussbaum, Martha. *The Fragility of Goodness: Luck and Ethics in Greek Tragedy and Philosophy*. Cambridge: Cambridge University Press, 1986.

Perelman, C. & Olbrechts-Tyteca, L. *The New Rhetoric: a Treatise on Argumentation*. Notre Dame: Notre Dame University Press, 1969.

Plato. *The Dialogues*. Translated by B. Jowett. New York: Random House, 1937.

Quintilian. *Institutes of Oratory*. Translated by H.E. Butler. Cambridge: Harvard University Press, 1958.

Rhetorica ad Herennium. Translated by H. Caplan. Cambridge: Harvard University Press, 1954.

Schaeffer, John D. *Sensus Communis: Vico, Rhetoric, and the Limits of Relativism* Durham: Duke University Press, 1990.

Scott, Robert L. "On Viewing Rhetoric as Epistemic," *Central States Speech Journal,* 18, 1967.

Scott, Robert L. "On Viewing Rhetoric as Epistemic: Ten Years Later," *Central Speech Journal,* 27, 1976.

Sherman, Nancy. *Making a Necessity of Virtue: Aristotle and Kant on Virtue*: Cambridge: Cambridge University press, 1997.

Toulmin, Stephen. *The Uses of Argument.* Cambridge: Cambridge University Press, 1958.

Vickers, Brian. *In Defense of Rhetoric.* Oxford: Clarendon press, 1988.

Walzer, Michael. *Obligations: Essays on War, Disobedience, and Citizenship* Cambridge: Harvard University Press, 1970.

Wander, Philip C. "The Rhetoric of Science," *Western Journal of Speech Communication,* 40, 1976.

Wellek, Rene and Warren, Austin. *Theory of Literature.* New York: Harcourt Brace Jovanovich, 1977.

Wells, Susan. *Sweet Reason: Rhetoric and the Discourses of Modernity.* Chicago: University of Chicago Press, 1996.

White, James Boyd.*When Words Lose Their Meaning* Chicago: University of Chicago Press, 1984.

White, James Boyd. *Acts of Hope: Creating Authority in Literature, Law, and Politics.* Chicago: University of Chicago Press, 1994.

Wieman, Henry Nelson and Walter, Otis M. "Toward an Analysis of Ethics for Rhetoric," *The Quarterly Journal of Speech,* XLIII, 1957.

Winch, Peter. *Trying to Make Sense.* Oxford: Basil Blackwell, Ltd., 1987.

Index